MARGARET Mc MILLAN
LIBRARY

HEAVEN IN THE CHRISTIAN TRADITION

Alinari

Christ Giving His Blessing. Mosaic from the apse of the Cathedral, Monreale

Alinari

The Triumph of the Cross. Mosaic from the apse of San Clemente, Rome

HEAVEN

in the Christian Tradition

BY

[illegible]ON

ULRICH SIMO

SALISBURY SQUARE · LONDON

MADE AND PRINTED IN GREAT BRITAIN BY
WYMAN AND SONS LIMITED, LONDON, FAKENHAM AND READING

For my wife

ACKNOWLEDGMENTS

The Bible text in this publication is from the *Revised Standard Version of the Bible*, copyrighted 1946 and 1952 by the Division of Christian Education, National Council of Churches, and used by permission, except in some special instances where the author has followed his own translation. Thanks are also due to the following for permission to reproduce extracts from copyright works: Harvard University Press (G. F. Moore: *Judaism*); the Loeb Classical Library, published by Messrs. Heinemann, for the translations of Hesiod, Cicero, and Philo; the Clarendon Press (R. H. Charles: *The Apocrypha and Pseudepigrapha of the Old Testament in English*); Martin Secker & Warburg Ltd. (Norman Douglas: *South Wind*). The author's debt to contemporary scholars is also acknowledged in the notes to the text. The substance of chapter II was given to and printed by the Victoria Institute as the Annual Address of 1957.

Preface

TEN years ago I prefaced my book *Theology of Crisis* with the motto: 'Tua Res Agitur'. Since then nothing has happened to lessen the reality of the crisis of our civilization. The human predicament has become more serious than could have been contemplated even during the last war. The 'matter' which men have to deal with nowadays is, as most of them realize, out of their control, and those who refuse to be lured by cheap escapes and avert their senses from the screens and voices of the electronic world around them must needs bemoan their lack of freedom to act: how can they shoulder the responsibility of this age?

In this situation most contemporary theology asserts that the Gospel makes us free; indeed, the drum of some theologians beats noisily to the rhythm of what is vaguely called 'existentialism'. But there is one fundamental difficulty: though we are exhorted to make decisions, and to appropriate the Gospel for ourselves, doubts assail our mentors. They grant that there is in the Gospel a large element of myth. The Christ, therefore, whom they wish us to encounter is nebulous and it is not always easy to understand why he should encounter us if he is *not* the Son of God, risen from the dead, triumphant over the whole world.

The scepticism of our age performs the useful service of stressing the old problems: it questions not only the status of Christ but the credentials of the records. As Christ is known through the traditions of the Church these traditions must be scrutinized afresh and critically in the light of what is now known of the ancient world; for this material proves beyond a doubt that the Christian writings accept the common cultural and scientific outlook of the first century A.D. Above all, a common cosmology dominates the scene.

In this picture of the world *Heaven* is very prominent. It is an exaggeration to say, however, that Heaven figures always and everywhere as the top of a three-decker universe. We are not compelled to dismiss the Oriental world-view as beneath contempt, even if it conflicts with modern knowledge. The point of this present enquiry is to show the Biblical use of the term Heaven. It may be said at once that it is rich and variegated and central to Biblical thinking.

In the present volume I begin by giving a short survey of some conceptions of Heaven outside the Bible. This chapter ends on a note of decline and an almost total eclipse of belief in Heaven. This leads to an examination of the Christian position in so far as it is derived from and supported by the Bible. I have consequently omitted every attempt to interpret the material from a modern point of view and hope to resume this task in another volume. Here I have not gone consciously beyond the terms of objective evidence; there I hope to give free rein to speculative theology.

The reader will appreciate that the evidence of the Bible is not objective in the sense that a mere quotation of a string of verses can be cited to make a simple point. There is a great complexity not only in our subject but in the Biblical evidence itself. Almost every passage has its own problems; these are listed and discussed in the relevant commentaries and lexica, whether they concern textual variants or obscurities of exegesis etc. I am indebted to these learned discussions, but I have kept the number of distracting footnotes to a minimum, lest the complaint, often heard today, be justified that a catalogue is all right for a record office but does not make a book. Hence a word about sources and commentaries must be inserted here.

In the two Testaments practically all the books illumine the subject of Heaven, but some are more important than others. Thus the Psalms, the Wisdom literature, and Daniel in the Old Testament, and Ephesians, Hebrews, and the Apocalypse strike a cosmic note which does not normally occur in the purely historical books. Nevertheless it would not be right to speak in this instance of an eclectic use of these books, unless, of course, any of these sources are considered as suspect and unrepresentative of Biblical thought. Hebrews is an important case in this context: if it be true, as is sometimes asserted, that, although canonical, the writer stands outside the main tradition of the New Testament, the chapter on the heavenly cultus loses its main support. The same applies to Ephesians and the victory of Heaven. I have taken the New Testament to be authentically representative of a very complex whole.

Without R. H. Charles's edition of the Apocrypha and Pseudepigrapha (1913, text, introduction, and comments) a work of this kind could not be undertaken. This does not mean, however, that Charles's curious approach in his life-long study of apocalyptic thought needs to be treated with more than respect. It is an almost inexplicable marvel that a man who devoted such immense labours to the subject found it really essentially disagreeable. Like everyone else who meets with much nonsensical phantasmagoria in the apocalytic imagination he could not conceal his dislike and even contempt for this madness. His approach was ambivalent. His last great work, the monumental commentaries on the Apocalypse (I.C.C., 1920) and on Daniel (1929), manifest both his love and impatience, which saved him from becoming a pure antiquarian dealing in archaic strangeness.

The apocalyptic books gathered together by Charles display a marked interest in cosmogony, a certain extravagance of style and a disposition towards the speculative and fantastic. Of these the most important, and to be the most frequently cited, are the book of Enoch, generally known as the Ethiopian Enoch; the Testaments of the Twelve Patriarchs, and the composite Jewish-Christian Ascension of Isaiah. A problem is raised by the so-called Secrets of Enoch, also known as II Enoch or the Slavonic Enoch. The date of this book is disputed. Charles includes it in the Pseudepigrapha and dates it about B.C. 30–A.D. 70 A. Vaillant, however, has shown convincingly in *Le Livre des Sécrets d'Hénoch* (1954) that it is a medieval product. Though it cannot rank as a contemporary document it may in a few places still throw light upon Biblical oddities. Otherwise it is as useless as the host of post-Biblical Gnostic literature which developed a veritable passion for cosmological and apocalyptic speculations and which interests us less for its contents than for the rebuff which it received in the Christian Fathers (especially in Irenaeus). The struggle between the Christian Faith and un-Christian cosmogonies begins almost in the Bible itself and the element of apocalyptic is the main battleground.

The attitude of theologians and historians to apocalyptic material deserves a book for itself. Some scholars, like Reitzenstein and Bousset for example, utilize it from a historical point of view and tacitly assume that its validity is nil. They belonged to a generation which could not sympathize with its message from within. Thus also G. F. Moore, whose *Judaism* (1927) is a classic, unsurpassed and invaluable, obviously favoured non-apocalyptic Rabbinic teaching and tradition. Although his work still puts his readers into his debt it must be recognized that the pendulum has swung away from his approach. The relevance of the Rabbinic traditions to the Biblical tradition constitutes one of the major problems of scholarship. Strack-Billerbeck's *Kommentar zum Neuen Testament* (1926)—unfortunately not yet translated into English—remains an indispensable tool by its citation of Rabbinic parallels. Yet, however tempting, these are not only later than the New Testament but came sometimes into being by way of reaction to the New Testament. On the other hand both Talmud and Midrash retain some traditions undoubtedly earlier than the New Testament. Here the problem of chronology cannot but cause a large margin of possible errors.

The cosmic tradition of the Bible and of Christianity owes an immense debt to Philo. Up to this day he occupies a controversial position; scholars cannot agree whether he initiated or merely followed the school of thought which sought to reconcile philosophy with the Scriptures. Nor is there any consensus of opinion about the quality of his work which some extol as wonderful and others belittle as a hotch-potch of eclectic inconsistencies. W.L. Knox (*Some Hellenistic Elements in Primitive Christianity*, 1942) did not credit him with originality. H. A. Wolfson (*Philo*, 1948) hails him as the patron of that allegorical method which, deplorably perhaps, obtained in Judaism, Islam, and Christianity, until the time of Spinoza. Philo is both a child of his time and a great pioneer. About his attitude to his predecessors among the Greek philosophers there is again more doubt than certainty. He is not merely a Hebrew Platonist and nothing else. Indeed, Wolfson's masterly survey shows persuasively that the Alexandrian was more concerned to adapt and accommodate the Greek heritage than to be ruled by it in any way. Philo's method, which is mostly one of commenting on the Scriptures, shows where his heart lay and where he desired to go. Yet it may be questioned with E. R. Goodenough[1] (*By Light, Light,* 1935; *Jewish Symbols in the Greco-Roman Period,* 1953–) what was the essence of that Judaism which Philo represents and to which he proceeds to adapt philosophy. If it be conceded that Philo is also steeped in Oriental mysticism a very complex picture emerges and the old problem comes acutely to the fore whether Philo was at all typical among the Jews in general, and of Palestinian Judaism in particular. Fortunately we have not to come to a decision on so subtle an issue. It is enough to bear the problems in mind, especially when we approach the relevant passages in the Fourth Gospel and in Hebrews. That both works show an awareness of Philo has been suggested with great force both by C. H. Dodd, *The Interpretation of the Fourth Gospel* (1953), and by C. Spicq, *L'Épitre aux Hébreux* (1953).

The New Testament and its precursors and contemporaries show that Heaven was in the Oriental world a key-concept of scientific thought, of all sorts of piety, and of theology. In the ancient world few, if any, stopped to define what they meant by Heaven. This looseness of the use of the word must in a certain measure persist here. What, for example, is the difference, in the Bible, between Heaven and sky? Or, between Heaven and the world? There is an epistemological puzzle at the very outset. Heaven means to people what they want it to mean, much in the fashion of Humpty Dumpty semantics. For the purpose of this study Heaven should be defined as the place which our eyes see, which our mind registers, and our spirit aspires to, as *above us*. In order to bring out the specific meaning of the technical term I have decided to give 'Heaven' a capital H throughout, even in quotations from sources and books where the normal usage is adopted. I hope this discrepancy will not cause any annoyance.

[1] Cf. the same writer's devastating critique of Wolfson's *Philo* in JBL, LXVII, 1948, pp. 87–109.

Though I venture to use Heaven as a technical term I am well aware that it was not originally used like that. I imagine that Heaven was at no time talked about in a more definite way than we talk about London or Rome: we may 'love London', or hate 'the London air', or 'try London for a job', or 'go out East via London', and in a thousand ways use and abuse a geographical term. The Biblical writers certainly thought about Heaven in the same liberal manner; their varieties of meaning are as great as those of their religious experiences. Thus extremes of literalism are balanced by extremes of metaphorical symbolism.

Unfortunately we cannot determine the feelings which certain words evoked among the communities now extinct; it is, indeed, difficult enough to do so among those still alive. We shall never know whether the Hebrews or the early Christians differed very much from ourselves in religious emotions. Did they conform to a certain standard of feeling and belief? It can be shown that what is now called individualism was not known in those epochs; on the other hand, a uniformity of belief, in the sense of defined agreement of dogma, was equally alien to priests, prophets, and people. It never existed because it was never sought until the split of Judaism and Christianity gave rise to it and promptly evoked a rigidity unknown in the Bible. The freedom behind the Scriptures must be borne in mind to understand the immense richness to be found there with respect to Heaven.

We have lost this freedom. Owing to our inability to think and feel Biblically we oscillate between literal fanaticism and liberal vagueness. Eschatology has become the special victim of mistaken methods. Some invent strange time-tables for the end of the world and the second coming of Christ and others explain these things away altogether. The Biblical conceptions of Heaven run counter to all such positions of either-or. They rest on the principle which may be summed up in the one word 'correspondence'. The wisdom of the Ancient Near East subscribed to the belief that in this nether world men experience life according to the eternal laws of creation. The earth corresponds to Heaven, and it also differs from Heaven. Correspondence includes both analogies and differences. In the Christian revelation this general principle is not violated but adjusted to the central figure of the

God-Man. Thus the Christian order claims to be the order of the whole world, both as origin and as end of all existence. It can be, and is, outraged and defied in the disorder of a fallen world of which sinful humanity is part. But even this passing order derives its reality (past, present, and future) from the cosmic order of God.

Heaven is a timeless theme and a rewarding one in the face of the ever-changing situation in the scientific world. Even Biblical exegesis cannot escape from the consequences of the vast findings of archaeology. The documentation of the middle of the twentieth century dwarfs that of only thirty years ago and will, no doubt, be dwarfed in its turn by what is yet to come. Ur, Mari, Nuzu, Ugarit, Qumran, Nag Hammadi have changed the climate of Biblical scholarship. The amount of re-writing that has to be done with respect to the history of Israel cannot yet be assessed. The theme of Heaven may, however, claim exemption from too much revision. The Biblical treatment has not been superseded but supplemented by the appearance of manuscripts and inscriptions. Thus the Discoveries from the Judaean Desert have shown, so far as their contents have been made public to date, that the Covenanters of Qumran took a great interest in heavenly things, especially in connexion with the book of Ezekiel and the heavenly Jerusalem.

Heaven suggests the themes of eternity above, which both edify men and challenge their ingenuity. Throughout Christendom, and also outside, men desire fervently to attain to an eternal end which corresponds to their moral and religious experience on earth.

CONTENTS

PRINCIPAL ABBREVIATIONS

ANET	*Ancient Near Eastern Texts Relating to the Old Testament,* Ed. J. B. Pritchard.
AO	*Der Alte Orient.*
ATAO	A. Jeremias, *Das Alte Testament im Lichte des Alten Orients* (1930).
BDB	Brown, Driver, Briggs, *A Hebrew and English Lexicon.*
CML	G. R. Driver, *Caananite Myths and Legends* (1956).
CQR	*The Church Quarterly Review.*
EB	*Encyclopaedia Biblica.*
ERE	*Encyclopaedia of Religion and Ethics.*
ET	*The Expository Times.*
E.T.	English Translation.
GFM	George Foot Moore, *Judaism in the First Centuries of the Christian Era,* vols. I and II (1927).
GJS	E. R. Goodenough, *Jewish Symbols in the Greco-Roman Period* (1953 ff.)
HTR	*Harvard Theological Review.*
ICC	The International Critical Commentaries.
JBL	*The Journal of Biblical Literature.*
JE	*The Jewish Encyclopaedia.*
JJS	*The Journal of Jewish Studies.*
JTS	*The Journal of Theological Studies.*
LXX	The Septuagint.
NSI	G. A. Cooke, *A Text-Book of North-Semitic Inscriptions* (1903).
PG	Migne, *Patrologia Graeca.*
PL	Migne, *Patrologia Latina.*
PW	Pauly-Wissowa, *Real-Encyclopädie der classischen Altertumswissenschaft.*
RAC	*Reallexicon für Antike und Christentum.*
RB	*Revue Biblique.*
RE	Hauck, *Realencyclopädie für protestantische Theologie und Kirche.*
RSV	Revised Standard Version.

SNTS	Studiorum Novi Testamenti Societas.
Str. B.	Strack-Billerbeck, *Kommentar zum Neuen Testament aus Talmud und Midrasch* (1928).
TWNT	*Theologisches Wörterbuch zum Neuen Testament,* edited by G. Kittel, subsequently by G. Friedrich, (1932– , in progress).
TZ	*Theologische Zeitschrift* herausgegeben von der Theologischen Fakultät der Universität Basel.
VT	Vetus Testamentum.
ZAW	*Zeitschrift für die alttestamentliche Wissenschaft.*
ZNW	*Zeitschrift für die neutestamentliche Wissenschaft.*

For abbreviations of the books of the Bible, of the Apocrypha and Pseudepigrapha, of the Dead Sea Scrolls, of Josephus and Philo, and of Rabbinical literature see also the respective Indexes.

The transliteration of the Hebrew follows the usual convention, except that soft ב = v (though the spelling of *Aboth* is retained) and ח = ch.

Chapter One

HEAVEN AND HUMANITY

THE religions of the world, except possibly primitive Buddhism, regard Heaven as an important reality. Their followers speak about and pray towards Heaven, for it is the obvious, self-evident, inescapable centre of man's most fervent hopes. Thither he looks for strength and gives thanks for the good gifts of life: from thence he hopes to receive a final reward for his aspirations upon earth. Yet, in spite of this general movement of man's faith to Heaven, it remains a strikingly elusive place. Perhaps it has the power of stirring deep feelings just because it can never be reached in this life nor be apprehended clearly by the human intellect. For man is born not only to look down to the earth and ahead to meet his kind but also to look up and around him, both as a spectator and as an actor.

SOME GENERAL CHARACTERISTICS

Frazer[1] has given a comprehensive picture of the place which the sky occupies in man's worship of nature. All the races are represented in the direct worship of Heaven, the great canopy which, to the uncritical sense, appears to cover the world: "no wonder that a phenomenon so universal and so impressive should at an early date have inspired men with wonder and awe and found a place in their religion".[2] Some tribes claimed to have come from Heaven. Among the Iroquois, for instance, the original female ancestress was believed to have fallen from

[1] *The Worship of Nature*, the Gifford Lectures for 1924–5.

[2] Ibid., p. 19.

Heaven.[1] Hence the worship of the sky had for some more than a feeling of the supernatural; the worship was associated with tribal solidarity. Moreover the sky was venerated not only for itself but for what it could and should give. Indeed, the dependence upon the sky also led to a struggle with the sky in the time of drought. The West African rain-makers were not content to ingratiate themselves with the sky but also threatened to set it on fire if it did not give the needed rain.[2] A distinction between a benevolent and a malevolent power in Heaven could not fail to arise.

In most mythologies the general chaos precedes the sky, and it is out of the original chaos that the world takes its origin. Hesiod sings of the traditions of Greece in his *Theogony*: "First chaos was, next ample-bosomed earth" (160); then "earth first produced the Heaven, whose starry cope, like himself immense, might compass her on every side" (173). The sky and the earth initiate a succession of events: "with Heaven consorting ocean from her bosom burst" (180). Ouranos and Gaia personify Heaven and earth, but these gods come to ruin "when vast Heaven came down from on high . . . desiring earth's embrace" (234 ff.). Then Kronos and Rhea enjoy the fruits of a treacherous victory, until their son Zeus ends their reign and triumphs himself in the sky, while Poseidon owns the watery realm and Hades the underworld. Thus the dominion of Heaven has changed hands.

In the Vedic religion, too, the sky is made out of the first sea or chaos after a great fight between giant powers. Then three Heavens—superior, middle, and lower—emerge, reflecting again a threefold division, albeit in the celestial sphere itself. It is not clear, however, why chaos led to existence and whether Heaven and earth are themselves gods, or were made by the gods, or even made the gods. In the song of Creation (Rigv. X, 129) darkness conceals the void and formless all. Then warmth and desire arise as mighty begetters, but one cannot tell whence the high and low realms originate. The principle of the union between opposites is a common theme. In China the male god

[1] Cf. ERE, IV, p. 127.

[2] Frazer, *Golden Bough*, I, p. 303.

Yang makes the sky with the female Yin, according to Li or natural law, by joining the light and the muddy matter. He represents the all-seeing, awful, wrathful sky and is represented by it.

These crude strands of mythology are easily reinterpreted in later times; in some myths the emphasis shifts from the simple worship of the sky to the complex tales about Heaven. A scientific interest ousts the purely religious wonder and investigates the manifold causes which may have contributed to the making of the universe. Against this the psychological approach, as for example in Buddhism, regards the material spheres of Heaven as stages of consciousness of life and beauty. Elsewhere the gods, too, are transformed and become in some measure independent of Heaven, though they make certain mountains their temporary homes. They are credited with great power, because they see everything from above, and with omnipresence, because "God is wherever the sky is". These sky-gods are connected with the heavenly realm of light and with the stars in particular, which serve as their eyes. They are "all-knowing because all-seeing and all-seeing because luminous".[1]

The regions on which the Christian interest must dwell in particular have yielded innumerable texts abounding with references to Heaven. In Egypt Re is lord over all; he declares: "Many were the beings which came forth from my mouth, before Heaven came into being."[2] He himself makes Heaven (Nut), which is the sky-goddess; she is held up over the earth by the god Shu.[3] But Heaven is primarily a place, with doors and the like, brilliant but unfruitful. The followers of Re go in and come out from thence. Most prominent of all, the Sun dwells in the sky and receives the homage of religious worship. When he sinks in the West he enters the night-Heaven.

In Mesopotamia, too, the myths of the gods and goddesses leave little room for an independent Heaven. In the Sumerian songs Heaven is a pure and peaceful place where the divine

[1] R. Pettazzoni, *The All-Knowing God,* 1956, pp. 12, 25.

[2] ANET, p. 6.

[3] ANET, p. 26.

residents have their being and move about.[1] In the famous Accadian myth of creation (Enuma Elish)—known in fact by its first line: "When on high the Heavens had not been named"[2]—chaos again precedes both Heaven and the gods; but once created, Heaven becomes an abode of social intercourse and hilarity for the gods. Marduk, the son of the gods, crosses Heaven like the Sun and splits Tiamat, the Deep, like a shellfish into two parts. One of these halves he sets up as the ceiling of the sky. The god, as the representative of his people, outstrips the celestial domain in power and significance. Marduk's temple tower, called Etemen-anki, was regarded as the cultic "House of the Foundation of Heaven and earth". Similarly in the Hittite mythology the gods sit in Heaven and listen to each other after the manner of kings.[3] Most familiar of all is the picture of the gods who appear and act in the *Iliad* (esp. Bk. XIV). Zeus is king and Hera queen of Heaven; the gods confer on the summit of Olympus where the golden throne stands and reaches into the sky. Heaven and mountain are almost identical as abodes of the weather-god: in Greece especially the mountains act as prophets of the coming weather which Heaven determines.[4]

From the Biblical point of view the Ugaritic texts excel all others in importance. These recently excavated documents from northern Syria, though gravely damaged and not easily put together, reveal the nature of the myth-ritual pattern which obtained north of Canaan and west of Haran at and before the time of the migrations of the people of Israel.[5] Of the hero-god

[1] ATAO, p. 26. Cf. S. N. Kramer, 'Sumerian Mythology', *Memoirs of the American Philosophical Society,* XXI, 1944, pp. 38 ff., for the fundamental cosmogonic concepts: Heaven and Earth (An-Ki), products of the primeval sea and the cosmic mountain, whose base was the bottom of the earth and whose peak the top of Heaven. An, the male Heaven-god in human form, carries off Heaven, Ki the earth, and together they produce Enlil, the air-god. Cf. also H. Winckler, *Himmels—und Weltenbild der Babylonier,* 1903, AO III, 2–3, esp. p. 11: "In erster Linie sind es stets die Himmelserscheinungen, welche das göttliche Walten erkennen lassen, und die Himmelskunde ist daher die Grundlage des ganzen Systems. . . . einer göttlichen und einheitlichen Weltordnung".

[2] ANET, pp. 60 ff. This myth, though much later than the Sumerian myths, is nevertheless continuous with Sumerian culture.

[3] ANET, p. 120.

[4] Cf. M. P. Nilsson, *Geschichte der griechischen Religion,* I, 1941, p. 367.

[5] Cf. CML, Introduction.

Baal, who conquers the sea and death and rides in the Heavens as victor, or upon the clouds, one lip to earth and one to Heaven, more will have to be said.

The world view of the Ancient Near East is as rich as its mythologies and cannot be reduced to a basic common denominator. Throughout, the reality of Heaven becomes part of its scientific interest, its imaginative art, its corporate worship, and its social traditions. It is an achievement of its culture that it sets Heaven within the whole pattern of life. No doubt the visible sky as well as the concept of Heaven stirred up different feelings and associations and nuances among the peoples; nevertheless the antique world always assumed the existence of a heavenly world. The world was a universe, alive, finite, crowded with beings; Heaven and earth were its chief components and they were related to each other. The *Corpus Hermeticum* (whatever its date, it certainly preserves typical beliefs) acknowledges the beauty of Heaven, which is the image of Egypt, and contrasts it with the earth from which ocean divides it. A gate opens into Heaven and its celestial spheres which constitute a harmony; the Law of Heaven is good, but war and fiery chariots are also known there. Isis is the queen of Heaven and the devotee has the power to travel through the spheres and hear the tongues, voices, and songs of Heaven and to acquire a heavenly body. Indeed, the speculation about Heaven in the Gnostic mysteries is less interested in the nature of the universe than in the participation of the heavenly realm through regeneration and illumination. The evil god of heaven and his demons shut the desired entrance and man must find the means of bliss to traverse the Heavens without the hindrance of a body. In the ether, among the stars, are the Elysian fields which the votaries desire for themselves.[1] The Milky Way serves as a road for the souls as they approach the realm of the Dead.[2]

In the developed mysteries of the Near East, Heaven is not only the goal to be attained but also the determining factor of human destiny. Astronomy and astrology were indivisible. The

[1] Cf. F. Cumont, *The Oriental Religions in Roman Paganism*, 1911, pp. 126 ff.; notes 64, 65.

[2] Cf. M. P. Nilsson, *Geschichte der griechischen Religion*, Bd. II, 1950, pp. 229 f.

whole world depends on the constellations of the stars. The universe and the world are ruled by an eternal necessity and this is made evident by the starry sky. The celestial writing manifests the future, and the astronomer or 'wise man' or 'star-gazer' determines the course of public and private life. The Ptolemaic system comprised both astronomy and astrology and reigned for more than a thousand years. Thus the belief that the heavenly bodies were alive and influenced man's destiny never died out. The Orphic doctrine that the wheel of birth and the stages of life depend upon the cycles of the circling stars crops up everywhere, even to this day. Even after the gods had vanished from the scene of popular credulity the hard core of celestial determinism remained. It can still be recognized in the names of the days of the week, dedicated, as they have been for centuries, to the Sun, the Moon, Mars, Mercury, Jupiter, Venus, and Saturn. Similarly, as weeks, months, and years revolve and return to their starting-point, the view of the universe as returning to its origin attracted common assent.

THE GREEK DEVELOPMENT

However strong the Gnostic appeal may have been, by no means all leaders and thinkers indulged in the fancies of the mysteries. The inconsistencies of the cosmic myths challenged the critical spirit of all ages. At Miletus, the place where the Aegean and Ionian civilization met, Thales (sixth century B.C.) made the first attempt to reach a scientific cosmology. Although introduced and indebted to Egyptian geometry, he proceeded to something new in the empirical application of his data. At least tradition credits him with opposing the mythical cosmology. From now on, in Greek science, the approach to the heavenly phenomena begins to be scientific though its success is vitiated by the lack of adequate means of observation. Pythagoras taught the existence of ten celestial spheres (stars, planets, sun, moon, earth, counter-earth) revolving in harmony, and empirical criticism failed him. Yet "the true hypothesis that the earth revolved round the sun was actually put forward by Aristarchus of Samos in the third century B.C., and his work was subsequently followed up by Seleucus of Seleucia who explained that the universe was heliocentric, that the earth revolved round the sun and rotated upon its axis".[1] Even Plato, whose influence was to become more far-reaching, states this astonishing fact (which was to be lost again for centuries); in the *Laws* (822 a, b) he clearly thinks of a revolving universe in which the earth also moves. But this theory is with Plato not a purely scientific proposition, for it is God, the 'best soul', who initiates the movement of the universe. Thus, although he opposes the crude myths, which he deems unworthy of belief—he alludes to Ocean and Thetis, the progeny of Heaven and earth, from whom the gods spring, without assenting to this belief (*Timaeus* 40 e, 41 a)—he again unites cosmological discoveries with moral and philosophical axioms.

The *Timaeus*[2] occupies the central place in classical cosmology and, through Philo, exercised a direct influence on Hebrew thought, both in New Testament and Talmudic writings. Plato assumes the existence of an eternal order to which the moral world of men corresponds. The soul is itself a counterpart, in miniature, of the soul of the world. Therefore it knows, even before birth, the universal order or harmony, which the visible architecture of the Heavens reveals in time. The material Heavens are below the supercelestial void (*Phaedr.* 247). Before the Heavens came into being there was no time, but time and Heaven came into being simultaneously and may dissolve together. Heaven is, in that sense, a copy of the eternal pattern and governed by the principles of the universe, such as rotation, affinity, and repulsion. The earth is within the Heavens and the planets act in the Heavens as the instruments of time. The stars are like them made of fire and round in shape and are distributed all round the Heavens as adornments, embroidering the whole 'cosmos'. At this point, however, the personal intelligences enter the universe, for the stars are equivalent to the heavenly race of the gods.[3] The universe is not a mechanical arrangement nor a dynamic revolution

[1] W. R. Halliday, *The Pagan Background of Early Christianity*, p. 209, with refs. to Cumont, *Astrology and Religion*, pp. 67–8, Heath, *Aristarchus of Samos*, pp. 301 ff., and Plutarch, *De facie in orbe lunae* 6; *Moralia* 922 f.

[2] Cf. F. M. Cornford, *Plato's Cosmology*, 1937. He opposes Taylor's theory in his *Commentary on Timaeus*, 1928, that the *Timaeus* is a spurious work. The relevant paragraphs are 31–40.

[3] As created by the Demiurge, cf. Rep. 508.

but rather the shining expression of a moral and intelligent pattern of supreme goodness. Hence Plato stresses the superiority of "higher and heavenly" things. The lower realm is good and harmonious only through the order imprinted upon it from above. The visible and the temporal must imitate the eternal forms to attain to reality and goodness. The world, as known on earth, derives from Heaven, the holy abode of divinity, which is made of the purest material after the eternal fashion. Thus the principle of correspondence affects the whole cosmology, macrocosm and microcosm achieving an essential parallelism. The higher illuminates and orders the lower, the smaller reflects the larger.

It is not surprising that Aristotle, anxious to save the phenomena (as it is said), accepted Plato's non-mythical approach but resisted a cosmology which imputes to Heaven a transcendental reality. Ironically the so-called empiricist, familiar to us as pointing to the earth as against Plato's gesture towards Heaven, insists that "the first Heaven must be eternal" (*Metaphys.* XII, 7) and is made of fire, a fifth element (*De Caelo*, I, 2). He holds that "the Heaven as a whole neither came into being nor admits of destruction, as some assert, but is one and eternal, with no end or beginning of its total duration, containing and embracing in itself the infinity of time" (*De Caelo*, II, 1). Following the observation of the data he dismisses the notion of a pre-existent idea of Heaven, and so restores the geocentric view to its former validity. He makes the fateful distinction between Ouranos and the "sublunary" region. The superior glory of Heaven's nature is proportionate to its distance from this world of ours. Yet even for Aristotle the traditional principle of correspondence remains in force. Despite the pronounced pluralism in his view of individual entelechies the world is still a universe and Heaven a principal part thereof.

At the dawn of the Christian era the Mediterranean world clearly possessed as great a variety of views about Heaven as there were mythologies, some of which were becoming defunct. Popular cosmology was not only based on the geocentric system but saw the whole world revolving in spheres of seven, guided by the principles of sympathy and correspondence. The dead hand of astrology coupled with unsound science triumphed in human affairs. Even the materialists and atomists were led astray by false presuppositions and arrived at detailed cosmologies as fantastic as their opponents'. These circumstances favoured the acceptance of Ptolemy's *Almagest* in the long period of scientific decline which followed.

SOME OPPOSING SCHOOLS

Cicero gives us a most interesting exposé of contemporary theories and the speculative feelings behind them in his *De Natura Deorum*. Velleius the Epicurean, Balbus the Stoic, and Cotta, the liberal and agnostic pupil of the Academy, speak as the respective leaders of their schools. On the whole Cicero is inclined to feel that Balbus's discourse "approximated more nearly to a semblance of truth" (III, 40), while Velleius supports Cotta's assaults on the traditional doctrines. Atomic materialism is seen to contrast with idealistic transcendentalism. The whole question comes to a head in II, 1: "When we gaze up toward the sky and contemplate the heavenly bodies, what can be so obvious and so manifest as that there must exist some power possessing transcendent intelligence by whom these things are ruled?" The dazzling vault of heaven, which all mankind invoke as Jove, testifies with its own evidence. Balbus interprets the phenomenon: "Has not man's reason penetrated even to the sky? We alone of living creatures know the risings and the settings and the courses of the stars . . . contemplating the heavenly bodies the mind arrives at a knowledge of the gods, from which arises piety with its comrades justice and the rest of the virtues, the sources of a life of happiness." Again the implicit parallelism decrees that the world is a universe in which Heaven and heavenly bodies exist providentially for the sake of gods and men. "There is no sight of which it is more impossible to grow weary, none more beautiful nor displaying a more surpassing wisdom and skill" (II, 61–2). Balbus speaks almost in the same vein in which Cleanthes the Stoic (301–233 B.C.) had addressed Zeus in his famous hymn: ". . . The whole order of the Heavens obeys thy word, as it moves around the earth."

In Book III, however, Cotta tears Balbus's assertions to shreds. The absurdities of the myths are once again exposed and he charges the Stoics with exceeding the vulgar stupidities in their deification of the stars. The argument from the awe-inspiring phenomena of nature is invalid, for experience teaches precisely the absence of a providential government. Virtue is not rewarded from Heaven and vice is punished, if at all, by man. The scepticism of the age comes out with great force. No more complete denial of a heavenly government and justice could well be imagined. Yet it must still be presumed that even the Epicureans would not have cared to deny the existence of the sky as a material fact. Their denial is, in fact, based upon moral and empirical grounds; for, even if the religious world-view be shaken, the celestial sphere as such is as real as ever.

From our point of view it is impossible to apportion soundness or extravagance to any set of cosmological views. Reason and mysticism mingle freely. The same Cicero, who gives a detached picture of what may be true, also amuses himself in recalling the very important Pythagorean blend of geometry and mysticism in the *Somnium Scipionis*. This dream is typical in that it views the universe in terms of mathematical and quasi-musical harmony and makes full allowance for grades of height and splendour in the spheres. Mystical emotion always goes hand in hand with scientific speculation and, for some, is definitely more important. The Emperor Julian tells us that his mind was so completely swayed by the light which illumines the Heavens that he desired not only to gaze at the sun but at the clear and cloudless firmament by night. His contemplation of the beauty of the Heavens, he insists, had nothing to do with science.[1] It is the effect which the visible phenomenon evokes which really matters, be it the subjective elation or the realization of the spiritual world behind the sensory object. The latter, Platonic, approach to the problem comes to the fore in Plotinus who asks, for instance, "what room, if any, there is for the arts and sciences in Heaven".[2] His answer is that in this pure All the symmetry of Beauty and Truth is eternal. Heaven is a spiritual state—"the Soul is the Matter of Spirit" there—whose immutable bliss consists in the union of

[1] Cf. *Hymn to King Helios*, 130 D.

[2] Cf. W. R. Inge, *The Philosophy of Plotinus* 1941, vol. II, pp. 86–91.

all that is, a felicity partly reflected below.[1] Against this Lucretius can be cited for the unmystical opinion that man is heavenly while he is alive on earth, for Heaven is Father of all.[2]

PHILO

Philo took upon himself the task of comparing and reconciling, if necessary, the different cosmic theories and the strands of Biblical revelation, as contained in the Scriptures of the Jews. Heaven is one of the virtuous mysteries, the soul's fatherland (Agric. 65), which is only fit to be studied by the initiated (Cher. 42). Its secrets do not admit of a ready answer: is Heaven of solid ice? or of purest fire? or is it made of a different, fifth substance? Is there any density upward from the firmament? Or is the sky merely a cover without depth? Are the stars animated and intelligent? Heaven is incomprehensible and the search after it is without result and fruitless (Som. I, 21–4). Nevertheless, something may and must be said, lest men worship the host of Heaven (Spec. I, 15; Her. 97). Heaven, being of infinite greatness, is not comprehended by anything, not even the void. There is no length, nor breadth, but a concentric whole, which is comprehended by God (Her. 228 ff.). Heaven pertains to the one undivided universe (Praem. 36), the one whole providential world which was originally planned and brought into existence after the beginning (Opif. 17 ff., 171). Earth and water are in the middle; air, fire and ether are above, and Heaven acts as the cover or limit (Plant. 2–3). A false etymology of Ouranos makes this point: ὅρος is limit, ὁρατός visible (Opif. 37). Heaven, then, is the Head of the universe (as of the ladder in Jacob's dream), the intelligible world of ideas or powers (Som. I, 184–8). There is a traffic of souls in the air, equal to the number of the stars (Som. I, 133–7) from whom they are, nevertheless, to be distinguished. The angels are words of God and move about the

[1] Cf. J. Moreau, *L'Idée d'Univers dans la Pensée Antique,* 1953, esp. for this verdict on Plotinus: "L'ontologie de Plotin, transposant le naturalisme en idéalisme, reliant aux exigences de la réflexion l'image biologique de l'Univers, achève l'élaboration de la cosmologie antique; mais en même temps elle édifie la conception du monde spirituel dans laquelle pourra se développer aux âges suivants, la théologie mystique" (p. 50).

[2] *De Rer. Nat.* II, 991.

minds of those persons who wash off every defilement and become the abode of God. These souls move through the air and they go to Heaven after death (Mos. II, 288, 291); the angels, too, traverse the spheres as souls without bodies, as the army and people of God (Sacr. 5), acting as commanders under God or as ambassadors who travel in the air (Abr. 115; Gig. 6; Plant. 14; Conf. 174; Som. I, 141). The Greek demons are in fact the angels of the Bible. The whole cosmos is alive with intelligent beings and the Cherubim are symbols of the rotation of the whole Heaven (Cher. 21 ff.). One Cherub represents the outer sphere of fixed stars, the other the inner sphere of the planets.

EARLY CHRISTIAN INTERPRETERS

The Hebrew-Christian tradition had no reason to quarrel with the multifarious aspects of Heaven, as we shall have occasion to show in detail. Philo had shown how cosmogony could be adjusted and allied to the data of revelation. The sky, as a physical and analogical reality above, did not contradict the Church's Creed. It was quite another and necessary matter to guard the faithful against the bizarre schemes of the Gnostics. From Irenaeus[1] we learn indirectly how their esoteric speculations invented aeons and emanations. The Valentinians observed the orthodox scheme of seven Heavens, whereas Marcus increased this by one to eight, and Basilides reached the impressive total of three hundred and sixty-five.[2] Paganism too, and, above all, the new enemy Mithraism, continued the worship of the heavenly bodies and fostered the work of astrologers and soothsayers.

Against this background it is all the more remarkable that the great Alexandrians of the critical period (*ca.* 180–230 A.D.) expressly set out to beat the Gnostics by insisting on their own knowledge, which included that of the Heavens. In St. Clement the references are incidental, as to the "seven Heavens, which some reckon one above the other",[3] or the fifth Heaven which he gets from an Apocalypse of Zephaniah now lost.[4] Origen

[1] *Adv.* haer. I, v, 2; I, xvii, 1 (A.-N.C.L.). Cf. Tertullian, *adv. Valent.* XX.

[2] Aug. *De Haer.* I, 4.

[3] *Strom.* IV, 5.

[4] Ibid., V, 11.

is more explicit and he exemplifies an attitude of both caution and interest. He protests against the fatalism derived from the constellations of nature and he seeks to safeguard the doctrine of Divine Providence by contrast.[1] But it is not a simple matter, for the heavenly government does not function without the employment of the stars; there are powers which direct men for good or ill. As long as paganism is kept at bay celestialism is perfectly right and even necessary. Origen speaks the common mind when he refers to the air between Heaven and earth as not devoid of living and rational beings. "The Scriptures, which are current in the Churches of God do not speak of 'seven' Heavens, or any definite number at all, but they do appear to teach the existence of 'Heavens', whether that means the 'spheres' of those bodies which the Greeks call 'planets' or something more mysterious".[2] We may vary, he admits, about the numbers, but we should be very foolish to ignore the upper world. "There is no doubt that something more illustrious and excellent than this present world is pointed out by the Saviour, at which he incites or encourages believers to aim. But whether that world to which he desires to allude be far separated and divided from this, either by situation, or nature, or glory; or whether it be superior in glory and quality but confined within the limits of this world (which seems to me more probable), is nevertheless uncertain, and in my opinion an unsuitable subject for human thought".[3] Origen truly shapes the Christian dialectic; the notion of the spatial ascent is to be retained, but cosmological fancies are discouraged since they so easily jeopardize true piety. It is enough to acknowledge that the created world is a universe and that the earthly and infernal realms are opposed by the celestial spheres and the super-celestial abode of God. Since, then, these worlds tower one above the other the soul also must ascend: "The pure in heart ascends to the region of the air until he reaches the kingdom of the Heavens, passing through those mansions which the Greeks call spheres and the Scriptures Heavens."[4]

[1] Cf. G. L. Prestige, *God in Patristic Thought,* 1952, esp. pp. 53–75.

[2] *Contra Cels.* VI, 21.

[3] *De Princ.* II, III, 6.

[4] *De Princ.*, II, XI, 6.

According to St. Basil, Heaven is distinct from the firmament outside the world, though not without relation to the world.[1]

SYMBOLISM

The West, however, being more practical and less allegorically minded, did not wholly accept the heritage of the East. At the end of the classical period St. Augustine formulated a doctrine of the City of God whose perfections and peace were of a Heaven less tied up with astronomy and cosmogony. He finds it, of course, appropriate to denounce in this connexion the mythical absurdities of Kronos and Ouranos, Saturn and Caelus. His own feeling he states in a reflection on II Cor. XII, 1–3, a passage to which we shall have to revert later on: "If we thus accept the third Heaven whither the Apostle is seized, in such a way as to believe that there is a fourth as well and other Heavens higher still, beneath which lies the third Heaven, just as some people hold there to be eight, others nine, others even ten . . . it is a wearisome thing to discuss whether they be material, as some do."[2] St. Augustine is obviously not even disposed to take an interest in the numbers or series of spheres and their component materials. Thereupon he anticipates a good deal of modern thought when he makes it clear that there are three types of things seen, as there are three types of vision: physical, mental, and spiritual. Hence there is first the material, Heaven, above the water; the second, seen in trances (such as St. Peter's vision of the sheet, Acts, ch. x), half material, half spiritual; and thirdly, the Heaven, purged from all sense experience, the Paradise of Paradises, which St. Paul beheld.[3] It is this last or third Heaven which is eternal. Both the Church and the earthly order derive their respective pattern and authority from this sole reality. For St. Augustine the cosmological side, strictly kept in bounds and simplified, is harnessed to the social and ecclesiastical concern. Having freed his terminology from the mythological taint, he abounds in the use of celestial origin and purpose to describe the Christian life on earth. Just because the earthly city was about to

[1] *Homil.* I, 5; PG XXIX, 13.

[2] *De Genesi ad litteram,* XII, ch. 29. Cf. *De Civ. Dei* X, 5.

[3] *De Genesi ad litteram,* XII, ch. 34.

be overwhelmed by the might of Darkness it was necessary to stress the indestructible radiance of the heavenly. Heaven is the transcendent order, the universal reign of Christ, the home of the Christian, the end of all creation.[1] The Church takes her beginning in the earthly Jerusalem in order to enjoy God in the heavenly Jerusalem: "Ab hac enim incipit, ad illam terminat".[2]

Even more important than the teachings of isolated theologians is the unanimous witness or early Christian art to the belief that the faithful are made partakers of the whole world by the merits and victory of Christ. The Byzantine mosaics which survive in the churches of Rome and Ravenna invariably portray Christ Triumphant on the clouds and in heavenly majesty, surrounded by Patriarchs, Prophets, Apostles, and his Mother. The worshippers who gaze into the apse have a foretaste of their goal, which is Heaven with the heavenly company. The motif is so common and so popular that it may be found even on a sarcophagos, such as that of Junius Bassus (+ A.D. 359) which depicts Christ standing upon the firmament, which is the veil which Ouranos spreads out over his head. The Kingship of Christ extends over the whole world and the Christian enjoys the benefits of his cosmic rule. The evidence of early Roman mosaics and paintings proves "how familiar . . . the symbol of the starry realm of Heaven was"; the ceiling of the Churches became the "Coelum".[3]

THE MEDIEVAL CLIMAX

The celestial tradition was certainly not lost during the barbarians' conquests in western Europe, and even Islam, notwithstanding the perilous attacks, spoke and understood the same language of a realm above. Clearly the medieval climax in theology, poetry, and art comes after a long continuous line of development. This does not mean that the orthodox view was not then in jeopardy. There were evidently doubts about the waters above the sky and that the firmament made a division

[1] *De Civ. Dei* XII, 16.

[2] Ps. CXLVII, PL XXXVII, 1929.

[3] Cf. J. Wilpert, *Die römischen Mosaiken und Malereien,* 1916, Bd. I, p. 55. See esp. plates 70–2 for the Throne in S. Maria Maggiore, pl. 116 the Heavenly City in S. Cecilia, Trastevere, and the relevant paintings of S. Maria Antiqua in vol. IV.

and that a plurality of Heavens really existed. The divergences of opinion about the world had also percolated down the centuries. Some believed the starry firmament to be composed harmoniously of the four elements whilst others postulated the quintessence as another special element. The never-ending riddle of the atmosphere, equated by some with the firmament, opened the way to many conflicting solutions. The authority of St. Basil, Strabo, and Bede and others favoured the existence of the empyrean Heaven as the highest physical immensity above the sky.

The orthodox theologians naturally defended the account of the creation as given in Genesis from which they derived the hierarchical structure of all being. According to St. Thomas Aquinas everything has its rightful place in the closed system of the universe, dependent upon the operation of the 'First Heaven', from whence the spheres have taken their origin. The graded universe embodies the principle of unity and separation; in the scholastic cosmology the heavens coinhere: There is only one universe for angels and saints.[1] The light is above the Heavens and the stars and the earth; more important, the spiritual universe towers above the physical. Hence the scientific interest must also be subjected to revelation. St. Bonaventura places a crystalline Heaven under the empyrean "for theological rather than physical reasons",[2] noting that eight spheres may have satisfied the pagan philosophers, nine were favoured by the more enlightened ones, and ten—i.e. the Heaven of immovable light, eternal rest and life—by the completely enlightened.

But even apart from theology the sky was still the same as that of the classical world. It would have been madness not to acknowledge the supremacy of the heavenly Power. Heaven manifested the Divine Will and Providence and constituted the goal of human aspirations. In frescoes and pictures it is furnished with angelic and saintly bands who surround the throne of God.[3]

[1] Cf. esp. *Summa Theol.* I, 61, 4; 66, 3; 68. The empyrean is the highest Heaven of creation (but not the Heaven of the Blessed Trinity), nextcome the crystalline and the starry Heaven of eight spheres.

[2] II *Sent.* 14, 2, 1, 1. See also Gilson, *La Philosophie de St. Bonaventura,* 1924, pp. 275 ff.

[3] Cf. the typical judgment scenes, such as Pietro Cavallini's (1293) at S. Cecilia in Trastevere *or the two examples given in the frontispiece.*

It was left to Dante to describe and bequeath to posterity what is no doubt the most perfect expression of this world-order, in which Hell opens its abyss to punish evildoers, Purgatory rises steeply over the Antipodes and receives the penitent who, deserving and wishing to be chastened for their sins, climb upwards to the earthly Paradise. The contemporary world-view did not contradict but supported this progress, tier by tier. The world, through which the poet ascends, can be mapped in detail. At the centre is the earth, motionless and massive, surrounded by the ocean and air and fire. Heaven leads to Heaven, the respective spheres of Moon, Mercury, Venus, Sun, Mars, Jupiter, Saturn, and the Stars succeeding each other, before the crystalline goal and summit of Paradise is reached, where the poet sees the snow-white rose, the blessed children and saints, the Virgin Mother and Christ. The mystical vision of God is the end of the All. Towards this centre of the sensible and finite universe the Angels, Archangels, Principalities, Powers, Virtues, Dominations, Thrones, Cherubim, and Seraphim gaze and minister in the corresponding order of ascending perfections and disciplines.[1] The effect on common piety is well known; François Villon (b. 1431) expresses it in his ballad, *Le Testament*, his mother lending the touching voice:

> Femme je suis povrette et ancïenne,
> Qui riens ne sçay; oncques lettre ne lus.
> Au moustier voy dont suis paroissienne
> Paradis paint, ou sont harpes et lus,
> Et ung enfer ou dampnez sont boullus:
> L'ung me fait paour, l'autre joye et liesse.
> (893–8).

Behind the medieval mentality lies the living feeling that the present world, and especially its churches, reflects in some essential measure the glories of the City of God. Those who sing of the heavenly Jerusalem

[1] Cf. D. Sayers, *The Divine Comedy* (Penguin Classics), for Dante's Cosmology in the relevant parts of the Introductions. For a detailed guide, M. A. Orr, *Dante and the Medieval Astronomers*, 1913; (new ed. 1955).

In hac urbe lux solemnis
Ver aeternum, pax perennis;
In hac odor implens caelos,
In hac semper festum melos!
Urbs caelestis, urbs beata
Supra petram collocata. . . .

or

O quanta, qualia sunt illa sabbata,
Quae semper celebrat superna curia!
. . . .
Vere Ierusalem est illa civitas,
Cuius pax iugis est, summa iucunditas
. . . .
Ibi, molestiis finitis omnibus,
Securi cantica Sion cantabimus. . . .

affirm even for themselves the possession of and the desire for some share in the light of the heavenly commonwealth. Their little world reflects the seat of David and all the other holy things, which now exist eternally (always: semper!) and unchangeably in Heaven. For enthusiasm and intensity of feeling, despite its great earthly limitations and offences, these centuries may surely be acclaimed as unique. Men lived in the belief that "he, who through his incarnation united earthly things with heavenly" could and would make them also partakers with the heavenly host.

UPHEAVALS

It would be inaccurate, however, to underrate the scientific differences between the different medieval schools. Aquinas, the Aristotelian, ascribed to Heaven a form and substance which contrasts sharply with the Platonic idealization of St. Bonaventura. More important still, the pure empiricism, with which, for example, Roger Bacon is credited, may have rebelled altogether against the dogma of the religious schools. It must be remembered that the Ptolemaic system of a mass of circles had really ceased to operate efficiently; it was both complicated and inadequate to the task of explaining the phenomena. Neither scholars nor ordinary laymen before the Reformation always gave their allegiance to orthodox cosmology.[1] It is said even of someone like Dante that his description of Hell, Purgatory, and Heaven was never meant to be physically accurate.[2] Men may have enjoyed the allegory of the *Comedy,* then as now, without placing their faith in the world-edifice behind the ascent. Yet it required scientific demonstration and not feeling or conjecture to end the Ptolemaic age. Clearly there had been anti-geocentric astronomers before Copernicus reached Bologna from Padua. Nicole Oresme in the late fourteenth century and the Cardinal Nicholas of Cusa (1401–61), for example, had anticipated the imminent changes. At the critical period (1496–1505) heliocentric notions were given the innocent-looking label 'Pythagorean', possibly to conceal their newness. They found a permanent place in 1543 when Copernicus published his *De Revolutionibus Orbium Coelestium.* Writing in the same year to Pope Paul III he refers himself to Cicero's *Academica* (II, 123) where the Platonic doctrine of the motion of the universe had already been stated somewhat obscurely. Like every great man he owed, and was anxious to acknowledge, his debt to precursors and contemporaries. He even retained a lot of Ptolemaic ballast and method: 'The Copernican view looked backward as much as forward."[3]

The Church accepted these findings readily: a heliocentric system need not offend the faith. The scenes of Paradise and the Ascension could be and were painted by the great masters as heretofore. The usual time-lag between theory and popularization also obtained in this case. Even Copernicus could still write in the old-fashioned language: "The earth conceives by the Sun and becomes pregnant with annual rebirth". The whole reorientation might have proceeded along calm paths of restatement if it had not been for the next stages in astronomical dis-

[1] Cf. For 'Criticism of Aristotle', A. C. Crombie, *Augustine to Galileo,* 1952.

[2] Cf. D. Sayers, op. cit., Hell, p. 14.

[3] Cf. C. D. Hellmann, 'Science in the Renaissance: a Survey', *Renaissance News,* VIII, IV, p. 193. Cf. E. Gilson, *History of Philosophy in the Middle Ages,* E. T., 1955, p. 518: "The theory of the diurnal movement of the earth was known by everyone in the Faculty of Arts at the university of Paris at the time" (fourteenth century).

covery and philosophical speculation. Even before Copernicus the new ideas had seemed to imply and had been attacked as veiled forms of pantheism. Though nothing could have been further from the purposes of Copernicus, Galileo, and Kepler than to alienate people from the faith in God and his providential order and the 'harmony of the world', these suspicions gained ground. It became both easy and advantageous to identify the new science with the blasphemies of the age.

And not entirely without reason: Giordano Bruno (d. 1600) was not concerned with minor matters, like the movement of the earth, but with the infinite space of the universe, in which the solar system is only a lowly member. Not only the sky is removed but earth is relegated to an unprecedented insignificance in a wholly new world without a Heaven. Bruno's pantheistic leanings cost him his life and made his theories heretical. When Galileo was condemned to protective custody (1633) the authorities reached a tragic turning-point. From now on the bad investment in the outmoded Ptolemaic system became a matter of faith, a test of loyalty. The Heaven of religion and the Heaven of science were cut asunder. New and various questions began to be asked: Was there a Heaven where God dwelt? Were other stars inhabited? Did other systems exist outside the solar universe? What if there was no system at all and a universe could not be said to exist? Science began to race towards complete liberation and a new world-view. Not many centuries hence and the revolution will be complete. Laplace will demonstrate the mechanics of the universe and, in his view, the existence of a Creator and Sustainer becomes an unnecessary hypothesis.

Oddly enough, there is no evidence that the Reformers championed the cause of the new science. Luther is accused of having revised Osiander's preface to the work of Copernicus so as to denounce more forcefully this "upstart astrologer" who dared to set his own authority above that of Holy Scripture. Luther, who has been hailed as "wrestling upward, pushing beyond the roof of the cloister to the blue sky, higher and higher, to the light" (Uhland), was not interested in cosmology, which, as part of philosophy, he wished to sever from his freed theology. When he interpreted Genesis in the old-fashioned way he neither was drawn into complex questions nor seemed aware of heliocentric possibilities. Heaven is still above and God dwells there.

It is one of the ironies of history that the school of Wittenberg committed itself to an irrational and unscientific bias which could not accommodate the giants of the age and their discoveries. Luther approved anti-rationalism, mocking openly: "The faithful strangle Reason and say: listen well, Reason: thou art a foolish blind wench".[1] And condemning Copernicus, his contemporary, he comments: "A new astrology was being made up to prove that the earth moved and revolved—not Heaven or firmament, Sun and Moon—just as if someone sat and were moved in a carriage or in a ship and thought that he himself was sitting still and rested while the ground and trees were moving. But so it is nowadays: if you want to be clever you invent something of your own. . . . That fool wishes to change about the whole art of astronomy. But Holy Writ testifies Joshua bid the sun stand still and not the earth."[2] Evidently even Melanchthon followed suit and Calvin, though often credited with a greater readiness to allow secular science its own place, had no use whatever for Copernicus. The same fatal argument is heard: "Who will venture to place the authority of Copernicus above that of Holy Scripture?"

The documentation of the sixteenth century on the Continent is lamentably meagre owing to the endless rule of violence for over a century after the Reformation. Luther's extreme view may not have been shared among the leaders, now mute, who were not wholly abandoned to religious and power politics. What did a man like Erasmus[3] think of the new astronomy? Was he interested? Would he connect its implications with a religious term like Heaven? It is impossible to judge how far a generation is aware of its own major developments.[4]

[1] See Luther on Galations, ed. Walch, VIII, p. 2043; cf. Dollinger, *Die Reformation*, I, 475–81.

[2] From Luther's *Tischreden*, ed. Walch, XXII, 2260. This chapter is full of praise for astronomy and abuse of astrology—Copernicus evidently serves the latter.

[3] Died 1536. The gigantic *Opus Epistolarum Des. Erasmi Roterrodami* yields three references to Astrology, one indirect contact with Copernicus (XI, p. 308), and nothing else.

[4] See e.g. H. Butterfield, *The Origins of Modern Science*, 1949.

THE NEW LOOK

It is not our intention here to attempt to summarize the extremely complex results of the cosmic revolution in the West. A chronological account of how the world reacted to the termination of its familiar conception of the general pattern of the universe would be totally misleading since there never could be, and never came into existence, a uniform new cosmography, to which all men alike could subscribe. Differences of education and interest as well as political considerations were of far greater importance in the succeeding centuries than abstract research. Nevertheless, it remained true that the earth had lost its Heaven, the universe had no roof to cover it and a new freedom invaded men's outlook. Before the religious reaction can be assessed it is both necessary and illuminating to enquire how the traditional belief in Heaven fared among the contemporaries and followers of the discoverers of the new world.

The ancient feeling for Heaven appears to have persisted for a long time.[1] Though secularized in a way, Heaven did not lose its wonder. If the new endless universe replaced the old it could evoke an even higher degree of awe. Not less but more amazement could be felt by those who appreciated the vastness of the immensity around the earth and who, with Pascal, could exclaim: "Le silence de ces espaces infinis m'effraie." The note of cosmic emancipation rings through the observations of men like Kepler and there is at first no momentous break between traditional religion and the new cosmology. In this radically new situation Heaven does not figure as an obsolete term but as a reality far greater and richer than the finite vault of old.

The most impressive witness for this continuity is of course Shakespeare. He is not in the least deflated in his celestial awareness by the heliocentric re-shuffle. In numberless passages Heaven is mentioned in the old sense, as if the very name arouses that peculiar feeling of dread and virtue. "Who ever knew the Heavens menace so?" asks Casca when the conspirators against

[1] And still does, especially among children and peasants: the sky is 'above'. The children's game of hop-scotch is typical for the power of the ancient world-view: in some countries it resembles the 'cosmic house' with the roof which bears the title of 'Heaven'.

Caesar fear the tumultuous night. Heaven infuses men and beasts with "all these fires to make them instruments of fear and warning unto some monstrous state". The classical view of the world as a universe is still alive: "the Heavens themselves, the planets, and this centre, observe degree, priority, and place, insisture, course, proportion, season, form, office, and custom, in all line of order." Moreover, man's felicity and misery can be measured, so to speak, in celestial relationship. The lover seeks his "sole earth's Heaven and Heaven's claim". The wide range of experience lies "between Heaven and earth", which only the imagination can fathom. To the unhappy, like Hamlet, "this most excellent canopy, the air, look you, this brave o'erhanging firmament, this majestical roof fretted with golden fire" appears but "a foul and pestilent congregation of vapours". Only to a few is it given to reach the door to the highest good, the greatest power and infinite bliss, to penetrate even to God himself: ". . . then my state, like to the lark of day arising from sullen earth, sings hymns at Heaven's gate." A multiplication of citations is not required to show beyond doubt that the new cosmology had not invalidated the ancient emotions with regard to Heaven. Indeed, only a hopeless pedant could have risen from his seat to protest against such archaic classicism in the theatre. There is no evidence that such a protest was ever registered, against Shakespeare or anyone else.

It may be argued, however, that Shakespeare reproduces the popular imagery before the repercussions of the revolution had really made themselves felt. Hence Milton's case is even more astonishing, for he certainly does not reproduce the common speech and deliberately creates the imagery of Heaven which, in a physical sense, was virtually lost in the seventeenth century. Milton probably knew more about these things than many of his contemporaries. He had met the ageing Galileo in his Florentine captivity and must have been deeply impressed by that martyr's struggle for a truth which the Protestant from the North passionately espoused. Yet he reopens, so to speak, the spectacle of a pre-Copernican world by writing in Biblical and classical terms.[1]

[1] His cosmic contention leads to obvious inconsistencies, e.g. *Paradise Lost*, II, 390 ff.; VIII, 34–8; 77–84. For the fascinating problems cf. for example, E. West, *Milton and the Angels*, 1955; K. Svendson, *Milton and Science*, 1956.

How could Milton the philosopher approve of Milton the poet who portrays the "vaulted expanse", through which a "high road" leads to "either end" of "the pillared frame, where earth and ocean meet"? What would Galileo—"the Tuscan artist who . . . through optic glass views at ev'ning from the top of Fesole"—have thought of his young admirer's "birth of Heaven and its progeny", the tale of Ouranos retold, of the throne of God in the Heaven of Heavens, peopled with angels and rebels soon to be cast out? Already the question arises whether men can halt between two opinions, engage in double-think and thus reconcile scientific truth with unscientific imagery. It is perhaps significant that Milton fails to regain Paradise and that the epic breaks off long before Heaven is reached. Although there is talk of ambrosia and banqueting no joyful ecstasy brightens the Elysian fields. The sky above can no longer invite the striving pilgrim and there can be no return to the lost celestial pastures.

The spirit of the seventeenth century presents the historian with notorious difficulties. At its beginning the pre-scientific cosmology still enjoyed the support of Church and University and the authority of the Bible and custom. When Cosmo de Medici III visited Cambridge in 1669 he attended a disputation condemning the Copernican system.[1] Yet the old order was on the wane and it is impossible to believe that someone like Milton did not know it.

But even those who did not know changed their tune. It is hardly probable that Bunyan, the possessed tinker, had any ideas about the universe as such; the new astronomy, if it had reached him, would have mattered less to him than events in and around Bedford. The pilgrimage to Heaven is consequently wholly unlike Dante's in conception. The fancies of his dream do not extend to the life and order of Heaven; the pilgrimage is to him more important than the pilgrim's haven, which, when attained, is given no further description than a few pages of Biblical quotation. This change of emphasis, this absence of a cosmic outlook, are typical for the new temper of the modern world.

By the end of the seventeenth century the triumph of scientific methods secured general assent for the new cosmology. Newton's

[1] Cf. C. H. Cooper, *Annals of the University of Cambridge,* vol. III, p. 536.

genius gave it the final stamp of irrevocable validity.[1] In the gradual reorientation the representatives of learning did not lose much time to postulate more speculative ideas, such as the habitation of other planets and the plurality of worlds. From the point of view of the physical sciences Heaven ceased to exist and yielded to concepts of a totally different kind.[2]

The story has often been told how the universe came to be regarded as the great machine of nature from which the supernatural had been banished.[3] Since then the changes have not been less revolutionary. Heaven has been brought within flying distance of men and what would have been hailed as a miracle only a short time ago is now a commonplace matter of fact. Only a few (like Saint-Exupéry) realize their privilege and tremble with ecstatic delight at this marvel of the penetration of the spheres. The machine is also mightier than men who are somewhat superseded by rockets and satellites which will soon be sent into the stratosphere and beyond to circle around the earth and perhaps the sun. Even travel between the planets is discussed as a possibility and may well be achieved about two hundred years after Kant's admission that Mars may be man's future home. At the same time telescopes of great power and electronic devices penetrate the distant nebulae while the theories of the quantum and relativity have outdated the universe of Newtonian physics.

In England a short-lived revival of Platonism at the beginning

[1] Newton ushers in the era which acknowledges the existence of a universe of science and another of faith. But he himself still held that his principles were such as to "evoke Faith in divine Being". He was annoyed and surprised by Leibniz's charge that he had postulated a super-mechanic who could not even create a satisfactory universe but must constantly repair its worn parts to keep it going. He refuted all accusations, not only by insisting that a personal and spiritual God had ordained the laws of this vast and complex machine, but by distinguishing between the period of the Old Testament as one of concessions and miracles and the Christian era in which men search, learn, and obey the divine laws which were no longer to be suspended. He also felt that the universe might well wear out and have to be re-created. Hence he was not averse to his own kind of apocalyptic and eschatological speculating. The cosmic picture of redemption is strong with him, his interest in chronology and prediction well known. The author of the *Principia*, the revealer of the absolute nature of space-time, is also the commentator of the book of Daniel and the Apocalypse.

[2] Cf. A. O. Lovejoy, *The Great Chain of Being*, 1948, with references to Fontenelle, Derham, Blackmore.

[3] E.g. B. Willey, *The 17th Century Background*, 1934; *The 18th Century Background*, 1940.

of the eighteenth century was soon followed by the establishment of empirical philosophy, whose anti-celestial bias, which interests us here, was complete. Heavenly thoughts were as fantastic as Heaven. Locke succeeded in showing that all those sublime thoughts, which tower above the clouds and reach as high as Heaven itself, take their rise and footing here. Thus the paradox came about that man in the infinite universe became earth-centred and himself the measure of all things, as against the medieval man who desired to leave the earth and whose thought was incomplete without Heaven. This process, which began with Voltaire and Hume, has reached its peak in the positivist position which cannot ascribe any validity to Heaven as an epistemological reality.

The political reaction to the new humanism pursued a similar line of this-worldly ambitions and achievements. Instead of looking for inspiration and consummation beyond this earth, men began to look for improvements by legislation on earth. The ideal of a cosmic harmony receded in favour of the ideal of happiness on earth. Hopes for the redistribution of power and wealth, the pursuit of liberal policies, and even social designs of a revolutionary nature replaced the religious cosmogonies and eschatologies. The new city of Man attracted more scientific blue-prints than the City of God had ever done. The realization of a Heaven-on-earth could be planned and ceased to be a romance of dreamers. It soon became the foremost concern of socialist advocates; thus even a Communist can say seriously: "Our country is not yet Paradise", not as an admission of failure but as a claim to the imminent attainment of Heaven, which is now identified with the economic optimum on earth.

When we turn to the cultural development of western Europe, however, we note with surprise the absence of a clear-cut logic. The empirical, earthly-political notions have by no means ousted the heritage of celestial thinking and feeling. Indeed, its richness is so immeasurable that a full account must be deferred and only a partial selection can help us out of our *embarras de richesses*. The truth is that for many centuries Heaven remained a living symbol and reality for the same humanity which had ceased to believe in its scientific existence.

The cosmic consciousness may be acclaimed as the heir to pre-scientific celestialism: it found an echo throughout the world with ever-varying degrees. For example, when Herschel "broke the barriers of the Heavens" and as the new discoveries became known a whole crop of theories appeared to account for the nature of the universe. In a notable early work[1] (1755) Kant speaks of the limitless waste of chaotic primordial matter upon which the laws of gravity operate, thus generating heat and producing rotation in the remotest nebulae. Such a theory of the Heavens establishes a common trend among great men to give the whole universe a cosmic interpretation. Although Kant obviously revised much of what he had said earlier he can still conclude his Critique of practical Reason with the famous words, presumably still to be seen as an inscription on his tomb in what was Königsberg and now is Kaliningrad: "Two things fill the mind with ever new and increasing admiration and awe, the oftener and the more steadily we reflect on them; the starry Heaven above and the moral Law within." Kant explains that Heaven stands for the undoubted existence of the world and that "my place" is therein. Everything extends endlessly away from me and annihilates my importance as an animal creature. I return to the earth from which I came but the intelligent consciousness apprehends and therefore stands above space. Heaven is complementary to the moral law within, for both Heaven and the moral law make man truly human by assigning to him a place in the universe. Yet Heaven is not to be thought of as a romantic notion but a spatial reality. Kant ends with a typical plea for the scientific method lest the interest in Heaven lead to the practice of astrology. All unscientific inclinations must be kept in check because Heaven becomes the source of an attitude of awe when properly discerned as the realm of universal determinism in which moral freedom operates in a problematical relationship.

The Kantian tradition, though assailed, has never been wanting in adherents who have been impressed by the close affinity between the natural and the moral order. They have succeeded in bridging a gulf which seemed to threaten mankind, ever since the sixteenth century, with a complete separation between the

[1] For a summary, cf. Abbott, *Kant's Theory of Ethics,* Preface.

universe of science and the world of moral aspirations. The end of Newtonian physics has not changed the picture. Thus Einstein, though opposed to all who wished to 'cash in' on the new cosmogony and insisting that Relativity is a purely scientific matter which has nothing to do with religion, encouraged belief in the rational aspect of nature and 'cosmic religion' in a special sense.

POETS AND ART

The restraints of science and philosophy do not limit the spontaneity of artists. In the new classical age the painters study the nature of the effects of light and paint the sky in all its moods. Poets appeal to the heavenly Muse to help them to sing heavenly songs. The Age of Reason retains its vivid sense of cosmic design. Heaven betokens the Creator and his providential care for, and the rationality of, the universe. Man as a rational creature enjoys the distinction of consciously contemplating its order. Dryden renders Ovid:

> Thus while the mute creation downward bend
> Their sight, and to their earthly mother tend,
> Man looks aloft, and with erected eyes
> Beholds his own hereditary skies.

Yet not man, but the visible world is evidence for the cosmic design. Addison states this theme with authority:

> The spacious firmament on high
> With all the blue ethereal sky,
> And spangled Heavens, a shining frame,
> Their great Original proclaim.

The silence of the spheres and the apparent lack of providential interest in man are difficulties, but they cannot contradict the impression which true rationality gains from experience:

> What though in solemn silence all
> Move round the dark terrestrial ball;
> What though nor real voice nor sound
> Amid their radiant orbs be found;

In reason's ear they all rejoice,
And utter forth a glorious voice;
For ever singing as they shine,
'The hand that made us is Divine'.

If this confidence is attacked with mordant wit, as by Voltaire, or with the zeal of social reform, as by Rousseau, or with the logic of pure empiricism, as by Hume, it remains surprisingly intact among the ordinary, conservative, and inarticulate masses, who value both the notions of moral felicity and of permanence in the world. Dr. Johnson is a massive defender of the popular view that Heaven is a moral necessity which offers permanent satisfaction for human endeavour. Though he considers London to be Heaven on earth he dreads death and yearns for the consolations of Heaven, where he anticipates many degrees of varying felicity. It is unreasonable to assume that this attitude was imputed to him by Boswell as one of his eccentricities. Rather it is a point of view which perpetuates poetic feeling in a rational manner.[1]

It would be idle to single out one particular strand in the complex web of Western cosmic consciousness. Goethe is perhaps the greatest representative of all the different aspects of Heaven which he, the enlightened humanist, the geologist, the empirical observer of the world, the theorist of the nature of light (and therefore passionate enemy of Newton), the anti-obscurantist in religion and admirer of Spinoza, held together in a gigantic blend of a cosmic unity. Goethe displays the classical reverence for Heaven, the visible phenomenon, studies the constellations at his birth, voices in his poems "the deep impulses and stirrings of Heaven", is "seized by celestial well-being", looks to Heaven for light and edification, for "as long as the gods grant us good sense and courage on earth we do not envy them their heavenly spheres".[2] Man's spirit he likens to the waters which

[1] Cf. for its classical statement O. Goldsmith, *The Vicar of Wakefield,* ch. XXIX.

[2] Ach, ihr Götter! Grosse Götter
In dem weiten Himmel droben!
Gebt Ihr uns auf der Erde
besten Sinn und guten Mut—
O, wir liessen Euch, Ihr Guten,
Euren weiten Himmel droben!

descend from and ascend to Heaven. The enigmatic Mignon sings of her flight from this earth to meet the heavenly powers who guide, and punish, in this life. They inspire men as of old. In his conversations with Eckermann, Goethe distinguishes genius by the ability to perceive the voice of the heavenly beings. Yet he mocks the old orthodoxy and refers jokingly to one of his early poems, a boy's couplets on Hell, as a "wonderful passport to Heaven". Despite his ironic comments he regards life after death as a legitimate demand and necessity. All these apparent paradoxes culminate in Faust: "Which idea did I endeavour to embody in Faust? As if I knew that myself or could talk of it: from Heaven through the world into Hell. . . ." Indeed Faust and Mephistopheles traverse the spheres as in ancient mythology. The gods and demons appear, the underworld and Helen of Troy acclaim their visitors; but at the end a Christian, Catholic Heaven —with children, angels, and saints—receives the striving hero, who had in his blindness mistaken the reclamation of earthly land as the fulfilment of the highest Good. Goethe's Heaven is pagan and mythological, Christian, harmonious, human and divine. Not one strand of reality can be omitted from this tremendous edifice of a cosmic mind.

It is not easy to account for the apparent decrease and virtual disappearance of the cosmic tradition in Western feeling. But a certain subjective, mystical attitude had always existed either in opposition to, or arising out of the feeling of cosmic affinity. An inner knowledge of heavenly mysteries was a favourite theme of Gnostic sects and it is to be found again in sectarian writings after the Reformation. Swedenborg (1688–1772), for example, after gaining an impressive reputation as scientist and statesman, "saw the Heavens open" and devotes vast and intricate columns to the spiritualization of Heaven. The esoteric knowledge of the universe comes through illumination within. Blake believes that "there is a full and entire Heaven in every man" and "that man should again converse in Heaven and walk with angels".[1] In his longing after the harmony of Heaven he shows his indebted-

[1] "Jerusalem in England's green and pleasant land" brings the ambiguity of a celestial term in a practical, geographical setting to a fine point. Its success as a hymn in secular societies is one of the funniest examples of unintentional poetic irony.

ness to Swedenborg. But the personal wish to "bring all Heaven before our eyes" (Cowper) expresses the feeling of many who prefer the personal possession of the transcendent to the apprehension of, and the absorption into, the universe. The approach is significantly subjective rather than objective.

The romantic movement developed the sense of cosmic delight with a strong personal flavour, but without the piety of former ages. Wordsworth uses the image of Heaven with typical frequency: "Heaven lies about us in our infancy", because we are innocent and free, part of nature; to be young is "very Heaven" because of the great opportunities of a full life: in short "the earth, and every common sight, to me did seem apparelled in celestial light." This transfiguration of earthly reality comes from the power of discernment in the beholder.

THE BEGINNING OF THE END

The subjectivization and the secularization of Heaven could not remain untouched by industrial and political events in the West. The romantic, neo-Gothic feeling, as expressed by some writers, indulged in celestial imagery and flights of the imagination which would have been foreign to the ancient world. In the nineteenth century the vagueness of the term Heaven becomes very marked: it may mean anything from unusual happiness to the life after death. Therefore it serves as an admirable *portmanteau* word which denotes a refuge from the appalling realities of life. In the new iron age Heaven seems to give rest both to the pioneers of wealth and the victims of poverty. Escape from this life is the merit of Heaven; the literature and the hymns draw heavily upon the debased coinage of this uncosmic celestialism. The retreat from metaphysical conceptions is again reflected in escapist poetry and fiction. For example, the drunkard Marmeladoff, in Dostoievski's *Crime and Punishment*, drinks in order to escape from the humiliations of an impossible life. When his employer consents to have him back he experiences his "seventh Heaven", though but for a few days. Heaven is freedom from economic perdition and the peril of being crushed to death by the machine.

The English hymns of this age abound in evocations of Heaven,

D

too tedious to be summarized here. The absence of the ancient cosmic motif is obvious. The assurance of cosmic hymns, like C. Wesley's "Come let us join our friends above", has faded and the themes of consolation and reward are now well to the fore: "Christians only fall asleep to wake again in Heav'n." The individual is made to sing: "Then in Heaven receive me!"; he will find compensation there for everything that has gone wrong here. This socially useful eschatology gathers to itself the whole apparatus of celestial beings, who lack only one thing, reality: "still through the cloven skies they come, with peaceful wings unfurled; and still their heavenly music floats o'er all the weary world. . . ." The greater the effort of descriptive realism, as in pre-Raphaelite art, the emptier the result. The verbiage of "angel faces, hosts of light, and stars upon their way" fails miserably.

The decline in the twentieth century is well known and requires little illustration. It is degenerate, like Proust's Baron de Charlus, who retains the old belief in Heaven with pious fervour. Heaven is as popular a term as it is meaningless in secular culture. Not a week passes without the publication of books or songs about Heaven in connection with fictitious dreams, loves, destinies, and the like.[1] "I dream of Heaven" is a typical proposition of contemporary 'lyrics' whose hall-mark is total unreality. Banal longings "to be in Heaven", "to walk in Heaven", "to kiss some heavenly mouth" evidence the last stage of the decomposition of a term, now not only meaningless but also repulsive. Few are the poets who desire to retain "One foot in Eden" (E. Muir), though there is at the same time a growing interest in the lost technique of ecstasy. Contemporary experiments claim to bring Heaven within man's reach by chemical means.[2]

[1] "Heaven" in blue velvet with frothy tulle clouds, is being blithely installed just now in one room at Dartmouth House, Charles St., where the Incorporated Society of London Fashion Designers gives its pre-collection party on Monday.

Diplomats, Cabinet Ministers, overseas fashion buyers, film and stage stars will thread their way by a snow-capped mountain and walk over clouds. The 300 guests will be received by——

Nineteen associate members are exhibiting in this highly unusual setting.

Two sketches given here show how amusing the exhibits will be. They have a stern purpose—more exports for Britain, as in the case of the two-foot-high angel which shows a miniature of a twin set. *Daily Telegraph,* February 1st, 1958.

[2] Cf. A. Huxley, *The Doors of Perception*, 1954; *Heaven and Hell*, 1955.

By the way of reaction against celestial hopes a mighty wave of disgust broke over the hypocritical celestialism. Even before the terrors of war exposed the hollowness of the hopes of the pre-Raphaelite Heaven, Nietzsche's scathing comments had set the pace. With what ecstasy he scoffed at the piety of his age! From quite a different quarter and with more enduring results the socialist protest hit the nail on the head with its ribald slogan "pie in the sky". This protest drew attention to the seriousness of the class struggle on earth. Then wars and revolutions furthermore helped to crush the celestial sentiment. As Bertrand Russell observed in 1935, Heaven had simply become the belief in life after death, which "has lost in vividness", as belief in hell has grown less definite.[1] In 1930 Freud mocked the celestial dope, "Eiapopeia vom Himmel",[2] with which "our governesses try to appease the strife of the giants, the real battle of life, between love and death". The governesses may have vanished, but not the scepticism. Most contemporary philosophers refuse to be drawn into a discussion of a meaningless term, such as Heaven. Statistical enquiries yield figures which show that "three-fifths of the English people do not believe in hell: 47% believe in a future life (34% men, 56% women) but differ about such topics as retribution, angels, rest, communion, reincarnation on another planet etc".[3] There is no reason to suppose that the proportions would be more favourable to traditional belief in other parts of the Christian world, except where the Catholic Church is still fully established.

The same reaction is to be observed among many poets and writers. Heaven is far away.[4] The Heavens are closed and thus "in the expanding universe hope too recedes".[5] This may cause sardonic amusement: when Aunt Helen died, writes T. S. Eliot, "there was silence in Heaven". Heaven is silence, nothing; or, worse still, it represents the old and somewhat disgusting habit men have of projecting themselves. The Heaven of fishes is mud,

[1] *Religion and Science,* p. 136.

[2] *Das Unbehagen in der Kultur,* p. 98.

[3] G. Gorer, *Exploring English Character,* 1955 pp. 252 ff.

[4] Rilke, *Eingang, Stundenbuch.*

[5] Ruth Pitter.

"celestially fair"; hence "in that Heaven of all their wish there shall be no more land, say fish".[1] Indeed, religion became decadent and soft when the old, war-like God of the tribes of Israel left the earth for Heaven; thus argues Chaim Breisacher, a Jew who ingratiates himself with the die-hard militarists of pre-war Germany by attacking the celestial transcendance of the Bible, in Thomas Mann's *Dr. Faustus*. Norman Douglas makes a similar observation: the paradisal grubs invent the whole proletarian, upstairs, or vertical type of religion: "they manufacture a god who approves of grovelling, a god who can look down upon them. They exalt this deity to an infinite degree in point of goodness and distance. . . . I disapprove of upstairs gods . . . if you rent a high attic overlooking my premises and stare out of your window all day long, watching my movements and noting down everything I do, why, damn it, I call that vulgar; vertical gods are inquisitive. I don't like to be supervised. I don't care about this *dossier* business . . . the peculiar position of the vertical gods necessitates a troublesome code of verbal signals, unintelligible to common folk, for the expression of mutual desires. You cannot have any god of this kind without some such cumbrous contrivance to bridge over the gulf and make communication possible. It is called theology. It complicates life very considerably."[2]

THEOLOGICAL ATTITUDES

The contemporary theological attitude to Heaven partakes itself of this 'complication'. Secular trends affect religious feelings; the Church's interpretations of dogma echo the world's sentiments. Consequently it can cause no surprise that a unanimous Christian opinion about Heaven does not exist. Many schools of thought try to come to grips with the basic difficulty that the modern world-view no longer supports belief in the ancient Christian Heaven.

One solution of the problem is to ignore and even to refuse to state it. Schleiermacher is perhaps the most notable patron of a whole generation of theologians who treat Heaven with complete indifference. In *The Christian Faith* (E.T. 1928) the term

[1] Rupert Brooke, *Heaven,* 1913.

[2] *South Wind,* 1917, Penguin ed., pp. 172–3.

does not even appear in the table of contents. Here is no accident, for this exposition of the Christian religion abandons its original, cosmic claims. The protagonists of this view in the twentieth century go even further and deliberately pull down the ancient, many-tiered universe and with it, as they insist, the myth of the heavenly Christ,[1] either in order to abandon every pretence of Christian belief or to reinterpret it in some contemporary form of thought. They dismiss all cosmological speculations as worthless and bestow them in the huge deposit of antiquities whose place is in a museum.

Some theologians, however, continue the struggle of reconciling the incompatible strands of scientific exploration and the Biblical tradition. Already in 1854, for example, C. W. Goodwin, writing in *Essays and Reviews* went out of his way to stress that Heaven, as mentioned in Genesis, chapter I, is not a poetical nor symbolical nor mystical term, but rather that the writers used it in, what we now call, a scientific-realistic sense; therefore, he argues, the whole account is no longer tenable as it stands, though "to be treated with respect as educational in a special way", i.e. in teaching unity of design and subordination to the Maker and Lawgiver. Goodwin may strike his readers as spoiling his own case, for why should a false cosmogony be educationally sound? One is inclined to suspect special pleading, as indeed with most attempts at reconciliation. The eirenic attitude is, however, typical of much of English theology. In *Foundations* (1912) the "geocentric picture now long outgrown"—with God seated in regal splendour on an almost material throne—is called fantastic and bizarre (p. 112). Yet the term 'heavenly' is still used quite freely to describe the ideal (p. 198), the eschatological future (p. 516). The Eucharist is enacted in Heaven—there Heaven meets earth (p. 392), for Heaven stands for the non-terrestrial,

[1] See *Kerygma and Myth*, 1953, p. 3; G. V. Jones, *Christology and Myth in the New Testament*, 1956, pp. 151 ff.; R. Bultmann, *Primitive Christianity in its Contemporary Setting*, E.T. 1956, e.g. p. 151: "In such visions or phantasies men still cling to the old idea of the unity of the cosmos . This was possible so long as the Stoic attitude of the freedom of the wise man from everything that happens in the outside world and the idea of the independence of the inner Ego and its relationship to the divine, universal law are not allowed to go by the board. Once that happens, however, the law which prevails in the world of the stars is seen in a different light."

the Other, the Greater, the Transcendent (p. 484). W. Temple is perhaps the finest exponent of this *via media*: in 1910 he attempted a review of "the Faith and modern thought" and regarded the universe as a rational whole. In his obviously much-dated idealistic exposition he is bold enough to include "the electric theory of matter" though he is already aware of the dangers that beset the amateur scientist who desires to buttress the *Sanctus*, with which he concludes, by means of theories of light and energy, Therefore the modern scientist, who is a Christian apologist, must hesitate before he commits himself to the view that the Heaven of religion may be equated with the expanding universe. He prefers to regard the former as a transcendent symbol of the latter and runs the risk of losing something of the simplicity of the original term in favour of scientific accuracy and honesty.

With astonishing freedom and unmoved by all concessions the traditional belief in Heaven also persists in modern times. Heaven is still a place, where virtue is rewarded, the end of life attained, and where God's own glorious Presence vouchsafes supernatural reality to angels and men. The beatific vision is granted to those who deserve the crown of perfection. Such a definition does not necessarily argue a return to obscurantism but an absence of concern for the scientific world-view. Barth, for example, dismisses the old bell-shaped bowl but does not borrow from the new cosmology. For him Heaven is a term within the structure of Christian revelation: "Heaven is the creation inconceivable to man . . . when we have reached what to us is inconceivable we have not yet reached God but merely Heaven."[1] It is the place where God dwells and which God has created, "the higher, invisible, we would say the spiritual and consequently the higher side of reality".

Thus the modern traditionalists concur with the general secular trend in stressing the moral, eschatological, and personal import of Heaven. Since all values are threatened and the world itself is in peril Heaven figures again as the macrocosm which the earth mirrors as microcosm. The twin claims that Heaven can be found on earth in a manner of spiritual correspondence, and be-

[1] Cf. *Dogmatics in Outline*, pp. 59 ff.; *Kirchl. Dogmatik*, II/1, p. 533 ff.; III/1, pp. 17–20.

yond in a new and felicitous existence, are of paramount importance to a generation facing persecution and death. The personal counsels of perfection—such as "If thou but greatly it desire, all Heaven is for thee" (Angelus Silesius), "He who carries God in the heart has Paradise" (Ignatius Loyola)—meet with ready acceptance in concentration camps. "No word means more to the believer at the present day than the word Heaven. To enter Heaven, to win eternal blessedness in Heaven, that is the essence of the religious hopes and desires of most Christians", wrote a priest before his execution in 1944.[1] Heaven is thus an experience of consolation by anticipation and participation.

None of these theological reactions to the modern situation can be considered satisfactory. They reflect the diversity of theological needs and interests but they leave untouched the one fundamental problem whether the Christian religion is essentially a cosmic fact. They present the indifferent world with the false alternatives that either Christianity is a belief which must be adjusted to empirical discoveries and therefore lacks an absolute degree of reality, or that an outworn symbolism may be used for certain religious ends which are themselves at variance with what is known of the nature of the universe. This split is not merely the traditional contest between science and religion; rather, it exemplifies the whole decadence of Western civilization which, having become entirely absorbed by its own pursuits in a non-transcendental universe, now reaps the harvest of this tragic isolation. Yet we are left with two positive values even in the theological stalemate of our times: on the one hand there is the integrity of purpose of the sceptics, on the other there is the sincerity of feeling among the mystics and martyrs of an eschatologically inclined generation. Both have their appropriate place in the Biblical tradition, but, as the following pages will seek to show, this tradition is richer than both.

[1] L. Stevenson, *Max Josef Metzger,* 1952.

Chapter Two

HEAVEN IN THE HEBREW TRADITION

NO specific Hebrew cosmology appears to have been held by any of the Biblical writers. Their view of the universe merely reflects the general non-scientific climate of thought of the Near East, which no technical advance and no astronomical discovery disturbed. The flint that first engraved the Hebrew word for Heaven, *shamaiim*, was directed by a mind whose cosmic information hardly differed, if at all, from that of the author of the last book in the New Testament who wrote *οὐρανός*. Thus in the Old Testament a Deborah may sing "The earth trembled, and the Heavens dropped" (Jdg. v, 4), and a St. John on Patmos in the New Testament may see "in Heaven an open door" (Rev. IV, 1). This generally accepted world-view permitted of endless deviations. The Bible never presents us with a precise definition but with a large variety of endless shades of meaning. One could evidently believe anything about Heaven without being suspected of betraying the right faith. But there was one exception to this freedom of thought: Heaven as a place does not admit of doubt. The vault rests upon pillars (Job XXVI, 11); God has prepared Heaven (Gen. I, 1; Prov. VIII, 27). The firmament divides the upper waters from the lower waters from which the world below is again separated. This firmament itself is Heaven, or perhaps the beginning of Heaven, the base of the vast world above (Gen. I, 6–8).

DERIVATION OF WORDS

An investigation into the origin of the word *shamaiim* is disappointing for it tells us as little as the etymology of, say, the English word Heaven (here the alleged connexion with 'to lift' is but a guess) or the German *Himmel* (sometimes connected with 'to cover'). The root meaning of *οὐρανός* is equally elusive. Only with the Latin *coelum*, which is akin to the Greek *κοῖλος* and its derivatives (hollow), are we on safer ground. The notion of a hollow and a high place, which covers the earth, used to express what people believed about Heaven in pre-scientific cosmologies, and this belief the Hebrews shared as a matter of course.

The Hebrew *shamaiim*—with which must be bracketed the Aramaic *shemaia*, the related *šmm* in Ugaritic, *šamu* in Accadian, *smv* in old South Arabic—fails to reveal its origin and therefore has also given rise to many a guess. It has been conjectured that the Accadian *šamu* denoted a cover or a roof; on the other hand, the whole family of related words may have signified height at an early date. In Hebrew the word always appears in what looks like a plural ending. This, it is generally agreed, adds nothing to our knowledge and may even mislead us if we conclude that *shamaiim* always denoted the layers of spheres of Heaven.[1]

The ancient speculative regard for a word strikes a modern philologist as absurd, but it deserves some respect, for, however artificial the associations, they shed a great deal of light on the Biblical conception of Heaven as a place. The great Jewish and Christian expositors of Scripture were scholars and yet took an interest in unscholarly plays on words; paranomasia was a time-honoured method of teaching essentials in non-academic circles.[2] Ordinary people could see with their own eyes that Heaven was a compound of fire and water, aglow with reds, pinks, and blues, full of wonders: did it not deserve to be called divine, to carry the name of the Lord? Thus the popular impression fills up the vacuum of linguistic obscurity. Imagination is stronger than semantics and grammar.

[1] Cf. C. Brockelmann, *Grundriss der vergleichenden Grammatik der semitischen Sprachen,* 1908, I, p. 232, for the dissimilation of u after m to i.

[2] Cf. E. G. Rashi, on Gen. 1, 8. See also A. Levene, *The Early Christian Fathers on Genesis,* 1951, pp. 135 ff.

In the Midrash on Genesis (Gen. R. IV, 7) examples of interesting conjectures, amounting to inventions, can be found. By slight changes in the spelling of the word *shamaiim*, or by the introduction of a new division of the letters of this word, the common form undergoes some strange changes: *sa-maiim* means 'laden with water'; *esh-umaiim* equals 'fire and water'; *she-maiim* is a later form for 'of water'. Indeed, the linking up of water (*maiim*) and Heaven (*shamaiim*) is very ancient: e.g. in Gen. VIII, 2 "the windows of the Heavens were closed and the rain from the Heavens was restrained". When God speaks there is a "tumult of waters in the Heavens" (Jer. X, 13), i.e. of the heavenly ocean. But the Rabbis go even beyond these ancient associations. They allude to *sammim* which suggest to them the different colours of paint of the chemicals which cause the glow of Heaven; they mention *shamam* to remind their pupils of the wonders from above; they speak of *shamim*, the weighing up of merits or sins, for Heaven is a place of judgment.

VISIBLE AND INVISIBLE

Before the conjectures, however, comes the direct experience by sight. Partly, at least, Heaven is visible from below, whereas to the other senses, except hearing, it is not known. But even the sight of men fails to penetrate the blue crust. The 'inside' of Heaven would be unknown except for the special event when the Heavens are 'open' to human discernment. This extraordinary experience belongs to the abnormal vocation and the privilege of prophetic seeing. It is, therefore, almost impossible to say whether such a vision can be classed with the normal process of perception. It varies according to the degrees of directness and only the recipient can measure and report the nature of his celestial contemplation. No doubt dream experience is the most common and is by no means lacking in reality. The Heavens are obviously more transparent by night than by day. Jacob dreams when he sees a ladder set upon the earth whose top reaches Heaven and angelic traffic moves up and down. This dream experience not only shapes the inner life of Jacob but serves as the true type of religious experience which Jesus commends: after obeying their call his disciples will partake of the celestial vision. The 'opened

Heaven' is to become a conscious reality for them (Jn. I, 50–1). Lest this be taken to be a metaphor one must recall Ezekiel's ecstatic vision (ch. I) through which the visionary transcends his place on earth, by the river Chebar, so as to approach the 'open Heaven'. His vision is the *locus classicus* of celestial visions and assures the hearer by its very detail that the experience entails the seeing of abnormal things and creatures which pertain to the divine self-manifestation.

The extraordinary experience stresses the contrast with the normal state, when Heaven is a closed place. Then experience must be content with the knowledge of Heaven's existence without a perception of its real nature. Traditionally it becomes a hidden and mysterious place which excites a constant interest, just because it is both concealed and visible, always above men, unattainable, and eminently desirable. The Hebrews 'consider' the Heavens; after a day's work they look up with admiration and ponder the size, structure, and meaning of this place.

SPECULATIONS

The immensity of Heaven suggests to the beholder the plurality of the spheres behind the firmament. "The Heaven, and the Heaven of Heavens" (Deut. x, 14; I Kings, VIII, 27) becomes the key expression and starting-point for speculative multiplications. The first popular division probably reckoned in terms of three Heavens. The Testament of Levi, before it suffered interpolations, tells of the first Heaven as a gloomy place where man's unrighteous deeds are seen and their punishments anticipated; the second Heaven contains fire and ice, ready for the day of judgment (III, I f.). In the third Heaven, God is enthroned and surrounded by his adoring angels (III, 4 ff.). But another tradition, defended by Rabbi Jehuda (b Chag. 12 b), refers to Deut. x, 14 literally and acknowledges only the existence of two Heavens, as if Heaven and Heaven of Heavens constituted two different realms. The Rabbis discuss the matter with noticeable restraint: the subject is not only elusive but possibly also suspect. Yet the opposing Rabbi (Resh Laqish) in proposing the seven Heavens has the majority opinion behind him. "The doctrine of the seven Heavens was prevalent in Judaism before and after the time of

Christ", says Charles, for the figure seven always seems to have proved irresistible. The passage in the Talmud actually mentions the names of these Heavens—they are not found in the Christian tradition nor in the pseudepigraphical writings. The arrangement of the seven Heavens seems arbitrary and forced, "puerile in the extreme" according to Charles. The first Heaven is the *Wilon*, a word borrowed from the Latin *velum* = curtain. It covers the stars and is renewed every day. This curtain, though based on Is. XL, 22, resembles the notion of the cosmic mantle or the divine cloak[1]; it is not part of the Christian tradition. Ascending from this lowest Heaven we come next to the *Raqi'a'*, the firmament, on which the stars are fastened, then to the *Shechaqim*, the place of grinding, a vaporous cloud, from which the Manna descends (Ps. LXXVIII, 23; LXXXIX, 7, 38); the fourth place is the *Zevul*, the eternal dwelling (I Kings VIII, 13), indistinguishable from the *Ma'on*, the holy habitation of Deut. XXVI, 15, and from *Makon*, the place of I Kings VIII, 39. The last name of all shows the ingenuity of the Rabbis. It is the *'Aravoth* of Ps. LXVIII, 5, which usually means deserts; but since God cannot very well ride "through the deserts" they conclude that it must be another name for Heaven.

Although the Christian tradition is free from these expositions it has its own difficulties. Jesus, Paul, and the early Church seem to have accepted the sevenfold cosmogony. The seven stars and the seven golden candlesticks of the Apocalypse (II, 1) are symbols of the early Christians' world-view in which Jesus figures as the light of the world in Heaven. This imagery is reminiscent of the candelabrum or *Menorah* of the Jews, itself a cosmic symbol of the light of the spheres.[2] The numerical order in this connexion presupposes respective degrees of both glory and virtue, and it is implied that there is an ascent from the lowest to the highest sphere. Thus "the Father's house has many stations" comparable to the floors of a block of flats. When Jesus promises them this accommodation in the future (Jn. XIV, 2) he knows that they will understand the meaning of being initiated into the order of the

[1] See R. Eisler, *Weltenmantel und Himmelszelt*, 1910.

[2] Cf. Philo, Mos. II, 102 f. The two branches of the Menorah and the seven lights represent the harmony of the planetary system with the sun in the middle.

universe, for the floors of the house represent the corresponding spheres of Heaven. The picture of the hero who traverses one Heaven after another until he reaches God's own domain was well-known and popular. Thus the Prophet in the Ascension of Isaiah advances in a manner similar to the Visionary of the Apocalypse. In the Ascension of Isaiah the Heavens are wholly without the taint of evil, probably because Christ has cleansed the Heavens. The distance between the Heavens is very great (VII, 28) The seventh Heaven contains innumerable companies of angels and just men, awaiting the exaltation of Christ and their own coronation (ch. IX). A similar order is symbolically alluded to in Enoch (chs. XXIV; XXV) where the seven magnificent mountains illustrate the progression. IV Ezra (VII, 81–98) distinguishes between seven ways of confusion or Hell, and seven ways of rest and Heaven.

Much later a further revolution altered the spatial arrangement. It appears that the seven Heavens became a favourite and discredited theme of the heretics, and, as Charles believes, unnecessary for orthodox thought. Illogically, however, instead of simply abolishing or simplifying the divisions of Heaven, the Christians actually increased them to ten. The date of the original addition remains unknown. The tradition of the ten Heavens represents the blending of the traditional system with Pythagorean thought and may have been favoured also by the assumed existence of ten orders of angels. Thus the passages in Dan. VII, 10 and in Enoch XIV, 17 ff., speaking of "ten thousand time ten thousand" suggest a pre-Christian date; yet in the Secrets of Enoch the reference to the ten Heavens in chapter XXII is rejected by Charles as a late interpolation.[1]

ST. PAUL'S TRANCE

The importance of the numbering of the Heavens from a Biblical point of view focuses mainly upon St. Paul's somewhat casual reference to his own experience in the following well-known passage: "I know a man in Christ, who fourteen years ago was caught up to the third Heaven—whether in the Body or out

[1] For the ten Heavens in later Judaism cf. *Monumenta Talmudica*, 1913, Bd. I., p. 195.

of the body I do not know, God knows. And I know that this man was caught up into Paradise . . . and heard things that cannot be told, which man may not utter" (II Cor. XII, 2–4). The Apostle does not only retain the veil of the secret lest the glory of the mystical trance be lost through boasting: he confesses his own ignorance about the actual occurrence and his physical condition at the time. The vagueness recalls Ezekiel's simple and non-committal description: "the spirit lifted me up between earth and Heaven" (VIII, 3). Nevertheless, the Apostle mentions the number of the *third* Heaven though he does not make it clear whether the penetration into the third Heaven and into Paradise are one and the same thing, as is most probable. Unlike the hero of the third-rate Apocalypse of St. Paul (esp. chs. XXI; XLV) the Apostle is silent about the first and second Heavens. Yet, notwith-standing the obscurity, "the condensed intensity of the narrative leaves little room for the play of fancy or exaggeration";[1] two things emerge with decisive clarity: there are degrees of Heaven and abnormal experiences, which when vouchsafed to some saints and others grant a momentary penetration into Heaven. The degrees of Heaven and the penetration are conceived of in spatial terms.

Assuming, then, the third Heaven and Paradise to be the same thing (as in Apoc. Mos. XXXVII, 5–6; XL, 2) it is still questionable whether St. Paul claims to have been translated to the highest or to an intermediary Heaven. The notions of Paradise—probably unknown among the non-Jewish Corinthians—are contradictory, although the term Paradise itself is of international usage. This Persian loan-word occurs in the Old Testament to describe the garden of Eden. It is a park or orchard: "I made myself gardens and Paradises" (Eccles. II, 5); Asaph is keeper of the king's Paradise (Neh. II, 8). This enclosure is plainly on this earth. At the same time Eden-Paradise, as the garden of God, gained currency, not only through the story in Genesis but also in Ezekiel's utterances (XXVIII, 13; XXXI, 9). It is still on earth, but the unworthy are expelled from it. Even the school of Enoch (LX, 8) retains the earthly Paradise, although apocalyptic writers tend to think of it more and more as a place out of this world.

[1] Cf. Plummer, 2 *Corinthians* (ICC), ad loc.

In Isaish LI, for instance, the consolation of Zion is not simply a return to the perfect garden but "her wilderness is made *like* Eden", a place of perfection. The comparison shows that already Eden-Paradise has been removed from this earth to a higher sphere. In the Apoc. Mos. (chs. XXXVII and XL) it is the place of transit for the just, who, with Adam, dwell there between Death and Resurrection.[1] In IV Ezra (VII, 36), it stands over against the furnace of Gehenna, with all its torments, for it offers endless delights. In Enoch (LXX) it is between Heaven and earth, at the remotest northern corner of an unspecified Heaven (LXXVII, 3), or at the East, the gates of the Sun (XLII). The Syr. Ap. Baruch, whose division of Heaven into five or seven is very ambiguous, places it in the fourth Heaven (LIX, 8) or very high; within its domains there are the beauty of the living creatures, which are beneath the throne, and all the armies of the angels (LI, 11). In the Talmudic tradition Paradise is not Eden, but rather a heavenly place of somewhat indistinct dimensions, suitable for mystic enquiry, with rooms or dwellings, commensurate with the record of men (b Chag, 14 b).

It is obviously not an easy task to explain St. Paul's account with reference to such a great number of potential parallels. Most commentators prefer the pre-Christian Testament of Levi (ignoring the later interpolations with the additional four Heavens), in which the hero ascends in his trance from a high mountain to the first Heaven of the sea, the second of brightness and height, and lastly the third of incomparable beauty. The first couple of Heavens contains armies, good and bad; these are set aside for warfare, retribution, and punishment. But the third Heaven is the highest and different, for it belongs to God (II, 5–III, 4). St. Paul has seen not only the immensity of the universe but has gazed upon the spiritual perfection of the highest realm. He does not report events in some intermediary sections of the universe nor does he wish to entice his converts with Gnostic speculations about emanations and spirits in the spheres. In his trance he has been made to follow the Messiah, the second Adam, to whom

[1] As also in the Secrets of Enoch, VIII, 3–5; Paradise is "between corruptibility and incorruptibility"; the Lord rests on the tree of life in the middle during his visits there.

God has opened the gates of Paradise for the salvation of the Gentiles (T. Levi. XVIII, 6–10). So Irenaeus (Adv. haer. II, XXX, 7) confirms the general tradition that the Apostle to the Gentiles reached the highest Heaven; there he obtained the celestial sanction for his mission, with which, after all, his work among the Corinthians is concerned. To conform them to the will of God he has seen the height and perfection of all things as they will be at their final state.

It must be conceded, however, that St. Paul's restraint is inexplicable, despite the apologies, made for him by commentators, that the Corinthian context explains it. Would someone thus initiated, albeit in a temporary trance, really wish to be silent about the highest Heavens? Hardly so: and indeed, the Apostle declares himself that he is willing to glory "on behalf of such a man". He looks upon the entranced visionary almost as another person, of whom he can speak objectively and *without* restraint. This high estimate on his part of visionary and vision confirms that the third Heaven and Paradise are for him the same thing, namely, the place which is highest in the world and nearest to God himself.

PARADISE, EDEN, JERUSALEM

Yet in the New Testament world of thought Paradise still oscillates in meaning between serene peace and final bliss on the one hand, and judgment on the other. The penitent malefactor of the Lukan tradition (XXIII, 43) cannot have expected anything but his entering upon an intermediate state; for him "to be in Paradise" must have been an expression readily understood (cf. Apoc. Mos, chs. XXXVII and XL). But even if Paradise was a place of retribution and even torment in Heaven (as e.g. in the Test. Isaac) the Lord's word still conveys consolation. Even in Paradise Jesus will be with him; the dead offender will not be left alone in the place of waiting to face the judgment.

The Christian tradition, however, is naturally far more concerned with the significance of Paradise for the godly. The destiny of the redeemed is of primary importance: "To him that overcomes (namely, in martyrdom), to him will I give to eat of the tree of life, which is in the Paradise of God" (Rev. II, 7).

There were those who looked for the triumph of the saints on earth and consequently placed the future Paradise on earth; others cared for the vindication of the righteous outside and apart from the earth and for them a celestial Paradise was even more attractive. All these ideas were popular and possibly intermingled with ease, so that the Paradise of the end of the world is thought of both as descending from Heaven to earth and as ascending from the earth into Heaven. In all these eschatological pictures, however, Paradise is no longer an intermediate clearing-house but the goal of the redeemed. God's park-garden cannot be far from his throne, for the tree of life which bears the fruit for the healing of the nations grows on the river-bank of the city of God (Rev. XXII, 2). Hence it is not surprising that the final location in the tradition places Paradise not on earth but in the Highest Heaven, following, at least in this respect, the highly individualistic account of St. Paul.

A similar, heavenly trend may be observed in the Christian tradition of Jerusalem, which, as we shall have occasion to show later on, altogether parts company with the Jewish ideology. The notion of a cosmic City of God was also known in Jewish circles: Adam, Abraham, and Moses had seen that imperishable city for which the godly are destined (IV Ezra VIII, 52), but the equation Jerusalem = Paradise (as interpolated in Syr. Ap. Bar. IV, 2 ff.) did not invalidate the political expectation of a liberated capital. The Christian stand against this earthly hope is deliberate. First St. Paul transcended the earthly conception by stressing the freedom of the exalted Jerusalem (Gal. IV, 24) at the expense of that below, and the writer of Hebrews makes the decisive identification, which his master Philo would have understood but hardly condoned: "you have come to Mount Zion and to the city of the living God, the heavenly Jerusalem" (XII, 22). It hardly matters whether the Romans had sacked the earthly city at the time of writing, for from now on, in Christian thought, it is this heavenly Jerusalem (Rev. XXI, 2) after which the Christians seek, and this sole abiding social reality is in Heaven (Hebr. XIII, 14). There stands the throne of God (Rev. IV, 2 ff.) with the fiery chariot (taken over from Dan. VII. 9–10, still found in b Chag. 13 a), the living beasts and the crystal sea. There the heavenly treasures are stored away (Mt. vi, 20) and rewards are bestowed in exchange for earthly title-deeds (Mt. xix, 21). The whole conception of the Christian life is linked up with the heavenly Jerusalem 'above', with foundations of sapphire, pinnacles of rubies, gates of carbuncles, borders of pleasant stones. All these things exist already in their perfection, since they came into being when God created the world.

PERMANENCE OF HEAVEN

The spatial paradox between the earth, the world, Jerusalem 'here', and Heaven, the City, Paradise 'there', which in this sharp form is peculiar to the Christian tradition, involves an even more complex temporal contrast between 'now' and 'then'. The Hebrew tradition, though not philosophical in outlook, had not been unaware of the two conflicting aspects of time: permanence and transience. Heaven and earth were originally created together by God as two distinct realms whose unity God had determined from the beginning. There was no question of an end. The Heavens, in particular, were made to stand for ever; God's faithfulness is often compared in the Psalms to the stability of Heaven, sun, moon, and the stars. Men swear by Heaven as a permanent witness (Mt. vi, 34). The Heaven of the Christian tradition—in which the Father dwells and from which the Son descends and from whence the Holy Spirit is received—is unquestionably felt to be stable and permanent.

Yet notwithstanding the Father's supremacy in Heaven, Hebrew feeling did not arrive at the obvious conclusion that the world 'below' is transient and the realm 'above' permanent. The unity of Heaven and earth appears to make such a division invidious. They were not only created together but they are also to be redeemed together. The prophet typically greets this eschatological harmony: "Sing, O Heavens . . . shout, O depths of the earth!" (Is. xliv, 23), for the universe is one.

This attitude enhances the problem of the present world which is evil and which must therefore tremble before God's coming judgment. The apocalyptic writers cannot but sentence the whole universe to dissolution. Heaven might have been exempted from this "rolling up like a scroll" (Is. xxxiv, 4) if the underworld at least had played a more important part in the Biblical tradition. But *Sheol* could not fill this part; despite its distance from Heaven it was held to be within God's control: "Though they dig into Sheol from there shall my hand take them" (Amos IX, 2), for "If I make my bed in Sheol, thou art there!" (Ps. CXXXIX, 8). The subterranean depth, with its dusty holes of death and pits of decay, still belongs to this earth and is too vague a place to account for the origin of evil and to accommodate the consequences of the reign of sin. Even in the New Testament the world is not divided into a Heaven which remains and an underworld which must perish; the fires of Gehenna, though eternally consuming the wrathful, the adulterous, and the proud, still recall the refuse of the valley of Hinnom outside Jerusalem and the burning-up of the rubbish; the threatening gates of Hades are figurative of the Church's trials, which are far more real than an imaginary realm under the earth. The truth is that the apocalyptic tradition does not locate evil under the earth at all, but above, in the air, reaching up even to Heaven. The chaotic forces, which God had "broken" (Ps. LXXIV, 13–15), the waste and void, which God had ended at the creation (Gen. I, 2), have not only entered the historical processes on earth but have also gone beyond the earthly confines and have polluted Heaven. Therefore both permanence and instability became in Hebrew feeling the warp and woof of the cosmic fabric.

The incursion of evil is a cosmic phenomenon. Different traditions combined to portray the present Heaven, or part of it, as unworthy of permanence on moral grounds. Since Satan and the fallen angels were deemed to have been originally celestial citizens it was by no means absurd to think of a Hell in Heaven. The rebels' corner is above; the Watchers spy out and attack the earth from the second or even from the fifth Heaven (cf. II En. VII, 1–3 as against II En. XVIII). The notion of a celestial place of punishment also supported the view that Heaven was a place of cruel sports where the wicked receive their recompense of torment. In Test. Isaac the visionary sees misshapen animals in Heaven; these were once human beings who are now exposed to retribution as the prey of lions and demons and the fire-flood. In the Gr. Apoc. Bar. (chs. IV–IX) the seer visits the third Heaven where horrible serpents lie in wait for punishment, almost as if the underworld had arrived in force in Heaven. It is true that the Jewish tradition never accepted such extreme fancies, but the law of correspondence decrees, more soberly, that there are always complementary parts, Paradise and Hell, even in Heaven (b Chag. 15 a; Midr. Ps. xc, 3).

THE NEW HEAVEN

The Christian tradition does not altogether cancel the sentence of the dissolution of the whole world. Heaven is a place no longer wholly clean but somehow implicated in revolt and in need of salvation. The work of Christ affects the heavenly topography and it may well be that some Christian writers assumed that the stability of the Heavens had been recovered by the saving work of Christ. Nevertheless the apocalyptic motif gained the upper hand, for it is commonly held that the final manifestation of Christ's glory coincides with a cosmic cataclysm. Heaven might have been restored its place of secure being, 'above' and 'for ever', but this was not to be. Indeed, Heaven tends to become an area of peril and conflict before the Last Day, instead of being a place aloof and safe. The Heavens "that now are", as opposed to the genuine Heaven, "have been stored up for fire" with the earth (II Peter iii, 7). Here cessation defeats permanence because God wills it so. The Heavens tremble, lose their light, and melt away, notwithstanding their immensity, beauty and strength. This great catastrophe precedes God's Judgment, which, according to the Christian Gospel, follows immediately upon the final appearance of Jesus Christ. The Markan Apocalypse (ch. xiii) combines the common material (as in Assump. Mos. x; En. lxxx; lxxxiii; IV Ezra v, 4; vi, 20; Sibyl. Or. III, 796 ff.) with the Parousia which governs the dissolution of the age both as cause and purpose. Thus a definite Christian bias severs the idea of the end of the world from the common stock of the myths of the chaos which engulfs the universe. This cosmic upheaval when "the sky vanished like a scroll that is rolled up" (Rev. vi, 12–14) comes as the climax of the judgment. In this catastrophe no place is found for the present Heaven.

The extreme Christian eschatology thus insists that Heaven,

i.e. the present, visible counterpart of earth, must pass away so that the perfect Heaven-and-earth may come. This perfect Heaven lies above the present cosmic vault and exists already in God and is anticipated by hope in the Christian believer, though it is plainly outside the present spatial universe and historical, transitory time. The last chapters of the Apocalypse fully reflect the hope of this Heaven as a 'new' place, which no longer provides for the exigencies of the present age but manifests the unbroken Presence of God.

In the Christian tradition, however, this new Heaven blends with some important characteristics of the old, for it fulfils the ancient feeling of, and longing for, cosmic perfection. The visible sky may recede in the apocalyptic writers' estimation but the bright firmament (Dan. XII, 3) and the transparent clarity and brilliance of the spheres must still give an intimation of God's glory. If even in ancient times "the Heavens proclaim God's glory and the firmament shows his hands' work" (Ps. XIX), by how much more must the blessedness of the new Heaven excel in light and purity! Thus the Christian tradition changed the apocalyptic expectation of destruction to that of a cosmic harmony to be attained. The cosmology of the Christian must therefore envisage not only what is 'above', or rather what is above the above, but also what is still to come. Heaven is the term which describes this place of the blessed future which is within man's reach. Transcendent in essence it becomes potentially accessible in the Church's faith and practice. When Christian preachers speak of Christ-come-from-Heaven and ascended-into-Heaven, and their congregations worship the present Christ in Heaven, they acknowledge, probably unconsciously, the manifold and paradoxical notions of the whole Hebrew tradition. But this paradoxical cosmology is itself the child of religious belief and it is the Christian doctrine of God which gives the Hebrew tradition its specific content.

Chapter Three

THE GOD OF HEAVEN

HEAVEN IS NOT GOD

THE Hebrew-Christian tradition associates God with Heaven. The latter is not to be regarded as a place for its own sake, but all its manifold aspects serve as a reminder that Heaven itself is under God. If Heaven is not always a clearly defined entity but rather a fluid term, it may be said at once that the term 'God of Heaven' also shares the same lack of precision. Yet a real connexion exists between God and Heaven and results from the operation of the principle of correspondence. Just as Heaven both resembles and contrasts with the earth so God also is said to be like and unlike Heaven. The phrase 'God of Heaven' is obdurate to closer definition. The genitive is even somewhat misleading, for it might be thought to imply that God comes out of, or derives from, Heaven in a mythical manner. But in the Bible God is not an afterthought, a personification perhaps of an existent physical reality. At least the first verse of Genesis guards against all possible errors; if "God in the beginning created the Heaven" God cannot have emerged from Heaven. An equally unacceptable notion is also destroyed by the preamble of creation: the God of Heaven is not confined to Heaven, as if he were only there but nowhere else. The God who created Heaven is also the God who created Earth and who performs his works in every part of the universe. The primary relationship between God and Heaven, therefore, is that of Creator and Creation, of Maker and Work. This doctrinal formulation reverses the genitive relationship decisively. God is the subject and Heaven the object in creation; thus God is 'God of Heaven' because Heaven is God's

Heaven, and not because he is Heaven's god. Therefore he is essentially known and worshipped as "one above the Heavens" (Ps. CVIII, 1–6).

Throughout the centuries common piety went a long way towards personifying Heaven without, however, identifying God with Heaven. The evidence of the Old Testament shows a striking consistency in distinguishing God from his realm above. Thus in Isaiah YHWH speaks "Hear, O Heavens" (I, 2) in a universal indictment of his people. Heaven as a metaphor for God is surprisingly late and arises out of the various attempts to counteract the use of the divine Name for magic spells. The need for a convenient substitute evoked the use of Heaven, among others. In the Rabbinical literature Heaven becomes accordingly a favourite cover-name.[1] From Heaven, it is said, comes help in war (I Macc. III, 18f.), for there the Covenant is laid up (I Macc. IV, 10). So *shamaiim* serves as an appropriate term for God, a name without the article. This Name is not to be profaned (Ab. I, 11). According to Philo, Heaven is the great "invisible god" (Aet. 10, 20). This close identification is familiar from the New Testament, too; Jesus asks in the Rabbinical vein: "Was John's Baptism from Heaven or from men?" (Mk. XI, 30) and leaves no one in any doubt that Heaven stands for God; Heaven and the throne of God and God are alternate terms (Mt, V, 34; XXIII, 22). Thus the Kingdom of Heaven is plainly the same thing as the Kingdom of God in the other Gospels. The Prodigal Son can exclaim: "I have sinned against Heaven" (Lk. XV, 18, 21) and St. John has no scruples in speaking about the gift "from Heaven" to which the Baptist testifies in the customary way as God's own (III, 27).

Nevertheless this imprecise use of Heaven for God as an expression of piety does not cover all the passages in the New Testament, least of all the famous petition: "Thy will be done, as in Heaven, so in earth" (Mt. VI, 10). God's rule in Heaven looms large in the New Testament because the faith in the Creator never permits the identification of God with his creation. Therefore God is held to be quite distinct from the place of his sovereignty.[2]

[1] Cf. A. Marmorstein, *Old Rabbinic Doctrine of God*, 1927, I, pp. 105–7.

[2] Rightly maintained by Cremer, as against Schürer, in RE VIII, pp. 80–4.

ORIGINS OF BELIEF

Such a far-reaching claim of monotheism is, however, hardly applicable to earlier centuries. Gen. 1, 1 is a doctrinal proposition of the Priestly school of Israel and no guide therefore to the origin of the belief in the God of Heaven. The close juxtaposition of gods and Heaven in other and related religions has led many scholars to explain the whole phenomenon by looking outside the Bible for origins of this Biblical belief.[1] Two basic assumptions are taken for granted in this connexion. First, it is asserted that the God of Israel was originally not a God of Heaven but the god of a place, such as Bethel or any other locality which had important cultic or political associations. Even the God of Moses is alleged to have been essentially a mountain god. Secondly, it is considered highly probable that the cosmic element, which pertains to a god of Heaven, was borrowed from foreign sources. Possibilities of contact were always present. In the Patriarchal age, for instance, the early Semitic belief in astral deities was a common possession. The migrations into Canaan would again encounter a myth-ritual pattern in which the gods of Heaven loomed large. The Egyptian worship of the Sun and of the King would provide encouragement to arrogate for the God of Israel similar status and powers. During the Babylonian Exile, too, every incentive would be given to exalt the God of Israel to cosmic rule, and this would not diminish during the Persian era and subsequently in Hellenistic times.

It will be noticed that this argument does not clearly distinguish between a common adherence to a common belief on the one hand, and an act of real borrowing from an alien culture on the other. The thoroughgoing evolutionists favoured its late entry into the religion of Israel: it was during the Exile that Yahweh 'grew' through syncretism into a god of Heaven.[2] Some historians[3] modified this view and claimed that earlier Canaanitish influence after the Conquest was responsible for what had become

[1] E.g. A. Alt, *Kleine Schriften zur Geschichte des Volkes Israels,* 1953, esp. 'Der Gott der Väter', 1929; O. Eissfeldt, 'Baal Samen und Yahweh', ZAW, 1939; D. Nielsen, 'Der dreieinige Gott in religions-historischer Betrachtung', 1942.

[2] Cf. B. Stade, *Biblische Theologie des Alten Testaments,* 1911, I, 291.

[3] Cf. G. Westphal, *Jahwehs Wohnstätten,* 1908, ch. VI, esp. pp. 250 ff.

a political necessity, and that in this way Yahweh took over the celestial prerogatives of his vanquished antagonists. The difficulty, however, with such views is the uncertainty of chronological development. There is no Biblical evidence for the sudden start of a belief, such as in the God of Heaven. We are not justified in saying, "here, at this point, Israel began to believe in a god of Heaven". What becomes apparent is that in the course of the settlement in Canaan the people began to copy certain institutions and beliefs, which were opposed by one section of religious leaders. Whether their assimilation brought them into contact with traditional cultures, of which they were really part, or with something wholly new, cannot be determined from the evidence. The Scriptures themselves merely suggest that the heavenly side of Deity received a varying degree of emphasis and favour at different periods and among different parties and teachers and schools. For example, Genesis and Exodus contain sources, which repeatedly mention God, or the Lord, of Heaven, while the prophetic books of Amos, Hosea, and Micah record words "roared from Zion", uttered upon earth. But even this distinction is perilous and unscientific, for the prophets were at least indirectly involved in the making of the narratives of Genesis and Exodus and were also servants of a "high God" (Micah VI, 6), despite their 'unmythical', this-worldly, political attitudes. Amos knows YHWH as One that "builds his upper chambers in the Heavens and founds his vault upon the earth" (IX, 6). The Old Testament in its present form no longer allows us to answer questions about isolated religious phenomena, and in the question which concerns us now we must be content to say that the God of Heaven represents an ancient tradition of belief, which became separated from the common myth of the Near East through the unique doctrine of creation.

THE HEAVENLY BAAL

The existence of this common myth is very well attested.[1] The Baal Shamem (Lord of Heaven) stands within a tradition of

[1] Cf. esp. O. Eissfeldt, op. cit.; J. A. Montgomery, 'The Highest, Heaven, Aeon, Time etc. in Semitic Religion', HTR. 31/1938, pp. 143 ff.; NSI esp. Nrs. 62, 64, 133, 134; ZAW, 1932, pp. 178 ff.

his own. Philo Byblius, who based himself upon the somewhat doubtful source of Sanchuniathon as an authority on Phoenician mythology, has been vindicated by recently discovered evidence in his dictum that the God of Heaven had been venerated in Syria during the second half of the second millennium B.C.[1] There is an ever-increasing evidence of his cultus. In the Ugaritic texts Baal is the hero-god who fights in the world with Death. The Jehimilk, Zakir, Zenjirli, Sefire, Palmyra etc. inscriptions prove that treaties and pronouncements were made and ratified by the invocation of his name. This Baal resembles Re, Apollo, Zeus, Marduk, and Ahurah-Mazda, but is not derived from these or any other gods who bestrode the Heavens as the sun and proclaimed their power every day. Baal is the lord of the world and rides upon the clouds from where he sends the thunder. His domain is obviously celestial. He is related to other deities, such as the moon and the thunder and Heaven. The storm-god Hadad of the Hittites, the Syrian El, Elyon, Sheme Marom and many minor deities overlap with Baal in scope until he usurps their place. This confusion may account for the fact that the Old Testament generally gives the impression that Baal is one of many Baalim. The Baal of Carmel, exceptionally, appears to be recognized in the singular (I K. XVIII, 19), though the king is accused of having followed the Baalim (verse 18). The multiplication of cultic shrines in Canaan gave rise to the prophets' indictment that the people worshipped earthly Baalim, and in this they were no doubt fortified by what they saw and heard in the centres of Baal worship. Decadence had overtaken the cult and the old Heaven-god Baal had been de-celestialized. Nevertheless, it is as a cosmic lord that he survived in the Hellenistic period.

THE CREATOR

The difference between the pagan gods of heaven and the God of Heaven in Israel became absolute once the doctrine of creation belonged to the faith of Israel. The Zeus of Antiochus, the common *Baal Shemain* of Hellenistic Asia, is roundly denounced

[1] Cf. Eusebius, Praep. Ev. I, 10. for references to Beelsamen whom the Phoenicians regarded as the Lord of Heaven. Cf. K. Galling, *Der Gott Karmel und die Ächtung der fremden Götter,* Alt Festschrift 1953, pp. 105–25 for the evidence from the Mar–Elias monastery of the god's colossal foot found on the spot.

as *Shiquz Shamam*, the abomination of desolation (II Macc. VI, 2; Dan. XII, 11). But when did the doctrine of creation begin to mark and uphold this absolute distinction? It cannot be imagined that 'the Hebrews' (if such a term has any meaning) accepted once and for all so difficult a proposition as contained in Gen. I, I. Certainly priests and prophets led the people in the belief, and even Amos may already refer to a long tradition when he briefly refers to God who makes the Pleiades and Orion (V, 8). Yet it was a tradition destined to be eclipsed for centuries. The great conscious dogmatists Ezekiel and the second Isaiah had to insist again that "he created all these things"; with much fervour the theme had to be restated. It is to this development that we owe the further refinement that God is said to have created the world *before* anything was made; this is almost certainly the correct rendering of "Bereshith . . ." of Gen. I, I and it prevailed.[1] This means that time and space were held to have come into existence when God uttered the Word of creation. The God of Heaven is not the sun in Heaven but exists before creation. The Hebrew dogmatists in their cosmogony part company with simple myths. Their God did not make the universe as a sculptor sets about his work, his materials being provided for him. They still speak of God as shaping and fashioning and carving, but the human analogy of moulding clay does not help here, for God does not create out of pre-existent matter. The "waste and void" of Gen. I, 2 is as formless and insubstantial as the darkness. Matter and energy are themselves made in the act of creation. The divine Potter (Is. XLV, 9) creates form, matter, space and energy at the same time. All arise at once, not fashioned by tools, carving, or digging into the primordial slime, but by his Word spoken in the void. In this way first Light and then Heaven come into being as his handiwork, not as the meeting of a divine mind with matter, but as his personal creation. Therefore Heaven also reflects the Creator's Being and declares his glory (Ps. XIX, I).

[1] The political situation in the era of Persian dominion favoured, but did not originate, this theological victory. Eissfeldt goes too far when he claims: "Weil die Vorstellung vom Himmelsgott damals den Juden von einer Macht nahegebracht wurde, die ihren eigenen Yahwehglauben nicht antasten, sondern schützen wollte, konnte die Yahweh-Religion auf sie eingehen und ihrem eigenen Gott das Prädikat eines Himmelsgottes beilegen." (ZAW, 1939, pp. 27 f.) Cf. Rashi ad loc.

This dogmatic position enabled the writers of the Old Testament to relate some very ancient strands of customs and beliefs without considering them detrimental to the belief that there is only one God of Israel who is Lord of Heaven. They feared no pagan infiltration despite the cultural environment of many high gods. Thus Genesis reports some very archaic and no doubt genuine names of the Patriarchal age. Isaac's God is called *Pachad* (XXXI, 42) and Jacob's *Avir* (XLIX, 24); these gods, 'dread' (or perhaps better: 'kinsman') and 'might', were originally separate deities; during the migrations in Syria the heavenliness of Baal became attached to them, unless they had already possessed it before. Awe and homage in a supernatural sense were due to a god of dread and might. Centuries after the Patriarchs the title *Avir* of Jacob is still used, now with deliberate intent of celestial might (Is. XLIX, 26; LX, 16; Ps. CXXXII, 2, 5). The doctrine of the Creator made the title perfectly safe in liturgical recitation.

TITLES: EL ELYON

This power of absorption knew no bounds. Only Baal remained an outcast from the beginning. Not so *El* and *El Elyon*, who as God and as the Highest obtained a firm place in the Israelite tradition.[1] There is no feeling of hesitancy in Gen. XIV, 18 ff. which describes Abraham's meeting with Melchizedek, the priest-king of Jerusalem. The alien priest blesses the father of the chosen race by *El Elyon*. Again the stranger Balaam knows and prophesies through his knowledge of this god (Nrs. XXIV, 16) and helps Israel thereby. The narratives accept the existence of the god who had a cultic place in Canaanitish worship.

The name El is probably both an appellative and a proper name, whose root meaning denotes strength, supremacy, and greatness.[2] The Ugaritic supreme god is called El; he is considered to be unique and to him man can and does entrust himself since

[1] Hebr., אל עליון.
LXX, Ὕψιστος (cf. Wisd. V, 15; VI, 3; II Macc. III, 31).
Vulg., Altissimus.
R.V., God Most High.

[2] Cf. A. Murtonen, *A philological and literary treatise on the Old Testament Divine Names*, Helsinki, 1952, which contains a full bibliography.

he is also merciful.[1] Although El appears at various places in Canaan he does not lose his supremacy through a multiplication of cultic centres. It is therefore wrong to assume that the El (or the 'plural' elohim) represents merely a local numen of some sort. El is a heavenly deity even if the myth at Ugarit places El in a pavilion on a mountain. There El presides over the gods of Heaven and the myth merely shows the close affinity which exists between mountains and Heaven: "El's home was both terrestrial and celestial . . . gods could travel vast distances with the speed of lightning".[2]

It is not known why and when El suffered a decline which the Ugaritic myths suggest rather than proclaim.[3] No doubt it reflected a change in political circumstances. When in the struggle for power El lost his place he had to yield to Baal though he had helped him in the struggle with Mot (death). Even if Baal won the succession at Ugarit, El may well have remained supreme in other parts of Syria. In any case, the Old Testament reflects the tension only by simple partisanship: Baal is the enemy, and El is God.

The name of the god Elyon raises further problems. The root of the word denotes height, and it is this concept of height which associates Elyon both with El and with Shamaiim, as for instance in the Sefire inscription of c. 750 B.C.[4] But it is as yet impossible to say with any certainty whether Elyon was known as a separate deity in the Canaanitish pantheon. He was not worshipped at Ugarit and does not figure in the mythology.[5] The evidence from the Old Testament places his cultic domain in the southern regions of the fertile crescent. Here El Elyon appears as one deity, almost as if the word Elyon merely emphasized adjectivally the supremacy of the High God. But this complete union does

[1] See esp. O. Eissfeldt, *El im ugaritischen Pantheon,* Berlin, 1951; M. Pope, *El in the Ugaritic Texts,* 1955, esp. ch. v.

[2] Albright in a review of Pope's book in JBL LXX, III (Sept. 1956), p. 255.

[3] Cf. J. Gray's comment in *The Legacy of Canaan,* 1957, p. 115: "The element of conflict between El and Baal has, we think, been greatly over-emphasized by Nielsen, Kapelrud, Cassuto, and Pope. . . . El resigns himself gladly to otium cum dignitate."

[4] For later evidence cf. also G. Kuhn, 'Ein Beleg für Elyon als phönizischen Gottesnamen', ZAW, 1939, p. 150.

[5] The word 'ln occurs frequently and means 'above'.

not appear in the Syrian epigraphy nor in the tradition preserved by Philo of Byblus[1] who distinguishes between El and Elyon and even claims that there was an intermediate stage between these gods' reigns. A family relationship must have existed in which the Phoenician El was grandson of Elyon, and Heaven (Ouranos) provided the link between the generations. It would be tempting to think that the Baal of Heaven is the same as this Ouranos, or the father of El. But since the Ugaritic Baal plainly supplants El, much as Zeus succeeds Kronos in Greek mythology, we are still left with an inconsistent picture of the strife among the gods.

Of this mythical background nothing remains in the Old Testament, except possibly, by way of reaction, its undisguised loathing for Baal, the usurper-god of Heaven. The Hebrew El Elyon has not engaged in a struggle among the gods. Since the God of Israel did not marry—the El of Ugarit had become parent of the gods with his wife, Ashera-Astarte—he never entered the fray of succession and sordid family strife. The polytheistic association is left a long way behind when, in the context of judgment, God addresses the rulers as Sons of Elyon who must die like men (Ps. LXXXII, 6).[2]

It is in the Psalter that the supremacy of God is denoted by the name Elyon, either by itself or as a compound with Yahweh (VII, 18; XLVII, 3) or Elohim (LVII, 3; LXXVIII, 56). The context is always one of strength. The exalted and unique supremacy of God in Heaven goes alongside his sovereign majesty in the world (LXXXIII). He is the King of the universe to whom reverence is due (IX; XCII). He protects those who trust in him (XCI) and receives cultic praise. The worship in Jerusalem reaches up to him (XLVI). Rebellion against him, when it occurs, is put down: to be 'like Elyon' is the temptation and sinful desire of angels and kings (Is. XIV, 14). The note of war is ever-present, and, with it, the noise of cosmic upheavals. Psalm XVIII gives

[1] Cf. Eusebius, *Praep. Evang.* I, X, 36 a–c; 37 b, 40 c.

[2] But cf. O. Eissfeldt, *El and Yahweh*, JJS, I, 25 ff., for a different interpretation. Psalm LXXXII is seen to "reveal a certain state of suspense" (p. 36) in the accommodation of Yahweh to El: Yahweh is one in the congregation of El; he is acceptable, all the other gods must die. El was the supreme God and never conceived of as a rival to Yahweh, but the latter inherited the special El qualities of creatorship and discretion, wisdom, moderation, patience, forbearance, mercy.

the classic picture of Elyon who intervenes when the earth shakes and the foundations are moved: he bows the Heavens and comes down; thick darkness is under his feet; he rides upon the Cherubim; as he utters his voice it thunders in Heaven. The Highest is, therefore, by no means a static God, confined to his supremacy, but one who adds triumph to his exalted height. He moves freely and, despite revelations in one place, like Sinai, precedes and follows his people without any restriction. The height of Heaven guarantees this freedom of movement.

The name of Elyon flows easily into the more general concept of the God of Height, the *Elohe Marom*, whose majesty and power are similarly celebrated in the Psalms and in the Prophets. Since God is on high he watches over every pious individual and delivers him from his oppressors, human and superhuman. God sends from his height and takes his friend (Ps. XVIII, 17) while he confounds the "high ones" (Is. XXIV, 21). The ethical content of height becomes very pronounced in such passages as Is. LVI, 15: God's exaltation is not removed from the lowliness of the contrite (cf. Ps. CXIII, 4 ff.). Sincerity of religion alone is heard "on high" (Is. LVIII, 4 f.), for, being on high, God "observes the nations" (Ps. LXVI, 7) and sees every heart's true nature (Jer. XVI, 17; XX, 12; XXIII, 23). Again it is the concept of height which encourages the universalistic concept of God. A God who is "lofty" sides with everything that is lofty in the ethical sense. He is wise and beyond all human censure, "in the height of Heaven" (Job XXII, 12). Thus the natural and spiritual qualities may be said to coincide as they meet in the final conception of the God Elyon in the heights.

The belief in God most High (Aram. עלהא ='Ilaha) as the supreme God—not as the highest god among high gods—became conventionally accepted in Judaism. "The preference for terms expressive of God's exaltation falls in with a marked tendency in the religions of the times, and notably in the religions of Syria".[1] For the Jews in the Greek-speaking world the acceptance of their Ὕψιστος was most useful. This title was particularly apt to stress tradition, to bring out the supernatural, to encourage worship, and to raise the great hopes of those who looked to the

[1] GFM. vol. I, p. 430.

Lord of the Universe for an amelioration and renewal of the earthly life.

JESUS 'ON HIGH'

The New Testament does not only continue to attribute unique exaltation to God who is understood to dwell in the Highest (e.g. Acts VII, 48) because he is Elyon-Marom, the Highest (Mk. v, 7). The demoniac knows this title and so do the Philippians (Acts XVI, 17). But as God is the Highest so Jesus also discloses in himself the divine exaltation: he is to be called the "Son of the Most High" (Lk. I, 32; VIII, 28) and his Mother shall be overshadowed by "the power of the Most High" (Lk. I, 35). After his Resurrection he is "exalted at God's right hand" (Acts II, 33). The Crucified has been exalted (Acts v, 31), foreshadowing thereby the exaltation of the humble to be children of the Most High (Lk. VI, 35; II Cor. XI, 7; Ja. IV, 10; I Pe. v, 6). That Christ shares the height of God, and therefore his power to move and to intervene and his right to receive thanks and praise, is commonly taken for granted. Christ is raised and sits above (Acts VII, 55; Col. III, 1 f.). St. John particularly insists that the Son shared God's supremacy from the beginning. The Son of Man did not have to ascend Heaven (III, 13) but has come down from Heaven in fulfilment of the Father's will (VI, 38). His earthly situation—"Is not this Jesus, the son of Joseph, whose father and mother we know?"—cannot obliterate his heavenly origin. The living Bread which is Jesus descends from Heaven (VI, 33, 35, 41, 50, 58). Such a descent from the Highest and out of the Highest has no counterpart in Judaism. Jesus is not a mediator out of the spheres but from 'above' (ἄνωθεν, ἄνω). The Rabbis would have agreed that the soul comes from above (whereas no evil comes from above), but Jesus does not simply come from 'above' in that sense; he says: "Ye are from beneath, I am from above" (VIII, 23). The distinction is total and the ambiguity of the word ἄνωθεν (also found in the equivalent rabbinic *millema'alah*) which may mean both 'from above' or 'anew', cannot lessen it.[1] God alone is the Highest and Jesus is exalted where he was before with God. The newness of

[1] Cf. O. Cullmann, *Der johanneische Gebrauch doppeldeutiger Ausdrücke als Schlüssel zum Verständniss des vierten Evangeliums,* 1948, Th. Z. 4, 5.

life of the Christian depends upon the supremacy of Christ and the supernatural begetting (III, 3). Therefore no one except Jesus can vouchsafe the new life for he mediates the life of God. The mediation is still conceived in vertical terms of descent from and ascent to Heaven. The Church's awareness of Jesus as ascended and therefore permanently placed in Heaven is the basis of the Preaching and Liturgy of the Church. The Ascension consummates the capture of captivity and the beginning of freedom (Ephes. IV, 9). Because Christ is "far above all the Heavens" (Ephes. IV, 10) he is acknowledged to be God[1] and Giver of all good gifts. Jesus is the Son of God who has passed through the Heavens (Hebr. IV, 14) and is made higher than the Heavens (VII, 26).[2]

The Christian view preserves in this manner the ancient feeling for the high God, and in particular for El Elyon; it extends to Jesus the unique status of God above all things and powers. He is high both in freedom from all restriction and in perfection. The great mystery how Jesus, once confined to one human body in one place, can be omnipresent and yet retain his personal identity is solved by the portrayal of his exaltation (Mt. XXVIII, 20). The whole of his humanity, assumed upon birth on earth, is carried outside all orbits of compulsion and coinheres with the Father above every created reality. The primitive ascription of height to God, embracing Father and Son, is in the direct, concrete and typically Biblical manner of thinking of and feeling after the inexpressible supremacy of God. The New Testament has little to add to the conception of the God of Heaven as the highest God except the central claim that he who suffered death upon earth is now enthroned on high.

SHADDAI

Despite his loftiness the God of Heaven is not excluded from his Creation. The exalted Christ is not felt to be taken away because he has been taken up. As the Heavens are places of power and life so the God of Heaven sustains his world with

[1] The gulf between Jewish and Christian interpretations of Ps. LXVIII sharply illustrates the gulf between both faiths. According to the Targum and the Midrash it is Moses whose receipt of the Torah is celebrated in verse 19.

[2] For a distinction between the Ascension as an event and as a Christian *theologoumenon* see A. M. Ramsay, *What was the Ascension?* SNTS, Bulletin II.

power and life. The tradition of the active God in Heaven is remembered in the ancient name of El Shaddai, the God of Abraham, Isaac, and Jacob (Exod. VI, 3). El Shaddai represents in the Old Testament the ancient belief in a sovereign God who acts from above,[1] distributing from on high the blessings and curses which determine life on earth like physical elements. Jacob blesses Joseph by Shaddai (Gen. XLIX, 25) and Balaam acknowledges him as his guide to the future (Nrs. XXIV, 4). El Shaddai is the protector of the wandering Aramaeans who depend upon him for light and food and defence (Gen. XVII, 1; XXVIII, 3; XXXV, 11; XLVIII, 3; XLIX, 25; Ps. XCI). He directs the sun and moon and controls the earth; he scatters kings for his and their sake (Ps. LXVIII, 14).[2] Shaddai rules over the natural universe and intervenes in human affairs in a unity of purpose. Although El Shaddai does not loom large in the later history of Israel—he is the 'archaic' God of the books of Ruth and Job; Ezekiel hears his voice in mystic vision (I, 24)—the conception of El Shaddai increased in importance through translations. All the Greek attempts at rendering the Name bring out his cosmic power: Shaddai is the Strong One, the All-Ruler, the God of Heaven, the Heavenly One; all these conceptions are later held together in the one suggestive *Παντοκράτωρ* of the Septuagint and the *Omnipotens* of the Latin. The Power here in question is absolute, cosmic power, the Might (Hebr. Hageburah) which knows no beginning nor end and which some Greek translators also endeavoured to bring out in the term self-sufficiency.[3] The Rabbis, under this influence, reached the same interpretation by a spurious rendering of the Name.[4]

YHWH

The El Shaddai tradition succeeds in ascribing the beginnings of revelation to the cosmic All-Creator by the epoch-making

[1] No explanation of the derivation of the Name can be given. The rt. שׁדה denotes 'to pour forth from on high'. The Accadian šadu = mountain.

[2] The rt. שׁדד denotes 'to deal violently'. Support for this derivation is found in Is. XIII, 6; Joel I, 15.

[3] *ὁ ἱκανός*, rare in LXX, frequently found in Aq., Sym., Theod., alluded to by St. Paul in II Cor. III, 5–6.

[4] שׁ + די

fusion of Shaddai and YHWH. The Lord of Moses and of all the subsequent history of salvation is not a new God, who acts only on earth and among Israel, but he is the same God who directed the fathers from Heaven (Exod. XXXII, 13): "I appeared unto Abraham, unto Isaac, and unto Jacob, as El Shaddai, but by my name YHWH I did not make myself known to them" (Exod. VI, 3). Yet he is the same God of Heaven. The connexion of YHWH with both Elyon and Shaddai is made evident by the compound expression YHWH-Elyon (Ps. LXXXIII, 19; XCVII, 9) and the complete identification between YHWH and Shaddai in parallelism, e.g. in Psalms LXVIII and XCI, and between El and Shaddai in the book of Job. The Lord YHWH is not a mountain El or a local deity, to be forgotten or to be left behind once the Midianite desert ceases to be the home of Israel; he is the Lord because he is above. He "sits in the Heavens" (Ps. II, 4); his throne is in Heaven (Ps. XI, 4). He builds his chambers in Heaven (Amos IX, 6) and releases water from the heavenly ocean (Ps. CIV, 13). The second Isaiah gives a classical formula to the cosmic being of the Lord, sitting above the circle of the earth (XL, 22), and Psalm CXLVIII invites the praise of YHWH from the whole universe.

There is no paradox in the Biblical writers' minds when they rejoice both in YHWH's participation in earthly exploits and in his exalted nature. Whether the name of YHWH helped them in their understanding of this role of YHWH we cannot tell unless the obscurity of the name, which may have been intentional, should yield to present attempts at elucidation. All such attempts will come to nothing unless they can explain why YHWH is a heavenly God who works wonders among his people, a God of nature who shakes the mountains, pours out fire, snow, hail, and rain from above, who makes the Pleiades and Orion and controls light and darkness from outside the realm of nature.[1]

Even the war-god YHWH is the Lord who rules above the Heavens (Exod. XV, 3 ff.). Since he rides upon the clouds he can and does intervene in hostilities. When he goes forth to battle,

[1] A. Murtonen, after examining all current etymological suggestions and dismissing them as unsatisfactory, turns to the Old Testament and explains the name as meaning *Lord* in the sense of master. Cf. op. cit. esp. p. 89. See also H. H. Rowley, *The Faith of Israel,* 1956, pp. 53 f.

marching from the field of Edom, "the earth trembled, the Heavens also dropped, yea the clouds dropped water" (Jdg. v, 4). This image places YHWH the warrior on earth and yet lifts him above the Heavens; therefore "from Heaven fought the stars, from their courses they fought against Sisera" (Jdg. v, 20). With this conviction in his heart Joshua prays to YHWH: "Sun, stand thou still at Gibeon; and thou Moon, in the valley of Aijalon" (Josh. x, 12). The martial lordship of YHWH is always a manifestation of his untrammelled cosmic power. The normal functions of the universe may be stopped by "the signs and wonders", as in Egypt (Exod. III, 20; x, 21; xv, 1–8). The history of Israel owes its significance to such typical tokens of rescuing power. Without the mighty hand of liberation in all trials the Lord would not be known in Israel as a cosmic force who rules the universe and history from above. This conception of God remains unmodified throughout the centuries of national existence: "He delivers and rescues, he works signs and wonders in Heaven and on earth" (Dan. VI, 27). His power over political affairs is but an aspect of his dominion in the universe.

The private revelations of the Lord to a few chosen individuals exhibit the same features. God acts supernaturally in his natural world. The fire which Moses sees in the burning bush (Exod. III) precedes God's self-revelation as YHWH. The great sight is caused not by the intense glare of the sun upon a dried-up shrub but turns out to be a fire that does not consume the shrub, a holy fire not of the sun or the stars but of the originator of all fires (Exod. XXIV, 17). The fire heralds the approach of YHWH and stands for his passionate love as heavenly God for his people on earth.[1] This tradition of YHWH and the fire subsists: he is a "devouring fire" (Dt. IV, 24).

The prophetic experience of God undoubtedly lies behind this recognition of Yahweh's cosmic sovereignty. Isaiah and Ezekiel, for instance, see the God of Heaven, albeit indirectly, in forms and likenesses composed of fire. But it is not in the name of the eternal fire that they proceed with their work on earth;

[1] For YHWH, the passionate and jealous Lover (Exod. XXXIV) see VT, 1956, 1, S. D. Goitein, 'YHWH the Passionate', anticipated by G. A. Barton, *Semitic and Hamitic Origins, Social and Religious,* Philadelphia, 1934.

rather it is in the name of Yahweh that they deliver the very oracles which are by nature fiery and dynamic, destructive of evil and kindling righteousness. How far are they removed from mystical speculations and quietist union with a cosmic force! Instead they stress the unity of their experience with the ancient self-unfolding of God as the all-conquering Yah (Ps. LXVIII, 4), whose warfare is not only their own but his purpose in the whole world.

It was left to the apocalyptic groups to cherish this particular aspect of Deity in their Messianic expectation. Its key text was old and to be found in the oracle of Balaam: "a star shall come forth out of Jacob" (Nrs. XXIV, 17). The ancient tradition, which enjoys the triple authority of El, Elyon, and Shaddai, suited the mystical and political tastes of the writers of the Testaments (Levi ch. V; Judah ch. XXIV) and of Enoch (ch. X) and of the Damascus movement, where the Community's scholars and leaders are given this important title 'star' (CD VII, 18). In the New Testament Jesus' birth is significantly greeted by the Magi with the question: "Where is he . . . for we saw his star in the east . . ." (Mt. II, 2) and at the end of the Apocalypse the risen Jesus refers to himself as "the bright, the morning star" (XXII, 16).[1] More important still is the Lukan saying: "I am come to cast fire upon the earth" (XII, 49) because it emphasises the unity of the work and person of the conquering Saviour who destroys evil and thereby kindles a cosmic conflagration of righteousness on earth. In view of this tradition one is tempted to accept the genuineness of the famous agraphon which Origen records not without some misgivings: "he who is near me is near the fire" (Jer. hom. XX, 3).[2]

In addition to the dynamic-martial note, however, the tradition of the heavenly God also brings out his essential being, for the sacred four letters YHWH designate God not only as alive and life-giving and acting from above. The common awe of this name preserved something integral in the divine answer in

[1] But this star-motif passes soon into the more important 'Jesus Sol Invictus' theme, based upon Mal. IV, 2 and then developed in Justin Ap. I, 67; Ign. Magn. IX, 1; Clement Protr. VIII; Odes of Sol. 15.

[2] Instead of emending πυρός to πατρός; cf. A. Resch, Agrapha, 1906, No. 150; J. Jeremias, *Unknown Sayings of Jesus,* E.T. 1957, pp. 54 ff.

Exodus III, 14: the I AM THAT I AM (Hebr. Eheyeh asher Eheyeh) is mysterious and not necessarily and always connected with action. Here was not a god who could be cited by name, but One who Is, and Will Be, what he Had Been and Is. There has been a tendency in recent years to belittle the metaphysical implications of this key passage, and inasmuch as the Old Testament is not concerned with metaphysics such restraint is wholly commendable. But the verb *hajah* in this context certainly suggests Being in a sense which is free from all contingent limitations of time and space. God's timeless existence is felt in his majestic presence and YHWH, which is his name to denote his Being, must become the Name which is unlike all other names and cannot be pronounced.

KYRIOS

When the translators chose the Greek *Kyrios* (never Yaweh) to represent the Name they must have been aware of their bold choice. Kyrios was then a vague term of secular and religious headship: there were many lords (I Cor. VIII, 5). But the Kyrios of the Greek Old Testament acquainted the whole Hellenistic world, and was meant to acquaint it, with the claims of YHWH, the only universal God of Heaven. Thus it was probably in the Greek-speaking communities that Kyrios-Yahweh was first prayed to as Lord in the most universal sense. The Hebraic custom of calling YHWH *Lord* followed, though even then a straight borrowing from Alexandria was avoided: instead of *Adon*, the simple equivalent for Kyrios, the curious and specially designed form *Adonai* was coined to convey the traditional picture of the God of Israel who is uniquely Lord over the whole world.[1]

This YHWH tradition of the God, who acts from and is above Heaven and who sustains everything with life because he is alive, enters the New Testament with unabated force. The man Jesus is called Kyrios in the Gospels. Here a provocative

[1] Cf. W. W. Baudissin, *Kyrios,* 1929, I, pp. 509 ff.; II, p. 241 ff. R. Pfeiffer opposes this theory and shows the subtleties of the issues involved (*Introduction to the Old Testament,* 1948, p. 94, n. 17). C. H. Dodd, *The Bible and the Greeks,* 1935, pp. 10 ff. steers a middle course: Kyrios translates Adonai. The Jews adopted the term in the Hellenistic world also to express their covenant relationship and this use "amounted in itself to a manifesto of monotheism".

oscillation of the term must always confound the reader: is not Jesus simply addressed as 'Sir', when the word Kyrios is used (e.g. Mt. VIII, 2, 6)? Kyrios in the Gospels recalls very unheavenly functions: the ordinary master owns property and slaves (e.g. Mt. XX, 8; Mk. XIII, 35; Acts XVI, 16) and is addressed and admonished on the grounds that he, the Kyrios, has a Kyrios in Heaven (Col. IV, 1). Jesus is Kyrios as a teacher among disciples (Mt. VIII, 21) and even refers to God as Kyrios (e.g. Mk. V, 19) and not to himself. Yet at the same time Kyrios is applied to Jesus and in some passages it is extremely doubtful whether God or Jesus is referred to. Who, for example, is the Lord in whose sight St. Paul takes thought for things honourable (II Cor. VIII, 21; cf. also I Thess. IV, 6; II Thess, III, 16, and, above all, the difficult *Maran atha* of I Cor. XVI, 22)? The key passage is in Phil. II, 11: "Jesus Christ is Lord to the glory of the Father." It recalls the Rabbinic exposition by Jesus himself of Ps. CX: The Lord's Son is Kyrios; David's son is not Kyrios (Mk. XII, 35–7). Whether suddenly or gradually, from the beginning or at the end of the Apostolic age, there bursts into the world the challenge of the cosmic Christ, the man Jesus who is Kyrios in the full, heavenly sense of Deity (Eph. VI, 9). And further still: the same title with its full traditional YHWH background is also made available for the Spirit: "now the Lord is the Spirit: and where the Spirit of the Lord is, there is liberty" (II Cor. III, 17). The gift κυρίου πνεύματος establishes almost accidentally the heavenly claim. The New Testament use of Kyrios certainly gives new meaning to the ancient cultic quest: "Who is the King of glory?" for the answer "YHWH strong and mighty, YHWH of the armed host" (Ps. XXIV) now requires further identification.

'OLAM

Yahweh-Kyrios is also lord over time; Heaven, as we saw, came to partake both of permanence and transience, but the God of Heaven is subject neither to beginning nor end. The first instance of the realization of the eternity of God probably occurs in Genesis XXI, 33, where Abraham calls at Beer-Sheba on YHWH El 'Olam.

The god ʻOlam is well known.[1] A cuneiform inscription over a gate at Karatepe refers to the eternal sun-god, Shmsh ʻOlam; both the sky and the sun were connected with ʻOlam, the god of time, whom the Phoenicians acknowledged. A reference to Bet ʻOlam in Shishak's list (926 B.C.) shows how widespread the cult of this Kronos figure must have been. At Palmyra, some eleven centuries later, the *Mare ʻOlam* is worshipped both as Lord of the world and of eternity.[2] But the eternal waned at the expense of the temporal. ʻOlam came to be used for the world of *passing* time, perhaps owing to Persian and Greek influence. In Ecclesiastes XII, 5 man's death is portrayed sadly as a journey to the house of ʻOlam, his "long home". The Greek equivalent (*Aion*), too, tended to lose the meaning of eternity; similarly the Aramaic *ʻOlma* is no longer the heavenly but the temporal and hostile world, the *kosmos* which is under judgment of death (Jn. XII, 31).

For the invading Israelites ʻOlam was a friend, the god of their fathers, of the past, and also of the future. YHWH is associated with ʻOlam (Exod. III, 15): "The God ʻOlam is YHWH the Creator" is the credal formulation of the second Isaiah (XL, 28). God is ever-present in and above nature and history, and there is no end to his Word, to his help, his salvation, his justice, and his goodness. His covenant love (Is. LIV, 8) and his personal love (Jer. XXXI, 3) are endless because the self-revealing God and eternity are one. Praise is due to him because his cosmic supremacy precedes time and exists independent of time: "Before the mountains were brought forth, or ever hadst formed the earth and the world, even from ʻOlam to ʻOlam thou art God" (Ps. XC, 2).

God does not belong to eternity as to something that is outside and above him; on the contrary he is lord of eternity (e.g., Ps. IX, 7). Space and time do not encompass him; as he is above the Heavens so he is beyond time (Pss. XLI, 13; CVI, 48). Both eternity and time exist through God, not as independent realms but as part of his creation (Eccles. III, 11). Therefore eternity is not greater than God but derived from him. It is God's own and

[1] Cf. E. Jenni, *Das Wort ʻOlam im Alten Testament* ZAW 65/1955, pp. 1. ff.

[2] Cf. NSI, p. 296; M. Lidzbarski, *Ephemeris für semitische Epigraphik*, III, 1915, p. 84, for the Nabataean Mare ʻolmah. For the Ugaritic use of ʻlm cf. esp. CML, B II IV 40: "El, Thy wisdom is everlasting."

unique eternity which the world does not share with him (Dt. xxxii, 39–40). But this does not mean that eternity isolates God from the world of time any more than the removal beyond the Heaven of Heavens separates him from the earth (Dan. xii, 7). The danger of a wholly remote God does not arise, since God, whom "Heaven and Heaven of Heavens cannot contain and comprehend" (I K. viii, 27) deigns to dwell on earth. The God of the Bible is heavenly because he is transcendent in his Being and immanent in the manifestation of his power. This is not a paradox because his cosmic lordship sustains the whole world by a personally conscious will. Having chosen to make himself known upon earth he reveals himself to the chosen who can apprehend him in his goodness and mercy (Exod. xxxiii, 19) and in the lowliness of his Wisdom (Mt. xi, 25–9) and the humility and obedience of his Servant (Phil. ii, 8). Before the world and its creatures were made, God determined that spiritual beings should know and love him as the Highest and the Strongest, as the Lord of all things and all eternity. To that end the transcendent God operates even in the history of men, the universal in the particular, the eternal in the temporal. The designation 'Olam acts as a guarantee that the saving events do not lose themselves on the rubbish heap of a human past but continue to be effectively present in the saving history of the whole world.

FATHER

The attributes of El Elyon, Shaddai, 'Olam, and YHWH are all gathered up in the final conception of God as heavenly Father (Mt. vi, 14; xi, 25).[1] In the Old Testament it is rare, since any intimation of physcial paternity would have been felt to be dangerous. Two Psalms (ii and cx) still show signs of the Israelite, or rather Davidic, version of that common pattern which ascribed not only divinity but sonship to the King. God who sits in the Heavens has not only adopted his ruler but declares himself to be his Father: "Thou art my Son, this day have I begotten thee."

It is, however, not possible to derive in a direct line the concept of the heavenly Father through the cultic sonship of the Messiah.

[1] For a full comparative study see F. H. Smith, *The Fatherhood of God,* D.D. thesis, London University Library.

Two Psalms are insufficient evidence for an extremely complex picture, in which, according to one text, the Messiah is even himself hailed as son and father (Is. IX, 6). It appears that the prophets were familiar with the cultic pattern of their age and that they rejected it. For them God's fatherhood is certainly heavenly and only heavenly: it is not to be represented in the royal cult. Hence they use the term metaphorically and corporately: the people are together YHWH's firstborn. "Israel is my son, my firstborn" (Exod. IV, 22): This motto proclaims the election of the people by the saving Lord and not the existence of a physical or mythical kinship. The Father who bought his enslaved son made and established his people, according to the Deuteronomic interpretation of Israel's history (Dt. XXXII, 6). But this fatherhood is eternal and not contingent upon political and even ethical disasters. Even to the dispersed, God continues to be their Father: for "I am a father to Israel, and Ephraim is my firstborn" (Jer. XXXI, 9). The Father's heavenly eternity is brought out with passionate clarity by the post-exilic prophet who prays: "Look down from Heaven" and continues: "For thou art our father, though Abraham know us not, and Israel does not acknowledge us: thou, YHWH, art our father, our redeemer from everlasting is thy name" (Is. LXIII, 16). The realization of God's saving Fatherhood leads to a recognition of his love and therefore evokes penitence and gratitude (Hos. XI, 1 f.). It sets the pattern of true behaviour without obscuring the infinite gulf between God and man, for "thou art our father, we are the clay, and thou our potter" (Is. LXIV, 8). We have all "one Father", and therefore treacherous behaviour among brothers is outrageous (Mal. II, 10).

In the prophetic tradition the Father in Heaven is neither despot nor a guarantor of nationalistic success but increasingly the guardian of the righteous congregation. Moore is right in maintaining that the belief expressed a feeling of intimacy rather than of separation.[1] In the inter-testamental period the Chasidim and their successors looked to God in Heaven for their vindication,

[1] GFM, II, p. 205: "The words 'who is in Heaven' have in them no suggestion of the remoteness of God, exalted above the world in his celestial habitation; they remove the ambiguity of the word 'father' by thus discriminating between God and an earthly father."

for God is the father of the righteous only (e.g. Sir. XXIII, 4; Wisd. II, 16).

Jewish piety became accustomed to invoke the Lord as "father and master" to express the unique relationship between the residue of the people and the God of the Torah, who was termed "in Heaven" to obviate confusion.[1] The connexion between the Heaven-Father of Judaism and the ancient Supreme God exists only by virtue of the fact that he is still the God of Abraham and of Moses. A far stronger cosmic note is found in Philo's casual references to God as Father. As usual he is concerned to mediate one system of thought to another tradition, and the concept of the heavenly Father aids him considerably in bringing out the universality of the God of the Scriptures and his cosmic sovereignty. "The supreme Father of gods and men" (Spec. II, 165) is likewise the god of the universe and of all men. So it can be said of Moses, as of all men, that "his father is God and his mother Wisdom, through whom the universe came into being" (Fug. 109).

The New Testament writers inherited thus a rich tradition of the Heaven-Father. There is no doubt that they insisted on the primary link between the new kerygma and the old belief: The Father of our Lord Jesus Christ is the God of the universe, of the Patriarchs and Moses, of the elect, Israel, and the prophets (e.g. Acts XIII, 17 ff.) He is the high God above, the supreme Lord, who watches over his people and guards the righteous. "Our Father in Heaven" is also invisible and unknown (Jn. XIV, 6) though every good gift comes from the "Father of lights" (James I, 17) whose cosmic and ethical perfection coinhere especially in the good order of things. The Father is not capricious but without variation. Therefore he is "not known" in the world of darkness, which the "Jews" represent in the Fourth Gospel (VIII, 54 ff.) and it is the task of the Messiah to reveal him directly to the elect. Jesus as the Son of the Father takes upon himself the very task of the Messiah which the Psalms II and CX delineate: the only-begotten of the Father fulfils the role of the King, yet not in a cultic sense but realistically.[2] The New

[1] Cf. Str. B.I., pp. 392 ff.; 410 ff.

[2] For the difficult ambiguity of *ὡς μονογενοῦς παρὰ Πατρός* cf. Commentaries on Jn. I, 14. The underlying *Ben iachid le'aviv* seems to favour a precise definition rather than a loose analogy.

Testament fulfils the theme of Fatherhood by the claim that the Son unfolds its cosmic being in his personal essence. It does not thereby sanction a type of piety in which every individual finds access to God as his father, for it still tempers the cosmic universality of the Father with the exclusiveness of election. The recipients of the Spirit of adoption in the Church may acclaim him as "Abba, Father" (Rom. VIII, 15), for they know the God of Heaven as the Father of the Lord Jesus Christ.

GOD, HIDDEN AND REVEALED

Unless God rends the Heavens to come down (Is. LXIV, 1) the Biblical tradition concedes to the sceptic that God is invisible and unknown. The principle of correspondence applies in the realm of ordinary experience. Just as none but the exceptional are granted the penetration of Heaven so none can claim to see the God of Heaven. He is always a hidden God, not in a metaphorical sense primarily, but as one whom the human senses cannot perceive. God dwells in "thick darkness" (Exod. XX, 21), clouds and darkness are round about him (Ps. XCVII, 2). Because God is thus beyond the human senses and the natural approach, there was in Israel the severe prohibition against the making of any representation of God or of any lesser image which might serve for religious purposes. The sight of the stars and the sun or of the King cannot compensate for the apprehension of the invisible God. Although there is no doctrine of the hidden God the second Isaiah certainly acknowledges a universal truth in the reverent address to the unknown God: "Truly, thou art a God who hideth thyself" (XLV, 15). This saying cannot be developed into an axiom of a doctrinal sort, but it would be rash to dismiss it merely as a quotation, on the prophet's part, from pagan sources. It is the necessary corollary of a heavenly God who does not unfold his Being.

THE "FACE"

The traditional form of God's self-revelation from Heaven is to be found in his looking-down from Heaven. God is said to be possessed of some bodily forms (arm, mouth, eye, face, front and back) which are analogous to human forms. That this is possible, despite the cosmic claims, is explained in the tradition of the making of man in Genesis I. Man, created in the image of God, is made after the divine likeness. The principle of correspondence does not press any identity but eases the conception of God's having and turning a face. This use of Face (Hebr. *panim*) comprehends both the Presence and Will in God's self-revelation.[1]

The turn of the celestial face bestows personal contact, face to face. The image of the face is taken both from the language of court circles and from the observation of lunar phases. God's face reflects, like a mirror, every change in his disposition. When God lifts up his face and shines on men they are honoured and certain of divine favour and compassion (Nrs. VI, 24–7). God appears in dreams and in visions and shows his face which resembles the human form (cf. Gen. XVIII, I where the angel of the Lord softens the starkness of the direct vision). In ordinary waking life men cannot see God and live (Exod. XX, 19; XXXIII, 20) for it is assumed that the impression is so tremendous and blazing with light that death must follow (Lev. XVI, 2). Against this background stands the revelation to Jacob who has seen God and whose life is preserved (Gen. XXXII, 30). Moses encountered God and may therefore say that his people have seen God "face to face" or "eye to eye" (Dt. V, 4; Nrs. XIV, 14). It is probably understood that the rule of the inability of human eyes to see God is not broken; for as the sun injures the naked eye so the Maker of the sun cannot be directly perceived. This is well brought out in the double tradition of revelation to Moses. God vouchsafed to appear to Moses but he put him in a cleft of a rock and covered him with his hand until he passed by: "thou shalt see my back: but my face shall not be seen (Exod. XXXIII, 18–23). These conflicting traditions indicate the nature of the problem as viewed by the Hebrew writers. They bring to a fine point the question of how the Lord of Heaven can appear to and dwell with his people. The Face of God is not comparable to a sudden and passing apparition but stands for the abiding and conscious and saving Presence of God. The purpose of God's heavenliness is not separation from, but a penetration of, the

[1] For a detailed comparative study see F. Nötscher, "*Das Angesicht Gottes schauen*" *nach biblischer und babylonischer Auffassung*, 1924.

whole universe by his Presence, the glance or look of his Face. His Face is turned from Heaven towards men so that he himself, or his Name, may dwell with them (Dt. XII, 5; XIV, 23; XVI, 2).

The form of the divine self-communication from Heaven is always either visual or aural, and very rarely both. But whether it be one or the other, it is always welcome and irresistible. Here again the principle of correspondence is unmistakably in operation: as the Heavens are pure and good and desirable so it is not open to question that the manifestation of God reveals him as eminently pure and good and desirable. It is also intelligible through the human senses of perception, and even despite the undoubted existence of false revelations and dreams and prophecies which are untrue (Dt. XIII) the Biblical tradition assumes that God can and does appear and make himself known to man.

GLORY

The visual knowledge of God derives from his effective penetration of the whole universe through glory. The divine glory is itself indescribable because it is not known upon earth (Ro. VIII, 18) but yet to be revealed. But there are degrees of glory found in Heaven and earth (I Cor. XV, 40) as among the stars: "one star differs from another star in glory" (I Cor. XV, 41). These proportions of glory do not however impair the absolute and distinctly unique glory of God. His supramundane majesty is guarded by his holiness, but it is a majesty which rules in freedom and cannot be confined to remote and extramundane regions. The concept of glory proved invaluable in making God's majesty accessible, for glory is not transcendental in a static sense. God can "fill Heaven and earth" (Jer. XXIII, 24), the whole vast universe like his house (Bar. III, 24 f.). Later comparisons of God's self-imparting from above strayed without success from this concept of glory: for instance, a cave may be filled by the overspill of the water, or a sponge may suck up water, without causing the sea any loss (Midr. R. Cant. III, 10; Aug. Conf. VII, V, 1), but the image somehow lacks in power.

The penetrating glory of God comes out of the celestial glory which surrounds and conceals the incomparable essence of his

Being. The imagery is again taken from the world of royal pomp and custom. But whereas a king is clothed in profane and changeable glory, such as Solomon's (Lk. XII, 27), God's cloak or train, which Isaiah saw in his trance (Is. VI, 1), does not belong to the perishable world. No human splendour can imitate the unique weight or radiance of this glory which is composed of light and fire. A cosmic kingdom constitutes the divine mantle of God,[1] but this fiery entourage is not identical with God nor even with God's glory. Inasmuch as it reflects the uncreated glory it serves in the revelation and declaration of the glory of God (Ps. XIX). The measure of the reflection determines the content or proportion of glory, and this is pre-determined by God in creating the world.

The use of the word 'glory'[2] would be highly ambiguous if every ordinary fire were considered to be an extension of God. It is true that light and warmth create a sight which may be the prelude to, or even the substance of, revelation. Every day and night may be called glorious because the sun runs the race from one end of Heaven to the other. But the inference that God can be directly apprehended by the glory of his works, that nature bears sufficient evidence in itself, is a grotesque distortion of the Biblical tradition, which sets the manifestation of glory firmly in the context of history, and, in particular, that of the Exodus from Egypt and the making of the Covenant. The flashes of fire and light are the physical counterpart of the spiritual unfolding of God. Glory, however, does not distinguish between these two aspects but rather unites them in the one act of visual appearance. God's glorious presence involves the accompaniments of celestial phenomena. God is seen like an erupting volcano and leads his people by a pillar of fire by night and as a cloud by day (Ex. XIII, 21). Both are thought of as the vehicles of God's active glory.

The history of the Exodus and the prophetic interpretation of its glory have become inextricably united in the Old Testament. The Covenant glory, which is celestial, becomes the focal point

[1] See R. Eissler, *Weltenmantel und Himmelszelt*, 1910.

[2] The Greek δόξα renders the following Hebrew terms:
כבוד, פאר, הדר, גאן הוד, עז, יקר, יפי, תהלה, תמונה, which render several aspects of wonderful and majestic strength.

and receptacle of prophetic experiences and messages of light. It ensures that there is no return to the pagan worship of light or the deification of the sun. On the contrary the manifestation of the glorious light leads to a deepening of the high ethical character of religion. The vision of the fire of glory becomes the authority for moral and cultic pronouncements. Isaiah identifies his perception of the glory with the "king, the Lord of hosts" (vi, 5) and infers throughout his ministry that the universal rule of the God of Heaven cannot and will not tolerate sin. In one place he describes the nature of iniquity with the significant denunciation: "Woe to them . . . that put darkness for light and light for darkness" (v, 20). In his consciousness of God and morality the light is the human perception and reflection of the glory of God. Therefore he begins a long tradition, highly developed in the whole book of Isaiah, that light is the dynamic principle of salvation and the end of historical existence. When YHWH "binds up the hurt of his people" the light of the moon shall be as the light of the sun, and the light of the sun sevenfold (xxx, 26). In the absence of righteousness the prophet's descendants walk in obscurity and they look for light (lix, 9). The whole Messianic hope coincides with the expectation of light in darkness (ix, 2 ff.), for when the light shines then the glory of the Lord rises up (lx, 1). The world's darkness awaits the glory of the Lord which all flesh shall see together (xl, 5). Thus the Exodus tradition is used as an inspiration for immediate reform and ultimate hopes: "all the earth shall be filled with the glory of the Lord": once the rebels of the Exodus had seen the glory, had disobeyed and yet been over-ruled (Nrs. xiv, 21 f.), and so it shall be again when the "Sun of righteousness" arises with healing in his wings (Mal. iv, 2).

A sharp distinction marks off the light of God's glory from the fire of the idol-maker (Is. xliv, 16) and the firebrands of man's devising (l, 11). There is only one glory and it cannot be changed (Jer. ii, 11). Ezekiel insists that the flashing fire and the surrounding brightness constitute "the appearance of the likeness of the glory of the Lord" (i, 28). He guards himself and his pupils against a complete identification of the phenomenon with the reality itself. The stages of God's self-manifestation can be noted without much difficulty: the Lord is in Heaven; his glory surrounds him and renders him invisible while partaking of his nature of light and fire; the shapes of blazing forms communicate to the entranced eye a likeness of the glory; the appearance belongs to the inspired perception of the moment. In this way the prophet avoids the pitfalls of the common mysticism of light and fire. To this end he connects his own vocation and strictly concrete prophecies with the unassailable and unique manifestation of the glory of the Lord (III, 12, 23), and therefore, though in exile, to the cultic glory of the Temple (VIII, 4; X, 4, 18; XI, 23). It is the unalterable glory of the Lord which survives all the vicissitudes of history and returns to the Temple of the future (XLIII, 2, 5; XLIV, 4). Thus the Ezekiel tradition developed the prophetic expectation in its cultic direction. The second Temple would fulfil this hope (Ezra VI, 12).

EXPECTATIONS OF GLORY

The cultus itself and individual piety celebrated and petitioned for the coming of the glorious light: "Lift up the light of thy countenance upon us, O Lord!" (Ps. IV, 6), for the axiom that the Lord is light (Ps. XXVII, 1) and that this light is reflected in human experience (Ps. XXXVI, 9) is a truth not confined to mystics and theologians but broadly accepted by all men. Indeed, the whole conception of the glorious Presence of the God of Israel not only was generally accepted but also lent itself to differing interpretations. The tolerance of Jewish belief allowed room both for a complete lack of interest in the cosmic glory of God and a zeal for its manifestation. Among those who were not indifferent to the tradition of glory we may distinguish those parties which looked upon the institutions in Jerusalem as the custodians of an ever-present glory, and those who broke away altogether from the institutional concept. It was the former who reaped the harvest of Ezekiel's work of Law and Glory.

The Rabbinical doctrine of the immutable *Torah* places the Law above the universe (cf. Ab. I, 2; Midr. R. Gen. I, 4; xii, 2;): the Torah is eternal, God's first possession; the universe is created after it (Ab. III, 14 and passim). The New Testament sayings about Heaven and Law take the same view: "It is easier for Heaven and earth to pass away than for one dot of the Law to become void." (Lk. XVI, 17; cf. Mt. V, 18 "till Heaven and earth pass away.") The reversal of ancient opinion is indeed remarkable. Formerly, the ethical and cultic order had been held to reflect the norm of the whole creation, but now the cosmic order of the universe reflects the Torah. In the early days of Israel the peasant elders had met at their gates to discuss and to decide cases in dispute. Then it had been their concern to uphold security and propriety and the ensuing rightness was no doubt felt to reflect the general order of things. Similarly, the grave ten 'words' or commandments had specified principles of righteousness which governed the whole world. Thus the Torah had always been more than a tribal code or a merely legal document. But after the Exile the Torah represents the heroic endeavour to show forth the acts of God in the calendar of earthly time and in a definite place. This Law of righteous life and true worship legislates against the darkness and chaos of a world without God and, having its authority from God, it is supernatural and permanent and glorious. Nothing visible or tangible can replace the Law.

The supremacy of the Torah supported the claims of institutional glory as long as this was politically possible and Jerusalem could be regarded as the place which God had chosen and the Temple the house where God dwelt. Pilgrims came up and acknowledged the glorious dwelling, the dwelling of God's glory (e.g. Ps. XLVIII; LXXXIV). Even then individuals felt impatient with the cultus. The Temple songs not only celebrated the praises of him "who has shone forth" (Ps. L, 2) but also appealed to the same God to come with fire (L, 3): "Thou that sittest upon the Cherubim, shine forth!" (Ps. LXXX, 2). Such prayers strike a discordant note, as if God were wont to withhold his glory and disappoint his worshippers by his absence.

The great crisis of the second century before Christ certainly reopened the issue of God's dwelling in cultic glory. During the Syrian oppression the glory departed from the Temple and this desecration changed not only the political but also the religious outlook with far-reaching consequences. Although the Maccabean victory and the re-construction of the sanctuary appeared to restore the former situation the scars of treachery and worldliness remained recognizable until the time of Jesus. The Chasidim who had resisted pagan pressure did not simply rejoice in victory. Their religious realism did not forsake them under the Hasmonean succession. The various sects, often disgusted with the priesthood, looked for another and worthier dwelling of God's glory than the cultic institution could provide. The importance of the discoveries at Qumran lies not least in the extensive documentation of the resurgence of the apocalyptic hope in Israel during the vital centuries before Christ. The Covenanters were traditionalists who cherished Isaiah's universal Messianic expectation within the particular framework of Israelite salvation. Above all, their awareness of the enormity of evil and the grandeur of their struggle caused them to take up the ancient threads of cosmic religion against the "dominion of darkness" (IQH XII, 6 f.). Apocalyptic feeling revived the almost obliterated belief in the God of Heaven as a supreme and dynamic force, whose dwelling is not on earth and not in a sanctuary. The place of glory is in Heaven and God penetrates the world with light and fire ere he consents to dwell with his people. This residence belongs to the future and perhaps to the end of the world. Thus the manifestation of the divine glory, of the visible part of his majesty, is not to be thought of apart from other events on a cosmic scale: the Shekinah[1] *will* appear; it has not yet appeared.

The book of Daniel sets the tone of the theology of all subsequent apocalypses, as the true representative of these times. God is the God of Heaven (Dan. II, 18, 19, 37, 44); Daniel and the saints are exiles in 'Babylon'. They cannot look to the cultus in Jerusalem for true worship. Just as Ezra and Nehemiah had prayed in a foreign country to the God of Heaven (Ezra I, 2; V, 12; VI, 9, 10; VII, 12, 21, 23; Neh, I, 4, 5; II, 4) and acknowledged his universal rule, so the heroic resisters of the second century find comfort in God's transcendence and seek freedom from local terror in the Babylon of their situation. It should be noted how the political anguish gives new support to the ancient

[1] Hebr. *shakan* = to dwell, hence Shekinah as a popular name for God's majestic Presence which had descended to dwell among men.

celestial conception. Kingdom, power, strength, and glory belong to God who gives them to kings and rulers (Dan. II, 37). All the qualities of Elyon (Dan. III, 26; IV, 2; VII, 18 ff.) and Shaddai and YHWH are developed to unparalleled heights of militant expectation. The result is that hope of salvation, as described in the key chapter VII, which hardly encourages a belief in a cultic or abiding Shekinah, but in the dramatic intervention of the God of Heaven and the vindication of the saints in Heaven. The most high God is the King and Judge, King "over the Heavens, judging kings and rulers" (as the writer of the Psalms of Solomon [II, 32–6] sums it up in his indignation at Pompey's profanities). He is the "ancient of days", the apocalyptic equivalent for the ancient 'Olam—eternity, or "father of years" as he had been called at Ugarit centuries ago. He is surrounded by white and blazing glory: "his raiment white as snow, the hair of his head like pure wool, his throne fiery flames, its wheels burning fire" (Dan. VII, 9). Fire issues forth from him and engulfs his endless train of attendants (Dan. VII, 10). Most remarkably there is in this vision no descent to the earth, no cloud or Shekinah to overshadow and guide Israel. On the contrary, one like a son of man, the Israel of the saints (Dan. VII, 27) is brought before God in Heaven to receive there his dominion. The later chapters, though much concerned with political events, do not annul this high cosmic note of redemption. The glory of God is a fiery power above and not an institution on earth.

In the apocalyptic circles mankind was looked upon as estranged from God's glory (e.g. Ap. Mos. XXVIII). After the Messiah's coming and after the judgment men would see it as a reward (IV Ezra VII, 91–7) as Daniel had already predicted (XII, 3). Here it is assumed to be in Heaven and only the glorified can approach it (En. XXVII, 3; LXIII, 2; LXXV, 3). But some ambiguity remains, for who are the glorified? In the Qumran scroll of "the War of the Sons of Light with the Sons of Darkness" the expectation is both political and eschatological. The war is against the Kittim (probably the Romans); the downfall of the Kittim coincides with the advent of salvation and the end of wickedness. It appears that the ranks are formed for military purposes on earth, but their standards bear celestial slogans, such as "the Glory of God". Similarly victory is not confined to territorial gains or earthly security but involves a cosmic change. Therefore the victorious sons of light pray: "Fill thy land with glory" (IQM, XII, 12). The Qumran document reflects the general Messianic hope that the Glory will appear and dwell among men when the war against all manner of oppression has been won with the help of God. This hope does not go outside history, but it involves cosmic participation. In short, when God gathers his people again the glory of the Lord shall once more be seen and not before (II Macc. II, 7–8). The 'How' and the 'Where and When' are left to the sectarians' interpretation.

THE SHEKINAH

Judaism under its Rabbinic guidance, however, recovered from these extreme views. Partly owing to its exacting reconstitution after the Fall of Jerusalem and partly owing to its final rejection of and reaction to Christian claims, the Rabbinic dialectic reverted to the moderate, pre-apocalyptic conceptions of the Shekinah and discounted speculations. Nevertheless, Judaism in rejecting the Christian solution to the paradox that the God of Heaven is above and yet dwells in his universe did not develop the concept of Shekinah to take the place of Christ. The references to Shekinah in Talmud and Midrash[1] are incidental rather than deliberate. What matters to the Rabbis throughout is the ethical and social aspect of tradition and not the transcendental speculation. The following allusions to Shekinah, chosen at random and impossible to date, are scattered over a very wide area. They confirm the absence of a consistency of thought.

On the one hand Shekinah is identified with YHWH and contemplated as enthroned in Heaven, excelling the sun in brilliance and ever present (b Sanh. 39 a). There are no descents at all and in the polemic against the Ascension there is the further denial that Moses and Elijah ever ascended up to Heaven, for it was the Shekinah's radiance which reached down to them (b Sukkah 5 a). On the other hand Shekinah is said to have rested among the

[1] Cf. J. E. ad loc.; also J. Abelson, *The Immanence of God,* 1912; Soncino Talmud, Index vol., p. 376; Str. B. I. 206 f.; II, 3.

prophets, even those of Baal (according to a very curious passage in b Sanh. 103 b), and to have deserted David (b Sanh. 107 a). Shekinah followed the exiles on their way to exile and out of it (b Meg. 29 a). The moving Shekinah rests upon the priests, even if unclean (b Yoma 56 b), the Divine Presence protects the sick (b Shab. 12 b), but withdraws from evil (b Sotah 3 b; Midr. R. Ruth I, 2), and especially from idolatry, murder, leprosy etc. in Israel. According to *Aboth* of R. Nathan (XXXIV, 8, where the text is slightly obscure) a tenfold descent of the Shekinah corresponds to ten events in the Bible: God's appearance in the Garden of Eden (Gen. III, 8), at Babel (Gen. XI, 5), at Sodom (Gen. XVIII, 21), at the burning bush (Exod. III, 8), at the Red Sea (Ps. XVIII, 9), at Sinai (Exod. XIX, 20), in the cloud (Nrs. IX, 22), in the sanctuary (Ezek. XLIV, 2), and in the future, at the defeat of Og and Magog (Ezek. XXXVIII; XXXIX), and triumphantly, on the Mount of Olives (Zech. XIV, 4). Ten stages of withdrawal are also recorded for the Shekinah's unwilling departure after the ruin of the first Temple: from ark-cover to Cherub, and thence to the threshold, to the court, to the altar, to the roof, to the wall, to the town, to the mountain, to the wilderness, and finally to its own place, i.e. Heaven (cf. b Rosh Hashana 31 a). The Shekinah's return to the second Temple was a matter of promise rather than of experience (cf. Targ. Hag. I, 8). Nevertheless, Israel was still surrounded by glory, both in Palestine and in the synagogues abroad (Mek. Ex. XII, 41). Just as a great man of distinction on leaving a city draws a number of ordinary people along with him, so the brilliance of the glory reaches far and wide among the people and even foreigners are under the wings of Shekinah (cf. Midr. R. Ruth V, 4). There also sprang up the pious belief, based upon Mal. III, 16, that when two men gather together to study the Torah the Shekinah is present (Ab. III, 6).

Throughout, the references to Shekinah concern human life and behaviour. Earthly duties are thought to go hand in hand with heavenly visitations, but the religious communion is not yet conceived of in mystical terms. It is the ordinary good life which both deserves and obtains the blessings of God's Presence: if men do that below which corresponds to that which is above, God leaves his household above and draws his Shekinah among the deserving. Consequently the saints in Israel are rewarded with the enjoyment of its light, both here and after death.

There was, then, in Judaism at no time a consistent system which set out to explain how God communicates himself to the universe by his glory and how he communes with his people. In its broadest Hellenized form Judaism would agree that light is a symbol of Deity in God's relation to man and the world, and it is this important aspect which Philo seized upon in his work, looking upon God as the archetype of all light, "prior to and high above every archetype" (Som. I, 75). Philo's half-scientific, half-mystical exposition of light came up against the same paradoxical issue as the Shekinah in Rabbinical discussions. How could light be heavenly, beyond, transcendental, of God, and yet also perceptible, here, on earth, among men? He distinguishes carefully: God saw before the beginning and was himself his own light, is apprehended by light and creates light by means of light (Praem. 45–6).

JESUS AND THE SHEKINAH

The New Testament acknowledges no outward authority in its treatment of the visual presence of God. The writers change and fit the existent tradition into their Gospel of Jesus Christ, but this change does not mean that they wholly abrogate the well-known words and associations. On the contrary: the glory-kavod of the Bible, the glory-Yeqarah of the Aramaic Targumim, the Doxa of the Greek Septuagint, converge upon the figure of Jesus, the focal point of the divine Presence who fulfils the expectation of God's visitation. This is the first complete departure from Rabbinic and Hellenistic Judaism, and from Gnostic sources of light-mysticism. Jesus is central, not only to contemporary and future living, but to everything that has gone before. Therefore even the traditions of glory, the tales of past Shekinah, are re-interpreted in the light of the one Person without whom they could never have occurred. Such a re-interpretation came to be called fulfilment, but it was a fulfilment of a revolutionary kind.

The humanity of Jesus contradicts some associations of the Shekinah. But the Gospels make no attempt to slur over the humanity of Jesus: he appeared and acted as a man. Yet he had come with glory and he had gone to Heaven. His Presence was assured to those who believed, though he was no longer visibly among them, until he should reappear in glory. The ancient paradox of the God above and his appearance beneath still exists, but it is wholly personalized. It is not a general question about light and the mediation of glory, but a concrete issue of the relationship in faith with God in Jesus. The Gospels do not deal with a metaphysical problem but set forth the manifestation of God in terms of human life and death. In this new tradition the Kyrios is Servant, the glory resides in a man who dies as a criminal. The paradox is sharpened and rendered concretely personal.

The humanity of Jesus conceals his cosmic lordship and glory. The world sees at times a man of Nazareth who lacks the lustre of royal glory. Jesus is not only poor and troubled, hungry and thirsty, but he prays to Heaven and lifts up his eyes to the Father who is in Heaven. He stresses his dependence (Jn. XI, 41). The son of Joseph, whom the crowds aver to know, is to their sight inglorious (Mk. VI, 1–6). Jesus does not himself act to make a divine impression (Mk. X, 18): his successful exorcisms, for example, are not to be broadcast to that effect (Mk. I, 34, 44–end).

The form of the Servant is not celestial but human. The Galilean preacher and teacher and healer has come to serve and even subjects himself to humiliation at the hands of men. Yet in the experience of the Church this humiliation represents the height of glory, for this glory does not emanate temporarily from outside to light up a particular scene but is the direct participation of God in man, the full turning of his *Panim* to blind, lame, and dumb humanity without God. In serving God comes to his people, who cast their shame upon his glory, their darkness upon his light. The Cross and not the sun is the symbol of the truth that the glory has come. Shekinah must be re-interpreted in its light.

The devotion of the apocalyptic tradition to the book of Isaiah pointed the way to the needed re-interpretation. Indeed, Jesus (Yesha) and the prophecies of Isaiah (Yesha-Yahu) become inseparable in the tradition. Just as the Covenanters of Qumran were deeply attached to this endless source of Messianic hope, the

Christian Community saw therein the *praeparatio evangelica* par excellence. Here was the portrait of the humiliated servant who was nevertheless God-with-us, Immanuel, the divine king, endowed with the perfect spirit. Unlike modern scholars these circles regarded the prophecy as one. The wonderful child, whose birth was certainly not described in ordinary terms,[1] was the same who was called "wonderful counsellor, mighty God, everlasting father, prince of peace" (Is. IX, 6) and again the same whom God elects to set up perfect law and order by redeeming men through death (chs. XLII, XLIX, L, LII, LIII). The Christian *testimonia* from Isaiah pass on easily from one section to another of this vast scroll about God's salvation, and the fact that originally centuries lay between their making does not affect their evidential usage. Thus the book of Isaiah is re-interpreted from the point of view of later events which are alleged to be the fulfilment of all these prophecies.

The climacteric portrait of Jesus is found in the last Servant Song (LII, 13–LIII end), a portion of scripture which was probably used liturgically by Jewish Christians as the most obvious prediction of the Saviour's death.[2] Here all the features of glory, found in the Immanuel prophecies, are resumed with dramatic suddenness: before the sufferings are described no doubt is left about the Servant's identity. With threefold emphasis proclamation is made of his majesty: he is high, lifted up, very lofty. His status is the ground for his success (LII, 13).[3] His subsequent humiliations and martyrdom and atoning sacrifice are not only no slur on his glorious self, but it is his glorious self which alone enables him to suffer and die and conquer.

[1] The 'almah-parthenos controversy has received a new impetus by the readings in the Ugaritic tablets: glmt occurs at K I IV 41; III II 22; NK I 7 (cf. CML ad loc.). Driver translates 'lass' throughout, e.g. "Lo! a lass shall bear a son". Mowinckel, however, acknowledges the 'mythical' tone and accepts its relevance to Is. VII, 14 and yet rather surprisingly opts for the old Jewish interpretation: Hezekiah is the as yet unborn son of the young Ahaz (*He That Cometh*, 1956, pp. 110 ff.).

[2] The oracle was originally also 'Messianic' in the Jewish tradition until "the history of Jewish exegesis of Isa. LIII is shaped increasingly by the opposition to Christianity" (J. Jeremias, *The Servant of God*, 1957, p. 75). It is also very probable that the same passage had once been used as Haftarah among the consolatory passages until it was eliminated for polemic reasons.

[3] The key-word Yaskil is also prominent among the Covenanters of Qumran: cf. e.g. Maskilin in I QSb I, 1; I QM X, 10.

THE HEAVENLY SON OF MAN

The interpretation is even more revolutionary than the original prophecy. It claims that the abiding Glory of God can be and is manifested apart from the usual phenomena of celestial light and majesty. In the process of salvation the High Lord is brought down to the inglorious miseries of human darkness and mortality, and yet it is YHWH'S Presence which is vouchsafed in the Servant's trials (LIII, 10). The Servant's humanity is not denied but rather stressed. He is not a mythical heavenly being, an angel, or a god, so common in the Near East, who in the person of the ruling king undergoes the seasonal humiliations to usher in the New Year.[1] He is Man, the Son of Man. The form of the Servant is human and not celestial; the enigmatic expression 'Son of Man', which Jesus uses for himself instead of the pronoun, retains apparently not a vestige of celestial relevance. But "who is this Son of Man?" (Jn. XII, 34). Here the pendulum continues to swing between the different expositions and claims, though they are not necessarily incompatible. Jesus may well have used the term as a simple self-description, regarding himself, as did Pilate, as the Man ("Ecce homo"), or, more particularly, as the ideal man of Israel, the representative of the *chasidim*, as in Daniel VII. Or again, the current Messianic development of the term may have pointed to the apocalyptic Son of Man who in Enoch is a celestial figure: "a heavenly being who really exists, and not merely a visionary figure of the future who does not yet exist".[2] He pertains to the hidden things and is with God. His righteousness is supernatural and his defeat of tyranny cosmic (En. chs. XLVI and LXXI). "Before the sun and the signs were created, before the stars of the Heavens were made, His name was named before the Lord of Spirits" (XLVIII, 2). He shall be the light to the nations and all who dwell on earth shall fall down and

[1] Cf. The relevant Psalms had prepared the ground (a) by exempting YHWH from any ordeal; (b) by linking the prophetic ideal of righteousness with kingship; (c) by stressing the humanity of the eschatological figure. Cf. A. R. Johnson, *Sacral Kingship in Ancient Israel,* 1955, esp. pp. 22 ff., 102 ff.

[2] S. Mowinckel: *He That Cometh,* 1956, p. 370. Cf. Bibliography ibid. According to Mowinckel, this Anthropos-Myth is an independent non-Semitic element, appropriated by the apocalyptic writers before the New Testament.

worship before him (XLVIII, 4 f.). The exalted ones are terrified when they see that Son of Man (LXII). Sinners descend to Sheol, driven from before his Face (LXIII, 10 ff.), for he is judge. With the dawn of the New Age, Enoch is translated to the enthroned Son of Man and to the Lord of Spirits whose unity above is unquestioned (LXX, 1).

The association of Heaven and Man in Enoch does not stand alone. Another tradition placed Adam in Paradise after death (Apoc. Mos. chs. XVI; XXXVII; II En. XLII). The Rabbis attached glory to a bi-sexual Adam whom the Angels worshipped before the Fall (b San. 59 b; Gen. R. VIII, 1; Vita Adae et Evae XII, 1). Philo interpreted the type of Adam in Genesis as a heavenly Man, to be distinguished from the earthy, empirical man (Op., 25, 134; L. A. I, 31 ff.; Conf. 146). It would have been easy, therefore, to establish the glory of Jesus as celestial, i.e. half mortal, half immortal, because, being the Son of Adam—as St. Luke's genealogy (III, 38) traces his descent—he was a heavenly creature. Possibly this was, in fact, done, for the great passage in I Cor. XV, 35–49 has not only a doctrinal but also a polemic ring about it.[1] St. Paul departs here from the accepted and somewhat Gnostic theme of the heavenly Adam. He cites Genesis to make his point: "The first man Adam became a living being, the last Adam a life-giving spirit." He does not place the first Adam in Heaven. The father of the race belongs to the realm of nature and to the earth and is mortal. In *contrast* to him there appears the 'last man', in whom the race reaches its end. His body is spiritual and he is "of Heaven" (verse 47). Jesus is accordingly not the first man, the Ur-Adam of mythology, but he is still the Son of Man who succeeds Adam, as the spiritual succeeds the natural. He is neither descendant nor simply son of Adam, but he is the true or last man, life-bestowing, heavenly. St. Paul's conception of the "man from Heaven" avoids the *Ur-Adam* parallels, Jewish or Hellenistic. Jesus is "God's Son from Heaven" (I Thess. I, 10), from which he descended to be "born of a woman" (Gal. IV, 4), and to which he returned until he will descend again

[1] Apart from commentaries ad loc., see esp. W. Bousset, *Die Religion des Judentums,* 1926, pp. 352–5; B. Murmelstein, 'Adam', *Wiener Zeitschrift für die Kunde des Morgenlandes,* Bd. 35; W. D. Davies, *Paul and Rabbinic Judaism, pp. 43* ff.

in glory (I Thess. IV, 16). Distinguished from all men, and yet the true man, Jesus is heavenly and yet of blood and flesh.

In the Synoptic Gospels Jesus is primarily the Servant who hides his glory. His works, it is true, are glorious and visible manifestations of his Power and resemble Yahweh's saving miracles as set forth in Psalm CVII. When he teaches and commands demons and forgives sins (Mk. I, 22, 27; II, 10) and especially when he rebukes the storm (Mk. IV, 37 ff.) he displays the Might which presupposes a divine and therefore cosmic origin. But the glory is not fully perceived; in St. Mark this pertains entirely to the Coming with judgment (VIII, 38; X, 37; XIII, 26). Even St. Luke does not wish to claim that he, who was born in and with glory (ch. II) and "glorified of all" (IV, 13) set forth this glory in worldly terms. It is left to Satan to entice Jesus to accept his domain of power and glory, which the Lord of the true glory rejects. Only once does the divine glory break through and become visible. The Transfiguration (Mk. IX, 2 ff.; Lk. IX, 28–36) is the one exception, the cardinal event of the Shekinah in the Gospels and also the crisis in the life of Jesus. Preceded by Peter's confession of "Thou art the Christ" (Mk. VIII, 30) it leads immediately to the anticipation of death and the Passion itself. Thus both confession and passion stand intimately connected with the revealed glory. The chosen disciples ascend and descend the mountain like Moses and see "face to face" not only the cloud and Moses and Elijah, the precursors in the supernatural meeting, but their own master, changed, transfigured, glorious. Jesus is not another Moses, for although he and his disciples are enveloped in the cloud from outside, the blinding and blazing light comes out of himself. He is the seat of the light, not less than the Shekinah which envelops them, but more inasmuch as the light stems from him. According to the Lukan account the disciples see him not only in glory but they behold "his glory" (Lk. IX, 32), that is they see him as he is in his full and eternal majesty of God. The cloud significantly comes *after* this manifestation, the Shekinah concealing what humans cannot see. The words from Heaven: "This is my Son", are in this context not 'adoptionist', as if Jesus were now only adopted 'Son' and elected to glory; they reassure the disciples of Jesus' humanity and stress the nature of the immediate task on earth: "hear ye him!" (IX, 35). They all return to earth and humiliation.

The full and explicit heavenliness of Jesus is reserved for the time after his death and burial. Then some of the restraint of the Messianic secret is relaxed so that at least the witnesses of the Resurrection and of the Ascension are aware of something wholly new. Jesus is not a vindicated martyr. He is not compared with the Teacher of Righteousness whose death the sectarians of Qumran mourned until he should be vindicated in the Messianic age on earth.[1] Inasmuch as Jesus did not clutch divinity and seize heavenly status in the fashion of Lucifer he is now endowed with glory and celestial power. The humiliated Christ is exalted, and this resurrection by God "gave him glory" (I Pe. I, 21). This glorification of Jesus is the central fact of the Christian proclamation: "The God of our fathers has glorified his servant Jesus" (Acts III, 13). The helpless victim of the Cross is "received in glory" (I Tim. III, 16), "crowned with glory and honour" because of the suffering of death (Hebr. II, 9). He now has obtained universal power, "authority in Heaven and earth" (Mt. XXVIII, 18), and Stephen sees him accordingly on God's right hand (Acts VII, 55). His Presence in extraordinary circumstances is perceived in exactly the same manner as the Presence of God in the Old Testament. A light shines and guides and comforts the perplexed and converts the rebellious. Thus the glory of Christ is seen, after his exaltation, both by St. Paul on the road to Damascus (Acts IX, 4) and possibly also by St. Peter with the angel in his prison cell (Acts XII, 7). One of the main points of I Peter is the categorical assertion that the glory of Christ is both celestial and accessible. The apparent paradox is resolved because the celestial Christ also suffered on earth; therefore communion with the celestial Christ is rendered possible in the communion of suffering. The partaker of the suffering is particularly qualified to anticipate the "glory that is to be revealed" (I Pe. V. 1). But this unfolding of Christ's glory is already an accomplished fact in Heaven and enjoyed on earth (I Pe. IV, 13).

[1] Cf. IQp Hab I, 4; I, 12; II, 15; CD I, 11. Jesus is not the object of affectionate blessings as invoked in IQSb.

THE PRE-EXISTENT CHRIST

Christ's exaltation not only reveals his universal and cosmic glory after the Resurrection but also his status in Heaven before his birth on earth. Pre-existence as such pertains to heavenliness, but it is an unsatisfactory term. All kinds of spiritual beings and realities are thought of as pre-existent in the ancient Near East. In the Jewish tradition, for example, Moses, the Patriarchs, and the souls of the righteous, as well as the Torah and Israel, are considered to have existed prior to their actual appearance on earth.[1] The Messianic oracle in Micah (v, 2) speaks of the ruler whose "going forth" is "from of old", from "ancient days". The pre-existence of angels embraces furthermore a class of spiritual beings which completely outnumbers human souls. If we add to this the Oriental and Hellenistic belief that cosmic beings and ideas were in existence before the visible world was ever brought into being we can measure the extent of the Christian task to show in what sense Jesus Christ is uniquely pre-existent.

In this connexion the famous passage in Philippians II, 6–10 has rightly occupied a prominent place throughout the centuries of Christian exegesis. If we accept the very persuasive theory that these verses are in rhythmic form, six strophes of three lines, and represent a *Carmen Christi* of unusual turns of thought, a "pre-Pauline, Jewish-Christian Psalm", nothing is taken away from the weight of its evidential value.[2] The Apostle builds the song into the main structure of his appeal to and exposition of Christ's triumphant humility.

The passage runs: "Be mindful then: this [you may also see] in Christ Jesus, who was in divine form and did not esteem God-likeness a good prey. . . ." The translation does not disguise the fact that "this section belongs to the most difficult passages of Pauline letters".[3] All commentators are agreed on the obscurity of words and syntax. The Philippians evidently knew their

[1] JE, X, p. 183.

[2] Cf. E. Lohmeyer, *Der Brief an die Philipper*, p. 8. His *Formanalyse,* based on the work of Weiss, has gained many adherents, though it leaves some questions unanswered. The strange ἁρπαγμός seems even stranger in a Psalm. Moreover, it is not easy to believe in a Hebrew or Aramaic original in this instance.

[3] Lohmeyer, op. cit., p. 90.

meaning for they were initiated and had to be "reminded" of what they had been told.[1] They would know the meaning of the key word μορφή and its allusion to the μορφή δούλου ('form of a servant', in the next verse); they would be more familiar than we are with ἁρπαγμός, a thing either snatched in robbery or yet to be snatched (*res capta* or *res capienda*, in the classical commentaries), and the connexion between this booty, which Christ forewent, and his self-humiliation as man in the death of the Cross.

The problem of the divine form is primarily religious and not philosophical.[2] It would be a mistake, however, to regard this 'hymn' as a separate theological document for it is manifestly not an isolated Christological excursus in the Epistle. Some commentators are in fact inclined to go to the opposite extreme and think of St. Paul's message only in a practical vein.[3] It is true that the Apostle appeals to the community to practise humility in their corporate life, but it is the humility of Christ which is the miracle to be considered and followed and it is therefore Christ's own metamorphosis, his change from the divine to the dying μορφή of man, which gives the eternal foundation to so great a change.[4]

Christ, before he became man, was a heavenly being, divine but not yet named Kyrios. The divine form was essentially his but he could and did detach it from himself. Before him lay still the temptation to snatch equality with God, to usurp the place of the Highest, to pursue a transcendental self-interest and to be God. This temptation, depicted as an earthly challenge in the narrative in Matthew IV, 1ff., was pre-existent with Christ

[1] Cf. M. Dibelius, *Die Briefe des Apostels Paulus,* 1911, II, p. 6.

[2] Hence Lightfoot's thorough analysis of μορφή and σχῆμα meets nowadays with little favour. Cf. J. B. Lightfoot, *St. Paul's Epistle to the Philippians,* 1903, pp. 132 f. for the conclusion that μορφή is used in a sense substantially the same as in Greek philosophy, i.e. it points to the intrinsic and essential nature of Christ's divinity, though "we need not assume that St. Paul consciously derived his use of the term from any philosophical nomenclature". Cf. also TWNT ad loc.

[3] So Vincent in ICC, 1897 ad loc., Bousset and many others.

[4] Cf. R. Reitzenstein, *Die hellenistischen Mysterienreligionen nach ihren Grundgedanken und Wirkungen,* 1927, p. 357, with refs. to II Cor. III, 18; I Cl. XXXVI, 2; Apul. XI, 30 as further evidence: the issue in question is not change of form or appearance but of nature or being (*Wesensveränderung*).

himself. It precedes and transcends the serpent's *Eritis sicut Deus* (Gen. III, 5) to which Adam, and before Adam the fallen Angel, had succumbed. Baal had ousted El; Christ, however, elects to tread the path of obedience and attains to the stature of Kyrios through giving up his divine form and surrendering himself to time and history and suffering. The paradox, as Lohmeyer shows brilliantly, lies in the *Kenosis*, the self-emptying of one who was of divine form in Heaven. The obedience of the Suffering Servant is the answer to the incomprehensible mystery. It is the causal nexus to God's deed in raising Jesus and exalting him to be Kyrios by name. Christ is 'more' after his triumph than before his renunciation from the god-like to the man-like (from the *Ke'lohim* of his pre-existent form to the *Kebarnash* of his earthly life). But this 'emptying' of himself does not by any means imply that the pre-existent Christ was not from before the beginning with God in Heaven or that his redeeming work precludes him from a cosmic role. The paradox of the Crucifixion does not obscure the eternity of the *μορφή*, "Kyrios due to its divine being and Kyrios again thanks to his own deed".[1]

According to II Corinthians the act of creation has been repeated on a higher level of glory in the redemption by Christ: Light has illumined our hearts "to give the light of the knowledge of the glory of God in the face of Jesus Christ" (IV, 6). Before he reaches this climax St. Paul urges the excellence of Christ's glory: the glory of Sinai points to the new ministration of glory (III, 8) which surpasses the former in bringing righteousness with abiding permanence (III, 9–11). St. Paul's slogan is not simply: "Jesus is the Shekinah", nor is the light which he proclaims part of a general mystical illumination. The Face of Christ is not that of an earthly hero nor an emanation from the beyond. The historical Jesus is the Messiah in whom all the prophecies of righteous kingship culminate. His Face brings together the elements of celestial and eternal glory as well as of the humanity of the promised Immanuel, the God-with-us, the Prince of Peace of the house of David, the King who rules in righteousness. The

[1] Lohmeyer, op. cit. ad loc. [my transl.]. Support for this interpretation is also found in JTS, X, 573; XII, 461–3; cf. ET, Oct. 1957 for the removal of *ἑαυτοὺ ἐκένωσεν* "from the arena of the kenotic controversy".

apprehension of the Person of Christ equals the knowledge of God's glory and in the Church the members reflect the radiation of this inseparable glory.[1] Therefore the gospel is itself also "light" and its rejection is the blindness which will not and cannot see the glory of Christ "who is the image of God" (IV, 4). The light dawns only for those who accept Christ's glory, though his earthly face, of his flesh, "we now no longer know" (V, 16). But this transience of "his person on earth" is no obstacle at all to the gospel of the glory of Christ; for "God was in Christ reconciling the world to himself" (V, 19). God's plan of salvation is from before the foundation of the world and, therefore, precedes Christ's manifestation upon earth. It is difficult to resist the conclusion that St. Paul preached a pre-existent Christ based upon a celestial unity prior to the creation. If the "form" of Philippians and the "face" of II Corinthians are used to interpret each other it would seem reasonable to allow that both "form" and "face" did not acquire glory through martyrdom on earth but mediated the divine glory from Heaven.

The great Christological statements in the New Testament succeeded in satisfying both Jewish and Hellenistic circles by means of the concept of glory. Jesus was glorious from the beginning, one in the cosmic glory of God himself, light of the eternal light, the Face or Image of God, the personal Presence of God. The humanity of Jesus on earth need not and does not disturb the concept of this eternal partaking in the divine glory. The problem which emerges does not concern so much the issue of Christ's pre-existence: the celestial origin of Jesus poses rather the question of the Sonship as related to the various ranks of the celestial hierarchy. This estimate of Christ, not content with simple exaltation and enthronement after the triumph of the Resurrection, but explicitly bringing out his celestial nature, cannot help questioning the status of Christ among the heavenly beings. An angelic element in doctrine might reduce Kyrios Christos to that of a *primus inter pares* and mar precisely the

[1] Cf. H. Kittel, *Die Herrlichkeit Gottes*, 1934, ZNW, Beiheft 16, esp. pp. 204 ff. He rightly insists that St. Paul sublimates the fundamental themes of Light and Power by drawing δόξα into the theological realm of justification and Grace. The Gospel is an εὐαγγέλιον τῆς δόξης τοῦ Χριστοῦ because of this new reality. This sublimation, however, does not imply a cessation from cosmic belief.

true heavenliness of Christ as God, for the true criterion of divinity is not only pre-existence in Heaven but pre-existence prior to the world of space and time.

The Epistles to the Colossians and to the Hebrews both answer to this need. Although from different hands and directed to different places they show clearly that the mediating role of Christ had impaired his heavenliness both among Jewish and Greek Christians. According to Colossians I, 15–17 the Son is not only the image of the invisible God (εἰκὼν τοῦ θεοῦ τοῦ ἀοράτου) for the purpose of redemption on earth, but the firstborn of all creation (πρωτότοκος πάσης κτίσεως) and thus in his own person the principle and purpose of the whole universe: "he is before all things, and in him all things consist" (αὐτός ἐστιν πρό πάντων καὶ τὰ πάντα ἐν αὐτῷ συνέστηκεν). Therefore the problem of the heavenly hierarchy does not really exist, for the Son has not, as it were, the pre-eminence among the cosmic powers but stands outside them, not in merit but in essence.[1]

Thus the concepts of light and glory, which may so easily obscure the unique transcendence of the Son (for even men are children of light and glory), acquire in connexion with Jesus the true heavenliness of God. The Son is the creative cosmic principle, the effulgence of his glory or constant brightness, the very image of his substance or distinct impress of his essence (Hebr. I, 3: ἀπαύγασμα τῆς δόξης καὶ χαρακτὴρ τῆς ὑποστάσεως αὐτοῦ). The filial uniqueness of Jesus determines the nature of his glory. It is not the emanation of the light from the sun, the radiation of light from light, and therefore not the temporal visible manifestation of God, as some notions of the Shekinah may have suggested. The Son belongs to the very extra-temporal and extra-spatial 'centre' of God, to the Glory from which all glories are derived, to the Father who has begotten him. Therefore the Son is worshipped by the heavenly hierarchy since the beginning of the world (Hebr. I, 6, quoting probably Dt. XXXII, 43 as given in LXX [B]). The kingship of Jesus is not comparable

[1] Cf. Philo, Op. 31; L. A. I, 33, 42, 53; III, 96; Som. I, 241; II, 45; Conf. 97, 146, for linguistic parallels of striking similarity. God is *not* εἰκῶν in Philo, but pattern and archetype; Logos is εἰκῶν with reference to God in antemundane existence, whereas Adam receives the divine image at Creation (Gen. I, 26, 27). The passage in Colossians takes this distinction for granted.

to any other. Inasmuch as he is king and priest he does not follow the pattern of kingship and priesthood but rather establishes it from the beginning. The themes of the Psalms (II and CX) are true of Jesus, king and priest, because he is from the beginning the effulgence of the glory in Heaven.

The conclusion that the Lordship of Christ is pre-existent because celestial is stated with apocalyptic emphasis in the classical 'Alpha and Omega' passage of Revelation (I, 8). Here it is not only taken doctrinally for granted but forms part of the whole message of martyrdom. Christians must endure with fortitude the onslaughts of the Evil One for Jesus is the beginning and the end (XXI, 6) the first and the last (XXII, 13). The Lord, Alpha and Omega, comes.[1] At his birth there was a wonder in Heaven and the beginning of cosmic upheavals (ch. XII). His Mother is "clothed with the sun, with the moon under her feet; and on her head a crown of twelve stars".[2] The Son is born and caught up unto God; King and his Kingdom belong to the heavenly realm, without beginning and without end.

Though a world of differences lies between the Apocalypse and the Gospel of St. John there remains a noticeable unity between these two works in their homage to the celestial and glorious Jesus. For the Fourth Gospel the ancient theme of radiance and light is wholly personalized in Jesus, the cosmic, filial focus of the true life-glory from the beginning. The Prologue demolishes every vestige of Shekinah associations which favour the reflection of glory; it is "his glory, the glory as of [the] only-begotten of the Father" (I, 14: δόξα ὡς μονογενοῦς παρὰ πατρός) which the apostolic community have seen when

[1] The Aramaic '*atha* (come) no doubt explains this symbol of *A* and *Ω*; these letters correspond to the א and ת in '*atha*.

[2] The composite nature of the chapter, which according to Charles (ICC, ad loc.) is wrested from its original context and a torso of a primitive international myth, makes the identification of the woman very difficult. The choice would seem to lie between a corporate view (i.e. the old, true Israel, the community of believers, the heavenly Jerusalem) and an individual (a sun-goddess in the original myth, but now the Mother of the Son). None of these conjectures "exclude John's having seen our Lady in this woman—how could he *not*?" (*A Catholic Commentary on Holy Scripture,* 1953, p. 1202). The cosmic note, which is established by the descriptive details, is seen to contrast with the power of Caesar (J. E. Stauffer, *Christ and the Caesars,* 1955, p. 177). For a figurative interpretation in which the Mother = Heavenly Wisdom and the Son = Logos, cf. G. H. Dix, JTS, XXVI, 1924, p. 1.

the Word became flesh and dwelt among them. The 'tabernacling' of Jesus recalls, it is true, the manifestation of God in the Exodus: "when Moses entered into the tent, the pillar of cloud would descend and stand at the door of the tent" (Exod. XXXIII, 9). The Hebrew *shakan* (dwell) and the Greek σκηνοῦν provided perhaps a happy meeting-ground through the accidental similarity of their consonants s-k-n: as God had dwelt with his Presence of Light in Israel so Jesus took up his abode among men, the Word in the Body, a temporary residence as in a tent. But this transitoriness of his dwelling does not spell incompleteness or partial manifestation. The fullness is granted in the only begotten Son Jesus who is visible (I, 16–18), whose Presence declares Grace and Truth with the momentous reiteration: "I am", a formula found throughout the Gospel.[1] Thus the Shekinah concept of glory provides here only a pointer towards the fullness which was to come; just as the Manna given from above, and the Serpent of Moses lifted up, serve as mental pictures, to throw into relief the 'how-much-more' of Jesus, so the light-radiance of the Exodus also, together with all the Oriental and Hellenistic concepts of light, converges upon Jesus who is the Light of the World, uncreated and without beginning. The Fourth Gospel, however, is far less concerned with the heavenliness of the glorious pre-existence and Heaven as the place of divine Being than is the Apocalypse. Heaven and the above (chs. III and VI) are wholly subjugated to Jesus as the unifying Person whose glory is given him by the Father, a glory no longer separable from truth and light as eternal realities outside space and time.

On earth, however, this glory of Jesus is not acknowledged and perhaps not even seen. In this respect there is a clear distinction between the cosmic glory which Jesus enjoyed with the Father as his Word (XVII, 5) and the inglorious residence among men. During his ministry Jesus is not visibly God because he is not yet glorified (VII, 39), or at any rate it is a glory which his enemies will not and cannot perceive because it is opposed to their own wishes (I, 5, 10, 11; VIII, 54). The apprehension of God's glory is no longer to be thought of in mechanical terms of

[1] For ἐγώ εἰμι as Messianic title see D. Daube, *The New Testament and Rabbinic Judaism*, pp. 325 ff.

merely registering light, but rather as the willing assent to know God in Jesus himself, as the "I am" of Abraham (VIII, 59). Since unbelief cannot penetrate to this vision of knowledge the glory of God must be conveyed in spite of darkness and through the means of death (XI, 4). The hour of the passion is the hour of the Son's glorification through suffering and death (XII, 23); the cosmic glory must now be made effectively known upon earth and it is something for which Jesus must pray (XII, 28) and which God confirms with a voice out of Heaven. The conflict with darkness is not only destined to glorify the Son, but God himself through the Son (XIII, 31, 32). The future glorification by the Spirit (XVI, 14) is the outcome of Jesus' glorification in which Father and Son have completed their work on earth (XVII, 4). The Son receives not an outward extension of glory, but God glorifies him with his own self, with the eternal, cosmic glory (XVII, 5). Death, Resurrection, and Ascension are thus different aspects of a divine activity and a divine self-manifestation and consummation. In this way the Fourth Gospel tends to abolish the old distinctions between Heaven and earth and between the Here and Now and the There and Then: the glorified Jesus belongs to a spiritual world which is successor to the old age which is passing away.

The followers of Jesus know the cosmic Christ not only in visual terms of glory but also in the dynamic-auricular experience of the Word and Wisdom. God gives his life in Word as well as in Glory. This unity of Word and Glory applies not only to the human apprehension of Jesus but also to his essential nature in Heaven. The complex of Word-Wisdom must raise problems similar to, if not greater than, the term of Glory to describe the Person of Christ. Again the double-usage, heavenly and earthly, imposes great caution. Clearly both *Logos* and *Sophia* pertain primarily to a world of experience which is not heavenly.

JESUS THE WORD

The Greek Logos is equivalent to the *word* of modern speech. Words are used to communicate messages and to recollect events in speech; claims, pronouncements, assurances, oracles, etc. are given and uttered, read or heard, understood, or ignored; they cannot be associated with the permanence and universality of cosmic significance. A "meaningful articulation"[1] aims at sense, but good sense, however valuable or religious, oratorical or simple, is not celestial. The contents and logic of propositions are complete in human discourse. Thus, in the case of Logos, the gulf between the mundane and the heavenly appears to be even wider than that which divides the light of the earth from the Light of God. Consequently the Johannine opening "In the beginning was the Word and the Word was with God" has always raised the question why the Evangelist seized upon Logos to represent the pre-existent, heavenly Christ.[2] The problem does not concern the heavenliness of the Son of God but rather the choice of Logos to represent him.

The concept of the heavenliness of the Word is partly to be found in Stoic teaching and especially in its influence upon Philo. One of the most important and perhaps insoluble questions of Biblical scholarship remains: "How typical was Philo?"[3] Is it legitimate to assume that Philo, a man of great distinction and some influence in Alexandria, was widely read and listened to as the head of a school? Even if this be admitted it does not follow at all that Palestinian Jews heeded his methods and interpretations and that Christian writers wished to emulate his style, vocabulary, and ideas. The Fourth Gospel and Hebrews stand in a peculiar relationship to Philo's work because their transcendental outlook and, above all, the conception of the pre-existent Word create the impression that they occupy, partially at least, the same ground. The exact nature of this relationship will always remain disputed, but few can deny that Philo was primarily a preaching theologican who blended many different strands of Greek theories and Oriental ideas and harnessed their speculative inferences to his own purpose of reconciling Jewish revelation and non-Jewish thought.[4]

[1] Aristotle, *De Interpr.* 16 b.

[2] E.g. Goethe: "Ich kann das *Wort* so hoch unmöglich schätzen" (*Faust* I).

[3] Cf. GJS, I, p. 6.

[4] The dependence of the Christian pupils on their master is analysed and brought to a brilliant conclusion by C. Spicq, *L'Épitre aux Hébreux,* 1952, ch. III: "on est en droit de penser à une dépendence littéraire et même de mentalité (p. 87) . . . on est amené à discerner la communauté d'esprit, de mentalité, qui a inspiré leur langage, leur prédilection et leur choix de tel thème ou de tel pensée, de tel mode d'argumentation (p. 90)."

In the 1,300 instances in which Philo speaks of Logos a richly manifold and inconsistent syncretism prevails, and one must therefore draw attention to his conceptions—rather than his conception—of *Logos*.[1] This makes the pursuit of our own particular quarry somewhat difficult and, it is to be feared, not a little arbitrary. Yet clearly for Philo there is a close link between Logos and the God of Heaven. He subscribes to the Stoic view which sees Logos as the law, the seed of universal reason, which creates the harmony of the world, for Logos is the unbreakable bond of the universe, the ruler and steersman of all (Plant. 9; Cher. 36; cf. Cleanthes, Fragm. 537). The intelligible universe is God's Son which he has consecrated to himself as his Logos (Spec. I, 96), and thus Logos also serves as model of the universe (Op. 25) and in one passage is even itself the universe (Her. 188), and in another is said to put on the universe as a garment (Fug. 110).

Evidently Philo is not repelled by the part which the world-principle plays in Stoic thought, for he can use the world's supposed existent harmony to good effect. God has brought it about by his own efficacious Reason which Philo identifies with *Logos* and not with *Nous*, for in the former he seeks and finds the necessary link with the Word, especially the prophetic *Davar*, of the Old Testament. Hence the vulgar personifications of Logos need not trouble him here, for Zeus, Hermes, Helios, Pan, and Isis vanish before the Logos, mysterious and incomprehensible as the God of the Old Testament himself (e.g. Deus 55 ff.). The almost personal being of Logos has determined the cosmic order of which it is ideally part.[2] The Logos of God occupies a position second to God (L. A. II, 86: δεύτερος ὁ θεοῦ λόγος) being

[1] Cf. PW XIII for Logos, XX/1 for Philo; TWNT art. λέγω; Schürer, *Geschichte des jüdischen Volkes,* 1909, III, pp. 706 ff.; Wolfson (*Philo* I, pp. 229–36; 327–8) detects three stages in the existence of the Logos: (1) the mind of God, identical with his essence; (2) a created thinking mind, identical with the totality of the intelligible world; (3) immanent in the world.

[2] The personal and impersonal aspects of Logos illustrate the fusion of the materials which Philo endeavours to assimilate. Logos as world-principle must be an 'it', whereas Logos as Davar can never be an 'it' and less than personal. Cf. also A. W. Argyle, *The Logos of Philo: Personal or Impersonal?*, ET, 66, 1954–5, pp. 13–14, for other aspects of the problem of the personality of the Logos, which the writer affirms against Drummond and Dodd.

the image (εἰκών) of the Highest (Spec. I, 81). This quasi-mystical conception of the Word puts it quite beyond the ordinariness of earthly use, such as the communications of men. It is true that man reflects the Logos, and this seems at first sight to contradict the heavenliness of the Word, but for Philo radiation is the divine process of being and does not diminish the transcendence of the source. Thus man is made after the image of God or the Logos without thereby dragging the Word from the supernatural world; rather the ideal man is a celestial being in the uninterrupted flow of rational illumination (Op. 25; Spec. I, 171). The Word may therefore be looked upon as mediating celestial being and the celestial outweighs here the non-celestial (Gig. 52; Mos. II, 133). The Logos is not God but rather of God, the essential emanation from above and beyond.

This usage prepared the ground for the propagation of the Logos doctrine, but it is also responsible for endless misunderstandings. The Christian writers contradict the Philonic position in essentials of such magnitude that it is impossible to detect a developing common trend. Philo's Logos occurs in a mixed collection of meditations, some of which are cosmic, but it does not enter the world of human experience on earth. The Johannine Logos is God and has become Flesh in Jesus, in Hebrews the pre-existent Word (=ῥῆμα with LXX) is spoken by God's Son. He alone is heavenly and not a principle of divine mediation.

If Philonic origins of the Word as the second Person of the Blessed Trinity have to be treated with great caution the Palestinian Hebrew tradition of the Word seems to yield even less grounds for the heavenly, cosmic interpretation. The Word in the Old Testament is not a person; rightly G. F. Moore pours scorn on "some older Protestant theologians", who "in their misdirected search for Christian dogmas in Jewish disguises found the *Shekinah* as well as the *Memra* (i.e. the Aramaic which renders the Hebrew Davar)—always the question-begging proper name with a capital!—to their purpose, and recognized in them the same 'hypostasis'."[1] There are, nevertheless, a few passages in the Old Testament in which the Word manifests an independent and eternal essence. In contrast to human perishability and

[1] Cf. op. cit. vol. I, p. 437.

the transitoriness of all created existence "the word of our God stands up for ever" (Is. XL, 8). It proceeds from above "as the rain comes down and the snow from Heaven", from God's mouth, and "it shall not return unto me void . . ." (Is. LV, 9–11). The meditative Psalm CXIX goes even further and ascribes to the Word an unchangeable establishment in Heaven: "Eternally, O Lord, thy word is set up in Heaven" (Ps. CXIX, 89). These feelings were abroad with respect to the Word; they cast a bridge to a metaphysical and even heavenly conception of the Word without direct borrowing from anywhere. Such is the confident belief of Hebrews in its immense opening: "God, having of old time spoken unto the fathers in the prophets by diverse portions and in diverse manners, has at the end of these days spoken to us ἐν υἱῷ.

In Hebrew thought the divine Word is dynamic and from beyond the earthly sphere; it enters historical existence in a personal manner; it becomes embodied in Law; it is creative in power: "by the word of the Lord were the Heavens made" (Ps. XXXIII, 6). The Gospels view the words of Jesus accordingly: they are at one with his Person, his work, his life, his exaltation. In general his words are not teachings in the sense of doctrine (I Tim. VI, 3 is an exception). His words are eternal and do not pass away as Heaven and earth (Mk. XIII, 31). Behind the word lies "the word of his power" (ῥῆμα Hebr. I, 3). This Word of the living Christ is heard and believed (Ro. X, 17) and dwells in the Church (Col. III, 16) and is also identical with the Word of the Old Testament, whether it be originally that of Isaiah or Moses or David (Ro. IX, 27; X, 20). Christ is the Word of God and the Word of God is Christ; this binds the old and the new together as prophecy and fulfilment. Past, present, and future are comprehended by the Word, the Mystery of the Gospel, which had been hidden and is now manifested (Col. I, 25–6). Therefore the Kerygma is the Word of God, for as Jesus spoke the word unto the people (Mk. II, 2) so the Church proclaims the Gospel, herself "born anew, not of perishable seed but of imperishable, through the living and abiding word of God". (I Pe. I, 23).

The New Testament believes in the heavenliness of the Word because Christ is exalted in Heaven. The Word is not a conceptual abstractum of the philosophers nor the religious comment on scripture of Mishnaic Judaism. It is not mythological, inasmuch as Jesus is the Word of Life which was "heard, seen, touched"; the broken grammar of I John, chapter I, underlines the claim that Jesus really lived on earth as a human being. This insistence naturally assumes that the Word is celestial, namely God's creative and eternal Word. This Logos became flesh when Jesus assumed manhood. No cosmic agency or principle, nor a mythical world-soul, but the self-revealing, heavenly Word, the creative "Let there be" of pre-cosmic beginnings has spoken in the redemptive "I am" of Jesus, who has neither beginning nor end (Hebr. VI, 20; VII, 3).

JESUS THE WISDOM

Moreover there can be no doubt that the Logos of the Fourth Gospel, and of the whole thought-world behind it, stands in an intimate relationship with Wisdom. Now this *Sophia* of the New Testament again seems at first sight not to support the heavenliness of Jesus, for, on the ordinary level of human experience, it is a virtue or skill for which men are famous. The wisdom of Joseph and of the Egyptians (Acts VII, 10, 22), for example, argues the profitable nature of prudence and sound sense, an attitude even of restraint which Christians are encouraged to emulate (e.g. Mt. X, 16; Col. I, 28; III, 16; James I, 5; III, 13, 17) even as the child Jesus grew and waxed strong becoming full of wisdom (Lk. II, 40). The wisdom of the world and of the speculative philosophers, however, ranks even as an enemy of true godliness, for it induces arrogance and a false sense of superiority (I Cor. I, 21f.; II, 1; II Cor. I, 12; Col. II, 23). Fleshly wisdom, in short, is only a show and removes men through its enticing qualities from the true path.

HEAVENLY AND WORLDLY WISDOM

Notwithstanding the human abuse of wisdom, however, the New Testament also regards wisdom as heavenly and identifies this wisdom with Jesus in several places.[1] The short Gospel saying

[1] The ambiguity of terms like 'wisdom' and 'spirit' is more pronounced in Hebrew and Greek manuscripts than in modern versions where the distinction between initial capitals and small letters—as also in this book—must prejudice the issue.

"Wisdom is justified by her own children (or works)" (Mt. XI, 19; Lk. VII, 35), read in the light of the 'greater than Solomon' passage (Mt. XII, 42) and the great invitation "Come unto me!" (Mt. XI, 28 f.; Sir. LI, 26–7) perpetuates an early tradition that Jesus on earth acted as the divine Wisdom. The Gospel of Christ is, therefore, the power and the wisdom of God, both for Jews and Greeks (I Cor. I, 24). This wisdom, it is true, leads to illumination and the practical experience of God among men on earth. But this fact points itself to the origin of wisdom, namely to Christ, "whom God made our wisdom" (I Cor. I, 30) and to God in whom wisdom and knowledge coinhere (Ro. XI, 33). Wisdom is thus mediated from God to man (Ephes. I, 8) and again ascribed in worship by the redeemed to God and Christ (Rev. V, 12; VII, 12). But "what is the wisdom that is given unto this man?" (Mk. VI, 2). What tradition lay behind the Gospel?

In the ancient Near East wisdom ranks universally high in the lists of acknowledged virtues. The maxims of Amenemope (possibly a distant source of much of Proverbs chs. XXII–XXVI) of the end of the second millennium B.C., the ancient Canaanite aphorisms of Phoenician origin ("Proverbs teems with isolated Canaanitisms"[1]), the place assigned to wisdom in Sumerian myths, evidence that the Hebrew Wisdom literature belongs to a wide cultural milieu and that Hebrew *Chokmah* in particular does not stem from a late borrowing from Persian sources.[2] It is no longer to be assumed, therefore, that the New Testament employment of *Sophia* constitutes a step into an alien, radically Hellenized world, with which Judaism was not or should never have been intimately conversant. The tradition behind the Gospels is as ancient as anything in the Old Testament. Yet the wisdom of the ancient Near East is, of course, as unheavenly in some instances as anything in the Bible. If wisdom is spoken of as 'she' this custom bears out that her femininity was very pronounced

[1] Cf. W. F. Albright, 'Some Canaanite-Phoenician sources of Hebrew wisdom', in *Wisdom in Israel and in the Ancient Near East,* Supplement to VT III, p. 9. See also O'Callaghan, 'The Great Phoenician Portal Inscription from Karatepe', *Orientalia,* 1949, p. 176.

[2] Cf. O. S. Rankin, *Israel's Wisdom Literature,* 1936, esp. ch. IX for "The conclusion that Wisdom in Judaism owes its origin to Iranian thought . . ." (p.252).

from time immemorial. She is not a specifically revealed, but rather a generally bestowed gift of the gods which poets praise in song and with which princes and kings are, or should be, endowed so as to rule successfully. The paean in praise of wisdom in Sir. VI, 18 ff. well expresses the tradition of royal wisdom as a glorious garment to be sought and to be worn.[1] This wisdom, salutary and grave, educative and civilized, appears to be entirely a social and also an individualistic possession. It seems far removed from that type of feminine deity which the prophets denounced as the great scourge of Israel, and equally unconnected with that wisdom of the skilled wise men, who opposed the true prophetic oracle by their ingenious devices (Jer. VIII, 8), the Chokmah of paganism in general (Is. XLVII, 10). Pharisaical learning flourishes in Wisdom's house of instruction and under her discipline (Sir. LI, 23 ff.). Such wisdom is no forerunner of the *Sophia* which the Pauline Christology so boldly enunciates; for Christ, the Wisdom of God, is for St. Paul on no account a personification of sound, beneficent, penetrating common sense or piety.

It is the *cosmic* tradition of wisdom which, kept alive throughout the centuries in Israel in the *Chokmah* circles, culminates in the New Testament gospel of Christ, the Wisdom of God. This wisdom is already found in the Epic of Gilgamesh as the immortality of the gods;[2] we find it again in the mythical progeny of the god El at Ugarit.[3] The overweening ambitions of annointed kings even fed on its supernatural authority. Thus Ezekiel denounces the prince of Tyre for arrogating to himself divine rights, being "wiser than Daniel". But this pagan excess of wisdom cannot last though its origin is from above (Ezek. XXVIII, 1–10), for YHWH stands in opposition to the cosmic wisdom of paganism.

When YHWH himself bestows the spirit of wisdom then the era of universal peace crowns the reign of the Son of David (Is. XI,

[1] cf. CML Anat, V, 38, 65; II Keret, IV, 3; also NSI No. 62, for inscriptions of Panammu, line 11.

[2] Cf ANET "Ninsum the wise, who is versed in all knowledge . . ." (III, Assyr.) Man's mortality is opposed to the gods' immortality (X, 3 Babyl.).

[3] CML "wise as El" (K. II, IV, 2) "Thy bidding, El, is wise, thy wisdom everlasting" (B II, IV, 41.).

1–9). In these passages the wisdom of God is still largely dependent upon its employment in the function of the state and establishes the title-deeds of the future King. But the concept of wisdom as an independent cosmic force comes as a great climax in the *locus classicus*, Proverbs, ch. VIII. Here wisdom is first introduced as the female *Chokmah*, who then begins to speak in the autobiographical first person. Clearly, *Chokmah* is no goddess, not even a dethroned deity, but a supernatural force of moral discrimination and of righteous power: "By me kings reign, and princes decree justice" (verse 15). She stands in an affective and intellectual relationship with individuals: "I love them that love me" (verse 17). But this is not by any means all: YHWH acquired her at the beginning of his way, that is at that beginning which preceded the beginning of creation (cf. Gen. I, 1). From eternity, before earth and deep and foundations and mountains were formed, Wisdom was set up. At the act of creation, when the Heavens were prepared and the firmament fixed, "I was there" (VIII, 22–30). Wisdom is the active, trustworthy, and delightful counsellor of God, the Lord of Israel. No man counselled God in the act of creation (Is. XL, 14), but Wisdom, unsearchable and hidden like God himself (Job XXVIII), is the cosmic principle of the whole creation which served God and is of God from the beginning.

This portrayal of wisdom as pre-existent and in a sense 'outside' God, as the architect of the universe who has built her house of seven pillars (Prov. IX, 1), did not fail to find a response in popular poetry. But the worship of wisdom as a goddess does not exist, for in Israel she is not, as for example in the somewhat Iranian story of Ahikar, "from the gods". There she is precious, "even to the gods, in Heaven she is established, because the lord of the gods has exalted her".[1] At the same time the Old Testament does not reduce *Chokmah* to simple angelic status, as a court expert or dignitary in the circle of divine servants in Heaven. No official dogma existed, but a reader of Sirach will be struck by the increasing juxtaposition of wisdom and instruction, almost as if wisdom had become the prerogative of the upper

[1] Cf. A. Cowley, *Aramaic Papyri of the Fifth Century* B.C., 1923, pp. 204–48, esp. lines 94 f.

class or the possession of rabbinical students, who put their neck under the yoke of instruction (Sir. LI, 26). In these circles the identification between wisdom and Torah was certainly assumed and by no means far-fetched (Sir. I, 1; esp. ch. XXIV). If wisdom symbolized the cosmic design and the supernatural favours of God, then Torah, or its spokesmen, could assert these very claims for the traditions of Israel as contained in the Law (Bar. III, 27 ff.). According to Philo, wisdom is of God and the source of all virtues (L. A. I. 64; II, 86–7; Migr. 134) and therefore related to the Law. Yet it may be questioned whether he or even the most thorough-going traditionalist would have claimed that Torah is, like wisdom, possessed of a spirit, intellectual, holy, unique of its kind and yet manifold, delicate, freely mobile, transparent, immaculate, distinct, impassible ... benevolent to man, steadfast, sure, free from care (i.e. self-sufficient), all-powerful, all-surveying . . . (Wisd. VII, 22 ff.). Here is a document, admittedly not typical for Palestinian thinking, which preserves for wisdom the unique status, "fairer than the sun and above all the constellations of the stars; being compared with light, she is found before it" (VII, 29). This universal, cosmic, celestial exposition approaches almost Gnostic overtones: Wisdom is "more mobile than any motion, pervades and penetrates all things through her pureness. For she is a breath of the power of God, and a clear effluence of the glory of the Almighty . . . an effulgence of everlasting light" (VII, 24–6).

Judaism curbed such excesses of praise and checked the personification of wisdom by the simple expedient of making *Chokmah* subservient to and included in the Law (e.g. IV Macc. I, 17; VII, 21–3; VIII, 7). Christian writings, too, show on the one hand a certain reticence which we have already described; on the other St. Paul indentifies Christ with the Wisdom of God. There is some evidence that he did so because he also identified Christ with the Torah.[1] The connecting links may be found in Colossians I, 15–18, where Christ fulfils as beginning, sum-total, head, and firstfruits the part which is assigned to wisdom in Proverbs

[1] Cf. W. D. Davies, *Paul and Rabbinic Judaism*, 1948, ch. VII "The old and the new Torah: Christ the Wisdom of God." For an interesting criticism "Christ was not a Law at all; he was the new Man" cf. A. T. Hanson, *The Wrath of the Lamb*, 1957, app. 4.

VIII, 22;[1] in I Corinthians X, 1–4, where the Rock Christ fulfils the image of the Exodus tradition as interpreted by Philo (Leg. Alleg. II, 21); in Romans X, 6 ff., where his joy in the accessible Christ recalls indirectly the words of Deuteronomy XXX, 11–14, which in Baruch III, 29 ff., refer to wisdom. But it is in his fight against Corinthian 'wisdom' that he unequivocally proclaims Christ the Wisdom of and from God (I, 24, 30). In this great transformation he places the risen Lord against human conceit and world-principles. Thus Jesus takes into himself all the floating concepts of *Sophia*, and even the feminity of the *Sophia-Chokmah* complex is absorbed into his masculine transcendence.

THE AMBIGUITY OF 'SPIRIT'

An even more radical transformation affected the use of the word 'Spirit', the Hebrew *Ruach*. The difficulties of the term are similar to that of *Chokmah*, with which it is occasionally connected as the "spirit of wisdom" (Exod. XXVIII, 3; Dt. XXXIV, 9). Spirit is primarily 'breath', whether of man or of God. God's breathing is operative in the universe (Gen. I, 2) and through this influence he controls all life, especially that of man. God is "the God of the spirits of all flesh" (Nrs. XVI, 22) and all human power, physical and mental, goes back to the life-giving act: "The spirit of God has made me, and the breath of the Almighty gives me life" (Job XXXIII, 4). The Spirit was probably conceived of as an immaterial substance which, like the air itself, produces life. Hence the whole breathing universe is 'spiritual', but the Spirit is not in a personal and transcendent sense God of Heaven.

Yet Ruach belongs to God in a sense which excels his other attributes, such as hands, eyes, or feet. The stormy Ruach is the physical accompaniment of divine activity: the Lord blows with his wind (Exod. XV, 10; Nrs. XI, 31). This blowing of wind reaches an important stage of development when the Spirit becomes instrumental in the inspiration of men. This inspiration

[1] The actual connexion hinges on the word *reshith* which occurs in Proverbs VIII, 22, and provides a bridge between Chokmah and reshith in Genesis I, I. Cf. C. F. Burney, *Christ as the ARXH of Creation*, JTS, XXVII, pp. 160 ff.

ranks higher than mere life itself: the Spirit comes upon the unsuspecting Saul and turns him into a different man and lends him abnormal strength and prophetic frenzy (I Sam. x, 6, 10; xi, 6). When Samuel disowns his king he anoints David "and the spirit of the Lord came mightily on David" (I Sam. xvi, 13). In the Elijah narrative (I K. ch. xix) the rock-breaking tempest heralds the Lord who is not physically present in the storm but, perhaps by contrast to earlier tradition, speaks by the still, small voice. The Spirit in the prophetic experience becomes less of an element of nature and more of a power of inspiration. Thus the Spirit is spoken of as 'given' to Moses and to Elijah and distributed among their servants (Nrs. xi, 17; II K. ii, 9) who, in the case of the latter, seek their departed master on earth "lest the spirit of the Lord has taken him up and cast him upon some mountain, or into some valley" (II K. ii, 16). The link is so strong that a prophet is quite simply "a man in whom the spirit of God is" (Gen. xli, 38).

In a few significant passages the Spirit is called 'holy'. The context in Isaiah lxiii, 10 f. is typical: in reviewing sins past and present the prophet lists the rebels' offence against God's holy spirit during the Exodus. Similarly the tenor of Psalm li is concerned with sin and the need for expiation before the climax is reached in verse 11: "Cast me not away from thy presence, and take not thy holy spirit from me." In this parallelism the spirit is not clearly defined but it is closely associated with God's forgiving presence, as for example, in the question "Whither shall I go from thy spirit? or whither shall I flee from thy presence?" (Ps. cxxxix, 7). In Ezekiel's vision the Spirit belongs to the realm of glory and appears with a following of the divine host (i, 12).

God's redeeming work culminates in the giving of the Spirit. The Messiah or "shoot out of the stock of Jesse" is the branch of the royal house who will be fully endowed with the spirit. At the beginning of Isaiah xi, 1–9, the Spirit contributes to royal dignity and power, to human civilization and the good of this world, but at the end spiritual government coincides with universal peace and a righteousness no longer of this world: "the wolf will dwell with the lamb. . . ." Ezekiel, too, strikes a worldly and an other-worldly note in the oracle of chapter XXXVII: the dry bones in the valley are brought to life by the *Ruach* of the four winds and the national resurrection of Israel is both a political and a 'spiritual' event. National existence and eschatological hopes are inextricably bound up together.

In the hope of redemption the Spirit is conceived of as a dynamic incursion from God, from outside and above. Thus the new covenant relationship in the redeemed world is spiritual. Jeremiah in his prediction of the new covenant dwells on the inwardness of the genuine relationship between God and man. This spontaneous and complete knowledge of God is his own work in the human heart and therefore universal and permanent. God who "gives the sun for light by day, the ordinances of the moon and the stars for a light by night" works on the same cosmic scale in redemption (Jer. XXXI, 35).

The second Isaiah also links the future with the past but he introduces something new: he places the Servant of the Lord[1] as the central, 'spiritual' figure of world-wide salvation. God elects his chosen and puts his Spirit upon him (XLII, 1) and this Spirit does not depart from him after the moment of inspiration is over, but rather leads the Servant forward to the ratification of the new covenant. He is himself the Covenant in his own person (XLII, 6) and embodies the prophetic inspiration which is upon him (LXI, 1 ff.). Through him the covenant becomes available to all: "This is my covenant with them: my spirit that is upon thee . . ." (LIX, 21).

This Messianic work evokes the theme of the restoration of the whole world and consequently the conception of the Spirit becomes increasingly celestial. In typically eschatological passages desolation overtakes the whole world until "the Spirit be poured upon us from on high" (Is. XXXII, 15), a cosmic force which God will pour upon all flesh when he shows "wonders in the Heavens and in the earth, blood and fire, and pillars of smoke" (Joel, II, 28–30).

[1] Although no unanimity exists as regards the identity of the 'Eved-YHWH there can be little doubt that he represents a soteriological and probably an eschatological figure whom God ordains to usher in his kingdom. The reading "I have anointed him" in DSIa at LII, 14 proves the popularity of the Messianic interpretation. See also my *Theology of Salvation*, 1953, esp. pp. 200 ff.

The eschatological oracles look to the future and are silent about the Spirit's share in the work of creation. Passages to that effect are altogether rare in the Old Testament. In Job XXVI, 13 the "garnishing of the Heavens" only hints at the Spirit's transcendent pre-existence, for the poet does not distinguish the Spirit from the hand of God. Elsewhere the Spirit and the Word are cited equally as divine expressions in creation (Ps. XXXIII, 6), and Wisdom and Holy Spirit as partners in the illumination and instruction of men (Prov. I, 23; Wisd. IX, 17). The reluctance of the Wisdom school in its treatment of the Spirit throws into relief the uniqueness of Genesis I, 2: "the spirit of God was hovering gently upon the face of the waters." In this Prologue the Spirit appears almost distinct from God as God. He is not merely a divine attribute or a metaphor for divine, creative action, but precedes God's Word of light. Later interpretations, however, failed to bring out the precise nature of this verse and exegetes were shy to stress the celestial nature of the Spirit as pre-existent and almighty God.

The comments on Genesis I, 2 in Judaism indicate the measure of the reluctance to ascribe full celestial status to the Spirit in a metaphysical sense. Partly the pneumatic element in Christianity must account for this timidity of treatment,[1] but the primary, positive reason must be found in the point of view which regards the Torah as sufficient for salvation and explicitly "not in Heaven" and not in need to be brought down to earth (Deut. XXX, 12). Accordingly the Spirit's part in the creation of the world is assumed to be relatively unimportant: "The wind from the Lord blew" (Targ. Onk.), "the spirit of mercies from the Lord breathed upon" the waters (Targ. Jon. and Jer.); in the Midrash allusion is made to the "spirit of Messiah", hovering like a bird, flying and flapping with its wings (Gen. R. II, 4). Against this exposition an isolated passage as "Thou didst send forth thy spirit" (Judith XVI, 14), even if uttered with regard to the creation, (cf. Ps. CIV, 30) does not materially change the dogmatic tradition. The Spirit, though distinct from God, and even personal (Mekilta Ex. XV, 2, 9), is not the *Creator Spiritus,* but created by God

[1] Cf. JE VI, 448; W. D. Davies, *Paul and Rabbinic Judaism,* 1948, pp. 219–20 and the whole of ch. VIII.

(b Chag. 12 a) and recognized as the spirit of mercy in action and active among men. What really matters is the national and political aspect of the Spirit's work, for it is admitted that the Spirit, once heard and seen, was lost at the Fall of Jerusalem and is found to be present only in a diminished manner and on certain occasions (b Yoma 21 b). Later sources discussed whether certain exceptional Rabbis were to be credited with the inspiration of the Holy Spirit (Tos. Sotah XIII, 2): the heavenly voice (Bath Qol), so it was said, had come to them from time to time as a kind of substitute (b Sanh. 11 a). But against this reticence it must also be noted that Judaism was not shy to retain the communal aspect of the Holy Spirit. Hope still remained for the future.

The Holy Spirit is especially connected with the future when the house of Israel will be reassembled by the four winds to the Holy Land where alone the Holy Spirit blows (based on Ezek. XXXVII, 12–14). Then all Israel will have the Spirit, all will be prophets. Whosoever sacrifices himself for the sake of Israel will have the Holy Spirit (Midr. R. Num. XV, 20); the Messianic ruler is given power by God's Holy Spirit (Enoch XLIX, 3; LXII, 6; LXVII, 10; Psalms of Solomon XVII, 42). The distinction between heroic and ordinary men is not to be pressed too far, however, for some at any rate believe that every soul is either inspired by or offends against the Spirit (CD V, 10; VII, 4). It is useless to look for doctrinal coherence; it is impossible, for instance, to infer whether virtue comes before, or as a consequence after, the Spirit has been given. The general feeling is that loyal devotion leads to the Holy Spirit and the Holy Spirit leads, as a reward, to the resurrection of the dead (Sotah IX, 15). Despite all inconsistencies the inspirational conception of the Spirit prevailed in Judaism (Targ. Jon. Is. XL, 13). As in the days of Elijah it is regarded as tangible stuff, or air and light and weight, for thus "it rests upon the prophets" (Midr R. Lev. XV, 2). It equips the good and the faithful and constitutes their reward. Some passages, it is true, go further than that and liken the Spirit to the Shekinah and speak of him as crying and even interceding with God (e.g. Midr. R. Lam. I, 45; Midr. R. Song of Songs VIII, 13), but the conclusion that "Christianity has received from Judaism only some formulas" for its doctrine of the Holy Spirit is irresistible:[1] he is not Lord of Heaven.

Pneuma, like *Ruach,* takes us back to the air we breathe: the hunter's scent, the breathing before a vowel, the spirits of men, and the spirits who exist without bodies, point to the principal phenomenon of breath.[2] In Greek thought this *Pneuma* also touches men and human affairs, as when men are possessed and enter a state of frenzy (Phaedrus 245 A). In Stoic speculations it becomes even a kind of stuff which penetrates the whole world. The universe is said to reflect on its different levels the world-soul, the one substance, which, like the fiery ether was believed to bind everything into one living whole. Thus the Spirit animates and maintains the universe; it is an element not entirely of this world, being both of and also above nature. Like the Hebrew *Ruach*, then, *Pneuma* can denote both the natural wind and the supernatural, abnormal, ecstatic influence. This double aspect of Spirit easily lent itself to a further and specifically religious development which reaches its climax in some Gnostic systems. Spirit serves as the medium between two worlds, just as the spirit of divination contacts the spirit of the oracle and thereby man knows the will of the gods. In the Hellenistic mystery religions the possession of the Spirit as the ground of religious experience is a common feature; this spirit turns ordinary mortals into *Pneumatikoi*, men illumined by the Spirit. They have direct mystical access to salvation and to the spheres of bliss.[3]

Philo adds little to this conception which requires our attention

[1] Cf. J. Lebreton, *Histoire du Dogma de la Trinité,* 1927, p. 155. Even the occasional convention which puts "Holy Spirit" for "God", e.g. Sotah IX, 6, does not invalidate this cautious appraisal of sources. Of the apocalyptic treatment Lebreton says pertinently: "dans l'ensemble de cette littérature manifestement la croyance aux esprits est alors beaucoup plus vivante que la croyance à l'Esprit" (p. 157). Cf. also J. Abelson, *The Immanence of God in Rabbinical Literature,* 1912, pp. 212 ff. "Rabbinic personification of Holy Spirit is but another means to express the conception of an immanent God" (p. 226).

[2] In common, of course, with the world-wide notion of spirit as the principle of breathing life, as in the Indian *Atman*, Iranian *Spenta*, Egyptian *Ba, Ka,* Latin *anima, spiritus.* Cf. TWNT, ad loc.

[3] The principle is much older than Gnosticism, cf., e.g. Plutarch's de Is. 40, for references to Dionysus, Heracles, Ammon, Demeter, Poseidon as the respective patrons of creation, destruction, reception, production, and the sea. The spirits of the gods prevail in their spheres. It is the job of the mysteries to unite human spirits with the divine.

here. His identifications are obvious and easy to follow. Ecstasy and inspiration are one and the same thing. The scriptural terminology accords with Greek usage, Ruach with πνεῦμα θεοῦ. Thus he pictures Abraham as a man of the spirit or an ecstatic. The possession of the Spirit leads to knowledge which is greater than the mere intellect of men. The divine Spirit is the 'other' which may even be in conflict with uninspired reason (Heres. 265). It is very similar to, if not the same thing as, Sophia (Gig. 22, 23), the knowledge and discernment of the incorporeal mind, created by God, after the order of the angels. Pneuma in Philo still covers the wide field of air as an element, of ecstatic inspiration, of cosmic penetration and mediation (Gig. 8, 9).

Despite its peculiar quality of ecstatic inspiration the Pneuma of the Greeks is even less transcendent than the Ruach of the Hebrews. Spirit is a label for many phenomena of religious experience, but not God in Heaven or of Heaven. It is, therefore, impossible to follow the argument of those who see in Hellenistic mysticism not only one but the most telling and effective source for the Christian doctrine of the Holy Spirit.[1] The whole Christian feeling, even more than the terminology, of the relevant passages militates against an identification between the human spirit and the Holy Spirit. The New Testament did not set out to extend the Philonic practice of equating the one with the other.

THE SPIRIT IN THE NEW TESTAMENT

It is of course to be admitted that the writers of the New Testament frequently speak of the Spirit in a manner similar to that of the Old Testament and of their own Rabbinic contemporaries and Hellenistic neighbours. In these passages the conceptions, which we have just examined and found non-transcendental and unheavenly, naturally prevail without apparently causing offence. It will suffice here to refer briefly to the survival of the

[1] For a most thoroughgoing advocacy cf. H. Leisegang, *Pneuma Hagion, Der Ursprung des Geistbegriffs der synoptischen Evangelien aus der griechischen Mystik*, 1922: The 'Pneumamotiv' is alien to the Gospels: only Luke knows what to make of it because he is familiar with Hellenistic mysticism. Thus the myths of God-in-man and of enthusiastic ecstasies secure an anchorage in the story of Jesus. It remains only to point out that such a Pneuma does not really become Kyrios, despite the Logion of the sin against the Holy Ghost (Mk. III, 28–30).

Spirit as the wind which blows from outside (Jn. III, 8), to St. Paul's praise of the Spirit as the source of human virtues and general gifts (if Gal. V, 22 f. is wrongly taken for that) and particularly his strange list of typical conditions, which includes the Holy Spirit among others (II Cor. VI, 6). In all these utterances the Jewish tradition of the Spirit as the Messianic gift and the Hellenistic hope of union by Pneuma play their part, though the blending is distinctly Christian. Thus the inspirational work of the Spirit is specifically promised to the persecuted in the hour of their need (Mk. XIII, 11; Mt. X, 20). Nevertheless, the manifestation of the Spirit in the inspiration of men, whether as individuals or in the Church, as in such passing phenomena as glossolalia or the universal gift of languages (Acts II), emphasizes the continuity between the different traditions and the central place which inspiration occupies in them. When, for example, St. Paul declares that "the Spirit himself (or itself?) bears witness with our spirit" he goes a long way towards a Philonic theory of mediation, in which Spirit meets spirit in the act of inspiration. If this were the only line of devotional and doctrinal writing in the New Testament it would be impossible to sustain the claim that the Holy Spirit is Lord in the same sense in which God is God of Heaven. But these earthly acts of inspiration do not necessarily of themselves invalidate the heavenliness of the Spirit.

In establishing our case we suffer inevitably from the Spirit's reticence to speak of himself which the Fourth Gospel records with prophetical intention (XVI, 13). We cannot enquire here why "the Gospels say so little about the Holy Spirit".[1] Yet an inadequate apprehension of the Spirit's divinity cannot but lead to a belief in spiritual emanations on the one hand and a confusion of Christ and the Spirit on the other. If the mediating features of the Spirit are esteemed to be his essential, or even exclusive, nature he must also cease to share in the reign of Glory and become an immanent force. Surprisingly the New Testament presents us with no direct evidence that such emanational views were ever held in the Church of the first century. True, the Holy Spirit appeared to be altogether unknown at Ephesus (Acts XIX, 2) but the intellectual problems which the Spirit's

[1] Cf. C. K. Barrett, *The Holy Spirit and the Gospel Tradition,* 1947, ch. X.

immanence must raise were bequeathed to post-Biblical Christianity, when the celestial imagery had weakened before other types of thought.[1]

First among the heavenly attributes we find height ascribed to the Spirit. Like the God Elyon, he is on high and acts from on high. Christ's baptism is from Heaven by the Spirit (Mk. I, 10). The symbolism of the Dove stresses the direction of the flight. St. Luke adds to the account that the descent of the Spirit took place in bodily form. The dove does not portray Israel[2] nor does it recall the emblem of the pagan goddesses (Astarte, Ishtar, Aphrodite) who adopted their sons. However enigmatic the symbolism of the dove may have been found at times, it does not hint at adoption; rather it demonstrates the heavenliness of the Son and his eternal unity with God. This is apparent from the words of the accompanying voice which in Mark and Matthew declare Jesus to be Messiah in terms of the elected Servant (Is. XLII, 1), yet naming him Son (*υἱός*) instead of the ambiguous Servant (*παῖς*). The Spirit acts here as the oil anointing the King (Is. LXI) and formalizes the royal appointment of Jesus on earth. St. Luke's substitution of Psalm II, 7 gives no ground for an adoptionist theory but rather enriches the account with a Son-of-David Christology, associating the whole complex of Isaiah IX and XI, Psalms II and CX with the Divine Son and the humble Servant so that the Oriental notion of the King anointed with oil as Son of God is shown to be but a type of the eternal and real Son of God anointed with the Spirit.

The dove stands for the lofty freedom of the heavenly God; in winged flight it resembles the "wings of the Spirit" (Odes of Sol. XXVIII, 15). The symbol suggests the Spirit's share in creation at the beginning, and in redemption at the end. The 'form'

[1] Cf. G. L. Prestige, *God in Patristic Thought*, 1952, pp. 34 ff., 80 ff., and 89 ff. for the remarkable identification of Holy Spirit with Wisdom in Irenaeus and Theophilus.

[2] As, e.g., in Midr. Ps. LXVIII, 14: "Why are the Israelites compared to a dove?" —"As the dove does not twitch so the Israelites do not twitch when slaughtered for the sanctification of the Holy Name; as the dove reaches safety only by flight so Israel saves itself only through the merits of the Torah. . . ."—The dove's wings shimmering in gold are compared to Mishnaic tracts. Cf. however Midr. R. Cant. I, 15: "The dove brought light to the world", where the comment goes back to Noah and the flood, though "my dove = Israel" in VI, 5.

withdraws after the Baptism of Jesus because the Spirit remains in Heaven; yet the Spirit is not restricted, for Jesus is also throughout his earthly life "full of the Holy Spirit" (Lk. IV, 1); "the Spirit abides upon him" (Jn. I, 32). There is no contradiction here, for God's presence in the universe is never regarded as having been impaired by the Incarnation of the Son of God on earth. Hence, according to the Fourth Gospel, Jesus on earth himself refers to the Spirit as not of this world (XIV, 17) and as one who is yet to come. The distinction between the Son and the Spirit is thus asserted, not in order to lessen the supremacy of the Spirit, but rather to enhance it. The Pentecostal outpouring again testifies to the heavenliness of the Spirit for the Pneuma comes from above (Acts II, 2). Hence St. Paul acclaims the Spirit as omniscient "searching all things, even the deep things of God" (I Cor. II, 10) and contrasts the Spirit with the spirit of man. Here the Apostle plainly associates the loftiness of the Spirit with the knowledge which only such loftiness can command.

The transcendence of the Spirit might be thought to have to be surrendered when the Spirit is experienced in action. But it should be remembered that this particular problem was already present—and solved—in the apprehension of God as Shaddai. The Spirit, like Shaddai, is omnipotent; indeed, he demonstrates his heavenly power by acts on earth. The Spirit drives Jesus into the wilderness (Mk. I, 12) and in his power Jesus returns to Galilee (Lk. IV, 14). St. John speaks of the Spirit as the dynamic principle of all truth, for the Spirit of truth proceeds from the Father (XIV, 17; XV, 26; XVI, 13). His existence is not detached, like a logical proposition in a vacuum, but he comes to establish truth in the whole universe. The personality of the Spirit becomes perceptible in this fight for the truth: like Shaddai, the warrior from above, he enters the fight against falsehood, and if he can be resisted (Acts VII, 51) this does not restrict his sovereign power but rather underlines the severity of the apocalyptic struggle. The power of the Holy Spirit (Rom. XV, 13) is directed against the spiritual dominion which opposes Christ; the unity between Christ and the Spirit in this struggle is complete without blurring the distinction between each. The conquest of the wicked principle by Christ, now with the Father in Heaven, is continued, and the victory imparted, by the Spirit of God and Christ (Rom. VIII, 9 ff., 26 ff.). The enemy is supernatural and can only be defeated by the commensurate Power. The "sword of the Spirit", made available on earth by "praying at all seasons in the Spirit" (Ephes. VI, 17, 18), annihilates "the spirit that now works in the sons of disobedience" (Ephes. II, 2) but can no longer entice those who are freed from the lusts of the world. In the combat against the "spiritual beings of wickedness in heavenly places" (Ephes. VI, 12) the Spirit comes to the aid of the faithful with intercessions of divine and inscrutable intensity (Rom. VIII, 26 ff.). Although the warfare has been spiritualized and universalized when compared with the skirmishes of the tribes of Israel, the Spirit clearly continues to play the part of the divine protector in Heaven. The fight on earth does not deprive him of celestial status and nature.

The most decisive recognition of the Spirit's transcendence is found in two passages which recall the name *'Olam* of God in the Old Testament. The Epistle to the Hebrews in an almost casual reference to the "eternal Spirit" (διὰ πνεύματος αἰωνίου, IX, 14) links the Spirit to Christ's self-offering in Heaven. The Fourth Gospel (IV, 24) by proclaiming "God is Spirit" (πνεῦμα ὁ θεός) in the controversy about true worship connects Spirit with God's essential being. The Spirit is not a mediating emanation in time but eternal with God and Christ, free from the partial, contingent and fleeting nature of material power. Hence absolute reality is ascribed to God in stressing his spirituality.

As the Spirit shares the attributes of divinity, which the ancient names Elyon, Shaddai, and 'Olam so significantly advertised, it follows that he must also share the Glory of God. The Matthean and Lukan records of the conception of Jesus are in this respect unique (Mt. I, 18 ff.; Lk. I, 15, 35 ff.). God's son is not physically conceived by man or angel; he is not a child of the gods. The Virgin's election shows no trace of the mythical marriage with a divine messenger. Behind the mysterious and yet simple role of the Mother of God one may detect several themes of the Old Testament: the Spirit constrains her within to bring to life the all-living; this Spirit is God, for "thy Maker is thine husband" (Is. LIV, 5). Even the secular and passionate love of the King for the maiden (in the Song of Songs) foreshadows God's search for the unique vessel to bear the Word. These themes must be in the Evangelist's mind, for according to his Gospel everything is predetermined from on high when the archangel Gabriel announces that the Holy Spirit will come upon Mary and that the power of the Most High will overshadow her. The celestial note is here sounded with breath-taking simplicity: from Heaven comes the angel who gives the tidings, from Heaven come the light and the darkness of the divine visitation, as in the days when God visited and abode in Israel (Exod. XL, 34 ff.). No explanation is thought necessary. Clearly the Spirit is not energy nor ecstatic inspiration, nor does he imprint the image of God upon a child already born; rather he dwells upon the Virgin of Israel as the Light and Glory of God. Thus the Spirit manifests his own divinity in the Coming of Jesus, for he joins the pre-existent Word to the flesh of humanity in the womb of the blessed Virgin.

This ministration of glory is reflected when Christ is born and brought to the Temple and the Holy Spirit possesses Simeon to prophesy the fulfilment of all things in the *Nunc Dimittis* (Lk. II, 25 ff.). For St. Luke the Spirit and the Incarnation are quite inseparable and this tradition of Christian birth and celestial Spirit comes to the fore again in the Lukan account of Pentecost (Acts II, 3). Here fire is the appropriate emblem of the Spirit and of the manifestation of glory. The juxtaposition of the Holy Spirit and fire in baptism is made by John the Baptist in his prophecy of universal judgment by the Messiah (Lk. III, 15 ff.). The holy *Ruach* will scatter the wicked like chaff and the holy fire will burn them up; but what works as destruction for the worthless, blows to assemble and revive the true Israel as in Ezekiel, and to rekindle her with the divine love (as the bush was set on fire and not burnt). Baptism of water and spirit, still contrasted here, become united in one single eschatological event in Jn. III, 5 when eternal life invades the dying world (III, 16). At Pentecost the Spirit supplies the Church with his own evidence of divinity (Acts I, 5; XI, 15 ff.). The experience is not from within nor the outcome of mantic dedication. The Spirit descends upon the new Israel and excels the wonders at Sinai. The holy congregation receives the fiery afflatus not as a temporary phase of its life but as its permanent life, not as a means to an end, but as the end itself. In this glorious life God possesses his people and the people know God in Christ. Such a knowledge is clearly opposed both to traditional Rabbinic teachings and Hellenistic mysticism and recalls the prophecies of the Old Testament. The unity of God and Christ and Spirit is to be found in the concept of glory, the focal point of personal Godhead, known especially among suffering Christians (I Pe. IV, 12 ff.).

St. Paul assumes this to be self-evident since he has himself experienced his conversion by the concomitants of the voice of Jesus and the light from Heaven (Acts IX, 3). After his blindness he received sight, baptism, and spirit (IX, 17 f.). He always speaks of the revelation of Christ in terms of glory and fire and light (e.g. II Thess. I, 3–12). The glory of Christ is not of the past nor perceived by mystical endeavours but by the free action of God: the glory of Christ is reflected by the Church and by every member 'in Christ'. It is this recognition which leads the Apostle to acclaim the Spirit as Lord, *Kyrios* of glory.

The ecstatic passage in II Corinthians III, 17–18, is so revolutionary that some interpreters[1] felt themselves compelled to infer that St Paul simply indentifies the historical Christ with the cosmic Spirit. After what has been compiled above from other writers it is, however, not proved that St. Paul's 'mystagogical' tendencies were solely responsible for the Apostle's ascription of Lordship to the Spirit. At the end of the same epistle he uses a formula in greeting—"The grace of the Lord Jesus Christ and the love of God and the fellowship of the Holy Spirit"—which does not admit a fusion or identification of Jesus and Pneuma. Similarly in the ministration of glory he distinguishes between Christ as the glorious image of God and the Spirit who enacts the transformation into that image. There is nothing obscure in the argument: the glory of Christ is a present fact in the Church, and it is the result of God's spirit: therefore the Spirit is Lord celestial.

St. Paul surveys the astonishing diversity of spiritual gifts as a transcendental fact in the Church. In I Corinthians XII he guards explicitly against the misconception of emanational spirits: "now

[1] e.g. W. Bousset in *Kyrios Christos,* 1913, pp. 142 ff.

there are diversities of gifts, but the same Spirit" (xii, 4), and the same Spirit is undivided and the sole ground for the confession of Christ as Lord (xii, 3) and the unity of all believers (xii, 12 ff.). The unity of the Spirit in himself derives from his lordship. Hence the Spirit is not to be confused with the sum-total of spiritual gifts: rather "the Spirit divides to each one severally, even as he will" (xii, 11). He wills because he is personal and transcendent. St. Paul never looks upon the Spirit as the group-spirit or as the inward principle of a pious community, but as the universal Lord who acts everywhere for the risen Jesus and governs the life of the Church before the consummation. This is the Spirit which the risen Jesus has bequeathed to the Church: "Receive ye the Holy Spirit" (Jn. xx, 22). The Spirit and the bride are wedded into unity (Rev. xxii, 17).

The omnipresence of the Spirit, which is a heavenly attribute of the Lord, accounts for the universality of the Church in the world. The exalted Jesus shares his abode with men everywhere and at all times because the Spirit unites them everywhere into the Kingdom of the world to come. Wherever Christians meet to break bread they eat the Lord's flesh and drink his blood and are thus quickened by the Spirit. Church existence is eucharistic and the sacramental presence of the forgiving and abiding Jesus derives from the Spirit's freedom (Jn. vi, 63; vii, 39).

The strangest and strongest evidence for the full divinity of the Spirit is to be found in the famous passage about blasphemy which Mark (iii, 22 ff.) and Matthew (xii, 24 ff.) connect with the Beelzebub controversy, whereas Luke groups it with the saying about persecution and witness (xii, 8 ff.). The uniqueness of the teaching and its difficulties are well known.[1] Jesus appears to draw a distinction between sins which can be forgiven upon repentance and one sin which places the sinner beyond reach of repentance. In this respect the Spirit occupies a sphere of reverence different from that of the Son of Man. The curse lies

[1] G. Fitzer, TZ, 13/3, pp. 161–82 gives a useful survey of exegetical attempts and their failure to date and endeavours to find a literary solution in a supposedly original text: "everything will be forgiven to the Son of Man, but if he blasphemes against the Holy Ghost. . . .": Jesus' very existence depends on the Holy Spirit. The text was altered to suit the Church's formative Christology. This ingenious 'solution' cannot stand up against the Lukan text.

upon the blasphemer in accordance with the decree in Leviticus XXIV, 15–16, and it recalls the severity to be observed against those who cursed the Name. The context of the passage in Luke implies that this 'anathema' (which differs from 1 Corinthians XVI, 22 and I John IV in the nature of the indictment, the Spirit and not Jesus being guarded against abuse) was needed against those who, either being obsessed by diabolical spirits or through sheer cowardice, blasphemed against the Holy Spirit. Whether they were guilty of formal apostasy or a much subtler offence, such as a distortion of all moral and religious principles, and that not without suitable spiritual self-vindications, we simply cannot tell; nor do we know whether the blasphemers were renegades in or aggressors outside the Church. The only thing which is clear is the Lordship of the Holy Spirit whose Name is holy. In Mark and Matthew the saying is more closely integrated into the Gospel setting. The power of Jesus to cast out demons ascribed by his enemies to Satan is in reality the power of the Holy Spirit (Matthew is concerned to make this clear in verse 28 where Luke has "finger of God") by which the Strong One is overpowered and his prey delivered (Is. XLIX, 24–5). Thus the Holy Spirit is seen here too as the conqering Lord (Yahweh-Shaddai) breaking into the dark kingdom and bringing in the deliverance of the Messianic Age.

The result of an examination of these passages indicates that the New Testament reflects a new and unique belief in the Ruach-Pneuma: the Spirit is heavenly because he is united with the Father and with Christ. This union did not begin at Pentecost but preceded the creation itself, for in the light of the Christian revelation it is imperative to interpret Genesis I, 2 as referring to the pre-existent Spirit and not to an attribute of God. The creative Spirit is then identical with the Spirit which inspired the prophets, proceeded in the Incarnation and Life of Christ, and governs the Church and sanctifies every member thereof.

THE HEAVENLY TRINITY

Consequently the whole conception of God as Trinity in Unity is not to be taken as an afterthought of pedantic dogmatists, even if the actual formulae in Matthew XXVIII, 19 and

II Corinthians XIII, 14 were in the first place spontaneous outbursts in hymnal form. These liturgical formulae not only asserted the present unity of Father, Son, and Spirit, but also the eternal quality of the divine union in Heaven. Thus the God of the Old Testament is not to be thought of as a different or older God, the God of the Jews (Marcion's "author of evils, a lover of war, inconstant in judgment and contrary to himself") as opposed to the God of the Christians.[1] Everything that had gone before was written not only for our learning (Rom. XV, 4) but as an enduring record of the identity of the God who had made and redeemed the world. Similarly, Jesus was not to be looked upon as one who had come to stay on earth for a few vital years but as the Son who had been in Heaven before time was made.

The trinitarian formulae did not merely pay lip-service to the monotheistic tradition but explicitly endorsed the ancient injunction to Israel: "Hear, O Israel, the Lord our God is one Lord" (Dt. VI, 4). When the problem of this unity had been approached at all it had proved intractable to the best minds in Israel. The Rabbis knew, of course, as did their contemporaries among the philosophers, that the oneness of God cannot be defended on the grounds of tribal or local considerations. YHWH was not just another protector of a nomadic community or the social and racial exponent of a people, the national figure and the owner of a cultic shrine. Such earthly conceptions certainly lingered on, as they do everywhere, but they did not answer the old cultic question: "Who is the King of Glory?" (Ps. XXIV).

Furthermore the Biblical tradition never attempted the useless task of locating God in the universe. His unity could not be pin-pointed as a place on a cosmic map. Again God is not to be thought of as co-extensive with the universe, for the All of creation is by God, made and sustained, and in no way equal to God. Totally foreign to the Bible is the thought of God as one in the mathematical sense of the word. The pagan tendencies to exalt one of their gods as chief god are as alien to the tradition as is the identification of God with one idea of the philosophical schools, such as Mind or goodness or any other.

[1] Cf. Irenaeus, *Adv. haer,* I, XXV, 1; III, XL, 2 (ed. Harvey); I, XXVII, 1; III, XXV, 3 (A.-N.C.L.); Tertullian, *Adv. Marc.* I, 27.

The perennial question "To whom then will you liken God?" (Is. XL, 18) must therefore evoke a series of denials. The transcendence of God is best brought out in propositions which affirm his absolute being by denying his dependence on contingent being. His unity is therefore incomparable except in such terms of revelation as he has chosen. These, as we have tried to show, are cosmic and transcendent, embedded in, and yet excelling, Oriental traditions. Thus the Christian conception of God does not subscribe to the Jewish belief that the Torah is this vehicle of revelation, though it is acknowledged that God is the only Lawgiver and that he has spoken by Moses and the prophets. But the Torah in its traditional form is a human, earthly document, to be apprehended as a pointer towards a living reality rather than to be taken for the reality itself. There is an eternal order whose outlines the Torah could only delineate, whereas Jesus Christ is its living image (Hebr. X, 1).

The positive assertion of the New Testament is that God is the Father of our Lord Jesus Christ in the knowledge of the Holy Spirit. This is the revelation of the one God which fulfils all previous aspirations after unity. It is a unity which knows no development, though the stages of human apprehension may and do vary. To Moses' perplexing question: "What is his name?" (Exod. III, 13) the deliberately obscure answer "I am that I am" ("Eheyeh asher Eheyeh") is now given definite content. The Names "Father, Son, Holy Spirit" are not names of gods nor earthly titles nor metaphysical speculations about Being. They assert a unity which is found only in God's heavenly pre-existence. God is One because none other existed before the beginning, before the creation, above all, outside Heaven and earth, in the eternal fellowship of glory, from which life and light are derived.

Chapter Four

THE SOCIETY OF HEAVEN

THE Bible views Heaven and Earth as one world. If the earth is spatial, so is Heaven. If the earth is inhabited, so is Heaven. The human race is not alone in the universe with God, for a host of others dwell in the spheres. Are they friendly or hostile to God, to each other, and to mankind? Are their desires good or bad or altogether outside the moral compass? Do they pursue an active existence? Are they superior or inferior to man? Do they entertain a rivalry of preferment among themselves? Can they be distinguished in respect of power and privilege? Do they exist for a time or for ever? What is their place in the creation and in the plan of redemption which God has revealed upon earth?

COMPLEXITY OF BIBLICAL ANGELOLOGY

These questions open up an immensely rich vista of thought. Local traditions and cosmic speculations of heavenly beings are universal and perhaps as old as the human imagination. East and West claim to know intermediaries who fly from Heaven to earth or hover above the earth. Human awareness of them is at times intense and at times casual. Some societies and individuals assert their presence while others ignore them. Some cultures express the belief in their art while others urge a pronounced disbelief. This Pro of belief and Contra of criticism is fully reflected in the Biblical writings and, therefore, in the Christian tradition.

The ubiquity of the heavenly powers is a constant theme in the Bible, but the importance attached to their part in creation and redemption varies enormously. Again the prevalence of a non-dogmatic attitude strikes us, for before heresy impaired the Jewish and Christian positions, and engendered the need for the fence of orthodoxy, the belief in angels and heavenly powers met with no restrictive measures. The secret of the Heavens included their inhabitants as well. The Biblical evidence does not suggest a primary line of development or a definite pattern of thought. There is no indication of a progressive movement. It is, for example, quite contrary to the facts to speak of a 'primitive' animism which changed into a polytheism with angels and demons, or to regard a pure monotheism, which knows no celestial beings, as the last stage. The question of the origin of the belief in these beings must now be pursued.

VARIOUS STRANDS OF BELIEF

According to Robertson Smith's almost classical view, "the oldest sanctuaries of the gods were originally haunts of a multiplicity of *jinn*, or of animals to which demoniac attributes were ascribed".[1] He connects these jinn with the ancient use of the term for God, Elohim, whose plural denoted the sacred denizens of the cultic places, viewed collectively. The Bene Elohim are not so much 'sons of God' as 'beings of the Elohim kind', namely the angelic beings who frequent holy places, such as Bethel and Mahanaim, even when they have no message to deliver (Gen. XXVIII, 12; XXXII, 2). The angels, then, "form part of the old Semitic mythology" which reaches into the Old Testament without belonging there properly. The angels have no distinctive individuality but simply form a 'class' of beings. Thus Jacob wrestles not with one angel but with Elohim (Gen. XXXII; Hos. XII, 4). This mythological view also lies behind the strange legend of the marriages contracted between the Bene Elohim and the daughters of men whose offspring were the giants (Gen. VI, 2 ff.).

According to Robertson Smith's theory the angels derive from a very lowly origin, for they are animals, or their vigour, projected into the air. A transfer of energy is to be observed here. The animals' strength and the fear aroused by it are now equated

[1] W. Robertson Smith, *Religion of the Semites*, 1894, pp. 445–6.

with the strength and fear aroused by the airy beings of El-(god) quality.

This conjecture, that the higher arises out of the lower, appears to receive further support from the evidence of spiritism. The cult of the dead does not necessarily imply the existence of ancestor-worship, but there can be little doubt that the shades of the dead (Rephaim) were continuous with those who had once lived. Having breathed out their last breath their spirit went floating on. The witch of Endor has no difficulty in conjuring up the ghost of Samuel (I Sam. XXVIII). In this instance, it is true, the ghost comes from below and can hardly be called a spirit of the air. Yet some spirits were alleged to have escaped upward (Eccles. III, 21), and it is to be noted that angels and wind-spirits (ruchoth, Ps. CIV, 4) are the same thing at times. This juxtaposition at least suggests a certain affinity between the angels and the spirits and therefore a source of origin which is wholly opposed to the totemistic view of Robertson Smith.

Another line of enquiry yields an even more disparate result. All literary critics of the Old Testament have had to account for the quaint phrase "the angel of Yahweh", which appears with considerable frequency in Genesis and Judges. They judge that behind it lies the process of substitution. Thus in Gen. XXXI, 11 the "angel of God" addresses Jacob in a reminiscence about Bethel. "It was clearly a very ancient spot . . . an El had already been worshipped there. An interesting sign of developed belief, due to overworking the passage at a later period, is that '*the angel of God*' says, 'I am the El of Bethel'. This angel replaces God at a time when God could no more be thought of as a local deity."[1] In other words, angels are dispossessed local gods.

These theories of origin fail, however, to explain the genuine heavenliness of the celestial beings. This feature is fully accounted for in a stellar hypothesis of angels. The stars in the firmament were considered to be alive since they were seen to move, though differently from sun, moon, and planets, which were held to be divine. But all the luminaries appeared to be driven by powerful

[1] Oesterley & Robinson, *Hebrew Religion*, p. 120, where this view is stated with more dogmatic conviction than is commonly found elsewhere. For a Catholic view of the *Mal'akh Yaweh* Problem cf. W. S. Heidt, *Angelology of the Old Testament*, 1949, pp. 70 ff.

agencies, namely the heavenly powers. Thus sun, moon, and stars ride in a chariot (En. LXXII, 5 ff.; LXXV, 3) through the gates of Heaven. The chariot of the sun became, of course, a popular picture everywhere. Forty angels pull this chariot (g. Ap. Bar. 6). The zodiacs and the spheres contain a corresponding number of leading angels, who are made both of fire and wind (on the first day of Creation Jub. II, 2). The stars are almost interchangeable with their patron angels or the 'sons of God' (Bene Elohim): "The morning stars sang together, and all the sons of God shouted for joy" (Job XXXVIII, 7). These stars are obedient servants; God calls them by name and they reply: "Here we are, present" (En. XLIII, 1; LXIX, 21). They shine joyfully for their creator (Syr. Ap. Bar. III, 34 f.) from whom "all the powers in Heaven received a commandment, a voice, and a light, comparable to fire" (En. LXI, 6). Innumerable is the crowd of heavenly powers (*αἱ δυνάμεις τῶν οὐρανῶν* Mt. XXIV, 29; En. LXXI, 8), the "ten thousand times ten thousand" (Dan. VII, 10), who belong to a universe peopled with star-angels or angel-stars. The heavenliness and the infinity of the angels are concepts derived from the observation of nature in the sky. The visible world dominates the feelings of the worshipping community; hence it is not surprising that the ancient cultus reflects the astronomical-astrological pattern of the universe. The cultus is never thought of as a man-made institution in which human beings are left to themselves. Not only angels share in the service of God but other living creatures also attend. These were originally represented in visible shapes.

THE SERAPHIM

The Seraphim were probably once guardians of the threshold and in some respects similar to the griffins (Eg. *šerref*) who can be seen on the tombs of important Egyptians. The link between Seraphim and the threshold is curiously still relevant to the mystical trance of Isaiah, for it is hardly an accident that both are mentioned in very close juxtaposition (ch. VI). Yet the same prophet also lends support to the theory that they were originally serpent-deities when he enumerates the Seraphim as fiery flying serpents among other dangerous beasts (Is. XIV, 29; XXX, 6). The two derivations are not necessarily mutually exclusive, for a fiery serpent may well be portrayed as a mythical guardian. In Israel the tradition appears to be ancient, for according to Numbers XXI, 8, Moses made such a burning serpent (Hebr. *saraph* = to burn) and put it on a standard in order to cure the victims of snake-bite. One is immediately reminded of apotropaic principles of healing and of the snake as an emblem of healing (Aesculapius). No wonder it survived in the cultus and was evidently disliked by the prophetic movement, for under Hezekiah the "bronze serpent that Moses had made" was removed (II K. XVIII, 4). Probably it had already acquired a heavenly association by that time, possibly by identification with the lightning. Yet it is due to Isaiah's unique contribution that the Seraphim survived as heavenly beings the purge on earth and became winged ministers of God. Their duties remained undefined but they were obviously not on the ground at all, but in the air and close to God in his revelation of glory.

THE CHERUBIM

The cultus itself has a power of transformation. Thus the Cherubim also illustrate the manner in which common, albeit foreign, mythological creatures are adapted to its use and made to join the heavenly host.[1] The earthy bull is already left behind when he is represented, in Assyria, for example, as a winged bull who became identified with the thunder and the thunder-clouds. In the Old Testament the Cherub is, first of all, the living chariot of the theophanic God (Ps. XVIII, 11; II Sam. XXII, 11), and later one of those who carry the flaming throne across the sky. Again, he acts as a guard of the garden of Eden (Gen. III, 24). His proximity to God is brought out in the phrase: "Yahweh Sebaoth, enthroned on the cherubim" (I Sam. IV, 4; II Sam. VI, 2). When Yahweh's dwelling-place was in the Ark the Cherubim flanked the sacred chest and God "sat upon the cherubim"

[1] Cf. RB 35/1926, pp. 328–58 where L. H. Vincent discusses modes of assimilation outside the Bible and the peculiar hybrid syncretism and symbolism inspired by the Cherub motif. In the same article P. Dhorme disposes of faulty etymologies, i.e. Kerub = (1) rt.rkv (to ride); (2) bull; (3) to be near; (4) bless, and insists on the Accadian root *karâbu* = devotion. The god kâribu acted as intercessor, the Ka-ri-ba-ti were orantes, male or female, at the entrance of the sanctuary.

(II K. XIX, 15; Ps. LXXX, 1; XCIX, 1). In the Priestly legislation the Cherubim are integrated into the pattern of worship, so that the mercy-seat (Ex. XXV, 18–22; XXXVII, 7–9; Nrs. VII, 89) and inner curtains of the tabernacle and the veils (Ex. XXVI, 1, 31; XXXVI, 8, 35) are worked "with cherubim". The finest descriptions are to be found in I Kings VI and in Ezekiel I. Their wings sustain the throne of Yahweh and manifest their celestial status. The all-seeing and hearing Cherubim own both features and powers which are elsewhere assigned to the ancient sky-god (e.g. Horus).

NO SIMPLE BORROWING

Owing to the obvious similarities of words and customs of worship, especially as they affect the world of angels, it has been supposed that the really vital source of Hebrew angelology must be sought in the Exile, when leading Jewish writers renewed their acquaintance, on the spot, with Babylonian and Zoroastrian religion. They could not help being influenced by the belief in Amesha-spentas, who watch from above, as the stars look down, and who lead the Yazatas, whose business it is to praise God and protect men, and under whom the innumerable multitude of Fravashis carry out an angelic ministry. Though the process was not one of simple copying, the Biblical grades of archangels, angels, and guardian-spirits, it is claimed, reflect the degrees in the Persian celestial domain.

This is not the place to weigh up the amount of cultural borrowing that may have been practised, consciously or unconsciously, in the Near East and among the Hebrews. What is more serious is that the reason for the borrowing has often been stated to be a practical, religious one.[1] Angelology, it has been asserted, became a virtual necessity to balance the increasing transcendence of God and to mitigate the effects of his remoteness. With God absent from the conflict some mediating powers had to intervene. The more pressing the political situation became the more public morale required a religious prop in Heaven

[1] E.g. Bousett, *Die Religion des Judentums im späthellenistischen Zeitalter*, 1926. pp. 321, 329; A. Kohut, *Über die jüdische Angelologie und Daemonologie in ihrer Abhängigkeit vom Parsimus*, 1866, pp. 2 ff.

and found it in angelology. Against this it must be urged that the belief in the heavenly host is much older than any post-Exilic sources. The God of Heaven, as we have seen, never became an absentee God and the belief in angels, after the Exile, never asserted free independence for the angels; they act under God without diminishing either his transcendence or his concern for the world. The angels do not spring from a leaning towards Persian dualism, but if they are to be considered in this context at all they serve as a theological weapon *against* dualism: no evil god or principle is cited as the cause of evil, but evil angels oppose God's heavenly host.

The attempt to segregate Jewish and non-Jewish strands in the origins of the Biblical portrait of the Society of Heaven is now generally abandoned and with it the explanation that Oriental cosmogonies introduced a foreign note into Hebrew religion. This is not to deny, however, that an apocalyptic interest in cosmic and universal events increased after the Exile and altered the prophetic concern for national issues.

ANGELIC APPEARANCES INFREQUENT

The fact that celestial visitors and voices appear in other religions neither invalidates nor confirms the Biblical position. The most important and independent strand of angelology that runs right through the Bible is the record of straightforward visual encounters of a few men with superhuman beings who are understood to reside in a higher sphere than the earth. Their appearances are rare; no reason can be given why Hagar, Abraham, Jacob, Moses, Balaam, Gideon, Manoah, David, Elijah, Elisha, Isaiah, Ezekiel, Zechariah, Daniel, in the Old Testament, and Joseph, Zacharias, the Blessed Virgin Mary, the Shepherds, Mary Magdalene, Peter, Philip, Cornelius, Paul, and the visionary of the Apocalypse, in the New Testament, receive supernatural visitors and see sights and hear words which are not normally granted to ordinary people. There is no Biblical psychology of the intercourse between men and superhuman, celestial beings. The events are narrated in a strictly matter-of-fact way, without leaving any room for figurative use or abuse to explain away the strangeness of this element. A stereotyped fondness for it would have favoured a constant employment of the angelic device, but the literary forms of the Bible display no such lack of invention. It must therefore be supposed that these experiences were recorded because they were reported by some individuals and became part of the oral and written traditions. They ranked as in no way inferior to other channels of revelation. What was said and heard on such occasions had the same worth as the oracles of God, given in prophecy and directions of conduct and cultus.

FIERY MESSENGERS

Of all the citizens of Heaven the angels appear in the most sharply distinguished part. They are made of finer material than men, but they are not immaterial.[1] They are not winged; this false portrayal is due to the confusion with the Seraphim and to the difficult text in Daniel IX, 21 (RSV.: "in swift flight"). The angels' form is not fantastic but beautiful and so impressive as to border on the divine. The angel of the Lord, who is admittedly a divine messenger in a special way, appeals to a sense of wonder. Therefore, as he appears to Abraham and Jacob, as narrated in the mysterious stories of Genesis, he seems almost interchangeable with God himself despite the homely intimacy of friendly hospitality. The theophanic angel is especially endowed with those proportions which convey to men the sense of the divine Presence. But this angelic dignity is not only beautiful but also dreadful, for the angel of the Lord is a numinous figure who must excite fear (Jdg. XIII, 6, 18). Jacob's experience at Peniel is illuminating, for he wrestles there with an angel who appears to him first as human and at the end of the struggle as God himself (Gen. XXXII, 22–end). The angels convey the divine glory in forms which resemble human figures. The "two men in white" at the Resurrection and the Ascension are angels (Lk. XXIV, 4; Jn. XX, 12; Acts I, 10), who simply resemble beautiful young men (Hermas Vis. II, 4, 1). Indeed the human features of the angels distinguish them from the brutal and beastly apparitions of the demons. Yet they are not made of flesh and blood and exist without sex and mortality (Mt. XXII, 3)

[1] Cf. e.g. Jdg. XIII, 20; Midrash on Ps. CIV, 4: messengers are made of wind, servants of fire.

though they are not incapable of folly (Job. IV, 18).[1] They are strong, but their strength is limited. The strong angel cannot "open the book" of life (Rev. V, I ff.). He achieves distinction mainly by visual impressions. His face shines in reflection of the Glory of God; therefore the burning face of a "man of God" is compared to that of an angel (Jdg. XIII, 6). David is esteemed an angel of God, for he creates this unique impression of fairness and goodness which is not vouchsafed to any except a few mortals (I Sam. XXIX, 9; II Sam. XIV, 17). St. Paul recalls his wonderful reception among the Galatians, who, despite some repellent feature or illness, received him "like an angel of God, as Christ Jesus" (Gal. IV, 14). In appearance, at least, the angels share the ecstatic effulgence of light with Jesus, the God of Heaven. This high fame applies also to the sense of hearing. The preaching of an angel from Heaven would persuade most men by his harmonious excellence of speech (Gal. I, 8; I Cor. XIII, I).

THE HEAVENLY COUNCIL

God is surrounded by a council of living and spiritual beings, among whom the angels are most prominent. This heavenly assembly of councillors (Hebr. *sod*) conforms to the pattern of an aristocratic monarchy. The Bene Elohim belong to the court of the King of Heaven and serve under him. They act as privy councillors in solemn debate, and their advice and approbation are sought after and given in confidential converse. Not only Isaiah, in his famous vision (ch. VI), but also Micaiah "saw the Lord, sitting on his throne, and all the host of Heaven standing beside him on his right hand and on his left" (I K. XXII, 19). Job's ordeal is enacted before them (ch. I). It was believed that God's words "Let us make man . . ." (Gen. I, 26) were addressed to this assembly. God's justice is administered in their midst (Ps. LXXXII) in "the council of the gods" (LXX: *ἐν συναγωγῇ θεῶν*), for they are, as it were, witnesses in the divine forum; therefore the Son of Man will testify for those who testify for him "before the angels of God" (Lk. XII, 8; Rev. III, 5). As the citizens of Heaven they defend the realm not only with wise decisions

[1] Cf., however, the strange tradition of the circumcision of angels in Jub. XV and the baptism of angels in Odes of Sol. IV.

but also with powerful intervention (II K. VI, 16 ff.). In every virtue they excel human beings. They ride and drive in thousands of chariots before and behind their King, whom they encircle as he delivers judgment (Dan. VII, 10). A large detachment serves the Messiah (Lk. XXII, 43), albeit without being called upon to intervene by Christ (Mt. XXVI, 53). When Jesus descends from Heaven it is "with a shout, with the voice of the archangel" (I Thess. IV, 16) and he returns "with his mighty angels" (II Thess. I, 7).

The *sod* or Council of Holy Ones (Ps. LXXXIX, 8) is the focal point of the Hebrew tradition of the heavenly society. Its suitability is extraordinary, for it provides outlets into every field of Biblical concern: the Council may act on the political horizon, or as a Law Court (Beth Din), or in individual inspiration, or in mystical converse. Earthly concerns depend upon its actions and earthly ranks and institutions correspond to the celestial reality.

RABBINIC MODERATION

The degree of importance attached to the celestial hierarchy varies enormously between different writers. Generally the Rabbinic traditions are moderate. In Judaism there was no 'doctrine of angels' and in the early Rabbinical sources angelic mythology "often seems to be an exhibition of homiletic ingenuity rather than serious opinion".[1] The Council[2] is composed, first, of the 'Ophanim, i.e. the chariot-wheels which through Ezekiel's vision acquired a semi-mystical and independent celestial reality (chs. I and X). The Chayyoth or 'beasts' are another class, also taken over from Ezekiel (I, 15–22); like the 'Ophanim they are in the highest story of Heaven, the 'Aravoth, where they support God's throne. The Seraphim continue to serve in their fiery role. The ministering angels, however, are the most important and outnumber all the rest, and among these the archangels[3]—Michael, Gabriel, Uriel, Raphael—lead the host, excelling all others in fiery radiance. Rabbinical Judaism, however, curbed the flood of all celestial speculations which led

[1] GFM, op. cit., vol. I, p. 404. Cf. Exod. R. XXXII; Lev. R. XXIV, 8.

[2] b Chag. 12 b.

[3] Num. R. II, 10. The number varies greatly, see below.

into and derived from theosophy. The angels "were not objects of veneration, much less of adoration; and in orthodox Judaism they were not intermediaries between man and God".[1] The Sadducees did not believe in angels (Acts XXIII, 8) and the Mishnah makes no mention of them.

APOCALYPTIC EXCESSES

The apocalyptic attitude, however, went entirely beyond the sober confines laid down by the Rabbis, especially in the matter of the classification of the angelic hierarchy. Even some canonical writings in the Old Testament indicate the popular esteem for this development. The ranks of the angels are brought into direct contact with the number of the spheres and associated with the planets. The "seven eyes" of the Lord, which run to and fro through the whole earth (Zech. III, 9; IV, 10), are the same as the archangels or princes of later Apocalypses, such as the Christian one, which says explicitly: "The seven stars are the angels of the seven churches" (Rev. I, 20) and distinguishes them individually from one another (chs. VII–X; XV; XVI), from ordinary angels and from the hurtful angels (VII, 1–2). The seven archangels had already appeared as "men" or executioners in the picture of the punishment of Jerusalem in Ezekiel IX. The astronomical-astrological outlook on history naturally linked both the stars and the angels with national fortunes and punishments; the highest angels, as leaders of their armies, represented the nations. Thus the exalted world of the spheres is politically attached to the earth and even to individual powers and régimes. Michael is the prince-angel of Israel (Dan. X, 13; XII, 1), by whom God sends eternal help to the lot of the redeemed and whose rule God exalts among the gods in eternal light (IQM. XVII, 6). Yet he is only one among others, for Persia, Greece, and presumably all notable dominions have their heavenly princes (Dan. X, 20; Targ. Jon. on Gen. XI, 7 f.). With that conviction national resistance is organized and success expected even against heavy odds. Judas Maccabaeus beats Nicanor by lifting the morale of his troops in recalling the angelic help given aforetime (I Macc. VII, 41). Thus the leaders of the Council espouse the causes of nations, and

[1] GFM, op. cit., vol. I, p. 411.

therefore some of the high ones are, in fact, subject to punishment. "The Lord shall punish the host of the high ones . . ." (Is. XXIV, 21), because they fought for the kings and peoples who are viewed with political displeasure.

The fusion of political and astronomical ideas led to the veritable abundance and disorder of the angelology which lies behind the Christian tradition. The pseudepigraphic systems do not aim at any kind of uniformity but accommodate angels, archangels, archai, forces, powers, lords, thrones, Seraphim and Cherubim in a multiplicity of celestial, meteorological, national and political constellations. The redactor of the Testament of Levi (ch. III) distributes the several classes to fit them into each layer of Heaven. The second Heaven contains the punishing angels, the third the powers of armies of revenge, the fourth the Holy Ones, the fifth interceding angels before the Face of God, the sixth angels who carry God's reply, the seventh thrones and powers. The book of Enoch also retains the figure seven, and in chapter XX an important list gives the names of the archangels: Uriel, Raphael, Raguel, Michael, Sariel, Gabriel, Remiel. Of these Michael, Gabriel, Uriel, and Raphael are the most important for the Christian tradition (the four "angels of the throne" of En. XL, 1 ff., where Phanuel is read for Uriel). Michael retains the function of protector ascribed to him in Daniel, which is supernatural and military. Raphael governs the spirits of men; in the book of Tobit he is one of the seven archangels, sent to heal Tobit and to unite a family whose prayer he brings before God. "I am Raphael, one of the seven holy angels, who present the prayers of the saints and have access to the glory of the Holy One" (XII, 15). The angels hold these prayers in their hands and offer them with incense (VIII, 2–5). Gabriel is the prince of Paradise, the leader of the Seraphim and Cherubim. Uriel is set over the army of angels and Tartarus; even the destructive angels belong to the celestial hierarchy (En. LVI; CD II, 6).

THE NEW TESTAMENT

The Christian tradition maintains a broad and variegated approach of its own. Both the Rabbinical caution and the apocalyptic freedom and exuberance are represented, and the canonical Scriptures also exercise their influence. The differences between the individual writers is therefore well marked. The Evangelist John, though commonly regarded as mystical, only rarely refers to angels, and, with the exception of the important quotation in I, 51, "Ye shall see . . . the angels of God ascending and descending . . .", he reports the common belief of others (V, 4). He is not really interested in the heavenly society; thus the cripple need not wait in vain for the angel's work at the pool of Bethesda for Jesus has come. The writer of the Apocalypse, however, is not only caught up into Heaven but also moves among the angelic host rather than among men. He is even warned not to worship the shining spirits (Rev. XXII, 9). For him the angels are all good and on the side of the Lord, and their unquestioned loyalty to the throne is more significant than their actual rank. Nevertheless, the heavenly order in respect of archangels, angels, elders, living creatures, the chosen of the tribes of Israel, and the multitudes of the believing righteous, is real and permanent, for it is in that order that they surround and worship the Lamb. The universality of their goal does not obliterate their distinctions, but the principle of rank is no longer one of power alone. The most intimate councillors of God are those who are worthy to be near him. They are made perfect and are exclusively engaged in adoration. In them activity and being have become one. They exist in Heaven because they adore God. The writer uses the vehicle of Apocalypse, with its extravagant pictures of cosmic degrees, to harness the ranks of the society of Heaven to their respective stations in the life of the Church of Jesus. This theological purpose unites all the writers of the New Testament, however much they differ in other ways.

An apparent contrast of attitude to angels can be detected even in one single writer; St. Luke may be said to exemplify the remarkable freedom which characterizes the New Testament teaching about heavenly beings. In the first part of the Acts much of the supernatural work is ascribed to the agency of angels. The celestial forces are as much at work in the Church as they had been, according to the Gospel of St. Luke, during the earthly ministry of Jesus. Then the birth of Christ had been announced by an archangel and celebrated by the host of angels; his Resurrection and his Ascension had been explained by "two men in white". So in the early Church "an angel of the Lord by night opened the prison doors" (Acts v, 19); an angel of the Lord directs Philip on his way (VIII, 26); Cornelius is approached by an angel (x, 3); St. Peter is liberated from his cell by an angel (XII, 7 ff.) and his friends disbelieve Rhoda's good news and assume her to have mistaken Peter's angel for Peter (XII, 5). Soon afterwards the wicked Herod is slain by an angel of the Lord (XII, 23). Moreover the preaching of St. Stephen, which is a typical sermon on salvation-by-Jesus, resumes the Old Testament tradition of angelic ministrations (VII, 30, 35, 38, 53). Indeed, Stephen, whose face looked like that of an angel (VI, 15), goes much further in ascribing events on Mt. Sinai to angelic mediation than the account in Exodus. Evidently the belief in the 'angel of the Presence' was a popular theme. However, as soon as the scene shifts to Antioch and the Pauline missions begin (chs. XIII ff.) all this is changed. There is no angelic participation in the work of St. Paul. When it could be expected, as when, for instance, the Apostle is liberated from prison in Philippi, the event is merely ascribed to an earthquake (XVI, 26). He traverses the Greek world and engages in many disputes as if both he and his opponents had never heard of a celestial society.

A simple explanation of this enigma might be found in St. Paul's own peculiar attitude to angelology, which will occupy us again later on. It will then certainly become apparent that he, who was a self-confessed debtor to Greeks and Barbarians and a Pharisee of Pharisees, shows hardly any interest in good angels, their titles and interrelations, but a great awareness of evil spirits. His familiarity with apocalyptic writings does not cause him to accept the angelology of Enoch or Jubilees or the Testament of the Twelve Patriarchs. He acknowledges the existence of angels (I Cor. XIII, 1) but repudiates, by silence, both their celestialism and the pagan notions of independent supernatural forces. He fights against the invasion of bizarre fantasies just because the Gospel is not enthusiastic madness. Since the things of Christ have not occurred in an esoteric corner his sober concern seems to curb flights of fancy. Yet he himself sees visions, not only of Christ, of the light of Glory, but also of "a man of Macedonia"

(Acts XVI, 9), who may well be meant to be an angel in the narrative, and, again, "an angel of the God to whom I belong and whom I worship" (XXVII, 23) stands by him during a terrible night at sea. He concedes that an "angel of light" (II Cor. XI, 14) is wonderfully persuasive. Some of the Pharisees in his defence even claim that a spirit or an angel might have spoken to him (XXIII, 9). So at least they liked to account for his inspiration.

A restrained angelology also characterizes our Lord's teaching in the Synoptic Gospels, outside the apocalyptic discourses. Angels come and go, look down upon the earth, give their reports in Heaven, and serve God. As in the Old Testament they pursue errands of importance and make common cause with the men whom they inspire. These things are taken for granted, but not stressed, in the following three important passages.

GUARDIAN ANGELS

A saying peculiar to Matthew (XVIII, 10) assigns to the angels the special task of representing every individual, however meek, before the royal presence. The angels of "the children" (whether literally babes, with most commentators, or the flock of humble, simple Christians, as held, for example by Montefiore) "always see the face of my Father who is in Heaven". Here the traditional aspect of the guardian angels as the supervisors of their charges on earth is deliberately transcendentalized. They are still thought of as private protectors, as in Jub. XXXV, 17 where "the guardian of Jacob is great and powerful and honoured, and praised more than the guardian of Esau". But the popular belief, as evidenced by later Rabbinic allusions, is also deprived of its fantastic features. Jesus knows nothing of two angels who accompany a man, winged and even ready to testify against him (b Chag. 16 a), nor does the problem of whether and how to ask a guardian angel to wait outside, while their charges fulfil the call of nature (b Ber. 60 b), concern him at all. The children's angel is not on earth, as for instance in the account of Moses' escape from peril when "an angel descended from Heaven and took the form of Moses, who thus escaped while they seized the angel" (j Ber. IX, 1). The phrase "see the face of my Father in Heaven" stresses the angels' superior, celestial status and their intercessory role in Heaven. It is as if every child came under the archangels' special care (cf. Tob. XII, 15) and as if the distinction between higher and lower angels no longer applied. It is therefore not necessary to follow Loisy's otherwise attractive opinion that these formulas are mere "theological euphemisms".[1] The evidence favours Edersheim's view that the New Testament offers here and elsewhere a radical departure from accepted Jewish angelology[2] and that Christ teaches not only the protection of "the children", but also that humility begins nearest the Throne of God: not the chiefest of the angels, who excel in power, but the most loving and humble cling to their Lord and therefore enjoy his closest presence.

As members of the *sod* the angels of the Christians have access to the Father and act as ambassadors at his court just as they act as his emissaries on earth. St. Luke also connects the angelic ministry specifically with the humble. In the parable of Lazarus it is the dead beggar who is "carried away by the angels to Abraham's bosom" (XVI, 22). Again the plural is somewhat strange, for this goes beyond the assumption that every man has his own tutelar angel for himself. The angels of the New Testament are certainly not a kind of double nor a spiritual replica, but separate, highly sympathetic beings who identify their own existence with that of morally striving men. One sinner's act of repentance on earth is hailed by the angels of God in Heaven with joy (Lk. XV, 10). What appears to man as unimportant is given by them an enthusiastic reception. Their interest in the practical world of man is intense, but their spiritual nature looks for those features of the world which are eternally significant. Their help and mediation are not even a luxury but a necessity, for as Jesus had received their ministrations in a world of temptation and wild beasts (Mk. I, 13) so his disciples may rely upon their continuation.

THE PROBLEM OF MEDIATION

It is in this matter of mediation, however, that the first serious divergence of views in the New Testament is to be found. In

[1] *Les Évangiles Synoptiques,* 1908, II, pp. 142 ff.: ". . . pour ne pas prêter a Dieu un sentiment humain, peut-être pour éviter de le nommer."

[2] *The Life and Times of Jesus the Messiah,* 1892, II, pp. 122, 142. Edersheim errs, however, in postulating an established angelology as such.

the story of Cornelius (Acts x) the angel assumes a central part. The form of mediation is direct. Cornelius is not a mystic but a man of prayer and good works. He experiences neither a trance nor a vision of God. The careful wording insists that "he saw clearly in a vision an angel of God" (x, 3, 22); the angel's mediation establishes contact between the Gentile centurion and the Jewish Apostle who saw the challenge and the implications of universalism in the image of a descending vessel "like a great sheet, let down by four corners upon the earth" (x, 11). Both the angelic encounter and the trance are of heavenly origin, but they are not the same thing. The angel is personal, an individual mediator between God and individuals. Similarly the seer of the Apocalypse, following the mystic experience of Zechariah, accepts not only angelic errands to himself but also relies upon angelic interpretations of given visions. The writer follows the tradition, of which Ezekiel is such an eloquent exponent, that visions are of immensely complicated imagery and that in these visions the interpreting angel—"a man" of the look of brass (Ez. XL, 3)—is himself part of the mediation of divine revelation. Thus the angelic ministry becomes inevitably linked with the communications between God and Man and it is frequently impossible in later times to judge whether we deal with genuine experience or a literary device.

AS VIEWED BY ST. PAUL

St. Paul, however, allows no such latitude to the mediating role of angels. In his controversy with the Galatians about the Law he cites the fact of the alleged mediation of the Law through the hands of angels. The Rabbinic background is far from clear. On the one hand the Rabbis cited the angelic mediation (based on Dt. XXXIII, 2) so as to enhance the glory of the Torah, whereas another tradition (bShab. 88 b, Cant. R. on Cant. VIII, XI, 2) asserts that the angels had opposed the giving of the Law at Sinai. However, the Christian preaching had to deal with the claim of the angelic mediation as a positive asset of glory and authority. But whereas St. Stephen in his speech accepts this fact as meritorious and accuses the Jews of disobedience (Acts VII, 53), in the fashion of Deuteronomic indictments, St. Paul deals quite differently with the matter in Galatians III, 19. In St. Stephen's speech the angels "are mentioned to glorify the law, being opposed to mere human ministers. Here the motive is different. The interposition of created beings is contrasted with the direct agency of God himself".[1] Therefore the Law also divides man from God and keeps him from union with God in Christ. Angelic mediation must be regarded as far from perfect and, for St. Paul, the angels' intervention is wholly suspect and not unconnected with the "rudiments of the world" (IV, 3) or material, cosmic elements over which the angels, in popular credulity, exercise their power.[2] Even in the unlikely case of an angel's mediation of the Gospel through preaching, no credence must be given to such a heavenly creature if his gospel differs from the Apostle's (Gal. I, 8). In Romans (VIII, 38) angels and powers are obviously enemies because they "separate us from the love of God". This strong language may be explained by reference to evil angels, but it may also simply refer to the dangerous habit of indulging in the worship or religion (θρησκεία) of angels, against which he warns the Christians, Jewish and Gentile, at Colossae (II, 18).

BY PHILO

What in St. Paul's treatment receives only accidental attention occupies the mind of the writer of the Epistle to the Hebrews as a problem to which he desires to give a systematic answer. It is very evident from chapter XII that his whole attitude to the heavenly society differs from St. Paul's for he portrays their ranks and order with almost ecstatic delight. But this love for the celestial society is really not comparable with anything else in the Bible, nor indeed with the Rabbinic or pseudepigraphic literature. If he is indebted to anyone it is to Philo whose angelology identifies the angels with "the army of incorporeal powers" (Plant. 14) and with the "divine, holy ideas" (Conf. 28). They carry out God's beneficent actions in the world and mediate his goodness, often as "the attendant messengers" in dreams (Som. I, 190 and passim). Therefore the angelic ministration always indicates a lack of permanence (Mut. 87), a sort of second-best

[1] J. B. Lightfoot, *St. Paul's Epistle to the Galatians,* 1892, ad loc.

[2] See pp. 163 ff.

quality when compared with God's uniquely excellent gifts (L. A. III, 177) and Philo appears in one place to recommend a somewhat nominal belief in angels, souls, and demons, all of whom are in the air and some of whom are holy and worthy (Gig. 16).

AND HEBREWS

But the fact of the pre-eminence of Jesus, viewed against the angelic background of a celestial society, gives the Epistle the mark of uniqueness. Far from belittling the glory of the *sod* or denying its reality or ignoring its function, the writer nevertheless must exempt the divine mediation of the Son of God from all angelic analogies. The God of Heaven cannot be mistaken for an angel. The Son is "so much better than the angels" because of his "more excellent name", that is his ontological heavenliness (Heb. I, 4–7). The angels are created and worship the God of Heaven, but they are not gods and do not save, however attractive such a drifting away (II, 1) from the truth may be. The humanity of Jesus admittedly makes him appear "a little lower than the angels" (II, 7, 9, quoting Ps. VIII), but the principle of salvation demanded from the beginning that men, and not angels, should be chosen for this purpose: "for surely it is not with angels that he is concerned but with the descendants of Abraham. Therefore he had to be made like his brethren in every respect. . . ." (II, 16–17). Hence the mediation of the Old Covenant or Word (II, 2), "spoken through angels", proved steadfast only as a preparation for the true Word. In the writer's mind the work of Christ excels the old by "so much more"; the *a fortiori* relationship acknowledges the part of the angels, without encouraging a belief in their mediation.

THE ANGELIC WARFARE

The apocalyptic strands of the New Testament, however, also resume those traditions of the *sod* which are not primarily concerned with the traffic between Heaven and earth. Apart from their participation in human affairs the counsellors stand on guard in Heaven in their own defence. Therefore it is their business to protect the righteous, whose allies they are, and to watch over the weak and pious: "he gives his angels charge of you to keep you in all your ways" (Ps. XCI, 11). This theme of martial assistance was tremendously popular. Even the non-apocalyptic Ben Sirach quotes the ancient story of the angel of the Lord who smote thousands of Assyrians by night (II K. XIX, 35; Sir. XLVIII, 21). The Temple resounded with the praise of the poor: "The angel of the Lord encamps around those who fear him and delivers them" (Ps. XXXIV, 7) and men on a journey gladly recalled the tradition of Moses who referred to the guiding angel in the Exodus (Nrs. XX, 16). Admittedly the presence of the protecting angels is hidden from the senses, but this deficiency gave point to the epic of Elisha's heroism who intervened successfully against Syria because he knew that the "mountain was full of horses and chariots of fire" and revealed the vision to his servant (II K. VI, 17). In the apocalyptic tradition, faith in angels amounts to vision. In the book of Daniel it is not only Michael who stands up for his people (XII, 1) but God delivers his servants from the lions' mouth by sending his angel (VI, 22). Nebuchadnezzar himself blesses God for the angelic deliverance of the men who endure the fiery trials (III, 28) and in his dream, which is a portent of his own lunacy and therefore of the end of his tyrannous rule, he has a vision of "a watcher and a holy one from Heaven". In the apocalyptic language the angel is a symbol of imminent liberation, of successful warfare and the triumph of the righteous.

The traces of this tradition in the New Testament are few but significant. The Lukan birth-stories proclaim the coming of the Saviour: therefore the stars blaze brightly at his birth and the angels precede the shepherds in their acclamation of the Messiah (II, 8 ff.). The pastoral and peaceful scene of the field near Bethlehem does not obscure but stresses the eschatological nature of the divine birth. The angels watch the son of God because they are themselves involved in the drama of salvation. Their first duty appears to be to protect the defenceless infant. The angel of the Lord prompts the flight into Egypt and later the holy family's return (Mt. II, 13, 19). Even more remarkable is the Lukan account of the Passion in a verse which many ancient authorities omit though it preserves a genuine tradition. According to Luke XXII, 43 an angel appeared to Jesus during the agony in the garden and strengthened the Lord. The Matthaean special source mentions the possibility of angelic intervention immediately after the Lord's arrest: the angels are pictured in military formation, standing at the ready and always in reserve (Mt. XXVI, 53). The saying may well reflect a need to explain why the angels failed at the crucial moment and permitted the Son of God to die: Jesus weighed up their ever-loyal readiness to intervene, but their destruction of evil at that hour would have been contrary to God's design of salvation. In other words, though they are powerful they cannot decide when their power may be used. It is clear that the angels are themselves subject to higher orders, especially in the eschatological struggle between God and evil.

The identification of the angels' struggle with the redemption of man goes further than the office of protection alone would indicate. It may be of help to remember that "there are different dispositions, partialities, and antipathies, among angels as in human society; there is no monotony of universal benevolence on high, nor is even justice dispassionate. And though there are no enmity, strife, hatred, or foes, in that place, still it is necessary for God to 'make peace in his high places' (Job XXV, 2)".[1] This contradictory, disharmonious note in the angelic society is partly due to the angels' traditional occupation with punishment. David had seen "the angel of the Lord stand between the earth and the Heaven, having a drawn sword in his hand stretched out over Jerusalem" and was too frightened to pass him (I Chron. XXI, 16, 30). The tradition of the destroying angel enlarged the theme of the protection of the righteous. The angel of the Lord not only serves as legal counsel in a forensic battle (as in Joshua's encounter with Satan in Zech. III) but also as the executioner after the verdict. Thus boastful Herod in the New Testament tradition comes to an ignominious end at his hands (Acts XII, 23). The destroying angels derive their power from the avenging Lord with whom they were sometimes confused, so that it was a matter of debate, for instance, whether the Lord himself or the angel had gone through the land of Egypt to execute judgment (Exod. XII, 12). It is not difficult to see that the presence of these "messengers of death", to whom the wrath of kings

[1] Cf. GFM, I, p. 407.

may be likened (Prov. XVI, 14), creates a tension in the heavenly society which itself calls for redemption. The Epistle of Jude and the Christian Apocalypse still retain the destroying angels for their part in the destruction of the ungodly. Plagues, death, and abyss are administered by the troops of Heaven, adding a catastrophic element to their campaign for righteousness. However, the central figure of the Lamb keeps their work in check and the punishing angels under Christ are no longer the national contenders who destroy the enemy of the side they happen to champion in a spirit of capricious *parti pris*.

CHRIST AND THE CELESTIAL SOCIETY

The war of the angels (Rev. XII, 7) is not merely a supporting campaign on behalf of struggling humanity. The heavenly council harbours no detached existence in apocalyptic thought, as if its members were merely looking on as a band of disinterested spectators. Michael leads his angels into a cosmic warfare of which all the tensions in the world and the earthly struggle are a reflection. The hierarchical order in Heaven is itself threatened from without and the earthly cause of God's redemption is the good angels' own.[1] The import of the Christian Apocalypse is the demonstration that the regional conflict occurs against a cosmic background. This widens the otherwise narrow rigidity of exclusive earthly concerns—whether of Israel or of the Church—to a supernatural universalism. The society of Heaven experiences the same crisis as the Church on earth. Both are found wanting and have to be refashioned and both look to Jesus Christ as the author and finisher of their re-creation. He is not only the centre of their adoration, but also the effective redeemer of their existence. They accompany him through his life and Passion to the tomb and hail his Resurrection and visit with him the place of the departed and flank his glory at the Ascension. They prepare for the final harvest, which is as much their own as that of mankind (Mt. XIII, 39). But notwithstanding their intimacy with God's plans they are kept in ignorance of the day

[1] Cf. IQH III, 35 f. in T. H. Gaster's translation: "... the hosts of Heaven give forth their voice, and the world's foundations rock and reel; when warfare waged by the soldiers of Heaven sweeps through the world and turns not back until final doom—warfare the like of which has never been". Cf. also IQM passim.

and hour of the end of Heaven and earth, the secret of the Father (Mk. XIII, 32). Until they mass under Michael for the final battle against the foe they must remain in a state of expectancy. Then they will come again with the Son of Man (Mt. XXV, 31) and gather the elect together from the uttermost part of the earth to the uttermost part of Heaven (Mk. XIII, 27).

These things are still of the future. The angels are also subject to the stress of the eschatological expectation and their ignorance of the date gives a dramatic urgency to their active ministry. The strange passage in I Peter I, 12 refers to their own need in the redemptive process: the preachers' evangelistic work by the Holy Ghost excites their interest and they desire to stoop down from Heaven to see the progress of the Gospel, probably as evidenced by the baptismal rite. They do not mediate the Gospel but, as they are witnesses in Heaven, they now extend their witness to the earth. At first one is apt to ascribe this activity to evil angels, whose spying is a prelude to their malicious interference, as we shall try to show in the next chapter. Here, however, hostility does not seem to be their motive but that form of self-interest which the eschatological situation causes everywhere in the Church: "the circumstances of the Church and the progress of its redemptive work are such as to excite the rapt attention of the angels".[1] If they peer into the baptismal secret it is not in order to vitiate its effects but in order to help it by their "contemplative share in the work of the redemption".[2]

THE CHURCH IN HEAVEN

After the final consummation the heavenly society achieves perfection at last. God unites for his glory's sake the new man with his truthful sons and holy ones (cf. IQH XI, 11f.). In his vision of the final state the seer of the Apocalypse removes the separation between the heavenly members and the earthly saints. All the "holy ones" are united in the multitude of the faithful: saints, apostles, prophets, the twenty-four elders, the martyrs, and

[1] Cf. E. G. Selwyn, *The First Epistle of St. Peter,* 1946, p. 138 for this quotation and a full discussion of the text.

[2] Ibid., p. 139, for a quotation from B. Weiss, *Manual of Introduction to the New Testament,* I, p. 355.

all the dead, great and small, recovered from the sea, Hades and death, assemble in Heaven and this humanity in Christ joins the celestial society. This is the new order which comes into being after the defeat of the universal enemy. The last chapters of the Apocalypse culminate in a picture which breaks new ground for it is now the Church of Christ which houses the ancient *sod* and fulfils its function. The heavenly society becomes grafted into Christ and ceases to stand over against human society: they sing God's praises in their respective choirs (Rev. v, 8 f.; xiv, 3; xv, 2 f.). This happy consummation is already anticipated in the potential union of the earthly and heavenly race (πατριά) which the invocation of Ephesians iii, 14–15 implies.

THE PERILS OF ANGELOLOGY

The unique contribution of the Christian Apocalypse in its treatment of the heavenly host can best be measured against the background of innumerable apocalypses which circulated at the same time among Jews, Christians, and Gnostics. In these the dualistic tendency becomes very pronounced. In Enoch the nations' guardian angels are the enemies of Israel, the seventy shepherds who exceed their hostile mission against Israel in the destruction of the sheep (lxxxix, 59 ff. and cf. Lk. x, 1–12 for a possible counter-motif). If these forces are to be identified with the angels who refused the Torah at Sinai[1] and are leagued together under Satan's command[2] the good angels must be portrayed in a more radical, dualistic manner than the Hebrew tradition suggests. In the Christian Apocalypse of Paul,[3] for example, they stand on watch for news and help the martyrs even to the end. They assume responsibility over their charges whom they are thought to resemble. In the battle of the faith they act as ministers of punishment. Hence even the good angels are involved in violence and forensic execution. The Enoch tradition goes furthest in the speculation of legendary heroes and supernatural helpers above.

It is impossible to say at which point the extreme apocalyptic

[1] Cf. Str. B. III, p. 49 f.

[2] Str. B. I, p. 142.

[3] In ch. viii; cf. M. R. James, *The Apocryphal New Testament*, 1924, p. 528 ff.

writings stand outside the main tradition and become frankly heterodox. However, when the angelic helpers tend to become gods and when their mediation arrogates to itself divine features we pass from Biblical to Gnostic-inspired apocalyptic. Among the Jewish-Gnostic emanations the most important is the enigmatic Metatron, probably the Next-to-the-Throne (*μετὰ* [*τὸν*] *θρόνον*), the celestial chancellor, or perhaps only an angel, Metator (Latin for 'measurer'), i.e. the measuring angel.[1] Such Gnostic inventions purported to come out of the text of Exodus XXIII, 21 ("My name is in him") which appears to have evoked this display of dubious ingenuity. As soon as the doctrine of emanation is brought to bear upon texts of this kind there is no end of possible beings who reflect divine radiance and pass it on again to some lower species. The "little Yahweh" in III Enoch, for example, is the product of the same reasoning and similar to the Christ of the Gnostics, who, apart from God, if not against God, is considered lord of the celestial forces.[2]

What is surprising under these circumstances is not the development of angelology but that its existence was tolerated at all. Important exhortations are uttered "in the sight of God, and of Christ Jesus, and of the elect angels" (I Tim. V, 21). The first-century evidence from Christian sources proves that belief in angels persisted and that restraint was by no means popular. Clement and Hermas simply agree that good angels exist and that they belong to the same universe which Christ has redeemed on earth. In the fifth vision the Shepherd of Hermas cites the evidently accepted tradition that the Angel of Penance intercedes with God for the penitent on earth. Again, Justin can reply soberly that Christians are not atheists and "worship the host of good angels" (Apol. I, 6). They were created at the beginning and exist permanently, not as emanations but as personal beings with quasi-human bodies and free and responsible natures. Nevertheless, the Gnostic impact kept angelology in check in the Church's doctrine; heretical extravagances, which the pseudepigraphical

[1] Cf. VT. I, 1951, pp. 217–19 for M. Black, 'The Origin of the Name Metatron'.

[2] Cf. Odeberg, III Enoch XII, 5. The date of this book is probably as late as the 10th *C.* A.D., but the traditions of Metatron are much earlier. Cf. *Pistis Sophia* 7 for Jesus, born of the seed of little Jao.

writings anticipate, were apt to sour the whole subject, especially concerning the ranks and the mediation of heavenly beings. Moreover, the Gnostics' endless spheres and corresponding emanations must distort the picture of creation altogether. Thus Ignatius concedes that "heavenly things", such as the places of angels and the gatherings of principalities, may actually cause harm among the Trallians, "seeing you are babes" (Trall. v). He restores the New Testament emphasis on Christ as the rightful Lord of the angels: "Let no one be deceived; even things in Heaven and the glory of the angels, and the rulers visible and invisible, even for them there is a judgment if they do not believe in the blood of Christ." (Smyrnaeans VI). As formerly in Israel all the tidal waves of speculation, no doubt released by the extreme pressure of political and social events, always flowed into monotheistic channels, so now in the Church Christ must be the focal point of the heavenly society. Thus the apocalyptic genius could still serve the new world-view of Christian institutions.

Chapter Five

THE ENEMY OF HEAVEN

THE preceding consideration of the Society of Heaven led to the surprising discovery that this society is, in apocalyptic thought, rent asunder and poised for war, not only on earth but in the very Heavens themselves. The good angels are keen sharers in the mystery of Christian redemption which they, like human beings, need in order to be set free from the attacks of evil forces. Their status after the triumph of Christ is infinitely safer and more felicitous than before the act of salvation began. Who, then, is the enemy of the celestial order and where is he to be placed in Christian thought?

THE EARTHLY ENEMY

Although the writings in the Old Testament display an almost constant awareness of the enemy, his identity is often quite ambiguous. Yet in the vast majority of cases the enemy is of this earth. There is to begin with the foe within the family: Cain kills his brother Abel. Children are seen to rise up against their father and destroy the family: the tribes of Simeon and Levi bring calamity and dishonour upon Jacob (Gen. XXXIV). Furthermore there is the hidden enemy within the camp and no peace can be had until he is exterminated, like Achan upon whom falls the lot of the guilt of private gain (Josh. VII). In the desert almost the whole congregation may be regarded as God's enemy and must be blotted out. Later Israel and Judah were locked in strife until the former vanished and with it an element of bitter enmity. But the traditional enemies of the Hebrews in Canaan are the tribes and bedouins in adjacent territories which never ceased to attack. Moab and Edom continued to be a thorn in the flesh of the remnant nation. Then the great world-powers, Assyria, Egypt, Babylon, Persia, Macedonia, the heirs of Alexander's short-lived empire, and lastly Rome herself were frequently regarded as nothing more than enemies. In all these traditions the earthly foe strikes from outside in a clash of national interests.

The prophets, however, always insisted that alongside the social and political enemies of this world there was to be numbered the enemy in the nation's heart and even in the individual. The most serious indictment is always reserved for the "sinful nation, a people laden with iniquity, offspring of evildoers, sons who deal corruptly" (Is. I, 4) of whom God will avenge himself (I, 24). The individual heart is "deceitful", "sick" (Jer. XVII, 9), stubborn and perverted (Ezek. XI, 19–21); the common pride and self-indulgence cause the enmity of sin and guilt; punishment becomes a moral necessity and men who sin act as their own executioners under God. Here man is the enemy; hence "the haughty looks of man shall be brought low" (Is. II, 11).

In view of the influence of prophetic teaching it would be absurd to assert that the Old Testament acknowledges a celestial enemy in many cases of struggle and suffering. On the contrary the avoidance of a mythical subterfuge to account for evil is remarkable. Terror, consumption, fever, famine, for example, are sent by God on those who break the covenant (Lev. XXVI, 16). It is the Lord who "will smite you with the boils of Egypt, and with ulcers, and with the scurvy, and with the itch, of which you cannot be healed" (Dt. XXVIII, 27). Hence Isaiah identifies the sickness of the nation with its revolt: the festering sores are incurable (Is. I, 5 f.).

"EVIL-DOERS"

There is, however, one enemy who does not fit into these relatively simple categories. The Psalmist (speaking in the enigmatic first person 'I') continually complains of and prays to be protected from his attacks and to be delivered out of his power. Now this evil-doer is sometimes, but by no means always, another hostile power on earth or the traitor within. In his great work Mowinckel suggested that these evil-doers inflict some form of disease on their victims by means of magical formulae. They are really magicians working with spell and net. But an examination of some passages shows that this concession to the supernatural does not go far enough and that this enemy often represents the enemy of all human existence who is rightly feared and whose onslaughts must be averted by solemn ritual.[1]

This enemy is in some measure still of this earth and often portrayed by the lion and the snake (Ps. XCI). He shows a close affinity with the desert *jinn* whose demonic animal nature enables him to raise himself above the earth and to float in the air. Such dangerous spirits are near the earth, though also in the air if not yet in Heaven. How far an earthly demon can outgrow the lower region it is impossible to say. Some demons—as, e.g., the Babylonian *šedu* or avenging spirits—assail men and beasts from Heaven and must not be confused with the *jinn*.

In the apocalyptic tradition the celestial enemy is not a raised earthly demon. He espouses the interests of Israel's enemies and brings about the despair of the age from above. If possible he would destroy the whole world for he personifies the destructive principle itself. His provenance extends to every known type of hostility on earth. In the Old Testament his origin takes us back again to the Council of the Bene Elohim.

FOES IN HEAVEN

The celestial enemy never appears as an identifiable person, such as the devil, in the early traditions of the *sod*. Thus the enticing spirit who is a lying spirit in Ahab's prophets (I K. XXII, 21 f.) is, in Micaiah's vision, among the host of Heaven and actually dispatched by God. He is as evil as the "evil spirit" (Ruach Ra'ah) who descends upon Abimelech (Jdg. IX, 22) and Saul (I Sam. XVI, 14). Yet he is among the Elohim, just as the Satan-Adversary is also found among them in Heaven (Job II, 1). These Elohim are potentially enemies in Heaven for they can turn to evil itself, oppose God and his angels, and ultimately become evil in essence. The picture of the assizes in Ps. LXXXII

[1] Cf. Gunkel's probably conclusive criticism (*Einleitung in die Psalmen*, 1933, pp. 176 ff.) of Mowinckel's brilliant but inadequate thesis which breaks down over his generalization of *'Aven* (*Psalmenstudien* I, 1913).

is understandable for they are now accused of apostasy as instigators of unrighteousness, associated with darkness. They are deprived of their immortality and sentenced to death. Judaism used the Elohim-concept to account for the existence of pagan gods, who were, after all, real for their own nations and often hostile to the Jews. Indeed, the Bene Elohim could be considered neutral until they had committed themselves politically; their true nature was made evident through the behaviour of the nations to Israel whose patrons they are until God abolishes their power and enters into their heritage.

These Elohim were, like the good angels, celestial from the beginning and associated with the stars and the spheres. It was always held that sun, moon, and stars had their favourites in battle and that they engaged in earthly strife. Thus the triumph of the central tribes of Israel was ascribed to celestial help (Jdg. v, 20). The stars' influence is noted in the calendars of the ancient world and solicited by the prominence given to them in its cultic ritual. The hostility of some astral powers could be evidenced by ill-luck or even the loss of battles. The hostile stars ranked equal with the presiding gods, determined human affairs and had to be placated together. The Mishnah preserves something of this tradition in the picture of God who sits in judgment over *all* the inhabitants of the world on New Year's Day (R.H.I, 2).

As the stars and the Bene Elohim are classed together to form the celestial hierarchy under God, so the hostile stars and the evil Bene Elohim also belong together. All stars display distinctions of rank by their brightness, as St. Paul notes: "one star differs from another in glory" (I Cor. xv, 41). Strangely enough the most luminous of all planets is singled out as an enemy. First associated with the pagan goddess of fertility and later with Venus, this star also personifies the arrogant defiance of God by all pagan pomp, but particularly the pride of the King of Babylon: "How are you fallen from Heaven, O Day Star, son of Dawn" (Is. xiv, 12). The oracle echoes the old tradition of El's unsuccessful counter-revolution to regain the sovereignty from which he had been deposed and is adapted for political purposes against rulers who would usurp God's place, ascend into Heaven, and sit in his seat (Ez. xxviii, 2–19). The attempted self-exaltation leads to a shameful downfall for the political move is not unconnected with a cosmic background. The evil angels, "the host of the high ones", will be punished because of their share in this ungodly pride (Is. XXIV, 21) and the dissolution of the Heavens coincides with that of the "host of Heaven", astral or angelic (Is. XXXIV, 4).

In later apocalyptic thought the disobedience of the stars gains momentum. As they are conceived of as intelligent and living beings they are also responsible for their actions. They transgress the divine commandment by failing to observe the times of their appointed rising. The book of Enoch is quite explicit on this point: "I saw a place which had no firmament of the Heaven above, and no firmly founded earth beneath it: there was no water upon it, and no birds, but it was a waste and horrible place. I saw there seven stars like great burning mountains, and to me, when I enquired regarding them, the angel said: 'This place is the end of Heaven and earth: this has become a prison for the stars and the host of Heaven.'" God has bound them until their guilt comes to an end, namely for 10,000 years (XVIII, 12–16; XXI, 1–6). In the Christian Apocalypse a third part of the stars are under condemnation (Rev. VIII, 12). The wonders in Heaven and the withdrawal of light testify to the insurrection of stellar-angelic forces against God and the Society of Heaven. Therefore the final judgment is heralded by the fall of great stars from Heaven (Rev. IX, 1).

DARKNESS

The most obvious celestial omen of hostility is the darkness, especially the extraordinary darkness which is opposed to light itself. It recalls the ancient tradition of the chaos when "the earth was waste and void and darkness was upon the face of the deep" (Gen. I, 2). It conveys the dread of distress and death and becomes a symbol of judgment: "Why would you have the day of the Lord? it is darkness, and not light" (Amos V. 18), a day of wrath, distress, anguish, ruin, devastation, darkness, gloom, clouds, thick darkness (Zeph. I, 15). The eschatological confusion on earth is directly related to the extinction of the light of Heaven so that even "the sun shall be turned to darkness and the moon into blood, before the great and terrible day of the Lord come" (Joel II, 31; Mk. XIII, 24).

The outer darkness corresponds to that within. The Qumran texts support the New Testament in regarding the darkness itself as morally corrupt: "from the fountains of darkness are the springs of perversity" (IQS III, 19); the deeds of the wicked are in darkness and all they desire is darkness (IQM XV, 9 f.). Men prefer darkness because they love evil (Jn. III, 19). It is a power which would overtake and overwhelm the light (I, 5; XII, 35). It has a dominion (I Pe. II, 9) which is opposed to God (I Jn. I, 5), being the complete denial of his glory. Judas walks into the night, the realm of treachery (Jn. XIII, 30) and Paul calls darkness, the devil's appropriate sphere, upon Elymas the sorcerer (Acts XIII, 10, 11). It lies over the land at noon during the Crucifixion (Mk. XV, 33). If darkness is perhaps too impersonal to be itself the celestial enemy it is at least the realm of his power, analogous to the realm of light in Heaven which belongs to God.

In the Biblical tradition no attempt is made to account for the rise of the celestial enemy and his obvious success which endangers the whole world. The good and omnipotent God is not opposed by an omnipotent force of darkness. The monotheistic fervour circumvents dualistic notions by the tremendous affirmation: "I form the light, and create darkness" (Is. XLV, 7) for neither darkness nor evil is independent in itself; for even though dark forces dominate the perverse and even tempt the righteous yet ultimately it is God who created these spirits of light and darkness, establishing every work accordingly (IQS III, 20–6), as manifestations of his power. By separating both, God prevents discord and chaos (Op. 32 ff.). The apocalyptic writers looked elsewhere to explain the presence of the enemy.

THE MYTH OF THE FALLEN ANGELS

The narrative in Genesis VI, 1–6, provided a suggestive answer. Taken by itself, in its proper context, this story of the mythological giants is perplexing enough. It recalls the dim past before history and treats of the wickedness of man on earth. No certain reason can be given why this terse account was inserted at this point of the narrative and at what period of the making of the Old Testament. Like so much in the great prelude in Genesis it forms part of a very ancient tradition which secured its perpetuation in the Canon when Monotheism had been established and ancient myths had become safe and could be adjusted to dogmatic rules. As the story stands it contains no reference to the Fall of the Angels. It hints at the empirical fact of the evil imagination in an almost casual manner; no wonder Philo allegorizes the motif most successfully to illustrate the descent of human souls from their true home (Gig. 12–15; 60 ff.).

Nevertheless, it is this particular story which the apocalyptic writers developed with freedom to their own use. In the book of Daniel "the watchers" appear in Nebuchadnezzar's dream and serve as the executioners of the Most High (IV, 13, 17, 23) and are not yet identical with the Bene Elohim of Genesis, chapter VI. But the Damascus movement already speaks of "the watchers of Heaven" who walked in the stubbornness of their hearts and fell from Heaven (CD II, 18). This theme is taken up by many pseudepigraphical writers and they may well have gone back to the original intention of the myth, namely the condemnation of the unlawful intercourse between the Bene Elohim and the daughters of man. Originally good (Jub. IV, 15), the watchers are caught in carnal lust and rebel against the divine order; before the Flood they have lost their privilege and smarting under the expulsion from Heaven they armed themselves to regain Heaven by force and to enthrone themselves there. For this purpose they war against humanity or try to enlist human beings in their ranks.[1]

The texts cannot tell us how far they express literal beliefs. In the more restrained allusions the tradition is made subservient to the general themes of the history of civilization and divine Providence. The book of Wisdom gives a brief, sober, and allegorizing glance at "antiquity when overweening giants were perishing" (XIV, 6) and Ben Sirah includes them in a survey of sinners and cites them for their subversive strength in pre-

[1] Cf. Enoch chs. VI–XI; Jub. ch. V; T. Reub. ch. V; T. Napht. III, 5; S. Ap. Bar. LVI, 10–13. For an interesting variation cf. Vit. Ad. chs. XII–XVII. The devil rebelled because of his refusal to worship Adam, conceiving himself senior to the despised "image of God".

historic times (XVI, 7). Baruch contrasts them and their war-like strength and folly with the true wisdom in Heaven and the greatness of Israel (III, 26–8).

In the book of Enoch the moderation yields to a radical, though still symbolical, belief in fallen angels. They no longer belong to a mythical past but are to be reckoned with as a power at the present time. In a dream vision of the deluge (ch. LXXXIII) Enoch blesses God and in this formal acclamation he states: "And now the angels of thy Heavens are guilty of trespass" (LXXXIV, 4). This point is taken up in chapter LXXXVI in a symbolic fantasy: A falling star (=Azazel?) arises and pastures among the oxen, who leave their stalls; the cattle live in promiscuity. Then many stars descend and join the first star and turn into bulls. They have intercourse among the cattle and beget elephants, camels, and asses. The oxen panic and are devoured (LXXXVII). Presently seven archangels appear and punish the fallen angels. The first star is bound hand and foot and is cast into an abyss. The progeny of sexual promiscuity slay each other and the remaining stars also perish (LXXXVIII). The earlier chapters elucidate the puzzling events for "these are the angels who descended to the earth, and revealed what was hidden to the children of men, and seduced the children of men into committing sin" (LXIV). The secrets of these angels concern sorcery, witchcraft, and idolatry, and the arts and industries of pagan civilizations. Mining and work in metals are suspect as derived from them and no doubt also because they lead to war. The angels are damned and have no repentance (LXV), they are held in check by the angels of punishment (LXVI), in a valley of fire and sulphur, in order to burn away their spiritual lust in their bodies (LXVII). These angels are the chiefs who seduced the Bene Elohim by enticing them to lust after women, by creating violence and war, and by propagating the decadent forms of civilization (LXVIII).

Two passages in the New Testament on judgment refer to the angels' disobedience as if it lay in the past. The writer of II Peter threatens: "If God did not spare angels when they sinned, but cast them into hell . . ." (II, 4) and in a similar vein Jude (v. 6) bids his readers remember "angels that did not keep their own position but left their proper dwelling". This optimistic estimate echoes the conclusion of the Enochian parable where the Son of Man sentences these angels from his throne of glory.

NON-MYTHICAL WATCHERS

St. Paul takes a very different view. He assumes the existence of evil angels in the present. "Do you not know that we are to judge angels?" asks the Apostle when he condemns the Corinthians' resorting to litigation (I Cor. VI, 2 f.). The members of Christ share in the sovereignty of Christ and are themselves involved in the final trial of the arch-rebels. St. Paul evidently dislikes rather than fears them. They are heartless spectators of the Apostles' humiliations (IV, 9). Their presence at the gladiatorial combat shows that they are not moved to compassion by the ordeal of the righteous. Yet they are not indifferent, for why do they attend the cruel display of privations and martyrdom? They are still bent on the conquest of the world and to that end they intrigue as ever before. Their spying impels caution: because of the angels "a woman's head must be veiled" (XI, 10).[1] Theirs is a perversion of the angelic curiosity; unlike the loyal ministers, who peer into the Christian secret, they continue in the illicit desire to lust after and mingle with women, who are therefore more vulnerable than men to the ambushes of evil power. They are watchers of and for evil and there may be said to be joy outside Heaven when men sin and do not repent, inasmuch as the cause of the celestial rebels increases in promise and Heaven itself may fall to them.

The evil angels' onslaught on humanity is, however, not to be identified with all evil as such. Over-simplification is out of place in the New Testament as it is in the Old. Thus an important passage in Mark reiterates the prophetic teaching that evil proceeds from within (VII, 21–3) and a warning in I Timothy IV, 1 even goes so far as to identify the seducing spirits with demonology, almost as if to suggest that too much concern with

[1] It remains debatable whether these angels act as guardians of the natural order or as envoys of the rulers of this world. The element of danger to which the women are exposed seems to favour the latter view. Cf. also for this *crux interpretum* G. B. Caird, *Principalities and Power,* 1956, pp. 17 ff. The reading in IQSa II, 8–9 favours the view that the good angels of the creation are present at the Church's meetings.

demons may work havoc with people's moral wills. But the Gospel narratives do relate the demons with the supernatural, even if local Palestinian belief may have associated them with earthly *jinn*. In the Markan Gospel they are primarily spiritual enemies—"unclean spirits" as of old (I, 23 ff.; III, 11; V, 2 ff.; VI, 7; VII, 25; IX, 25)—who sense the advent of Jesus as a disaster for themselves. They inhabit their victims as forces from outside and resist expulsion until the power of God proves stronger than their own. Their immense power testifies to something resembling angelic status (cf. Jub. X, 5; CD XVI, 5; Vit. Ad. XVI) which enables them to evaluate events in their proper light: the conflict with Jesus concerns their whole campaign in the universe. They must resist, otherwise they are lost. The events surrounding the restoration of the Gadarene demoniac illustrate the rightness of their fears. The drowning devils are captured in the swine and rendered harmless by their removal from the air (Mk. V, 13). Therefore the place under the earth, whether it be called Hades or the pit or the abyss, is assigned to them not as their true domicile but as a place of punishment when their exile from their heavenly home is finally established.

The most comprehensive and remarkable passage is found in Luke X, 17–20. The mission of the seventy is probably, as we saw, the counter-stroke against the nations with their seventy angels. In it culminates the subjection of demons to the Name of Jesus, who, in his reply, immediately links this exorcism of evil powers with the expulsion of Satan from Heaven. The comment retains the flavour of the oracle in Isaiah XIV, 12: the vision of Satan, falling with the suddenness of lightning from Heaven, belongs to the eschatological Now, the switch from the old to the new age, evidenced by the acts of power. The cosmic event crowns the victory over the angelic dominion.

SATAN

This expulsion of Satan necessarily raises the question whether it is the result of Christ's work on earth, as traditional exegesis maintains, or the fall before the Flood.[1] Before the final clash,

[1] For the import of the difficult tenses—ἐθεώρουν (impf.), πεσόντα (aor. part.) see commentaries ad loc. and pp. 178 ff.

at any rate, Satan's power is not diminished. His presence on earth, on the contrary, helps his angels to mobilize their full strength—"serpents, scorpions, all the power of the enemy" (Lk. x, 19)—against which Jesus now formally pits his own power. The context clearly expresses the belief that the evil powers also are organized as a hierarchical body. In another account of an exorcism (Mt. xii, 25 ff.) the point is specifically made that the kingdom of Satan is undivided. Jesus by the power of the Spirit of God breaks into this stronghold and robs Satan of his goods and therefore challenges the enemy to reveal his full, celestial strength. Needless to say this is not an enemy to be loved, for God himself shakes the foundations of the Kingdom of Satan. Its powers are not to be underestimated. "Rejoice not that the spirits are subject unto you," warns Jesus (Lk. x, 20) in anticipation of the full unfolding of the enemy's might. He would undermine the Lord's own army; therefore Satan "asks" for Simon (Lk. xxii, 31) in order to counter-attack and break into the defences of the Kingdom of God. The disciples' safety lies in their names being "written in Heaven" and in Jesus' own intercession in Heaven against Satanic enticements (Lk. x, 20; xxii, 32).

The celestial ranks of evil are headed by the chief enemy or the Satan of the New Testament. This conception swallows up the names and functions of leading figures (En. ch. vi) such as Azazel, Mastema (Jub. x. 8; En. viii, 1; IQS. iii, 20 f.; CD iv, 13; v, 18; viii, 2; xvi, 5), and Sammael (Asc. Is. vii), who ambush the godly and obstruct the course of righteousness. In the New Testament there are not many Satans (as in En. xl, 7) but only one Satan with whom Belial or Beliar, the great figurehead of evil in apocalyptic literature, the Greek Diabolos, the Prince of this world and God of this aeon are identified. Even the popular term of abuse 'Beezeboul' loses its independent ring when Jesus identifies the power with Satan (Mt. xii, 25).[1]

[1] Cf. also Mk. iii, 22, Lk. xi, 15, Mt. x, 25 for the same strange form Βεεζεβουλ which does not occur in Jewish literature and has nothing to do with the Baal Zebub, god of Ekron (IIK. i, 2) nor with Baal Devav, god of enmity. If Baal Zebul is the original reading the name designates an evil heavenly power, Lord of the Zebul, which is reminiscent of the epithet zbl of the Ugaritic Baal (cf. CML, B I VI 10).

The Christian interpretations go in many respects beyond the Jewish conception of Satan, where despite his evil commission he still retains constant access to Heaven, if only to accuse the guilty and to obtain permission to capture the booty of their souls.[1] As in the book of Job, he appears as a kind of public attorney or prosecutor; as in the early parts of the Old Testament (e.g. Nrs. XXII, 22) the Jewish Satan is still an earthly adversary: he tempts as he had tempted David (I Chron. XXI, 1) and opposes the priests as he had fought against Joshua until rebuked by God (Zech. III, 1). When legend adds that as 'hassatan' has the numerical value of 364 Satan's power is in abeyance on the 365th day, namely on the Day of Atonement, one cannot help feeling that the whole figure, though celestial, is perhaps a little legendary altogether.[2]

The picture in the New Testament is more threatening. The Epistles to the Corinthians are particularly revealing just because they are not primarily apocalyptic in character. The "rulers of this world" are totally devoid of God's eternal plan for the world; their share in the Crucifixion is proof of their ignorance which is due to their separation from God (I Cor. II, 8). The power of Satan is formidable and still extant after the Resurrection. A fornicator, a so-called Christian, is to be expelled from the Church in the name of Christ (V, 3 ff.). His punishment consists of being "delivered to Satan for the destruction of the flesh", for he is "the natural ruler where God's authority is disowned".[3] The thought of the consequences of such a handing over to Satan is notoriously difficult and concerns us here only to the extent that it suggests that Satan can still destroy the flesh but is no longer able to ruin the spirit or carry away a soul for himself. On earth he certainly continues in his role as tempter. He entices men and women to infidelity (VII, 5). The end of the age brings the whole pattern of temptation and destruction to a head (X, 6–11) and Christ must rule until all his enemies—false

[1] bBaba Bathra 15 b f.

[2] bYoma 20 a.

[3] Cf. R. S. J. Parry, op. cit., ad loc. and ad II, 6. The passage also reflects the almost paradoxical belief that Satan and Belial act as punishing angels of sinners. This office does not imply that its holders are righteous, but rather as in many unhappy modern camps and prisons, wholly corrupt.

sovereignty, authority, and power—are abolished (xv, 25). Death (Thanatos) is personified as the last power to be overcome (xv, 26) and again seems far more terrible than the angel of Death in Judaism (b Avoda Zara 20 a–b). Similar ideas recur in the second Epistle to the Corinthians. Satan sends a messenger to torment the Apostle with a thorn in his flesh (xii, 7) and attacks the community with cunning plots to obtain an advantage (ii, 11). He still wields the power of furthering his lying apostolate by putting on a mask and posing as a member of the heavenly host, "an angel of light" (xi, 13–15). His heavenly guise enables him to give visions and inspirations, though Satan is, in fact, no longer admitted to the heavenly host; he is plainly the enemy of God, the mythical monster, the Antichrist, the Devil, who will bring his subversive lawlessness to a terrible climax before he is finally unmasked as a liar and deprived of all power (II Thess. ii, 9 f.).

Again the documents do not tell us whether the Apostle and the recipients of his letters took these things literally or left a considerable margin for symbolical interpretation. St. Paul's interest, we may be sure, is never in 'Satanology' as such, but in the missionary experience of diabolical interference.[1] But he manifestly thinks of this interference in terms which include the outside, supernatural world where rebellious powers are let loose which affect the whole universe. For this reason there can be no compromise between Christ and Belial (II Cor. vi, 15), for this fight unfolds the meaning of the whole history of the universe. Satan is god of the perishing aeon and claims adherents from those who perish in it (iv, 3f.) and no longer see the light in their dark world where demons and the demonic cause irreparable damage. Such a Satan certainly does not belong to a world of metaphor or mythological exaggeration nor indeed to a prehistoric past. Inasmuch as the enemy is worshipped and served as, or in the place of, God, he is 'real' and enslaves humanity as lord (Ro. i, 25) and therefore must be bruised by God shortly (xvi, 20).

Christians may not doubt the existence of evil angels though they are free from the constraint of these demonic powers. The gods in Heaven and on earth (I Cor. viii, 5) resemble the idols

[1] Cf. M. Dibelius, *Die Geisterwelt im Glauben des Paulus,* 1909, pp. 190 ff.

in that they exist for those who serve them (VIII, 4), and not for those who know that there is only one God (VIII, 6). Nevertheless, the illusory character of the evil powers does not lessen their menace, and St. Paul is very chary of commending a simple optimistic disregarding of their existence. Even in points of diet and general conduct it is still imperative to withdraw from communion with devils, however unreal they may be for Christians (X, 19–21). There is after all a table and a cup of devils.

COSMIC FORCES

St. Paul's lack of interest in the ranks of evil angels does not, however, deprive them of celestial functions. He complicates the matter—for us, not for the original recipients of his warnings—by the use of the ambiguous term 'beggarly elements' (Gal. IV, 9), for he seems to identify these angels with the *στοιχεῖα*, the 'letters of the alphabet' or rudiments of the world (Gal. IV, 3).[1] The Jews did not generally hold that the elements and their angels were anything but good (cf. En. XLI) and Philo agrees with this tradition (Cher. 127) though he also links them with the gods and regards them as lifeless matter, incapable of movement, and the raw material, so to speak, for shape and quality (Cont. 3–4). In what sense, then, did the Apostle speak of 'rudiments'? Only a few ancient commentators looked upon them as unheavenly elements, such as inadequate beginnings or modes of teaching (e.g. Jerome, following herein the meaning of Hebr. V, 12). The majority discerned some cosmic elements, whether physical, astral, angelic, or spiritual. This broad association with supernatural realities seems to be demanded by the context in which the 'rudiments' are placed in the Epistle to the Colossians where philosophies and traditions, cultic observances and angels are equally involved in the indictment (II, 8–20). It further appears that the characteristic feature of the 'rudiments' is that they exercise a wrongful and somewhat impersonal compulsion on those who ought to deem themselves free.[2]

[1] "Seldom can a word have had a more interesting etymological history" comments G. H. C. Macgregor, *Principalities and Powers,* NTS, I, 21.

[2] A theme further illumined in the early 3rd-century 'Bardaisan'; cf. W. H. P. Hatch, JTS XXVIII, 1927, pp. 181 f.

Of deterministic forces in the Hellenistic thought-world there was no lack, and it may well be that St. Paul means to comprehend them all. It seems very unlikely that air, fire, earth, and water can be referred to in these passages, except as far as they may be said to belong to those fundamental notions as well as to those elementary forms of religion which endanger the freedom of Christian converts. It is true that for St. Paul the Law, though good in itself, brings about the logical sequel of sin, guilt, and death (Ro. v, 12 ff.) and in that sense must bring a Judaizing community back into bondage. But if the denunciation of the 'rudiments' has an anti-Judaistic ring about it at all this may well point to sectarian Jewish beliefs rather than normative Judaism with its great stress on moral freedom (cf. the famous passage Ab. III, 15 "right of choice is granted").[1] The apocalyptic movements had developed heavenly determinism to such a degree that it was not always very different from fatalistic predestinarianism.

This determinism, whether in religion or philosophy, ultimately always goes back to some cosmic principle. The promiscuity of good fortune and life's dependence not on merit but rather on the constellations (*mazzal*) evidence the compulsion of destiny (b Moed Katon 28a). The Rabbis do not subscribe in general or without contradiction to planetary influences and they even struggle against the "dismay at the signs of Heaven" (Jer. x, 2) and read freedom from, or favour of, astral constellations into the tradition of Abraham's call (Is. XLI, 2). Nevertheless, "not the constellation of the day but that of the hour is determining" and every planet makes its contribution: the sun gives distinction, Venus wealth and immorality, Mercury wisdom and a retentive memory, etc. (bShab. 156 a).

These Jewish reminiscences reflect the unbroken common tradition of elementary powers to which, in Babylon, even the high gods were subjected, their fate also depending upon the writing of the sky. The Olympic gods, and particularly Zeus, were not free and almost like mortals had "no release from predestined calamity" (*Antigone* 1337 f.). Nemesis, Moira, Tyche, whether

[1] For the difficulties of translation and meaning in the full context cf. Danby's note on the variants (*The Mishnah,* 1938, p. 452); also the note in the Soncino Talmud ad loc.

as gods or as concepts, determined the fate of men because they lived in a universe of elementary cosmic causes. Stoic teaching connected Providence with both Fate and Nature.[1] Since, then, the world is admittedly sinful it follows that this universe of necessity is governed by evil powers. No wonder the Colossians emulated their Galatian brethren in the endeavour to placate them and to get on good terms with them. St. Paul acknowledges their power, though in a sense very different from the astral-cosmic tradition of the offenders. They believe in accommodating Christ to them, he believes in Christ's exposure of their non-entity through his abolition of their power.

THE REBELLIOUS UNIVERSE

The awareness of evil in the New Testament inevitably stresses not only the popular belief in diabolical forces but also their astonishing presence in all circumstances. "Be sober, be watchful: your adversary the devil, as a roaring lion, walketh about, seeking whom he may devour" (I Pe. v, 8). The mobility of the enemy corresponds to his ability to act everywhere and at the same time, and this distinguishes him altogether from an ordinary earthly enemy. He exercises special power in the air. The present condemned age is governed by "the prince of the power of the air" (Ephes. II, 2). The Ascension of Isaiah describes the hero's meeting with the Satanic host at the firmament; its members are all engaged in fighting each other out of envy and it is their struggle until the Parousia which 'this age' reflects upon earth (ch. VII). Elsewhere some evil angels ask Michael for their transfer into the good camp (g. Ap. Bar. XIII, 2). These attractive speculations deviate from the main Christian tradition, however, which maintains the axiom of Satan's "undivided Kingdom" (Mk. III, 23 ff.). Desirable though it may be thought, the enemy does not weaken himself by internecine war before he deploys his maximum strength, even if hatred and envy are his characteristic qualities.

Satan is the devil, who acts as the lord of this lost world of

[1] Cf. Cicero, *De Fato*, for the logic and nuances of the tradition: Chrysippus steers a middle course between fatalism and freedom and makes imporant distinctions between primary and secondary causes and external and internal factors (39 ff.).

envy and delusion. In this part he appears to Jesus in the Temptation and offers his realm as a bait (Mt. IV, 8–10). It is the present world, not only with its political constellations of power but also the supernatural reality which lies behind and controls the same. The concept of 'this world' occurs with the sharpest possible theological edge in the Fourth Gospel (XII, 31; XIV, 30–1; XVI, 11). Whereas the Prince of this world is, in Judaism,[1] merely the angel who unites the whole life of nature by supervising the elements and arranging the calendar and therefore indirectly controls the affairs of the world, the Johannine use of the term is not in the least this-worldly. This ruler is not prince of Rome or some local deputy, who causes or condones persecutions, but a symbol of cosmic hostility. He reigns in his sphere until Jesus is "on high" and ready to lift all men up to himself (XII, 32). His clash with Christ is always thought of as an encounter in the air. Even at the Parousia the Christians are caught up in the clouds and meet the victorious Lord in the air from which the Prince of this world has at last been finally expelled (I Thess. IV, 17).

This concept of evil powers under a personal leader implies a metaphysical world-view which is neither dualistic nor monistic. Evil on earth is real because it reflects a cosmic disorder which if it were not redeemed and conquered would bring to an end the whole creation. Hence the warfare waged by the soldiers of Heaven penetrates the whole world for it is the cause of Light itself which battles against darkness. The New Testament endorses this view of the enemy and the Epistle to the Ephesians gives great prominence to it. A great division runs through the whole created world: some "thrones, dominions, and principalities or powers" have indeed remained loyal to the purpose of their creation and co-inhere in the divine economy (Col. I, 16) but the "principalities and powers in heavenly places" (Ephes. III, 10) remain the enemies of Christ even after having been exposed in their true nature (Col. II, 15).[2] They are spiritual

[1] Cf. Str. B. I, pp. 31, 142, 745.

[2] This apparent contradiction between the views in the two Epistles gives, however, little support to the alleged non-Pauline authorship of Ephesians, for ἀρχαί and ἐξουσίαι may be either good or bad in this tradition. In view of Ephes. III, 1–13 and IV, 1, Pauline authorship seems only improbable if Collossians is also dismissed as a non-Pauline forgery with cosmic interests.

powers, superior to man both in situation and power. They may best be recognized in their dark rule of those spheres of the world which they (κοσμοκρατόρες τοῦ σκότους τούτου, Ephs. VI, 12) are still permitted to govern, such as the very human levels of social and economic pressure and compulsion, though their nature is essentially spiritual, wicked, and heavenly (VI, 12). The seriousness of the final exhortation in this Epistle excludes the possibility of the author's accommodating himself in expression to Hellenistic thought or indulging in apocalyptic exaggeration. This is the enemy who had originally a place in Heaven and who lost his celestial status through deliberate rebellion against God. His following is numerous and powerful and espouses the evil cause in the universe in the hope of usurping God's sovereignty and of establishing a permanent realm of universal darkness by the delusion of the spirit. His society is bound together by self-interest and fear. He marches from strength to strength so that the whole world lies under his dominion, since everything organized as if God did not exist "is placed in the sphere of his influence" (Westcott on I Jn. V, 19), until God himself calls a halt and a turning-point in this battle is reached.

Chapter Six

THE VICTORY OF HEAVEN

THE theme of war is continuous throughout the Bible and, if possible, the New Testament deepens the awareness of hostility and the intensity of combat. In every war the nature of the enemy must determine the nature of the victory; what then was Christ's victory and whom did he fight? Among theologians there is no general agreement here. It is relatively easy to see that the enemy in the New Testament, who is defeated, cannot be identical with the enemies whom Jesus commands to be loved (Mt. v, 44), nor can the evil which he overcomes be identical with the evil which one is not to resist (Mt. v, 39). This use of the word 'enemy' is altogether new and unique, for is it not of the nature of an enemy to fight so as to prevail and to avoid defeat? Can Jesus, for example, desire his disciples' defeat?—Moore comments on the "utopian strain in the teaching of Jesus as it is reported in the Gospels. . . . Much else in the Sermon on the Mount is so impracticable that many modern scholars think it necessary to save Jesus' reputation. . . ."[1]

The so-called 'interim ethic' of non-violence is said to be, following A.Schweitzer, a perfectionist rule given only in anticipation of the imminent crisis that ushers in the reign of God. But this critical attitude tends to ignore the historical fact that the early Christians behaved in a very surprising manner and looked upon war in their times very differently from most of their fathers and contemporaries. They follow the example of

[1] Cf. GFM, II, p. 151. Moore traces the utopian strain back to the idealism of Deuteronomy and finds it on a lesser scale in Judaism. Cf. also Str. B., I, p. 341, for Rabbinic teaching on the virtue of pliability in conflict and readiness to yield.

Jesus who appears to have shown no interest in the battle against Rome; the disciples after him do not interpret the Jews' resistance as a righteous cause. More remarkably, Jesus in his own time did not stir up a revolutionary party, however revolutionary Galilee may have been. But if neither the military nor the social conflict gained from his support or leadership it should perhaps be born in mind that the great prophets, for instance Isaiah, Jeremiah, and Ezekiel, had already discarded this kind of external warfare as irrelevant.

THE AMBIGUITY OF WARS AND VICTORIES

The Dead Sea Scrolls testify to the complex notions of war and victory before and at the time of Christ. The prominence of the Isaiah scrolls suggests that the Covenanters at Qumran subscribed to the many strands of teaching on salvation in that prophetic school. They were steeped in the apocalyptic and eschatological expectation which looked forward to God's reign (Is. LII, 7). This was to be preceded by the victory over Egypt (ch. XIX) and Babylon (chs. XLVI–XLVII), not so much in a military as in a supernatural sense.[1] Egypt evoked the tradition of the defeat of chariot and horse, Babylon that of pomp, idolatry, and religious festivals, of Marduk, the slaying of the primeval monster, the death and the resurrection of the god, his marriage, coronation, and enthronement. The victory over Egypt and Babylon was the "new thing" of redemption (XLII, 9; XLIII, 19) which would miraculously transcend even the liberation of the Exodus from Egypt. It would be neither political nor mythical but God's own work from above, wrought by his Servant on earth by sacrifice unto death. Its effects would be universal, "unto the ends of the earth" (XLV, 22) and for all time (LV, 13). It would be a triumph over the earth and her workers of wickedness and terror (XXIV, 3 f.; 17 ff.). The prophetic school associated this victory with cosmic signs (XXIV, 23), when "the windows on high" are opened (XXIV, 18) and God visits the "high host on high" for punishment (XXIV, 21).

[1] I have argued elsewhere against the usual interpretation of Babylon in the Second Isaiah as a political power and nothing else; cf. *A Theology of Salvation*, 1953.

AT QUMRAN

The Convenanters linked this supernatural crisis with the struggle of their own community in their own times. At least this must be our conclusion if we may assume with most scholars that the scrolls in the caves really represented their convictions.[1] The Zadokite Fragment, which was in any case known elsewhere too, writes of a controversy which God has with all flesh and in which the Teacher of Righteousness[2] fights with the man of lies. The community of the new covenant looks forward to the rising of the Star of Jacob "to break down all the sons of Seth" (VII, 20), and welcomes the destruction which Belial causes in Israel because of fornication, wealth, and the defilement of the sanctuary (IV, 13–18). The tone is apocalyptic and the warfare is consequently concerned with more than the vindication of a sectarian minority against the ruling caste of priests in Jerusalem. At the same time the community's rules are not only strict and austere but also ensure a disciplined, almost puritanical life on earth. As the warfare is this-worldly and other-worldly, so the expected victory is over enemies in both worlds.

The Habakkuk Commentary is even more explicit on the double nature of war and triumph. Here the personal conflict rages between the righteous teacher and the wicked priest. The associations of the battle are manifold: there are those who "will act treacherously at the end of days", i.e. in the eschatological battle (Hab. I, 5); there are the Kittim, no doubt a politico-military power, either Greeks or Romans (I, 6 ff.); there is the 'house of Absalom', a party in Israel which condones all the evils (I, 12). All the nations are under God's indictment (I, 19). Clearly the Community's stand is against the whole world.

The Manual of Discipline makes membership conditional upon a decision for truth and love, while the members live in the age of Belial. Their order reflects that of the eternal council and the community is in that sense already triumphant and eternal (IQS

[1] And not what was left of orders, completed in the scriptorium, without being collected, nor a 'library' in our sense of the word, nor a dump of condemned manuscripts.

[2] Or 'right teacher', indicating an office rather than a particular holder of that office.

I, 18 ff.). The fight in the soul of man is, however, still continuing, and the spirit of truth is opposed by the spirit of lies. These correspond to the prince of light and the angel of darkness. The spiritual universe is thus represented in the Community. The struggle in the heart of man is inseparable from the cosmic array of powers (IQS IV, 18). Since the righteous partakes of the divine order and of light, having left far behind the dark places, his war is not of the ordinary kind: he will not render to a man the recompense of evil. He comforts himself both with the perfection of the cosmic order of light and the vengeance which will overtake the men of lies (IQS X, 10, 18 ff.). The pacific nature of the Community is against ordinary violence, but it acknowledges the "War of the Sons of Light with the Sons of Darkness".

This War-scroll mixes all the motifs of conflict of the previously mentioned documents. Again Belial and Kittim and traitors are identified with the troops of darkness. The eschatological setting goes hand in hand with dates and figures. The battle standards e.g. "Glory of God", "War of God", "Vengeance of God", "Peace of God", declare the nature of the hostilities and the dedication of the troops (IQM III, 1–IV, 9). Military realism blends with a celestial ideology directed against the troops of Belial. According to the Thanksgiving Psalms the leader of the righteous is immune against the assaults of the assembly of the wicked and undoes the devices of Belial. God has lifted him up, after eschatological birth-pangs, to the height of Heaven and his triumph comes to him after enduring the onslaught of chaos: the host of Heaven utter their voice . . . the war of the celestial army penetrates the world until the end. The whole corpus of hymns represents the theme of cosmic victory through suffering on earth by an unnamed servant (op. IQH III, 8–19; VII, 1 ff.).

VICTORIES: COSMIC AND EARTHLY

The Hebrew tradition of warfare and victory does not speak of the simple distinction between earthly and spiritual conflict. It is, therefore, misleading to assume a prevalence of patriotic and even chauvinistic notions of redemption at the time of Christ, for the desire to be free from Roman oppression coincided, at least for some, with the longing to be rid of sin and supernatural enmity. It remained open for different points of view to gain their adherents. The Rabbis became in the end chiefly interested in the effect which war must exercise on men and their keeping of the Torah; thus they came to distinguish between obligatory warfare, which exempted men from both duties and privileges, and voluntary conflicts. Such a distinction, however, was not easily made before the Fall of Jerusalem and the end of the Jewish state. In the first century B.C. civil wars raged and were regarded by some, and not without reason, as holy wars (cf. T. Jud. XXII, 1; T. Zeb. IX, 2–5, which refer to uprisings at the time of Aristobulus II and Hyrcanus II). Victory became therefore a somewhat ambiguous term, for it might denote a simple military decision (cf. Josephus Ant. VI, 145) or the victory of the spirit over the base passions of men (L. A. III, 186), or the advent of God's forces on earth, as in apocalyptic circles. The hope of salvation oscillated between these poles and derived its impetus and richness from the diversity of conquests to be attained.

The difficulties of portraying the warfare of Jesus are well known. The failure to give a reasonable picture of the conflict is due to a general inclination to forget the Jewish background, and thus to ignore the paradox of this-worldly and other-worldly levels. The Gospel narrative is largely, though not exclusively, concerned with a conflict on earth. Jesus meets all sorts of people, e.g. Sadducees, Pharisees, Herodians, zealots, secularists, lawyers, tax-gatherers, priests, and local officials—who attack him or whom he challenges. Even his own intimate disciple can on a certain occasion be a "Satan" who must be overcome (Mk. VIII, 33). Jesus the prophet encounters sin everywhere in the manner of the great prophets. Indeed, one can read the greater part of the Synoptic Gospels without sensing behind the terrestrial enemies the presence of that foe who has revolted against God and who now endeavours by all means within his power to use human beings for his own end. Yet the same Gospels consistently claim that the Good News concerns a victory over sin and death and the devil. The clash of powers goes beyond the aura of street brawls (e.g. Lk. XI, 53–4; Jn. VIII, 59) or Temple incidents (Mk. XI, 15) or public controversy in general. It culminates in a Death which defeats not the victim but him who appeared victor, the enemy who belongs to another world. The Gospel is only what it is because it makes the sweeping claim of the universality and permanence of this victory. It never questions its own authenticity because of its dealing with earthly events in the past. The temporary and earthly victories of Jesus do not count for much in themselves: one is never told, for instance, whether a healed mother-in-law or a raised Lazarus profited a great deal from the extension of life on earth. The miracles have a claim to eternity which brushes aside the notion that Jesus won a particular victory in the past. Rather, that earthly warfare in the past, which the Gospels preach, engaged supernatural forces which descended to the earth and into the history of mankind. Consequently the war and the triumph are really a heavenly mystery though partly enacted on earth.

A HEAVENLY SECRET

Since 1901, when Wrede published *Das Messiasgeheimnis in den Evangelien*, special attention has been drawn to the different aspects of secrecy in Mark's Gospel.[1] Before his radical enquiry into the paradox that Jesus is portrayed as veiling himself in revelation, it was common to explain the *mysterion* of the Gospel as due to the Lord's self-restraint which he also enjoined upon his disciples. Wrede showed that this point of view is untenable in the light of the different strands of the *mysterion*-context, which comprises encounters with demons, teachings of parables, and clashes with his own disciples. All these three converge upon Mark IX, 9, the climax of the *mysterion*-teaching after the Transfiguration: "He charged them that they should tell no one" until after the Resurrection. Why did Jesus say this? Wrede's method was of a more lasting importance than his own solution to the problem, which ascribed the secrecy to the Evangelist's purpose

[1] Cf. H. J. Ebeling, *Das Messiasgeheimnis und die Botschaft des Marcus-Evangelisten*, 1939, for a complete historical summary of theories; cf. also A. Schweitzer, *The Quest of the Historical Jesus*, 1910; *The Mystery of the Kingdom of God*, 1925: Schweitzer opposed Wrede though he also insisted on the secret of Jesus' Messiahship as central to the understanding of his life (p. 6). "Suffering is the way to the revelation of messiahship" (p. 223), for "with death comes the Kingdom" (p. 271) in Jesus' mistaken eschatological hopes.

of showing Jesus as Messiah—a strictly unhistorical invention on his part. Wrede ignores the fact that the *mysterion* is itself part of eschatological thinking and resumes the ancient cultic practice of enjoining silence upon those who attend to cosmic secrets. In the Old Testament the inner connexion between secrecy and cosmic religion is brought out with great force in the word *sod*, which, as we have seen, describes the company of God's intimate council and also the secret counsel which may be revealed (e.g. Amos III, 7; Prov. XI, 13). Similarly the *raz* which Daniel is called upon to interpret (II, 18 ff.) is a heavenly secret which is veiled until God chooses to reveal the same. The apocalyptic circles regarded themselves as guardians of secrets which were eschatological and cosmic (En. IX, 6; XLIX, 2; CIV, 10; CD III, 18).

An eschatological understanding of the Gospel interprets the element of *mysterion* not so much as a human disposition to prefer silence for some tactical reasons, like propaganda and security, but rather as the only suitable means whereby the heavenly and pre-existent Son of God can enter history and be recognized by faith. That Jesus is himself the Kingdom and that therefore cosmic history is enacted on earth is not a message peculiar to Mark but accords with Pauline preaching. The paradox of Mark IX, 9 is itself not a peculiar *cri de coeur* uttered by Jesus on a particular day in a certain passing situation, but rather supports a basic eschatological understanding of the Gospel. Secrecy befits the Victor from Heaven on earth and the nature of his victory.

The Messianic secret comprehends both the identity of the Messiah and his acts on earth. Until victory is complete, and perhaps even after it, the secret is kept. Both men and "the rulers of this world" were ignorant at the time; otherwise they, which includes Caiaphas and Pilate as well as supernatural powers, would not have crucified the Lord of Glory (I Cor. II, 7), thus unwittingly sealing their own doom and the world's salvation. Only after the victory is revelation given to some by the preaching of the Gospel, and even the heavenly powers, who had until the day of Jesus Christ failed to detect God's plan, are being initiated into the mystery now (Ephes. III, 9, 10).[1] The modern

[1] Through the Church! This is a unique conception. Cf. R. Leivestad, *Christ the Conqueror*, 1954, p. 155.

objection that an earthly event is not likely to have celestial repercussions does not arise where the traditional world-view of correspondence obtains. The earth even takes precedence over Heaven because the victory occurred here; the centre of redemption is in the place which God has chosen.

JESUS THE CONQUEROR

The Messianic secret obscures not only the identity of Christ but also his role as conqueror. Although his name is Jesus—he is not merely Immanuel, as one would expect after Isaiah VII, but Joshua-Jeshajahu, the liberating victor—his pacific interpretation of salvation almost belies his name. But this interpretation does not eliminate the motif of war. Mary magnifies God for the great tidings, for showing strength with his arm, scattering the proud, putting down princes and reversing the whole known order of things (Lk. I, 46 ff.). When Jesus announces the Kingdom it turns out to be the contradiction of human customs and institutions. This crisis is not peace but war: "Do you think that I have come to give peace on earth? No, I tell you, but rather division" (Lk. XII, 49–53). But the realm into which Jesus breaks is, as we saw before, not simply the natural world of human making, but the universe, alienated from God. He is stronger than Satan who can no longer guard his goods in the peace of diabolical purpose (Lk. XI, 20–2). The evidence that Jesus regarded his fight as the clash between God and the Prince of this world comes to a head in his encounter with the devils. The fighting with human beings and with non-human enemies occurs on the same front, almost as if they were inextricably united. Yet it is important to note from the start that the warfare is always realistic and not a mock affair, a sham performance. The contestants are equally conscious of their interests and they are never anything but responsible for their actions and attitudes. Thus the fight with the demons is also a moral one.

OVER THE EMPIRE OF EVIL

The paradox of human responsibility, on the one hand, and of enticements, seductions, temptations, possessions, all procured by Satanic means from outside, on the other, is typical of the many instances of Jesus' work of exorcism. The evil human impulse in full flower—which St. James' Epistle later describes: "Each person is tempted, when he is lured and enticed by his own desire. Then desire when it has conceived gives birth to sin, and sin when it is full-grown brings forth death" (I, 14)[1]—is complementary to the work of the devil. Hence the terrible sentence of judgment: "Depart from me, you cursed, into the eternal fire prepared for the devil and his angels" (Mt. XXV, 41) assigns the condemned (the ungenerous and indifferent) to eternal punishment in company with Satan. He is the enemy who has sown the tares and prevented the sowing of the good seed of the Word of God and stands invisibly behind all human evil (Mk. IV, 15).

The conflict of Jesus with the demons is therefore of central importance, for in them he meets, on earth, the power of the fallen angels. "The enemy is not Rome, but Satan and his hosts of spirits . . . the metaphysical conflict has become central to the same extent as national redemption has been relegated to the circumference".[2]

Yet the demons should be called 'heavenly' rather than 'metaphysical', for they are not philosophers' concepts, lying dormant until used, but aggressive powers in their hatred for God and their opposition to his designs. Satan's attack on Christ after the Baptism and the descent of the Spirit (Mk. I, 12, 13) is typical; the supernatural arena is now situated in the desert, the home of the demons. Once again the full circle of ideas is achieved inasmuch as the beasts loom so large in the background. In fulfilment of Psalm XCI it is part of the Messiah's task to conquer these and to render the poisonous beasts harmless (cf. Is. XI, 6 ff.; Ez. XXXIV, 35; Lk. X, 19), for these also belong to Satan's host. The presence of the good angels emphasizes the nature of the battle, which, according to the fuller account in Matthew IV and Luke IV, is not only a moral test but an ordeal. The very allegiance of the Son of God is open to doubt; Satan represents the principle of insubordination in Heaven; the ancient theme of the angels' envy of God is at work, but the

[1] A process of degradation reminiscent of the spirits of Beliar and their treatment in T. Reub. III, 3–6; T. Asher I, 2.

[2] Cf. Leivestad, op. cit., p. 40.

Son's loving fidelity to God settles the issue, ends the tempter's hopes, and opens up the chapter of direct attacks. From now on the battle will be between Jesus and those who are possessed by Satan; healing, forgiveness, and, above all, exorcism issue from the decision against the enemy.

The demons excel men in angelic power; they know more than men. The man with the unclean spirit in the synagogue at Capernaum is not astonished at the teaching and the authority of Jesus, as are the rest of normal people: "What have we to do with each other, Jesus of Nazareth? Thou hast come to destroy us. I know who thou art, the Holy One of God" (Mk. I, 24). The victim of madness does not merely display the mantic gift of detection, but, being possessed, he really knows the nature of the encounter. The unclean spirits recognize his divinity, which remains a secret to men: "he would not permit the devils to speak, because they knew him" (Mk. I, 31). The conflict is a bitter one and for the raging demons the advent of Jesus is a torment (Mk. V, 7). They fear exactly what they have administered to others.

As the Satanic forces have enslaved their victims—for example, by binding a woman for eighteen years with the bond of sickness (Lk. XIII, 16)—so, in the great reversal, they will themselves lose their liberty. Until then they enjoy their freedom and they increase: "When the unclean spirit has gone out of a man, he passes through waterless places, seeking rest but he finds none", until he returns to his cleansed and polished house with a whole company of new devils (Mt. XII, 43–5). Ordinary methods of exorcism do not prevail against his angelic power. Even those who shared the vision of the divine glory cannot expel the unclean spirit in a possessed boy and only the Master can rebuke it (Lk. IX, 39–43). There are clearly degrees of possession, dependent upon the rank of the members of the Satanic hierarchy who possess men. But the "word" of Jesus is always irresistible: "They brought to him many who were possessed with devils; and he cast out the spirits with a word" (Mt. VIII, 16), and it does not seem that a believing disposition on the part of the sufferer is a conditional requirement. Some of the healed do believe and, now in their right mind, and, no doubt, with a remembrance of the "word" spoken over them, join the body known as the Disciples (Lk. VIII, 2–3). Their new status probably shocked the good Pharisees who failed to see, or did not wish to perceive, the inner connexion between the healing and the new existence of the possessed. They interpreted the exorcisms as tokens of a falsely assumed earthly prerogative and therefore mistook the word of Jesus in his acts of forgiveness of sins. They knew less than the devils, namely that "the exorcisms themselves are regarded as a victorious combat with the devil and his kingdom".[1]

THE DEATH OF CHRIST A COSMIC VICTORY

The Gospel tradition agrees that the ministry of Christ leads up to the climax of the Passion. It is, therefore, somewhat startling to find that the death of Jesus seems to lack at first sight the celestial setting which one might expect. The Markan account is particularly restrained and non-mythical. Death is not personified. The actors and their actions are caught up in the political world, the motives are human. The place of execution is on earth. The only reminder of the watching interests in the universe occurs in XV, 33: "When the sixth hour had come, there was darkness over the whole land until the ninth hour", for the universe of light mourns the horror of the Crucifixion. This is the eschatological sign of the withdrawal of all radiance and it confirms the terrible seriousness of the death of Jesus. The power of Satan's darkness is made manifest in slaying the Light of God on earth.

The earthly rulers, however, are themselves really tools of demonic powers, for this is their hour because it is the hour of the power of darkness (Lk. XXII, 53). Consequently there is temptation on every side. Simon Peter is in dire peril and his fall and restoration issue from the struggle between Satan and Christ (Lk. XXII, 28 f.). But the same enemy enters Judas so successfully (Lk. XXII, 3) that this traitor becomes a symbol of the incarnation of Satan. When he goes into the night, God is glorified in the imminent expulsion of the Prince of this world (Jn. XIII, 30–1; XIV, 30; XVI, 11). Because Judas is Satan no pity is shown for him in the tradition; he is not one of the men who are ignorant of the im-

[1] Leivestad, op. cit., p. 47.

port of their actions (Lk. xxiii, 34), but, like the devils, he is both cognizant of and responsible for his outrageous evil. It is therefore felt to be appropriate that the death of Jesus leads to his own suicide (Mt. xxvii, 3 ff.) or accidental death (Acts i, 18). Even belated repentance (Mt. xxvii, 3) cannot help him, for his self-destruction anticipates the upheaval of the whole diabolic empire.

Jesus speaks of his own death as a necessity and an accomplishment (Lk. ix. 22, 31). Having cast out devils "today and tomorrow" he is "perfected" on the third day (xiii, 32). The Passion is not a mechanical completion of the prophecies nor an enactment of a cultic sacrifice but two worlds clash when Jesus is led away to die. His earthly arrest and humiliation, the trial, verdict, and execution are stages of a cosmic ordeal which he has chosen to endure in order to reveal his power over all cosmic forces of evil. He is the Son of God whose glory will be seen after the trial (Mt. xxvi, 64) in which he refuses angelic help (Mt. xxvi, 53) so as to attain to the absolute victory. A combat between heavenly armies is ruled out. It is precisely his death which shakes the powers. Earthquake and darkness respond to his death at the moment of his dying (xxvii, 50–2). The natural order is defeated; the tombs yield up their dead. Therefore the Fourth Gospel interprets the Passion as a royal enterprise in which the other-worldly Kingdom defeats 'this world' (xviii, 36). The *Tetelestai* ("It is finished", xix, 30) affirms not submission to death but Christ's all-embracing conquest over the world of darkness. The *kosmos* without God is overcome (xvi, 33).

THE SUBJUGATION OF DEATH

St. Paul also declares the Passion to be the unique means of liberation, for the victory of Christ has brought defeat to death, the principle which is itself lord of the corrupt order of sin. Jesus encounters death as the primary enemy in his dying. The universal principle which feeds on corruption is personalized as the 'last enemy' (I Cor. xv, 26). His ranks are composed of the enemies of God: sinners, the ungodly, even 'ourselves' (Ro. v, 10). Man's place in the chain of sin and death is central for through man sin entered into the world and the dominion of death prevails where men serve sin (Ro. vi, 16). Christ became exempt from this dominion through his obedience: as he "died to sin" (Ro. VI, 10), neither committing sin nor yielding to evil in any point, but rather achieving in his death the perfect image of God, death could only kill him by ending its dominion.

The celestial nature of the atonement is not pressed here, for the conquest concerns sinners set free on earth. But if it is recalled what the Satanic enemy is elsewhere in St. Paul's thought it is difficult to confine his estimate of the victory exclusively to men who happen to be alive at the time. The kingdom of sin-and-death is an independent dominion which Christ has ended: "for to this end Christ died and lived again, that he might be Lord of both the dead and the living" (Ro. XIV, 9). The whole vista of the past opens up as Christ reclaims from death what, through the power of sin, had become the property of death. The unearthly world must yield up its booty. The descent of Jesus into the abyss (Ro. X, 7) evoked the sweeping claim that Christ preached unto the "formerly disobedient spirits in prison" (I Pe. III, 19).

The personification of death as the enemy is taken further in I Corinthians XV where the polemic starts from the fact of the Resurrection of Christ. The Apostle concedes that Christians still die or 'fall asleep' but the ordinary end of human life does not militate against the absolute victory over death. Christ is alive and in his risen state he continues the warfare of the Messiah. The enemies upon which he treads are the superhuman powers whose rule and sovereignty are headed by death (25–6). But the destruction of death has begun; he can no longer boast of victory. Throughout the Apostle carefully avoids a borrowing from paganism. The subjugation of the powers echoes the favourite Psalm CX of the victorious Priest-King. The personification of death leads to the challenge of a personal address: "O Death, where is thy victory? O Death, where is thy sting?" In the original prophecy (Hos. XIII, 14) these words had been a threat to Ephraim, introduced by the question: "From the hand of Sheol shall I deliver them? From death shall I redeem them?"—The plagues and the sting of death were destined for the unrepentant. St. Paul retains the personification of death and the death-sin sequence, but he changes the threat to an assertion of victory: death is not only countered by virtue and even sinlessness, but "swallowed up". Here he alludes to the passage in Isaiah xxv, 8 which had looked to the future, if not the end; it had adapted the common motif of the slaying of the monster, of death or *Mot* of the Ugaritic myth, to bring out the eschatological triumph of YHWH. St. Paul's quotation changes the future to the past (aor. pass.), for 'it' has happened, and he also replaces the "for ever" (Hebr. *lanezach*) by "into victory" (*eis nikos*, thus taking *lanezach* in the Aramaic sense).[1] This victory over and abolition of death belongs to the eternal plan of God (II Tim. I, 9–10); all later admonitions are based upon this objective verity which does not depend upon anyone's decision or insight.[2]

THE TRIUMPH OVER DEATH

This objectivity is necessary to sustain the thesis of a celestial, cosmic victory. A Messiah who died and rose again could easily find faith on earth during the life of the generation to which he belonged but hardly after its extinction. The New Testament takes it for granted despite its eschatological point of view that the victory of Jesus is of a lasting and universal efficacy. This is not entirely because he died unto death and survived, but because God triumphed in raising up Jesus from the dead (I Cor. xv, 15). The glory of the Father operated then (Ro. VI, 4) and the love of God in Christ Jesus continues the conquest (Ro. VIII, 37–9). The victory of Christ must be understood as God's own conquest and is, therefore, valid for the whole world.

The Ressurrection does not make Jesus into a perpetual sojourner on earth, as frequently portrayed in nineteenth-century piety; the risen Lord has not completed his conquest until he be "received up" (Lk. IX, 51; Acts I, 9; Jn. XX, 17). The simple account in Acts I, on which the Markan and Lukan secondary verses lean, brings out the passivity of Jesus who receives the reward which God has prepared for him. In the manner of Elijah (II K. II, 11) Jesus is carried off and vanishes from sight in a cloud. Unlike Enoch, the hero of a typical ascension of

[1] The LXX (except Q mg.) has the strange reading: "Death has eaten up with might" or "Death prevailing swallowed them up"; the Hebr. is ambiguous. St. Paul stresses the great reversal by making death the object. In the quotation from Hosea he changes the δίκη of LXX to νῖκος.

[2] Cf. G. Aulen, *Christus Victor,* 1931, ch. IV, esp, pp. 82 ff.

apocalyptic Judaism, who traverses the Heavens (chs. LXX–LXXI) to return and report on what he saw, Jesus penetrates to God himself and remains above the Heavens. As against the common mysteries of the East which link death and exaltation (traces of which may be found in T. Levi XVIII, 3) the exalted Jesus cannot be separated from the real, meek servant of the Lord who was the prophet from Nazareth. The whole Jesus is received up into Glory, for thus God seals his triumph over death.

CHRIST'S COSMIC ENTHRONEMENT

The Ascension, as it has come to be called, should therefore not be looked upon as an extension of the Resurrection or as another 'event' in the history of salvation.[1] It is the appropriate and necessary sequel to the Incarnation itself as well as the withdrawal before the Return. The Fourth Gospel expresses this in a manner foreign to apocalyptic extravagances by meditating on the question: "Who has ascended to Heaven and come down?" (Prov. XXX, 4). Dismissing Enoch, Moses, and Elijah, as well as all pagan claims, the Gospel answers: "No one has ascended into Heaven, but he who has come down from Heaven, the Son of Man who is in Heaven" (Jn. III, 13). The Word in Heaven, having come near to man in fulfilment of Deuteromony XXX, 12–14 ("not in Heaven, but very nigh"), has returned to the Father.[2]

Yet this triumph of Christ demonstrates the dramatic element of conquering kingship. Two Psalms, which themselves treasured the ancient themes of royal progress in procession towards enthronement and coronation, illustrate the force of the primitive preaching. Psalm CX provides the text for St. Peter's development of the Messianic exaltation: David, who had been crowned and enthroned on earth, did not ascend to the Heavens; rather, like all earthly kings, he inherited a temporal kingdom in the earthly rite. But Jesus has received an eternal kingdom and sits in

[1] For the historical problem cf. A. M. Ramsay, SNTS, Bulletin II, pp. 43 ff.; C. F. D. Moule, ET, April 1957; R. Seeberg, *Lehrbuch der Dogmengeschichte,* 1920–33, I, pp. 75–7.

[2] Not in a vertical direction, but in a gentle hovering motion to the East. Cf. the relief on the door of St. Sabina in Rome and F. J. Dölger's comment in *Sol Salutis,* 1920, p. 159.

Heaven at God's right hand (Acts II, 33–4). Psalm LXVIII strikes so martial a note of triumph—"kings of armies did flee apace . . . when the Almighty scattered kings"—that it is not as fully used in the Church's preaching as one might expect. Jesus is already invested with royal power in the portrayal of Ephesians IV, 8 ff. which quotes Psalm LXVIII, 18. [1] In the Psalm the victorious king exploits the victory by bringing in the captured and distributing his booty on earth (cf. Jdg. V, 12); Christ "when he ascended up on high" distributes the fruits of the supernatural freedom. His footstool is made up of the defeated enemies whom God puts under his feet.[2] This subordination of the evil celestial powers, who could and did separate men from God (Ro. VIII, 38), began to take effect when Jesus "passed through the Heavens" (Hebr. IV, 14), where they operate. Christ's dominion extends now over the spheres and their rulers, whose defeat cancels once and for all the cosmic enmity which threatened not only man but the whole creation: "Jesus Christ has gone into Heaven and is at the right hand of God with angels and authorities and powers subject to him" (I Pe. III, 22).

The elimination of enemy interference is the prelude to Christ's distribution of the eternal gifts.[3] The coming of the Holy Spirit is Christ's own reward in Heaven, the Father's promise which is now shed forth, visibly and audibly (Acts II, 33). As the "accuser of our brethren is cast down which accuseth them before our God day and night" (Rev. XII, 10) the new creation of the Spirit (Ephes. IV, 11 ff.) may not only enjoy his fruits (Gal. V, 22 ff.) but even rely upon his constant advocacy as Paraclete. The "sword of the Spirit" supplies the people of God with the conquering power of the Word in Heaven (Ephes. VI, 17).

[1] In an adapted form which posits many problems. The change concerns not only the persons (the 'Thou' of the Psalm becomes the 'He' of Ephes.) but also the verb *laqach* (receive, take) becomes *chalaq* (to apportion, give), as also found in the Targum.

[2] The 'redeemed' are the liberated captives according to Justin and Theodoret, but Chrysostom thinks of Satan, sin, and death as the captives now brought under control.

[3] Abbot (ICC ad Eph. IV. 10) supports von Soden's view that Christ's Katabasis follows his Anabasis in this passage because it deals not with Incarnation and Ascension but with exaltation and the giving of gifts.

THE CONTINUITY OF THE WAR

This conception of Christ's victory is familiar to all lovers of art, but far less familiar in its implications to religious thought. It abrogated the expectation of a politico-supernatural conquest in the future and put in its place the paradoxical notion that the eternal war has already been won and the king of righteousness been enthroned while great battles remain to be fought.[1] The King's exaltation ushers in the era of the Spirit on the one hand and an increase of warfare on the other. The evil powers are exposed but they are enemies until they cease to exist altogether. It is this 'until' which gives Christian eschatology its peculiar flavour (Ps. CX. I, still quoted in full in Acts II, 35; I Cor. XV, 25; Hebr. I, 13) and does away with any illusions of perfect peace, when men and beasts live again, as in the golden age, in perfect harmony without an enemy. Rather, the re-making of the universe is catastrophic in the apocalyptic sense and the victory of Christ leads to a dialectical process of building-up and throwing-down, in the typically Biblical rhythm of construction and destruction (cf. Jer. I, 10). The New Testament reflects this double experience, for the fruits of Christ's exaltation are both of peace and war, joy and dread, order and chaos.

The "persecutions in the world" confirm the continuation of the crisis in the world which Jesus has conquered (Jn. XII, 31; XVI, 33). The Now of Christian experience is, however, only possible because the exalted Christ himself confronts the hostile aeon. The earthly *mysterion* now becomes an eternal heavenly one, for "he who was manifested in the flesh, justified in the spirit, seen of angels, preached among the nations, believed on in the world, received up in glory" (as the hymnal creed has it in I Tim. III, 16) is still resisted by some persistent cosmic enmity, which is reflected in such enemies, Satan's agents, children of the devil, liars against the Holy Spirit, as Ananias, Elymas, and many others (Acts V, 3; XIII, 10). The enemy's onslaught—whether in or outside the Church—is against Christ and can be conquered only by Christ. The harassed followers are united with him;

[1] For an expanded thesis of this eschatology cf. O. Cullmann, *Christ and Time,* 1951.

therefore angels, principalities, things present or future, height or depth cannot "separate us from the love of God, which is in Christ Jesus our Lord" (Ro. VIII, 37–9). Unless Christ held celestial power his followers could not be expected to oppose so massive a host of evil, met with both in the inner, moral struggle as well as in the fight for the proclamation of the Gospel.

THE CHURCH VICTORIOUS

The celestial victory belongs to the Church by the power of the abiding Word (I Jn. II, 13–14), made effective in the defeat of the 'evil one'. The conflict is, however, not confined to a narrow ecclesiastical sphere, for everything that owes its existence to God and has remained faithful to the principle of reality and truth is engaged in the struggle against and the victory over the world (I Jn. V, 4). The present victory is the extension of the victory that has been achieved: "It is by the introduction of the spiritual, the eternal, that we obtain a true standard for things, and so can overcome the temptations which spring out of a narrow, temporal estimate. And this holds good not only of man as a whole but of each power and faculty, with which he is endowed." It is this vista of the eternal alone which justifies the unique use of the word νίκη: the victory which has conquered the world "was gained upon a narrow field, but it was world-wide in its effects"[1], and the confessional faith (πίστις only here in St. John's Epistles, never in the Fourth Gospel) in Jesus is the means of appropriating the triumph everywhere and for all time. Thus the individual believer becomes the victor (I Jn. V, 5), not by an act of courage and inspiration but rather by his participation in the cosmic truth.

The heavenly powers learn the secret of cosmic redemption when they see the operation of faith and truth in the Church. This new fellowship reveals in its human structure God's purpose for the world. Jews and Gentiles, formerly in bondage to the elements, hated each other, but now their cessation from strife announces also the subjection of these hitherto uncontrollable forces (Ephes. III, 1–10). This reconciliation on earth is not a social event among many: it presents a direct challenge to the

[1] Westcott, *The Epistles of St. John,* 1892, p. 180.

whole universe still at war. Christ has broken down the middle wall of partition, and the new creation, of Jews and Gentiles, brings peace to near and far (Ephes. II, 11–17). "God was in Christ reconciling the world to himself" (II Cor. V, 19), and in the new era of reconciliation both men and spiritual powers are assigned positions of loving concord.

IN THE NEW ORDER

The victory on the Cross has begun to restore the original order which the hostility of some heavenly powers had deranged. Jesus Christ has become the apex of the new world and it is not to be supposed that the heavenly powers are only defeated. They are also to be re-made according to the purpose of creation: "in him were all things created, in the Heavens and upon the earth, things visible and invisible, whether thrones or dominions or principalities or powers: all things have been created through him, and unto him; and he is before all things, and in him all things hold together" (Col. I, 15–17). The recital of the unique place of the pre-existent Christ and the created orders under him would lack point without the assertion that all things had returned to him from whom they took their origin. The cosmic redemption is already seen in its fulfilment. The blood of Christ has wrought a change in Heaven (Col. I, 19–20)[1] If it were not so it would be impossible to speak of Christ as the *Pleroma* (Col. I, 19; II, 9) in whom "God dwells bodily". This notion of fullness answers the Jewish-Gnostic case: neither emanations nor angels are needed in a redeemed universe to supplement belief in Christ; no distance of time or space separates God from any object of his love. The *mysterion* of Christ who comprehends all reality, both created and redeemed, secures release from the exigencies of time (Col. IV, 3–5).

The Epistle to the Ephesians further unfolds the nature of the

[1] For a discussion of the complex problems of Col. I, 20 cf. RB 55/1948; R. P. B.–N. Wambacq gives an invaluable survey of identifications of τὰ ἐν τοῖς οὐρανοῖς. (Origen: evil angels; Chrysostom: angels and men reconciled: Calvin: good angels; Beza: dead before Christ; Meyer: angels and demons; Haupt: chiefs of the nations; Ritschl: angels of the Law &c.) and prefers himself to think in terms of satisfaction made to the guardians of lawful order by the blood of Christ.

spiritual universe in the age of redemption. The inaugural hymn (I, 1–14) pronounces a liturgical blessing, praising God for Christ's abolition of cosmic enmity. This blessing is itself "in the heavenlies" (I, 3: ἐν τοῖς ἐπουρανίοις). This expression has counfounded many commentators: it appears to be a cultic one, of Mandaean origin, and it is not found elsewhere in the New Testament. In meaning it oscillates between the heavenly spheres, where the work of Christ is consummated in reconciliation, and between the very partakers of this reconciliation. The redeemed sit with Christ in the heavenlies (I, 20; II, 6); there, through the Church, God's wisdom is made known to principalities and powers (III, 10). The Church's position is heavenly, comprising all the generations that ever lived; the new fullness of Christ operates in this spiritual universe. This final reintegration brings everything to a head (Ephes. I, 10). Christ is the divine summary of all being and in him the ultimate secret of God's will is made wholly known.

COSMIC UNITY

Nevertheless, the divine recapitulation, this ἀνακεφαλαιώσασθαι τὰ πάντα ἐν τῷ Χριστῷ, unless it be taken as no more than a figure of speech, raises a metaphysical problem: what is this cosmic society which enjoys the new universal harmony? It is clear that, set up "upon the *heavenlies* and earthlies" (ἐπὶ with a strange dative), it commands the loyalty not only of men, Jews and Gentiles, but also of non-human spirits and powers. The inhabitants of the spheres are brought into the living wholeness of Christ, from whom they derive their life and unity. Since, then, the reconciliation embraces all the powers of the world, the new society must also include all the living members of the cosmos.

This conclusion is not without its difficulties. A smooth intercourse between men and angels does not only baffle the imagination but it also goes beyond other relevant passages in the New Testament. There the problem of the unity of Christians is solved by the concept of the Body of Christ which achieves organic coinherence (I Cor. X, 17). As Christ had a body on earth and continues his Sonship in Heaven in his glorified Body so the members of Christ enter into his mystical Body (Ro. XII,

5), the extension of the incarnate and glorified Christ in which the many became One (I Cor. XII, 20, 27). The Fourth Gospel uses the metaphor of the Vine and the branches, deeply rooted in Israel's history (e.g. Ps. LXXX, 8 ff: "Thou hast brought a vine out of Egypt"), to bring out the harmony of the mutual indwelling of Christ and his Church. In Colossians another change of emphasis occurs, for Christ is now not so much the body (possibly a dangerous concept among Gnostic myth-makers) as the head of the body (I, 18; II, 19). The imagery brings out the heavenliness of the Lord and the earthly humanity of the members and suggests "that only mortals are to be included in the Church . . . that the Church is not a cosmic Body . . . that the Church consists of redeemed humanity, and that the heavenly powers, and all creation are excluded from it."[1]

The complementary teaching in Ephesians, however, puts such a cautionary attitude to shame. To this writer the triumph of Jesus was from the beginning cosmic in intention. The notion of an independent world, existing outside the Body, is intolerable since everything that is called into being must stand in a living relationship with God. The Church as an enclave in the universe would be as foreign to him as it would be unattractive to the recipients of his Epistle. In the end such an institution would be essentially meaningless and quite disproportionate to God's act in Christ. The new fellowship of love is heavenly because it flows with the life of him whose fullness fills all in all (I, 23). The work of apostles, prophets, evangelists, pastors, and teachers (IV, 11) is not designed for an earthly building-site but for the housebuilding of the Body to the glory of God. Therefore the gifts of the victorious Christ transcend all others and the process of building never ends; the house is not completed for it must grow in proportion to the measure of Christ's own eternal

[1] E. Best, *One Body in Christ,* 1955, p. 126. Best sets out to refute the majority view of the Church as a metaphysical organism of cosmic dimensions. The argument is too intricate to be summarized here; it seems to the present writer to fail because the author extends his thesis to Ephesians as well. Here he seems to ignore (a) the feelings and presuppositions of a people for whom metaphor could not be what it has become for us; (b) the division of the heavenly powers which makes their share in the pleroma and their militancy against Christ perfectly intelligible. For the issues raised by the Body of the 'Urmensch' as applied to Christ see p. 89.

being (IV, 13). The mystical Body is analogous to the glorified Body and the infinity of the living Christ prohibits a closure as if everything were finished.

Human relationships reflect this cosmic unity: fatherhood and family life and marriage are not to be thought of as separate islands of unity but as derivative; every fatherhood is named after the Father (Ephes. III, 14), every marriage involves the unity of Christ and his Church (V, 32). Of every microcosmic unity on earth it may be said: "I speak in regard of Christ and his Church." Christ having gathered the whole world unto himself has brought all his members into unity with each other.

This mystical note of union in Christ makes no concession to Gnostic schemes of salvation, with intermediary stages of intimacy. The Church, as Israel of old, is 'the bride' of the Lord. Even in pagan days the bridal mysticism had been freed from the usual licentiousness; Hoseah had looked forward to the restoration of unfaithful Israel to her true lover (II, 16 ff.; Is. LXI, 10). Even the Song of Songs had been included in the Canon and its erotic theme interpreted as God's love for Israel. Now the unity of Christ and his Church is preached as the fulfilment of Love on a cosmic scale (Jn. III, 16). The seer greets the descent of the new Jerusalem, "made ready as a bride adorned for her husband" (Rev. XXI, 1) and with the Spirit utters the supplication "Come!" (Rev. XXII, 17).

HEAVENLY CITIZENSHIP AND EARTHLY DUTIES

The celestial commonwealth (Phil. III, 20: *τὸ πολίτευμα ἐν οὐρανοῖς*) under Christ's victorious sceptre prevails in Heaven and upon earth (Phil. II, 10), thus fulfilling the political strands of eschatology. The Christian, to use a modern idiom, is no longer in need of a visa in his passport: he is a full citizen of the new cosmic order with access to his King. This citizenship makes all earthly materialistic desires irrelevant though it does not remove him from earthly scenes of activity. The missionary task on earth postpones an immediate departure for the realm of glory (Phil. I, 21 ff.) and keeps him where he has not "an abiding city" (Hebr. XIII, 14).

This dual function of citizenship does not obliterate the victory of Christ but merely reflects again the paradox of the new eschatology: Jesus has ascended into glory and must reign until all his enemies are either drawn into his fullness or finally defeated at his Coming. The Church cannot be more than Jesus nor can it escape from this tension. Thus even Ephesians ends on a note of triumph which still summons to battle against the rebellious powers in heavenly places (VI, 12). The wrestling against flesh and blood on earth is, when properly understood, a cosmic engagement which can be won, and only won, by God through the Spirit. Whether all these powers are meant to, or will, avail themselves of Christ's reconciliation remains a problem as acutely unsolved as in the case of mankind.

The apocalyptic tradition (Mk. XIII; Mt. XXIV; Lk. XXI) even strengthens the paradox: with the fall of the earthly Jerusalem the end has not come, but the whole future is full of troubles. An almost general apostasy features a new stage in the strife when the closest bonds of family loyalty are ignored and treachery is rife. The hatred against the Christians is so great that even endurance equals victory. They can do no more than be prepared for their tribulation and speak without preparation in their defence and pray for some mitigation of the horrors. When the chaos, which shows not a single vestige of Christ's new order, is at its height of perdition and misery Christ intervenes. Then it becomes apparent that the earthly abominations are, in fact, celestial upheavals: "the powers in the Heavens will be shaken". The consuming fire of God burns up the perishable things of the world in this last upheaval (Hebr. XII, 26 ff.) before Christ descends with his "sign", which is probably the Cross.[1]

Although the world had not come to an end and the Church continued to increase in numbers and in disciplined organization the eschatological hope remained alive or, if inclined to flag, was fanned into a new blaze by the force of history, especially at the time when the Roman State, under Domitian, seriously endeavoured to arrest the success of the movement. Now defeat seemed nearer than triumph and the cosmic consolations far off. Even if it is difficult to agree with Charles that the Apocalypse teaches the continuance of the warfare against sin "in contradis-

[1] Cf. the difficult *σημεῖον ἐκπετάσεως ἐν οὐρανῷ* in Didache XVI, 6.

tinction to the rest of the New Testament" he is certainly right that "the chief theme of the Apocalpyse is not what God in Christ has done for the world, but what he will yet do, and what the assured consummation will be".[1] The seer insists that the hour is still unknown (Rev. III, 3), but like Daniel he introduces a numerological element by multiplying the battles, which are not necessarily consecutive but different aspects of the same thing or of local conditions. Thus there are limited periods of distress (ten days, II, 10; three days and a half, XI, 9) as well as the millennium (XX, 1–6), both the end of hostilities and again the prelude to Satan's release (XX, 7).

THE VICTORY OF THE LAMB

Throughout the victory of Christ is discerned in martyrdom. The victors are those who remain true and faithful in the face of adversity and persecution. For them the fruits of victory will be available after death. The constant refrain assures them: "To him that overcomes, to him I will give . . .": life, and not death, is the result of their dying (II, 7, 11, 17, 27; III, 5, 12, 21). The Christian's victory on earth is not confined to the earth, for both in significance and in reward it is heavenly. The clash with the enemy on earth leads to the same apparent defeat which Christ suffered before, and inasmuch as Jesus conquered death through suffering, his followers also overcome cosmic powers of evil while they are overcome of them. During the battle the saints receive no supernatural help, for "the beast was allowed to make war on the saints and to conquer them" (XIII, 7). The specific virtue of their warfare lies in their unaided stand and integrity. The Christian witness *will be* granted to eat of the tree of life (II, 7); he shall not be hurt by the second death (II, 11) but will eat of the hidden manna and obtain a white stone upon which a secret name is written (II, 17); he will be clad in white garments, his name will be preserved in the book of life, Jesus will confess his name before his Father and his angels (III, 5). Jesus will make him a pillar in God's temple (III, 12): in short, redemption lies in the future with its blessings of the coming world when the martyr will be pronounced a son of God (XXI, 7). For the seer

[1] *Revelation of St. John*, 1920, pp. xv, cix.

the beginning of eternity is found in the living testimony for Jesus in this world, a testimony which must culminate in resistance against the enemy of Jesus and in sacrifice.

This enemy comprises now all the forces of evil active on earth and the identification between the supernatural and the political foe strikes an ancient note: "The great dragon was thrown down, that ancient serpent, who is called the Devil and Satan, the deceiver of the whole world—he was thrown down to the earth, and his angels were thrown down with him" (xii, 9). The prophetic past tense looks to the future; the prehistoric fall of the evil angels leads now to the post-historic winding-up of their power in their final expulsion. The "war in Heaven" has begun with the birth of the mysterious child (xii, 5) and his removal (Vulg. *raptus est*) to God's throne, while the woman, mother of the child, endures persecutions in the desert (xii, 6, 13). Despite the confused imagery it is clear that the seer thus explains the troubles of the Church in the world, while her Lord is already conqueror in Heaven and Michael guards the celestial realm. Christ's exaltation is indeed the direct cause of the increase of the devil's formidable power on earth. The evil powers hope to defeat the saints and thereby seize their last chance of regaining lost dominions. As their strategy unfolds, the cosmic setting of their attacks becomes more pronounced. A Satanic trinity has been detected in the league of the dragon (Satan), the first beast with kingly functions, and the second beast with prophetic functions. Thus the evil cosmic principle as well as the secular arm and the religious-cultural society combine to achieve their triumph on earth which must be complete except for the followers of the Lamb. Even after the so-called battle of Har-Magedon (xvi, 16) and the apparently final execution of the unholy alliance (xix, 19) Satan, released from prison, attacks Jerusalem where Christ and the saints reside in glory. This attack is short and this time the penalty is final: the host of Satan is cast into the lake of fire (xx, 7–10).

Though victory recedes into the eschatological future the Victor himself, invisible and not immediately present, loses none of his majesty. Sitting amidst the seven candlesticks (i, 12 ff.), the exalted Christ enjoys and imparts the heavenly victory and combines the dazzling radiance of God with his own humanity. He is the Son of Man who died and lives for evermore and holds the keys of death and Hades. In Heaven he receives the worship of angels, creatures, elders, and the whole righteous host of Heaven because he is "worthy" to receive their homage together with God. The grounds of his worthiness are stated in chapters V and VI. He has prevailed because he was slain as God's Lamb. But this Lamb is also the Lion of Judah who will yet roar again and fight; slain from the foundation of the world (XIII, 8) he is full of wrath and ready for vengeance in answer to the beseeching "How long?" of the almost desperate martyrs (VI, 10). Although the actual operations of war are largely left to Michael and angelic intermediaries there is one exception: when the Lamb opens the seven seals the first unfolding manifests a white horse on whom rides the royal conqueror. The splendour of the image contributes to its ambiguity, which has defeated commentators for centuries. He rides in company with war, famine, pestilence, and death; the image anticipates none too happily the vision of "a white horse and its rider, called Faithful and True" (cf. VI, 1–2 ff. and XIX, 11–16),[1] who is obviously Jesus, the Word of God and the fierce and wrathful executor of God's vengeance. The Christ of the *Dies Irae* (centuries before its composition) leaves his throne and the evil world trembles with anguish. Victory is achieved by supernatural means as the heavenly host follow him upon white horses, "arrayed in fine linen, white and pure" (XIX, 14). The conqueror who returns from Edom with his garments dyed with the blood of the enemy (Is. LXIII) was the precursor of the heavenly victor who treads the winepress of God's wrath (Rev. XIX, 15). After Satan's last attempt the old earth and Heaven flee away at the sight of God's presence (XX, 11). The old order has passed away and all warfare is over. The new world is lit by God's glory, which all the powers acknowledge (XXI, 22–XXII, 5).

[1] Charles comments op. cit., p. 164: "The two riders have nothing in common but the white horse"! M. R. James, however, while full of admiration for Charles's erudition, warns against his tendency of tidying up the inconsistencies, particularly by means of textual rearrangements (JTS, 1921, p. 388). This criticism can now be tested against the massive and probably definitive work of Josef Schmid, *Studien zur Geschichte des griechischen Apokalypse-Textes,* 1955–6.

The great differences of the conception of Christ's victory in the New Testament focus the historian's attention on the complexity of the background to early Christianity. What was known, believed, and loved in one place was not necessarily known, believed, and loved elsewhere. Yet the central thread of the tradition is always recognizable and explicitly stated: Christ's victory is not a local, passing, earthly event, but a cosmic, lasting, and transcendental reality. Every desire for freedom could be satisfied by such a Gospel. Whereas the Jews lost Jerusalem in a vain and tragic war and their leaders repaired to Jamnia to salvage the fragments of a long tradition in opposition to Christ's victory, and whereas Rome brought home many bitter fruits of victory, the Church could offer a victory over all earthly power, the threats of possessing demons, the might of the stars, the dominion of fate, the hold of death, the realm of the devil, the universe itself, in the name of the crucified and glorified Conqueror.

Chapter Seven

THE LIFE IN HEAVEN

A LIFE-ASSENTING TRADITION

LIFE, according to the prophets and poets of the Bible, is a gift from God, wholesome and profitable. Even the tormented Job curses the day of his birth and longs for death only because God has cheated him of a good life. If he could be vindicated he would once again taste the sweetness of living. The epilogue (Job XLII) expresses popular feeling, if not the author's original intention: a happy ending cancels the tribulation, and God blesses Job with more property and good things than he ever had. Life is good. Even the very Hellenized 'Preacher' does not bemoan the ingredients of life but the failing of strength, the transitoriness of happiness, the vanity of all endeavours, when "the silver cord snaps and the golden bowl is broken" (Eccles. XII, 6). The cessation of life is its one great fault. Even evil and sin cannot annul the goodness of life, which is inspired by the breath of God and sustained by obedience to God. Thus Jeremiah, proved right in all his predictions of disaster, can still advise the survivors of the catastrophe of the fall of Jerusalem: "Build houses and live in them; plant gardens and eat their produce. Take wives and have sons and daughters . . ." (XXIX, 5 ff.). Life must go on through the generations. God has set before man a path of life and of death (Dt. XXX, 19), and those who choose life enter into a covenant of good life and loyal service (IV, 1; V, 33). God satisfies his people with length of days, with long life (Ps. XCI, 16; Prov. III, 2), which is handed on by children to children. But this long life is not everlasting life for man is mortal. "All go to one place; all are from the dust, and all turn to dust again" (Eccles III, 20). Life draws nigh to Sheol and from the pit there is no recall (Ps. LXXXVIII, 3 ff.). In Adam all die and death reigns (Ro. V, 14–18) and even Christians "fall asleep" (I. Cor. XV, 6).

How could the creative spirits of Israel simply acquiesce in human mortality? It is, of course, possible that they entertained with their faith in the living God also some hope of individual life after death. The argument from silence is often pressed too far; it does not prove that Isaiah or Jeremiah, for example, expected nothing beyond death just because they do not refer to such an expectation. More cogent, perhaps, is the absence of a prophetic tradition that Moses and the great founders of the schools lived on in Heaven. Elijah, and possibly Enoch (Gen. V. 24) are quite the exception among the heroes of Israel, but their translation to Heaven really circumvents the problem of death.

PROPHETIC THIS-WORLDLINESS

The prophets' primary task was to fulfil their respective functions: the seer had to interpret the present and predict the future; the herald of the divine oracle had to announce the will of God; the watcher must assume responsibility for his people. When the prophets, therefore, thundered against social and religious abuses in the name of God they were not concerned with a personal Hereafter any more than with a future of world-shaking miracles. Salvation must be enacted here and now; such a conviction leaves no room for eschatological fancy. If something can and must be done this action is human and upon earth.

Nevertheless, when the prophetic victories became enshrined in formal legislation, as in the code of Deuteronomy, the question arose how long this achievement was meant to last. Prophetic action cannot evade the problem of duration, especially if it be remembered that ecstatic experiences last but a very short time and even dynasties and institutions can be measured in decades and centuries. The prophets, however, do not shrink from the challenge of time. They cannot consider God's work among men to be only of temporary relevance, for righteousness and truth are essentially timeless. The Torah does not reckon at all with an end; the Covenant is "for ever" (Jer. VII, 7), sun and moon being faithful witnesses (Ps. LXXXIX). But how can a completely this-worldly outlook satisfy so great and sweeping a claim?

AGAINST PAGAN HOPES

This terrestrial, non-eschatological standpoint also came into conflict with pagan notions of immortality. We do not know, of course, whether every Canaanite believed that he would live after death with his people or in some other form of existence. His ritual certainly must have stimulated the desire and may have conveyed some sense of probability. The king survived death in combat, nature passed from death to life, the sacred marriage rites linked life with human sexuality.

The popularity of Baalism in early Israel is enough evidence for the attractiveness of fertility religion. If paganism could hold out the hope of immortality in such a tangible manner how could a non-eschatological tradition hope to be successful? The prophets countered this belief on the grounds of revelation and its implicit morality. They turned their own celestial traditions into an ally in the fight. They agreed that men live in a living universe. All sorts of beings, good and bad, exist in the spheres, but human beings share the universe on earth. Israel's vocation is for the promise of the good land, the blessings on earth, the service of this life. The conception of God as the high Lord who is present among his people rids them of an interest in cosmic migrations. The belief in the ordered universe which God has created as Heaven and earth excludes the pagan thesis of migration. Men do not live elsewhere after their death. There are no ranks of honour among the departed in proportion to the layers of the Heavens or the brightness of the stars. Just because the world is made by a good Creator death can be boldly taken in its stride.[1]

The affirmation of life as belonging to and coming from the self-revealing and loving Creator-God in Heaven proved stronger not only than the Canaanitish paganism but even than the influences of more important cultures in Africa and Asia. In these

[1] "Hinter der pessimistischen Todesauffassung steht die optimistische Schöpfungsbetrachtung"—O. Cullmann, *Unsterblichkeit der Seele und Auferstehung der Toten*, TZ, XII, 2, p. 138.

Heaven loomed large as the home of some departed spirits. In Egypt, for example, the hope of an upward migration was strongly entertained, suggested, as it appears to have been, by the smoke of cremated corpses and the bird-like escaping breath of the dead.[1] In Mesopotamia the soul is frequently portrayed as travelling to Heaven in God's chariot on the third day after death.[2] This recalls the Oriental world-view that man is in some measure a fallen god who still remembers Heaven and is animated by a divine spark. This flame of life is directly obtained from the fires which shine in the ether. Life is therefore one with the stars in the world. The power of astrology rested not only on the alleged pleasures and profits of prediction and fortune-telling, but on the supposed intimacy which united all souls to the world: "the soul returned to Heaven after death to live there among the divine stars. While it remained on earth it was subject to all the bitter necessities of a destiny determined by the revolutions of the stars; but when it ascended into the upper regions, it escaped that fate and even the limits of time; it shared equally the immortality of the sidereal gods that surrounded it."[3] No Old Testament prophet could have agreed to any order in which the initiates ascend from zone to zone until they reach the last stage of everlasting happiness.

The prophetic conception of the one God, YHWH Lord of Heaven, excluded the individual from the pagan hope of life, forbade the deification of kings and notables, and in general retarded the development of belief in a personal life after death.[4] This negative attitude persisted even when despair mingled with the prophets' political and social endeavours. Jeremiah can burst into passionate soliloquies of grief which anticipate the inevitable doom and destruction of his foolish people; he can see the earth waste and void,[5] the Heavens without light and the end of all

[1] Cf. J. H. Breasted, *Development of Religion and Thought in Ancient Egypt*, 1912, pp. 109 ff.; E. Langton, *Good and Evil Spirits*, 1942, pp. 77 ff.

[2] Cf. W. Bousset, *Die Religion des Judentums im späthellenistischen Zeitalter*, 1926, p. 500.

[3] F. Cumont, *The Oriental Religions in Roman Paganism*, 1911, pp. 125–6.

[4] Cf. O. S. Rankin, *Israel's Wisdom Literature*, 1936, p. 177.

[5] Supposing Jer. IV, 23 ff. to be genuine.

known civilization; yet this does not induce him to seek for compensation elsewhere. Even before Jeremiah, Amos proclaims the Day of the Lord as a day of darkness in which cosmic forces cause universal ordeals (v, 18ff.) and Isaiah pictures the awful ruin of Jerusalem (ch. III) without looking for an answer in the beyond. It is true, a strong apocalyptic feeling lies behind many oracles, for the prophets begin to be disillusioned about improvement by progress and the possibilities of moral reformation; even in Israel the European motto applies: "Plus ça change, plus c'est la même chose." But this realization does not lead the prophets to postulate individual salvation or eschatological consolations; instead they look for the coming of a new world, for even earthly success seems too paltry a thing when human disorders are on a scale such as necessitates a cosmic conception.

THE NEW WORLD

Assuming that supernatural forces are at work and that angelic wars spill over into human affairs it is no longer sufficient to preach and exhort in earthly terms alone. Memories of Elijah and his chariot of fire and of Elisha's heavenly host stir; the ancient hopes of the golden city, of the perfect garden, of God's marriage to his people, and of the royal banquet live again. The Second Isaiah in particular announces the end of the old things and the coming of the New (XLI, 22; LII, 1ff.; LIV, 55; cf. LXI, 10). After the Exile, prophecy makes increasing use of the ancient apocalyptic images of its mantic forbears in order to jump the confines of merely earthly concerns; it looks for the Kingdom of God in the setting of a new Heaven and earth to crown the history of God's acts on earth.

Notwithstanding this immense widening of the prophetic vista, from Israelite parochialism to universal salvation, the doctrine of life after death still remained surprisingly restricted. Famous apocalyptic passages may now easily be read in a spirit hardly intended by their authors. The opening of the graves and the reanimation of God's people in Ezekiel, chapter XXXVII, refer to the possibilities of national resurrection, conceived on a miraculous scale. Even the anonymous author of "Thy dead shall live; my dead bodies shall rise" (Is. XXVI, 19) still views the resuscitation of the people as the primary token of God's apocalyptic favour in the future.

THE VINDICATION OF THE GODLY

The essential link between death and life in these and similar passages is the typical Hebrew element of *vindication*. God is the Redeemer of Israel, the next-of-kin, so to speak, who will not let his Holy One see corruption (Ps. XVI, 10). The righteous nation does not deserve extinction, the holy must not go into perdition and be cast into the pit. They have a sacred cause which cries out for vindication. The vindication of the innocent righteous, who are killed, forges ultimately a strong link between the individual's death and his restoration. The martyr must be shown to be in the right though he dies (Ps. XXIII). The Servant of God, who is smitten and who suffers death, must be rewarded with life: he prospers and is exalted (Is. LII, 13–LIII, end). When the wicked are destroyed God takes the pious man to himself with glory (Ps. LXXIII, 24 ff.). But these apocalyptic passages which assert a positive belief in personal life after death are rare in the Old Testament. Only in the second century B.C. does the vindication of the pious on a broad scale become a practical proposition and a moral necessity. The political and cultural exigencies of the Hellenistic world demanded a positive eschatology, which nevertheless preserved the integrity of the prophetic position. This compromise comes to a fine point in the Maccabean conflict. The dead are not dead; not only the righteous but also the unrighteous have to give an account of themselves: "Many of them who sleep in the dust of the earth shall awake, some to everlasting life, and some to shame and everlasting contempt" (Dan. XII, 2). The vindication of the righteous is ultimately the vindication of God himself.

But how and where is such a vindication to be effected? The old conceptions were not helpful in solving this new problem. Job's vindication, for example, though something of an enigma owing to textual confusion, was probably thought of as occurring on earth (XIX, 25 ff.). The scepticism of Qoheleth tilted altogether against the righting of wrongs after death, for then man returns to dust and the spirit leaves the corpse after its short residence, thus ending the ambiguity of human life (Eccles. III, 21; XII, 7).[1] The Sheol of tradition is certainly not a place for vindication and personal justification: "there the wicked cease from troubling; and there the weary are at rest . . . the small and the great are there . . ." (Job III, 17 ff.). To look for a moral reversal of fortunes and a conscious experience in such a place and in such conditions is absurd.

The Platonic teaching in its popular Hellenistic form seems to offer advantages here which the Jewish tradition could not supply; yet its influence was much less extensive than might be expected. Thus the writer of the Wisdom of Solomon succeeds in combining a doctrine of immortality with the desire for vindication: "The souls of the righteous are in the hand of God, and no torment will touch them" (III, 1). The saints do not die, they are in peace, they have stood the trial and God empowers them to reign in their vindicated state: "the righteous live for ever and in the Lord is their reward" (V, 15). This reward is continuous with and proportionate to their labours on earth. They owe their extension of life to their performance on earth and moral retribution constitutes the *raison d'être* of their eternal life. Nevertheless, the author seems more interested in the consolation of the bereaved than in the state of the dead in their new life which remains obscure. Philo, however, goes further and accepts the common belief that God gives a life whose nature is rational as well as ecstatic (Fug. 198; Som I, 151; Conf. 12 f.).

The Rabbinic conceptions retain a great freedom of belief. Every individual is judged according to his deserts at the great assizes. The revivification of the dead could not be presented within a consistent framework, since the connected Messianic hopes varied enormously. Would the dead of Israel arise alone to enjoy the blessings of their own land? Would this precede, or coincide with, or come after, the day of the Messiah? Was such a particular rising to be differentiated from the Last Judgment when all men would give an account of themselves? Every

[1] N.B. the famous discrepancy between the MT and the LXX. The former (followed by AV, but not RV) embodies a dogmatic alteration in support of the idea of the ascent of the human spirit to Heaven after death without an intervening rest. The author's intention, preserved in the LXX, was to reject all notions of immortality.

question allows of a variety of answers. According to IV Ezra VII, 37 Jews and heathen are eligible to receive sentence to happiness or torment for all the nations are raised from the dead; some Rabbis, however, excluded the Gentiles from a portion in the World to Come,[1] whereas they claimed that all Israelites will be saved at the end. The righteous Jew, immediately upon his death, enters upon a blessed state. His soul is bound up, for safe keeping, in a "bundle of life" (an ancient conception, cf. I Sam. XXV, 29) and stored away in the heavenly treasuries, either in the highest Heaven, or Paradise, which may either be a place of transit or the final assignment of bliss.[2] Whether final or temporary, the upper world and the resurrection of the dead meet in Rabbinic Judaism, albeit without dogmatic insistence.

CHRIST AND HIS PEOPLE

The New Testament confirms the eschatology of the Hebrew tradition. Basic is the axiom that the Patriarchs are with God who is not the God of the dead, but of the living (Mk. XII, 26 f.). But the central fact that Jesus Christ has been raised from the dead and has ascended into Heaven adds further complexity. He has conquered Death and yet men die; He has overcome the world, yet the end is not yet and the Church must show forth his death until he come (I Cor. XI, 26).

The old prophetic concern for the 'here and now' comes to the fore in the Johannine conception of "eternal life". This life has the quality of the heavenly life, but it is lived on earth by men who believe in Jesus. Even before death and the last day the believer has eternal life (Jn. VI, 40) and does not perish subsequently (X, 28). The knowledge of the one true God and of Jesus the Messiah is itself eternal life (XVII, 3). The union of God and Christ and the believer is the fulfilment of the promise of eternal life (I Jn. II, 24, 25). Althought the Christians are in the world, upon earth, they are not debarred from the vital experience of eternal life. Thus John releases himself and his readers from a purely apocalyptic interpretation not only of Jesus but also of

[1] The opposite opinion, however, prevailed.

[2] Cf. IQH II, 20: "I thank thee, O Lord, because thou hast put my soul (nephesh) in the bundle of life."

eternal life. If this can begin on earth in such perfection it cannot depend on astral progress and spatial success. St. Paul echoes this prophetic directness: God renders to every man his due, to the seeker after godly virtue he gives "eternal life" (Ro. II, 7), which is the free gift of God in Christ Jesus our Lord (Ro. VI, 23). In his thought Christ and the ethical and religious decision are central: spatial and temporal considerations secondary or non-existent. Even the "heavenlies" in the Epistle to the Ephesians are not so remote as to be attained only after death. The blessing in "the heavenlies in Christ" is obviously already enjoyed on earth and the cause of profound thanksgiving (I, 3–22). Since Christ is Lord of the universe it would be intolerable for his followers merely to await life in Heaven.

Since the Christian belongs to Christ on earth he partakes already of life though he is not in Heaven. If he keeps Christ's word and is thus morally united with Christ he escapes from the experience (vision) of death (Jn. VIII, 51). Small wonder that the Jews are said to have misunderstood Jesus; basing their argument on the current saying "some will not taste of death at all before they see the Kingdom of God come with power" (Mk. IX, 1; Jn. VIII, 52) they point to the absurdity of all such claims. Is it not a case of clear hallucination to speak of the exemption from death when the individual's physical death remains beyond dispute?[1]

The Johannine position is intentionally paradoxical: The rule that "a grain of wheat fall into the earth and die" (XII, 24) applies to the Christian as it applied to Jesus. Indeed, the end of the Gospel makes it clear that popular misconceptions about the deathlessness of the beloved disciple had to be dispelled. Apparently those who held the conviction that "we know that we have passed out of death into life" (I Jn. III, 14) were apt to shelve the crisis of physical dying.

The possession of life on earth is, therefore, to be contrasted with the simple fact that all men die. The life which the Christian tastes on earth has a deathless quality; indeed, the life in Heaven

[1] The almost offensively crude realism of the description of the corpse of Lazarus (Jn. XI, 39) suggests that the Evangelist even wishes to stress the certainty of physical death.

is the fullness of that state which was begun on earth. Therefore the "eternal life" of which St. John speaks is, like the Kingdom of God in the Synoptic Gospels, a consummation to be achieved in Heaven through faith on earth. The believer's union with Christ on earth involves the active assent of the whole personality, and it is part of this assent to look forward to the judgment, when God pronounces his approbation on the faithful. This decisive confession of faith before death is not the heavenly life itself but rather the qualification for it. The ancient link of vindication, which binds life before and after death into a whole, is in Christian experience enriched by the continuity of faith.

UNIVERSAL JUDGMENT

The New Testament does not assert, however, that Christians differ from ordinary mortals in passing through the gateway of death and judgment. Typically St. Paul comments: "For we must all be made manifest before the judgment-seat of Christ" (II Cor. v, 10). He envisages here everyone's ascent to Heaven after death and accepts the apocalyptic thesis that judgment is given at the heavenly assizes. Even St. John, quoting Daniel, endorses the belief in a universal resurrection to life or to condemnation (v, 29). Commentators who pronounce this verse a gloss forget that Christianity is not a sect, providing for some initiated only who ascend to Heaven, but the revelation of God which deals with all men for whom "it is appointed to die once, and after that comes judgment (κρίσις)" (Hebr. IX, 27). The universality of this turning-point embraces not only individuals but whole nations, Churches, and groups of men. The Apocalypse regards the heavenly life as the outcome of a succession of universal judgments which Christ executes upon the nations and those who are taken from among them (v, 9; IX, 15). Never is there the slightest hesitation to ascribe cosmic universality to the whole process of death, judgment, and life.

Since Christ is the judge of all men it is obvious that the death of individuals and the judgment of the world are related to each other by the simple fact that the same Judge must decide their case. Hence a forensic atmosphere certainly combines with the detailed working-out of Christian eschatology. But the timing of the assizes is unknown and nothing but confusion has resulted from the identification of the appearance of the dead before the Judgment-Seat and the final sentence on the whole world before Christ's final appearance in glory. The New Testament refrains from giving a chronological account, not only because this is impossible but also because of its constant eschatological expectation. Thus even the concluding sentence of Hebrews IX: "Christ having been offered once to bear the sins of many will appear a second time, not to deal with sin, but to save those who are eagerly waiting for him" does not specify the time or place of this event. The author does, however, stress the point that before the Parousia of Christ men are *waiting* and this tradition is firmly incorporated into Christian eschatology. The heavenly life before the end finds men still in a state of expectation. Judgments proceed continuously until the final Judgment. The Apocalypse distinguishes between the vindication of the saints, immediately after their martyrdom, whereas the vast mass of the dead stay in death, without taking part in the first resurrection, and are in fact only summoned to the final assizes (Rev. xx).

Even without the further complication, which the "thousand years" (Rev. xx, 2, 4, 5) adds to Christian eschatology, it is clear that the universal appearance of men in Heaven is not to be thought of as natural progress. Judgment is always a dramatic event which involves the participation of the heavenly courts (Rev. v). It is not only the gateway to eternal life but it also reveals a divine activity which is itself a wonder and far more than the mere assembly of a court for the hearing of a case. St. Paul regards the change from death to life as a mystery (I Cor. xv, 51). Incorruption does not organically follow upon corruption. Without Christ's Resurrection men perish, and communion with Christ on earth alone is not life (I Cor. xv, 18). The conquest of death through Christ is as dramatic as the judgment. Here the analogy of the seed (xv, 36 ff.) must not be mistaken and must not obliterate the discontinuity in the change from dishonour to glory, from weakness to power, from the natural to the spiritual body. This is not a gradual transformation, but a sudden *crisis*: the trumpet shall sound (xv, 52); whether for the last day or for 'our change' is quite immaterial. The naked man cannot wait after death but requires "a building from God, a house not made with hands, eternal, in the Heavens" (II Cor. v, 1 ff.). But he has no title-deeds to this house: the resurrection of the dead is not to be taken for granted but to be attained by being apprehended by Christ (Phil. III, 10 ff.). Since God is the author of our resurrection much more is still veiled than unfolded. The end, when Christ has subjected all things to himself and hands the Kingdom to the Father, involves dimensions entirely beyond human ken (I Cor. xv, 28).

THE HEAVENLY BOOK

Judgment through and in Christ brings men to life in Heaven. It is given out of the heavenly book which contains the lists of eligible citizens (Lk. x, 20).[1] The motif is ancient and common. Moses, for instance, assumes that his name is written down in God's book and the Lord assures him that only sinners are blotted out of this book (Exod. XXXII, 32 f.) Moses himself numbers the children of Israel by their names (Nrs. III, 40). To have one's name cancelled amounts to death; therefore evil-doers are "not to be written with the righteous" (Ps. LXVIII, 28). This book which is deposited in Heaven acts like a ledger from whose evidence there can be no escape. There the future is written out in advance (Ps. CXXXIX, 16) and from thence retribution proceeds (Dan. VII, 10). The recorded facts vindicate the saints and entitle them to their entry into Heaven (Mal. III, 16; Dan. XII, 1; En. XLVII, 3). St. Paul mentions his fellow-workers "whose names are in the book of life" (Phil. IV, 3) and together they make up the "assembly of the firstborn who are enrolled in Heaven" (Hebr. XII, 23), especially in recompense for their fortitude on earth (Rev. III, 5). The reverse of the picture is meant to be frightening, for those who are not written down in the heavenly book must come to perdition (Rev. XIII, 8; XVII, 8; XX, 15). Their names are erased after the opening of the incriminating tables on which all the offences have been recorded

[1] Cf. L. Koep, *Das himmlische Buch in Antike und Christentum*, 1952, esp. p. 38 for the supposition that the book of life is a metaphor which has grown up in Biblical soil.

(En. XCVIII, 7 f.; CIV, 7; CVIII, 7; s. Ap. Bar. XXIV, 1). In the preaching of Jesus, easy-going fatalism, whether optimistic or pessimistic, meets with the challenge and the warning that men must give an account of every idle word in the Day of Judgment (Mt. XII, 36). The heavenly mystery must act as a moral force on earth.

THE HEAVENLY TREASURE

The judgment out of the book presupposes that the past is stored up until the Day of Judgment. The New Testament reflects the common teaching that man earns a good treasure in Heaven while on earth, and that this treasure is itself preserved in the heavenly treasuries. In Tobit IV, 7–10 the well-known formula reads: "Give alms . . . according to your means: for you store away a good deposit for yourself against the day of necessity, because alms delivers from death", presupposing that the works of the just are stored up with God; according to IV Ezra VII, 77 the just are shown their treasures on the last day, which are kept in the heavenly store-chambers (s. Ap. Bar. XIV, 12) to be opened at the assizes (XXIV, 1). The Jewish tradition continued to value good works as an assurance of a good future after death. The good man reaps the capital sum after having paid the interest in premiums.[1] The least ambiguous use of this motif occurs in the Sermon on the Mount. Jesus teaches the eschatological axiom that treasures on earth are not worth having. Whether the property in question is private or public, material or cultural, is not further discussed. The point is that in the passing world it is not safe. The true incorruptible treasure is in Heaven, for in the heavenly treasury the deposit cannot be assailed and loss is impossible. Riches on earth disqualify from wealth in Heaven; indeed, poverty and self-abandonment now warrant the future treasure in Heaven (Mt. XIX, 16 ff.) Self-reliance is the surest way to eternal poverty. Richness in good works, which means the voluntary giving away of wealth, lays up the much-needed eternal currency as a good foundation (I Tim. VI, 17–19). This conception need not be taken in its obvious, materialistic sense of a commercial exchange. The mental and moral and

[1] Cf. Str. B, I, pp. 430 f. for Rabbinic parallels.

emotional riches of Christ, held together by Christians, constitute not only a claim on the heavenly bank but also an absolute possession at all times (Col. II, 1–3). But even the spiritualized belief in eternal treasure bases itself upon the traditional concept of the heavenly treasury: from there Jesus gives the living bread (Jn. VI, 33 ff.) to those on earth, and the "hidden manna" and the "white stone" to the Christian victor and martyr (Rev. II, 17).

"HOW ARE THE DEAD RAISED?"

Although the heavenly life clearly depends upon the translation of men to Heaven, the New Testament retains a marked silence on the means whereby the dead reach the desired goal. The Corinthians' question "How are the dead raised?" (I Cor. XV, 35) evokes an impatient reply which carefully avoids an answer on the point of transport. The Apostle is not drawn into an argument about the Styx or anything of the sort. More seriously, despite the tradition of the Lord's Ascension and the Apostle's own experience of a temporary removal to Heaven, the New Testament nowhere asserts that all ordinary mortals will also be translated after death in a like manner. The Pauline assertion "God raised the Lord and will also raise us up by his power" (I Cor. VI, 14) leaves a large margin of unanswered questions.

In some pseudepigraphical works the concessions to the imagination go much further. Frequently the hero is bodily translated into Heaven before he can receive his revelation. Isaiah, for example, is said to leave behind his body during his trance while his spiritual self converses in Heaven (Asc. Is. VII, 5 ff.). This and similar passages recall the popular theme of the ascension of Elijah in the chariot of fire (II K. II).[1] Though this belief is perfectly orthodox no similar claim is made for Christians; a flight of the expiring spirit to Heaven upon death is also absent from the early Kerygma. On the contrary: "no one (and certainly no soul) has ascended into Heaven" (Jn. III, 13) for Christ is unique. The visionary of the Apocalypse is no exception to the rule; he is simply admitted to Heaven through an open door while

[1] E.g. Enoch *passim*; g. Ap. Bar. 11, 1 ff.

he is alive. Of the dead nothing is said except that they appear before Christ.

The New Testament appears to reflect the Rabbinical suspicion of speculation; both religious traditions in their several ways discourage a pseudo-mystical approach, especially in regard to the Merkabah[1] (Chariot), which in popular credulity supplied the ferry service between the two worlds. In a world where Gnostic teachers influenced many, dangerous meditations on the theme of Ezekiel's vision (ch. I) were not permitted, or, at any rate in later Judaism, withheld from all but the initiates who could be trusted not to abuse esoteric knowledge. Such caution was not due to dogmatic prudery but was well-advised in a climate which favoured the mysterious accounts of the souls' travels on the path of the dead from earth to Heaven.

In the pagan myths the dead heroes reach Heaven on foot or horseback, in flight or swimming or sailing, generally against immense obstacles in many places. Monuments of the Roman period show in reliefs how the soul travels to its destination. Especially the deified emperors attain to their apotheosis in Heaven in the manner of Hercules. The celebrated Igel monument near Trier, erected by the rich mercantile family of Secundini, probably in the latter half of the third century, obviously identifies the deceased with Hercules in his ascent to Heaven. Even ordinary mortals were heroized and caught up by the sun. The theme of an astral apotheosis is conveyed by the star-spangled canopy above the bier of a Roman military official at Amiternum and the famous ivory leaf of Constantius Chlorus in the British Museum. The apotheosis of Marcus Aurelius depicts the steed, the winged angel, Selene with her stag-drawn chariot, accompanied by the evening star and heralded by the figure of Night, Ocean, and by the chariot of the sun rising above Terra Mater. In the sepulchral iconography the defiance of death is often symbolized by the soaring eagle and the radiant corona or wreath. However varied the visual evidence may be, it testifies to the complete success of Oriental eschatology in the West. At least the desire to soar after death, above the earth, into the spheres beyond

[1] Cf. JE, vol. VIII, pp. 498 ff.; G. G. Sholem, *Major Trends in Jewish Mysticism*, 1941, pp. 40 ff.

the sky was intense and probably very widely spread and accepted.[1] It not only depended upon but even governed Gnostic cosmology.[2]

THE RESURRECTION OF THE FLESH

It is obvious that Christian preaching could not compromise with such notions of apotheosis though it proclaimed the attainment to eternal life in Heaven. The Apostles' Creed with its *Carnis Resurrectio* puts up a barrier against confusion. The clause is not so much proof of the Jewishness of the doctrine as of the acceptance of the pagan challenge.[3] The strange expression does not derive straight nor solely from Jewish sources.

Judaism had its own difficulties when it came to describe the revivification of the dead and was not averse to the doctrine of the immortality of the soul.[4] The resuscitation of the flesh was then considered by some, as it always will be, to be undesirable, because of its well-known fragility, and unsuitable precisely because its components are very unheavenly: "flesh and blood cannot inherit the Kingdom of God" (I Cor. xv, 50).[5] Nevertheless the Resurrection of the Dead (the Hebr. *Techiat hametim* equals the Greek ἀνάστασις νεκρῶν) was also conceived of as the Resurrection of the Flesh in Jewish and Christian circles of the first century,[6] and thence perpetuated in the provocative *Carnis Resurrectio* of the Latin Church. The historians of Christian dogma[7] agree that the choice of the expression is not accidental,

[1] Cf. W. Bousset, *Dir Himmelsreise der Seele,* Archiv für Religionswissenschaft IV, 1901, pp. 136 ff., 229 ff.; for a different view see A. Dietrich, *Eine Mithrasliturgie,* 1910, pp. 181 ff. For sepulchral art in the Roman world cf. A. Strong, *Apotheosis and After Life,* 1915.

[2] Cf. G. Quispel, *Gnosis als Weltreligion,* 1951, pp. 40 ff. The planetary gods act as somewhat crude and stupid non-commissioned officers to guard the way to eternity, but once they are given the password they show themselves as friendly and even helpful fellows.

[3] Thus Justin insists that Christian Life after death is in no way connected with pagan ascensions (Apol. I, 54). The myths of Hercules were invented in imitation of Ps. xix, 5. Cf. M. Simon, *Hercule et le Christianisme,* 1955, esp. p. 197: "Entre la mort du Christ et son ascension s'insère la résurrection glorieuse de son corps 'spirituel'", for which the myth of Hercules offers no equivalent.

[4] Cf. GFM, vol. II, pp. 380 ff.; Str. B. IV, p. 1131.

[5] Cf. Kant's protest, *Religion innerhalb d. Grenzen d. blossen Vernunft,* II, 1, c.

[6] Cf. RAC, *Auferstehung,* with refs. to σάρκος ἀνάστασις in Kleine Texte, hrsg. v. H. Lietzmann, 17, 18.

[7] Cf. M. Werner, *Die Entstehung d. christl. Dogma,* 1941, pp. 135, 288, 396.

nor merely spontaneous, but a deliberate, anti-heretical slogan, directed against the Gnostic infiltration of ideas. In particular, the clause *Carnis Resurrectio* combats notions of universal immortality. The Church maintained not only that unbelievers cannot receive spiritual bodies but also endeavoured to show that the whole order of salvation is complete. This includes the mortal bodies of those whose flesh-bodies had become spirit-possessed or "temples of God" (I Cor. III, 16; II Cor. VI, 16), or "temples of the Holy Spirit" (I Cor. VI, 19). Had not Isaiah predicted that "all flesh shall see the Lord's glory" (XL, 5)? Had not Christ's flesh-humanity been raised, and, through him, the whole of humanity? Therefore the life in Heaven and the flesh are not themselves incompatible.

The post-Biblical evidence is fairly consistent. In the Epistle of Barnabas (XXI) the beautiful vessel (τὸ καλὸν σκεῦος) appears in the general Resurrection. Clement of Rome alludes both to the salvation of the whole body (I Cl. XXXVIII, 1) and to our flesh in connexion with that of Christ (XLIX, 6). Baptism and the Holy Spirit have had their effect upon the flesh and it will be judged and raised (II Cl. IX). Ignatius speaks of the essential union of flesh and spirit, ἕνωσις σαρκινὴ καὶ πνευματική (Magn. XIII, 2). Athenagoras (Res. ch. VII) describes the ἀνάστασις σωμάτων and Tatian (Address to the Greeks, ch. VI) stresses earthly reality in the Resurrection. Irenaeus repeats the same themes of wholeness and identity with respect to the resurrection and the flesh (adv. haer. I, X, 1; II, XIX, 9; III, IX, 1; V, XIII, 2, 3; XX, 1 [A.-N.C.L.]). The whole Pauline teaching is now re-interpreted with a sharp twist and I Corinthians XV is used, *per impossibile*, in support of the resurrection of the flesh. The exposition on the theme of the flesh of Jesus, as given in comments on John VI, serves the same purpose, and this despite the assertion that "the flesh profits nothing" (VI, 63). At the beginning of the third century Tertullian in his *De resurr. carnis* could present the Christian world, in the interest of rewards and punishments, with an "eloquent panegyric of the flesh".[1] Against this success no Platonic reaction, even if led by Origen,[2]

[1] J. N. D. Kelly, *Early Christian Creeds,* 1950, p. 164.

[2] E.g. in *De Princ.* II, X, 3; *c. Cels.* V, chs. XIV ff.

could prevail. His plea that the spiritual body alone is capable of inhabiting Heaven failed. The astonishing fixity of Christian dogma[1] certainly owes nothing to the tentative formulations of Rabbinic Judaism.

THE HEAVENLY BODY

Credal slogans, however, are not enough to clarify our problem of the translation of human mortals into Heaven. The silence of the New Testament stands as a persistent defence against apocalyptic and Gnostic speculations. The only reality which is to be commonly acknowledged is that Christ has gone to Heaven to prepare a place for his people where he will receive them into communion (Jn. XIV, 3). Christians die with Christ in Baptism and are raised like Christ (Ro. VI, 4, 5). Such a belief requires a unique treatment. Neither the reassembly of the material physical components nor the spiriting away of disembodied spirits appears to provide a satisfactory means to describe the access of the dead to Heaven. It is to be doubted whether a 'materialistic' or a 'spiritual' theory is more likely to succeed. The relevant data of the problem are the perishability of human mortals and the eternal abiding of Christ in Heaven with whom the dead are to live. This paradox is not resolved along materialistic or spiritual lines of thought. It is, for instance, not after entertaining materialistic views that St. Paul favours an immaterial continuity in I Corinthians XV, which he discards in II Corinthians to make room for what is commonly called 'an altogether spiritual conception.'[2] In neither case does the Christian, or man in general, grow into Heaven, but in each he is changed, both inwardly and outwardly, either by means of a new body, or a new eternal house in place of the dissolving earthly tent.[3] But when does he reach this heavenly state? To this un-

[1] For detailed treatment see W. Haller, in *Zeitschrift für Theologie und Kirche,* 1892, 'Die Lehre von der Auferstehung des Fleisches bis auf Tertullian'; J. T. Darrach, *The Resurrection of the Flesh,* 1921.

[2] For a detailed discussion Cf. W. D. Davies, *Paul and Rabbinic Judaism,* ch. X.

[3] Bultmann comments on so-called Pauline inconsistencies: "This contradiction betrays how little difference it makes what images are used to express the fact that 'life' has a future beyond life in the 'flesh' (*Theology of the New Testament,* vol. I., p. 346, E.T.).

comfortable question scholars have given widely varying answers. If St. Paul links the resurrection with the Last Day in I Corinthians xv there must be a waiting period for the dead until they are summoned to their new existence. What becomes of them in the intervening period before they go to Heaven? Do they moulder in their graves and are their bones reassembled when the trumpet sounds? The theme is not absent from the New Testament: "Many bodies of the saints who had fallen asleep" had been raised and emerged from their tombs (Mt. xxvii, 52 f.), and "all who are in the tombs" will hear the voice of the Son of Man (Jn. v, 28). As against this prevalent logic of later Christendom the contribution of II Corinthians can hardly be ignored, where the succession of the house for the tent occurs immediately upon death and where the horror of the naked corpse is particularly set aside. Dr. Davies concludes his long discussion of the problem with the attractive verdict that Paul's reconciling idea is to be found in his belief that "the Age to Come eternally existent in the Heavens had already appeared in its initial stages in the Resurrection of Jesus. Already the resurrection body, the body of the final Age to Come was being formed. Paul had died and risen with Christ and was already being transformed. At death, therefore, despite the decay of his outward body, Paul would already be possessed of another 'body'. The heavenly body was already his."[1] Thus both continuity and discontinuity are vouchsafed to men in Christ inasmuch as Christ changes the form of our humble body and conforms it to his own body of glory (Phil. iii, 21).

Such a position is clearly consistent with the Johannine view of eternal life. It places every human death within the great framework of salvation, but it does not state how the dead body is related to the glorified body in Heaven. The immediacy of the possession of life in Christ would seem not to permit a link with the earthly body, once it is left behind. But it must be remembered that the heavenly realm itself is still in a state of flux until the final Day of Judgment, and while it may be urged that all Christians go to Heaven in their new bodies after death they cannot possibly reach a final state until after the great reversal

[1] Op. cit., pp. 317 f.

when all nations are summoned to judgment. In view of this further complexity intermediate stages cannot be wholly ruled out.

INTERIM STATES

We have already shown how the celestial topography accommodates both those awaiting judgment, though dead, and the living, in Paradise.[1] When Enoch traverses the spheres he sees the righteous and the unrighteous in their respective places.[2] It is possible that for St. Paul such a scheme is superseded (despite his vision, II Cor. XII, 4), but its acceptance is echoed in the eschatology of the "many mansions", whose existence Jesus specifically confirms (Jn. XIV, 2). Abraham and Lazarus are above (Lk. XVI, 22); the humbled evil-doer is translated to Paradise after his crucifixion (Lk. XXIII, 43).

This interim state is wholly opposed to all notions favouring the loss of personality. The individual retains his identity and is not absorbed in Christ. Having been rescued on earth he experiences the fruits of victory in the borderland between two worlds. The seed which was planted here comes to fruition there; the treasure which was invested here is enjoyed with interest there. The self which died in Christ here rises to be with him there in a station appropriate to the judgment of each individual person. In this interim state the soul remembers the past and anticipates the future. It has entered upon the penultimate stage in which some uncertainties and contingencies are still found. The transformation from the earthly to the heavenly life cannot be completed before the work of Christ and the re-creation of the universe have been achieved. Even for those who are admitted to life after death there remains the waiting as for the multitude of the dead.

CONTINUITY AND DISCONTINUITY WITH FORMER TIES

The heavenly life which the New Testament suggests belongs almost entirely to this penultimate stage; yet it would be a mistake to draw too hard a distinction here between it and the last

[1] Above, pp. 46 ff.

[2] Chs. XXI–XXXII.

and final condition of the resurrected life of man. Throughout, the imagery presupposes that for human beings, however transformed, life remains human. It is true that in the controversy with the Sadducees Jesus refutes their case by the positive statement that the dead are "like angels in Heaven" (Mk. XII, 25). This would at first give the impression that human mortals lose their essential humanity through the transformation of death and resurrection. Against this it should be observed that the proposition states an analogy of status in Heaven and, more definitely, the cessation of marriage and sexuality in the life after death. It is nevertheless an astonishing statement (Mt. XXII, 33) for it runs counter to the popular notions of celestial blessings, which, *a fortiori*, must excel those on earth. It has even been thought to reflect the Church's preference for virginity on earth (cf. I Cor. VII) which was itself the result of eschatological expectation. In any case, it throws up the problem of transformation in the most radical manner. The propagation of the species is no longer required and the curse on Woman and Life is reversed (Gen. III, 16 ff.).

THE HUMAN FAMILY

The heavenly life anticipates the age to come to such an extent that it reflects its conditions, and these stress the lack of continuity between life on earth and life in Heaven. The passage just quoted, if pressed to its logical conclusion, abrogates not only that essential human faculty of sexual love and relationship and the need for procreation but even the very survival of family ties. The earthly relationships do not appear to be translated into Heaven. It is never said of the Christian that he "is gathered unto his people, old and full of days" (Gen. XXV, 8; XXXV, 29), as of Abraham and Isaac; he does not "go to his fathers in peace". It is indeed remarkable how the New Testament lacks an awareness of the problem. Farewells are solemn, but the consolatory note of 'meeting again in Heaven' is not struck (cf. e.g. Acts XX, 38). In the Lazarus story Martha evidently holds that the long delay before the resurrection at the last day divides brother and sister without offering an interim consolation. Again, St. Paul's admonitions towards good family relationships never evoke the threat of a meeting hereafter. But the argument from silence must not be pressed too far. The parable of Dives and Lazarus at least suggests some form of recognition and the absence of a gulf between those who belong together (Lk. XVI, 19 ff.). It is in fact difficult to believe that brotherly love and solidarity —the Philadelphia of the New Testament—can be broken by death. The mutual abiding in love is eternal life, according to St. John; the disciples will see Jesus again (Jn. XVI, 22), not only in this life but also in the life to come. It follows that they are not likely to be deprived of their own mutual company. Similarly the Pauline conception of the Body (e.g. I Cor. XII, 27) and of the household cannot favour a sudden disruption and cessation of membership after death.[1]

The New Testament keeps silent on the relationship between the members of earthly families in Heaven. The problem of fathers and sons, mothers and daughters, must be solved on earth. If families are split in their religious allegiance on earth the ill cannot be healed hereafter. Furthermore there is a fervent eschatological impatience with the rigidity of narrow family ties which enlarges the whole conception of the real family (Mk. III, 31–5; Lk. XIV, 26). In answer to Peter's statement "we have left all and followed thee" Jesus promises his disciples a twofold recompense: a much wider family on earth, with persecutions, and "in the world to come eternal life" (Mk. x, 28 ff.). Here on earth the natural ties of the blood are transcended and in Heaven they do not prevail. Eternal life is actually contrasted with home and hearth.

The severity of the texts must, however, be balanced with such later evidence as we possess from the Roman catacombs. The general background is joyful and very human. In beautiful landscapes children are seen at play and the newly alive attend banquets unless they are happily asleep. The setting is one of

[1] Cf. J. A. T. Robinson, *The Body*, 1952, esp. pp. 51, 78. Robinson holds that "nowhere in the New Testament has the resurrection of the body anything specifically to do with the moment of death. The key 'moments' for this are Baptism and *Parousia* (p. 79). "The house not made with hands, eternal, in the Heavens, the οἰκοδομή from God (II Cor. v, 1) is the Body of Christ, the Church (76 f.), not the individual's new body. If this is correct the individual survives death *only* as organic member of the whole Body, and then hardly in a conscious state, though in Heaven.

hope and does not exclude the probability of a blessed reunion of loved ones in Heaven. Christian funerals were both austere and joyful and thus combined the ascetic and the natural feelings about the continuation of earthly love in Heaven. In some typical scribbles a surviving lover addresses his departed love: "Vivas in Christo, in Bono . . . vivas in Christo, dulcis, semper vivas in Deo"; beside her he would soon rest on earth and wait not only for the resurrection but for the meeting with her. Although liturgical references to "in caelesti regno", "in caelesti sede" are relatively rare the private feeling of affection goes much further. The departed has "gone to God", is "received or accepted by God", "lives with Christ", "is among the angels", "among the saints", "refreshed and joyful among the stars". This hope is often portrayed by the flight of the dove which symbolizes the flight of the spirit to the great social realm in Heaven, or by the lamb on the way to join the blessed flock of the Shepherd.[1]

PROPERTY

We are not faced with a double eschatology which entertains incompatible views about the life in Heaven; rather the positive hope derives from the acceptance of the austere teaching about family rights and their resolution in the concept of the family of God. Sacrificial living on earth prepares for life in Heaven and particularly concerns the key issue of family life, namely property. As the Christian abandons property in service on earth so he is not burdened with any assets or liabilities in Heaven. 'Lands' pass out of the orbit of Christian concerns. The rights and privileges, which are most fully valued on earth, as well as the title deeds to property, no longer avail in Heaven. The rich man who stores up goods is simply a fool because his life is required of him suddenly and his riches remain left behind on earth (Lk. XII, 16 ff.). The treasure to be seized in Heaven is not continuous with earthly riches. On the contrary, the reversal is most marked, for the poor own the Kingdom of God (Lk. VI, 20). Earthly notions of investment, profit, and inheritance fail to apply. The real man is himself, naked and stripped of things: "We brought nothing into

[1] Cf. G. B. de Rossi, *La Roma Sotteranea Cristiana,* 1867, esp. Tomo II, Tav. XXX ff.

the world, and we cannot take anything out of the world" (I Tim. vi, 7). The heavenly treasure exposes the futility of all former deceits. Although the early Church clearly has to rely upon contributions and welcomes the gifts of property on earth, no such transactions of property are thought of in Heaven. Thus the life in Heaven dispenses with one of the most substantial earthly activities.

THE END OF THE LAW

The abolition of private interests and group concerns inevitably implies the end of a good deal of legislation. The heavenly state no longer depends on the compulsion of the Law. Jesus Christ has mediated the new Covenant whose coming Jeremiah had prophesied, and this covenant of spontaneous right-doing makes the old redundant (Hebr. viii, 6–13). The old way of life has reached senility after its maturity and is to be replaced by life itself: the new creation needs new things (II Cor. v, 17). The whole conception of secular government also must vanish. The Apocalypse contrasts Babylon, the type of government by tyranny, with the heavenly Jerusalem and celebrates its downfall (Rev. xiv, 8). The kingship of Christ and the thrones of Israel in Heaven pronounce the doom on Gentile rule and the authority of the great (Mk. x, 42). Just as the codes concerning property cannot apply in Heaven, so lawyers, officials, and judges are dismissed from the scene; therefore power in all its degrees is entirely irrelevant to the new mode of existence. The accumulation of human strength, as that of human wealth, has lost its point. Subversive activities and enslaving suppression have no part in the new society's life.

The few glimpses of the heavenly life in the New Testament stress the denial of earthly rights and customs, a denial enunciated upon earth and accomplished in the New Age. Thus the typical tensions—as between men, nations, and races—which are the ingredients of constant warfare on earth disappear. The conflicts which arise with the clash of hostile carnal appetites have lost their cause. Sin which coincided with the pursuit of self-interest no longer attracts, and the natural Law, which governed human life from birth to death in a strict sequence of cause and effect, is also done away in the reign of Christ. Since sin and law are dead letters in Heaven the New Testament depicts the heavenly life as a new existence for new men (Ro. VI, 4; Jn. III, 3). They tread a "new and living" way which by-passes the veil of Law (rent through Christ's death, Mt. XXVII, 51) and gains access to Heaven by this road "of his flesh", from which the old barriers have been removed (Hebr. X, 20)'[1] The Holy of Holies was barred in the Temple; in Heaven God's Presence is accessible.

THE NEW LIFE

It is impossible to exaggerate the newness of the Life in Heaven. The typically religious activities and experiences known on earth also become redundant. St. Paul in I Corinthians XIII draws a clear picture of the transitoriness of prophecy, knowledge, faith, and good works; in a rhetorical style, which is nevertheless used to express a realistic theme, he insists on the nature of our earthly religious state as wholly inadequate: we know in part, we see in a mirror, in a riddle. But it does not follow that these childlike activities have to be developed. They must be allowed to expire when they become useless, as they do in Heaven, where everything is self-evident and not in need of religious exposition or implementation. The Apostle's insistence on Agape steers the course of his argument: what counts both on earth and in Heaven is the single-minded Christian loving devotion, the desire of all desires, purified and eternally valid. In the enjoyment of Agape, both given and received, the new creature stands out from the old; thus, and thus only, he may be said to preserve his identity in the eternal world, even when all things around him change beyond all human imagination.

STILL HUMAN

The new creature in Heaven need not divest himself wholly of his humanity or human experience. In this respect the Resurrection Body of Jesus foreshadows the manner of life lived in Heaven. We have become united both to the likeness of his death and of his Resurrection (Ro. VI, 5); the identification reminds us,

[1] Taking the two genitives *καταπετάσματος* and *σαρκὸς* to stand in a brachylogy of opposites; cf. Spicq, ICC ad loc.

in the few reports of Jesus' appearances after his Resurrection, that the Lord lived for forty days on earth in that human Body in which he ascended to Heaven. Just as he was not a ghost, the new man in Christ is not a ghost. As he could see and hear and move and taste and eat and be touched, so the spiritual bodies not only continue but transcend the use of their faculties in the flesh. The heavenly life is full of sensory living.

IN THE HEAVENLY CITY

The classical image in which continuity and discontinuity fuse is that of Jerusalem, the heavenly city. Despite its popularity in subsequent centuries it does not appear to belong to the original Kerygma. The only Jerusalem, of which the Gospels speak, is the actual city (e.g. Mt. v, 35), the seat of much opposition and blindness, the place where the Galilean Saviour must suffer, the Jewish capital which must henceforth be levelled down to the ground, in fulfilment of the rejection of Jesus, who wept over the city. Yet it would not be true to say that there is only an escapist romance of a new Jerusalem which the fall of the old in A.D. 70 inspired. The theme is an old one in Jewish apocalyptic thought and lends itself to Christian adaptation. Haggai had said: "The latter glory of this house shall be greater than the former . . . in this place will I give peace" (II, 9).

The idealized picture of Jerusalem dates from the Exile after the fall of the city in 586 B.C. The pattern of the new city, whose name is "YHWH SHAMA" (Ezek. XLVIII, 35), occupies the last nine chapters of the book of Ezekiel. Some scholars believe them to be genuine reminiscences of the old, and hopes for the new city, by the prophet himself; others ascribe the contents to the designs of the priests of a much later age.[1] Apart from setting up Jerusalem as an ideal yet to be realized the prophecies do not attain to the celestial note. The latter is found in the second Isaiah, although here again the political and earthly orbits still encompass the heavenly. However, Zion, as the bride of God (XLIX, 16 ff.) whose innumerable children extend their habitations (LIV, 2 ff.) while the city is built up by God on sapphires and precious stones (LIV, 12 ff.), tends to become otherworldly too. There

[1] Cf. R. Pfeiffer, *Introduction to the Old Testament*, 1948, pp. 525 ff.

God's disciples live in peace (LIV, 13) and thither the nations flow (II, 2 ff; LVI, 7).

With the development of Jewish cosmogony, and in particular the parallelism of Heaven and earth, later Judaism exalted this ideal Jerusalem into Heaven. The Targum to Psalm CXXII, 3 reads: "Jerusalem, built in Heaven as a city to associate with that on earth"; God will not dwell in the upper city until the lower be rebuilt. The destiny of both is linked. According to b. Chag. 12 b, God's dwelling par excellence, Jerusalem, is in the Zevul, the fourth Heaven. In s. Ap. Baruch, IV, 2 f. the heavenly Jerusalem is pre-existent. Adam, Abraham, Moses are shown the city, which according to this tradition is the same as Paradise. According to IV Ezra, VII, 26, this "invisible city" pertains to the Messiah's age; it is open for the new generation which finds there perfect felicity (VIII, 52). The just go there after death: "The saints will rest in Eden, the just rejoice over the new Jerusalem" (T. Dan. V, 12). In the apocalyptic tradition the earthly Jerusalem recedes; God has made the city in Heaven against the time of the new age which culminates in the succession of the new to the old (cf. En. XC, 28). But the Rabbinical tradition held such expectations to be quite misleading, for after the fall of Jerusalem in A.D. 70 (and even more after A.D. 135) the political situation did not warrant celestialism at the expense of earthly measures of reorganization. Indeed, the by now important role of the Church—her interpretation of the fall of Jerusalem above all—could not but move the Jewish leaders to oppose the universalization of religion in the shape of a heavenly Jerusalem.[1]

St. Paul's appeal for the freedom from Law makes controversial use of the symbol of the City (Gal. IV, 24 ff.) In a typically Rabbinical argument he allegorizes the nature of the two covenants, comparing the one of bondage to Sinai and that of freedom to Jerusalem, above and free. Even at a time when the earthly Jerusalem could still assert her considerable authority the Apostle alludes with surprising familiarity to the other city in Heaven in order to fight the Judaistic tendencies of his converts. The

[1] For the extreme complexity of this issue cf. S. G. F. Brandon, *The Fall of Jerusalem and the Christian Church*, 1951; for the Jewish development of Temple ideology cf. H. J. Schoeps, *Aus frühchristlicher Zeit*, 1950, pp. 175–83.

earthly Jerusalem receives in this context solely condemnation and it is impossible to judge how, if at all, the Apostle conceived of the similarity and the difference between the earthly and the heavenly cities. It is enough for him to stress the loftiness and the freedom from restraints in the city of God. The Epistle to the Hebrews takes us much further. Having been written at a time when in all probability Jerusalem had been captured by the Romans and the Christians had reacted to her fall not with lamentation but with re-orientation, the writer can use Jerusalem without equivocation: "You have come to mount Zion and to the city of the living God, the heavenly Jerusalem" (XII, 22). The triumphant statement addresses all Christians who "have here no abiding *Polis*", but seek of necessity that of the future (Hebr. XIII, 14).

IN HEBREWS

The writer develops a theme which we find not only in apocalyptic literature but also in Philo. "The city of God is called in Hebrew Jerusalem and its name when translated is "vision of peace". Therefore do not seek for the city of real being (τοῦ ὄντος) among the regions of the earth . . ." he urges, for it is part of his philosophy that "Heaven is ever melodious, producing, as the heavenly bodies go through their movements, the full and perfect harmony". (Som. I, 35–7; II, 250). Needless to say this heavenly life is universal and open to all, whether they belong to the commonwealth by birth or by their deliberate choice of religion (Spec. I, 51).

In the Epistle to the Hebrews, too, the true Jerusalem is pre-existent and the prototype of the earthly and, indeed, of all tokens of order on earth. In the heavenly *Polis*, founded and governed by God, absolute stability and security are found. Here all the spiritual orders meet in a myriad society in solemn assembly; angels and the first-born of the Church occupy their respective stations. The punctuation of Hebrews XII, 22 makes it difficult to decide whether innumerable companies of angels and the society of the Church constitute together the citizenship of the heavenly state in equal proportions or not. Quantitatively, both the angelic and the saintly orders are without end; qualitatively, most of the former were higher in rank (Hebr. ch. I) until Jesus, whom the angels serve, returned to Heaven. Now unity of love and service enfolds all the spiritual kinds. The lustful union of angels and man (Gen. VI, 4) is redeemed by the perfect harmony of the victorious throng of this city; it includes "the spirits of just men made perfect" (XII, 23), whose Judge is God. The author shows no hesitation in extending the covenanted mercies of Christ also to those who have gone before, such as the Patriarchs and Prophets, and who are found acceptable in God's judgment. The city is the theocratic state of the beginning, which as pattern preceded all copies, and of the end, which justifies all eschatological hopes. Therefore Christians do not even wish to build or reside in a falsely permanent *Polis*, which both experience and revelation demonstrate not to exist on earth. The felicity of the abiding city alone deserves the service of the pilgrim: it is the joy set before him, the end and fulfilment of striving. God acknowledges those as his own "who desire a better, namely a heavenly, country": for them he has prepared a city (Hebr. XI, 16).

The ideology of the heavenly Jerusalem is other-worldly and has no precedent outside the Christian experience.[1] The city is not only new and in the future, but it is already in existence in Heaven and welcomes those who have accomplished their earthly pilgrimage. It is the goal of all the living who endure to the end. Having acquired his passport on earth, by membership in Christ, the Christian may claim citizenship in this heavenly commonwealth (*Politeuma*, Phil. III, 20). He has become a full citizen of the new cosmic order, replacing thereby all the minor deities and astral powers which had usurped the right of celestial residence. The status is that of "συνπολῖται τῶν ἁγίων καὶ οἰκεῖοι τοῦ Θεοῦ (Ephes. II, 19). It follows that every citizen takes cognizance not only of God and Christ, but also of his fellow, practising that very same inter-relationship of Love which he had begun to acquire on earth.

[1] A detailed examination of the abundant new material at Qumran has not yet been made possible and may require a qualification of this verdict. But however other-wordly the heavenly Jerusalem of the Covenanters may have been it could not be for them the City of Jesus Christ unless and until they themselves had become Christians.

IN THE APOCALYPSE

According to the Apocalypse (Rev. III, 12), however, this present commonwealth is not identical with the new Jerusalem, but only a foretaste of the same. There Jerusalem descends from the re-made Heaven to the newly fashioned earth and evidently binds Heaven and earth together in one. The description in XXI, 11–21 portrays the Holy City both as continuous with the lay-out of and opposed to the life of the earthly Jerusalem, having contrasted its glory with the shame of the murderous Sodom and Egypt of the Crucifixion (XI, 8) and the cosmopolitan Babylon of chapter XVII. Whereas Babylon endeavoured to raise itself up into Heaven (Gen. XI) the new Jerusalem is God's gift from Heaven. Above all, the description supernaturalizes the earthly expectations and fantasies: the wall, the gates, the foundations, the measurements, the materials, the streets, retain the imagery of city reality, but they are no longer of this earth. The symbolism brings the transformation to a fine point[1]: the new Jerusalem has no Temple, because God and the Lamb are the Temple (XXI, 22). The harmony and perfection of the city are worked out by the principle of the cube: length, breadth, and height are equal (XXI, 16). The names of the twelve tribes of Israel, inscribed on the gates, (XXI, 12) and of the twelve Apostles of the Lamb on the foundations (XXI, 14) guarantee the unity and wholeness of the People of God, gathered together from the beginning to the end.

We are here not concerned with the outward appearance of the city but the kind of life that it affords to those who have survived death. Chapter XXII stresses the fruitful and peaceful character of this existence, portrayed again in direct opposition to the life on earth. The servants' activity in this uncursed universe is that of homage to God: they serve, in the liturgical sense, as formerly, with prayer and sacrifice. They contemplate the Face of God in constant vision (XXII, 3–4). What this means in terms of human experience is further brought out in VII, 15–17: the perpetual service of God spells the end to all suffering. Neither the appe-

[1] For the connexion with Old Testament and Rabbinical ideas, cf. Str. B. III, pp. 573, 795 f. for the details cf. Charles ad loc.; A. Farrer, *A Rebirth of Images*, 1949, esp, ch. VIII.

tites nor uncongenial surroundings shall harm the servants: "they shall hunger no more, neither thirst any more, the sun shall not strike them, nor any scorching heat": theirs are the waters of life, in complete fulfilment of the great prophetic themes. Above all, the whole past of incomprehensible ills is now resolved: "God shall wipe away every tear from their eyes." This picture of eternal life not only confirms the transitoriness of previous suffering but also provides the final Amen to the Beatitudes in the Sermon on the Mount. The comforting in the Kingdom of God of all the disinherited and the satisfaction of all those who hungered and thirsted after righteousness had been placed in the future (Mt. v, 3 ff.): this future has now become the present, the Service and the Vision of God supplying all that is needed for eternal life.

THE VISION OF GOD

How far does the heavenly life fulfil the goal of mystical endeavour? The pagan mysteries rewarded their initiates with beautiful sights towards which they progressed through illumination and purgation. The ἐπόπτης (initiate of the great mysteries) longed for a permanent vision and union and to this end the individual mystic underwent trials which made him equal to the gods, if successfully endured. It is, of course, obvious that the Christian faith and practice did not confirm the devious means by which such a heavenly existence was to be gained. But if the Christian Kerygma attacked the pagan cults, did it necessarily invalidate the hopes of the pagan world that the heavenly state could be reached, howbeit without the deification of the initiate? How, in fact, does the picture of the heavenly Jerusalem tally with "the belief that some men at least had seen God, and had found in the vision the sum of human happiness ... attainable by all".[1] Everywhere the vision of God had been offered as the *summum bonum*: now the Jewish-Christian Apocalypse offered it again as the fulfilment of God's Reign and the reward for Christian testimony on earth.

Both the terms and the substance of the offer probably differed

[1] K. Kirk, *The Vision of God*, 1931, p. 54. Chs. I and II are highly relevant to the whole problem of the Christian claims in their historical setting.

from what was commonly expected by many a convert. If they looked for "eternal life", as pagan mystics would have done, they must have been disappointed. The fact that the Apostles so frequently meet with and write against apostates and renegades is easily explained by the Gentile mystics' disillusionment. Instead of the hoped-for degrees of advance in illumination they had to accept the Gospel of the Kingdom of God whose righteousness must first be apprehended on earth before it can be experienced in Heaven. They had to learn that there was no separate and higher law for mystics and mystical vision. The vision of God is not left to promiscuous chance but comes through obedience; it does not depend upon successful initiations but on the practical acceptance of the truth. Only those who fulfil God's will on earth, as it is done in Heaven, may aspire to the reward in Heaven, where the perfection on earth is consummated in the Kingdom. Thus the extravagant hopes of mystical progress are constantly checked by the ethical demands of the Law of God.

The eternal Law, of which not one jot or dot will pass away (Mt. v, 18), is none other than the everlasting covenant which God ratified in Jesus. Therefore Jesus reiterates in the Johannine farewell discourses that, in the keeping of his commandments, union with God, or eternal life, is already found on earth. The pattern of the life is given. The vision of God in Heaven is, therefore, a new crowning experience, but its ethical content is continuous with the loving knowledge of God, obtained on earth. Nothing is rescinded in Heaven, either of the Lordship of Jesus or of his preaching. The Life is Jesus (Jn. xiv, 6). On earth the way—which is Jesus—was "straitened" (Mt. vii, 14); in Heaven this discipline, if not austerity, is still characteristic of life. In Heaven, however, the way is not enforced by necessity; the moral affinity between God and Man excludes external forms of rigorism. A freely-willed discipline adumbrates the loving relationship between God and Man. The Vision of God is inseparable from it. Hence the Christian mystic cannot be classed among mystics in a general manner. The moral and personal links with Jesus explain the fury of pagan mysticism in its fight against Christianity whose covenant relationship implies the corporateness of the vision throughout; indeed, "the experience of the Church makes up for the deficiencies on the part of the individual; even those who have *not* seen are blessed because they share in the Church's belief (Jn. xx, 29)".[1] This does not mean, however, that a kind of ecclesiastic allegiance replaces the forbidden private mysticism in order to secure the vision. If such perilous views appeared later they cannot claim Biblical authority. In the New Testament God's eternal perfection both demands and offers a greater reality than vested interests can command.

If we may speak of Church life in Heaven it must fully take into account the social structure of the heavenly society. The New Testament keeps a guarded silence about the relative positions of the celestial orders and human beings. It is not even possible to say which of the angels and archangels and powers are viewed as superior or inferior to the souls of men.[2] With the abolition of constraints no interest can be taken in such questions. This does not mean, however, that the corporateness of the celestial life omits reference to anything but human existence; rather men live side by side with the spiritual beings of the whole universe. The importance of the Apocalypse lies in its unique recapitulation of Old Testament and apocryphal images, such as the "four living creatures", angels and spirits. It projects into the heavenly spheres that ancient strand of prophecy which conceived of salvation not only as the defeat of evil powers but also as a newly-found concord: "the wolf shall dwell with the lamb, and the leopard shall lie down with the kid; and the calf and the young lion and the fatling together; and a little child shall lead them" (Is. xi, 6). Thus the heavenly life reflects the triumph of love in a more than human society, the earthly life being immeasurably transcended in this infinite encampment of peaceful creatures. The Child as the harbinger of peace leads the hitherto violent into a life of active harmony (xi, 8). Playing and feasting and enjoyment of one another are the features of this tradition of the social joys of the heavenly family. An absorption of the individual in the corporate is not necessary because the spiritual

[1] K. Kirk, op. cit., p. 108.

[2] Probably the angels of nature, who do not keep the Sabbath, were considered lower, the angels of the Sabbath, higher than man. Cf. Charles, ad Rev. iv, 8.

bodies coinhere in the Body without loss to themselves. They radiate the life which they receive.[1]

THE EXALTED CHRIST

The central figure of this life is the exalted Lord Jesus. To be with Christ or in Christ (Phil. I, 23) guarantees not only eternal life, but full communion with God in the blessed fellowship: "where I am, there shall also my servant be: if any man serve me, him will the Father honour" (Jn. XII, 26). The Johannine discourses expound the mystical realism of the heavenly life. "The Lord did not cease to be with the Father, and therefore in Heaven, while he lived on earth . . . wherever he is, there is Heaven."[2] The principal point is that the vision of and belief in Jesus both prepare for and vouchsafe the vision and knowledge of God: "he who has seen me has seen the Father." (Jn. XIV, 9). The indwelling of the Spirit accomplishes in men the union in Glory. Again it is the Apocalypse which translates this teaching particularly to the heavenly realm: the Lamb of God is surrounded by his adherents, the Lord by his people, the King by his subjects, the Light by the glorified. Eternal life is equated with the following of Christ. The imitation of Christ crowns all endeavours, for the mighty acts, the signs and wonders, done upon earth, are the sole reality in Heaven. Although no needs of healing or forgiving exist now, the love which prompted these miracles prevails completely. The Life in Heaven is, therefore, a procession behind and the adoration of the Lamb. Where he goes, the blessed people go; whatever he does they emulate; what he wills they give. The apprehension of him who has apprehended his loved ones, the reply of love to the first love, this conscious growth into the depths of divine love, as expressed in the filial devotion to the Father, summarizes the Life in Heaven, the fulfilment of something barely begun upon earth where discipleship had met with estrangements and deviations at so many turns.

[1] Cf. Richard Baxter, 'He wants no friends': "centred all in thee, members, though distant, of one Head; in the same family we be, by the same faith and spirit led . . . the heavenly hosts, world without end, shall be my company above".

[2] R. H. Lightfoot, *St. John's Gospel,* 1956, p. 132. This point is also made by Calvin, *Inst.* II, XIII, 4.

As might be expected, the pictorial art of early Christianity brings out the peculiar feeling of the celestial existence centred on Christ. Everywhere Christ, replacing gods and emperors, enthroned in majesty within the mandorla, faces the onlooker. He is removed from all the conditions of time and space, in his pre-existent state, to which the glory of the Resurrection is added, and by his intimate glance draws in the beholder.[1] Christ, the new Sol Invictus, radiant with Easter light, receives his own, perhaps as the great Fisher of men—"the human soul typified by a fish and plunged in the waters of Baptism, is drawn forth by the Angler, washed and reborn into a new, divine life of Grace—a positive conception of restoration to a supernatural plane of which the pagan world seems to have had no inkling"[2]—or as the Good Shepherd who completes the rescue of the lost sheep in Heaven where they surround him with grateful and adoring love. The individual soul on its journey to Heaven is never identified with the ascending Christ but rather prayers are offered to the effect that the deceased may go to Heaven like Elijah: "Libera, Domine, animam servi tui N. sicut liberasti Eliam de morte communi." Similarly the very ancient imagery of the ascending Elijah serves in early Christian art and rids it thereby of the suspicion that paganism has crept back into Christian salvation.[3]

The unity of the ascended Christ and his flock restores to each member a status of Christ-likeness. The divine image, which was lost, shines forth from every face: "we shall be like him, for we shall see him as he is". This bestowal of the ἑικὼν τοῦ Θεοῦ upon the saved in Heaven led later writers to speak of deification in a sense which would have been impossible to New Testament writers. The imitation and following of Christ, and especially the ascension to Heaven to be with Christ, seemed to imply θεοποίησις or θέωσις, not only as a goal but as present reality. Hippolytus concludes his Refutation of all Heresies with the affirmation

[1] Cf. A. Strong, *Apotheosis and After Life,* 1915, for the significance of the 'primitive', non-Hellenistic frontality of the Saviour's position.

[2] J. Toynbee, J. W. Perkins, *The Shrine of St. Peter,* 1956, pp. 116 f., for a description of Tomb M, Pl. 32.

[3] Cf. H. Schrade, *Zur Ikonographie der Himmelfahrt Christi,* 1930, pp. 81 ff.

that the obedient and regenerate disciple resembles God, having become immortal and deified. Irenaeus acclaims the regaining of the divine image[1]; later Athanasius can claim boldly: "He became man that we might become divine".[2] But Biblical eschatology clings to the ancient images of human fellowship rather than God-likeness.

SYMBOLS OF UNION WITH GOD: THE BANQUET

The favourite symbol of the fellowship in Heaven is that of the sacred banquet. It pertained to the Messianic hope that the righteous would partake of the good meal which is freely given (Is. LV, I ff.). In the tradition of Israel God was known as the rock of living waters (Ex. XVII, 6) and the bestower of bread and plenty; indeed, in the age of the Messiah the redeemed feast upon Behemoth and Leviathan (IV Ezra VI, 52). The community at Qumran, however, anticipated the heavenly meal in their own austere way.[3] The parable of the marriage feast (Mt. XXII) and of the great supper (Lk. XIV, 6) assumes the current belief that "Blessed is he who shall eat bread in the kingdom of God" (Lk. XIV, 15). In the Gospel teaching, however, it is not the heavenly life so much as the earthly challenge which matters: rather readiness and worthiness should be shown, lest the terrible happen and "none of those men who were invited shall taste my banquet" (XIV, 24). The Apocalypse describes the marriage supper of the Lamb and can state freely: "Blessed are those who are invited to the marriage supper of the Lamb" (Rev. XIX, 9), for the privileged partakers of the Banquet have qualified for their attendance. Further than this "fellowship with the Father and with his Son Jesus Christ" (I Jn. I, 3), the Bible does not go. No Homeric touch of the luxuries consumed, of ambrosia and nectar, is to be found.

[1] Adv. haer. V, XVI, 2.

[2] *De Incarnatione Verbi* LIV, 3,

[3] Cf. IQSa 2, 17–22 for references to sacred food and the order at table. M. Burrows comments cautiously on alleged similarities between Qumran and the Lord's Supper: "There is little in the Gospels to suggest that the fellowship of Jesus and his disciples had any such formal structure as that of the Qumran community.... The meals of the covenanters give us a concrete example of one such model...." (*The Dead Sea Scrolls*, 1956, p. 333).

THE REST

Similarly hardly any light is thrown on the nature of the work by which the Lamb's followers serve their Lord. The paucity of interest in heavenly labours can only be explained by the general distaste for work, conceived of as toil and almost as punishment for disobedience: "Cursed is the ground because of you; in toil you shall eat of it all the days of your life . . . in the sweat of your face you shall eat bread" (Gen. III, 17 ff.). Nothing could be more opposed to modern feeling than the hope that in Heaven the grief of work (Eccles. II, 23) will end. True, there is a work of God, and the Pauline Epistles recognize the worth of godly labour, e.g. I Cor. XVI, 10. But even the Apostle hardly holds more than that "your labour is not vain in the Lord" (I Cor. XV, 58). Good works on earth are rewarded not by a continuation of activity but by a cessation from toil: "Blessed are the dead who die in the Lord henceforth." "Blessed indeed," says the Spirit, "that they may rest from their labours, for their deeds follow them" (Rev. XIV, 13). This view, however extreme, is typical; for the enjoyment of the fruit of the tree of life and plenteousness and goodness (IV Ezra, VIII, 52) would be disturbed by duties. Even the famous passage in Jn. IX, 4 with regard to "the night when no man can work" does not exalt work for its own sake but stresses the 'givenness' of the opportunity of life when man can work. Nevertheless, it is possible that the Johannine view of work is more positive and that he associates work with God and with Life to such an extent that it is almost impossible to conceive of eternal life apart from work. The Fourth Gospel is wholly convinced of the activity of God in Christ; it is an eternal fact, a metaphysical reality: "My Father is working still, and I am working" (V, 17). This doctrine of the ever-working God affects the whole. Belief in Jesus is the supreme work of God (VI, 29). The injunction not to work for the meat which perishes but for the meat which abides unto eternal life (VI, 27) at least suggests that the reward of life eternal also brings the opportunity to take a share in God's "strange work" (Is. XXVIII, 21), even as fellow-workers with God (I Cor. III, 9).

Cessation from work, however, rather than promotion in

tasks to be performed, is the prize. Those who live in Heaven do not act; they see and they hear; they are at peace and they rest. This particular theme of the heavenly life must be understood in the broader setting of the Peace of God and the Rest of God. The state of the dead who sleep in death cannot be equated with the glorious rest "which remains for the people of God" (Hebr. IV, 9). This is the sabbath rest which God enjoyed at the end of creation (Gen. II, 2; Ps. XCV, 11; Hebr. IV, 4) and which Jesus entered when he sat down on high. The Lord's intercessory work is not incompatible with the rest; the Epistle to the Hebrews envisages the Sabbath rest as the fulfilment of salvation.

The author again draws upon current traditions to bring out the divine nature of the Sabbath by way of contrast. The Creator's Sabbath coincided with his "all is well" at the end of the creation, but the serenity of his rest accords ill with the Hebrews' historical failure to achieve *menuchah* (rest) in the promised land. There had never been a cessation (*shabbath*) of fighting (Hebr. IV, 8). Yet all men long for peace and rest in the 'today' of their existence. Our author links his theme with the exhortation of Psalm XCV but he is clearly influenced too by Philo's identification of God's 'today' with the eternal 'always' (L. A. III, 25; Fug. 57). The rest of the Christian is eternal for Christ shares the eternity of God's Sabbath (Hebr. IV, 10).

The *Shabbath Shabbathon* (Ex. XVI, 23; XXXI, 15; XXXV, 2; Lev, XVI, 31; XXIII, 3) pre-figured in the Torah the eschatological hope that there should be a cessation from all work so that men might be free to enjoy God's work: hence the characteristics of Sabbath-joy and consummation which Psalm XCII brings so vividly before the congregation. In Judaism the Rabbis recall the eschatological link; the day is to be one of entire rest, without the preparation of meals and commerce, for so the just will rest, seated with crowns on their heads, delighting in the splendour of the Shekinah. The keeping of the Sabbath saves from eschatological woes and brings redemption to Israel (bShab. 118 b), for Sabbath, rest and everlasting life converge (Tamid VII, 4). The Sabbath gives a foretaste of the world to come with the fulfilment of all desires (Midr. Gen. R.X, 9; Ruth R.III, 3). According to Jub. II, 30 the Sabbath rest belongs both to the creation and to the end, both to earth and to Heaven. Philo goes much further than this and speculates freely about the unique significance of the figure seven. The seven-stringed lyre serves best the principle of harmony in a universe which reflects the perfection of the figure seven on every level. The Sabbath is not symbolic of rest in a negative sense, for God rested on the seventh day from the creation of mortal beings to turn to the formation of eternal, rational, and virtuous forms. The Sabbath serves as an allegory of God's creativeness in its cosmic manifestation (L. A. I, 8 ff.).

If for the Jews the Sabbath observance was the "symbol of adhesion to the covenant religion and the condition of the participation in the coming restoration with all its blessings"[1] the eternal Sabbath in Heaven is in Christian thought the very fulfilment of these blessings. In Judaism the restrictions and their exceptions became the hallmark of true allegiance throughout the centuries, the touchstone of earthly conformity to the Law of God. The Christian tradition, on the contrary, seizes on the festal character of the rest (Neh. VIII, 9–12), eating and drinking before the Lord being its joyful expression (Dt. XII, 6 f.; XII, 18; XIV, 23–6; XVI, 10 f.). What is really new in the Epistle to the Hebrews is not the seriousness of the warnings against rebellion, nor even the note of cheer in the sabbatical message, but the translation of the earthly institution to its original celestial context. The Sabbath is the Lord's (cf. Ezek. XX, 12 ff.) and the Son of Man is Lord of the Sabbath (Mk. II, 27). Redemption having been achieved the redeemed also rest, with their Lord, from the week of trials: "enter thou into the joy of the Lord" (Mt. XXV, 21). Just as the Sabbath is set aside for the peace of the community so the heavenly Sabbath is dedicated to the Peace of the universe. The Holy War is at last at an end. The true King of the new Jerusalem follows the type of the ancient king of Salem, or Peace (Hebr. VII, 2); on earth, before his Passion, he was hailed as conqueror, in the name of the Lord and with the shout: "peace in Heaven, and glory in the Highest" (Lk. XIX, 38). After his Resurrection he said to them: "Peace be unto you!" (Jn. XX, 19, 21, 26). It is this Peace

[1] GFM, vol, II, p. 24. Moore scorns the anthropologists who speak of the Sabbath as an ancient taboo-day; cf. pp. 21 ff. For the Messianic Sabbath in later Judaism, cf. L. Ginzberg, *The Legends of the Jews,* I, 1947, pp. 83–6. The Sabbath saves Adam from fire and perdition and continues to grant him celestial light.

of God and of Jesus which significantly begins and ends most of the Epistles of the New Testament and which, according to the Epistle to the Hebrews, is attained in Heaven in the Sabbath of the everlasting Covenant. It is no longer to be sought or to be enjoined, but it is the natural state of the heavenly life. The Blessing is no longer given, for the life itself is the Blessing.

The Sabbath in Heaven is a continual feast day and the participants are released from the burden of toil so as to be free for the worship of God. This is the real meaning behind the idea of the eternal Sabbath and its peace. The four beasts in the Apocalypse (IV, 8), like the Seraphim in Is. VI, offer endless homage to the true God: they make Sabbath, without day and night. The four and twenty elders lead the heavenly Church in the ministry of Glory (IV, 4, 10; V, 11 ff.), for it is in the performance of worship that the whole creation is united and continues its active life in perfection.

THE PROBLEM OF TIME

Is the heavenly life or Sabbath to be thought of as an experience in or outside time? The passages which have been investigated use temporal adverbs and descriptions: we speak of the state of the dead after death and before the final judgment. We invoke. human analogies of activities which most commonly occur in space and time. Even the remodelling of Jerusalem stresses the spatial aspects, and the apocalyptic portrait of life is given in sequences of experience and speech. Thus it does not seem legitimate to equate eternal life with timelessness. On the other hand the abolition of the powers of the stars, of the rotation both of sun and moon, of the calendar itself, together with the grand themes of Rest and Peace and the eternal Sabbath of ceaseless Worship, tend to make the temporal conception of life meaningless and therefore unreal. If God, in whose eyes "a thousand years are only a day" (Ps. XC, 4), be the only centre of reality from which everything else is derived and reflected, and if the adoration of the Lamb constitutes the sole state of blessedness, it is certainly justifiable to abandon the scheme of time and space and to put in its place a divine simultaneity.

An irreconcilable tension prevails because the heavenly life involves both temporal experiences and simultaneous felicity.

This difficulty is not overcome by the plea that the temporal conception represents Hebraic, and the simultaneous, Greek feeling. The Christian blend of feeling is far too complex to take sides in party fashion and usually wishes to retain both the field of time ('eth) and timelessness ('olam) in the heavenly life, The contradiction is sometimes solved by drawing a perfectly legitimate distinction between the life before and after the final judgment. In the so-called Millennium the elect still await salvation; after the judgment they enjoy it outside time. But the trouble with this solution lies in the enigmatic character of the life of waiting,[1] which can hardly be called a heavenly existence; furthermore, the simultaneity of the final state, though one of perfect service and adoration, differs too much from the oriental "God-in-All" philosophy to be identified with it. Even the final state is a personal, human state and, therefore, never quite severed from dynamic events.

The best illustration of our difficulty comes from the Apocalypse itself. In chapter IV the scene of homage shows the adoration of the four beasts. Their attitude, as that of the Seraphim in Isaiah chapter VI, certainly symbolizes timeless worship; but the twenty-four elders, who follow in their demonstration, are emphatically worshipping as creatures made in and for time. Charles[2] stresses with almost comical precision that theirs is no continuous action. They are probably neither angels nor men but the heavenly representatives of the faithful of the twenty-four orders (I Chron. XXIV, 7–18). Thus in one passage, admittedly mixing two themes, both views are entertained in a typical manner. The Christian feeling, no less than the Scriptures, refuses to make a decision which is philosophical rather than religious.

FINALITY

Nevertheless, the answer to our problem has far-reaching religious possibilities. It cannot help raising the extremely controversial issue of the *finality* of the state of the dead, not only

[1] Cf. O. Cullmann, *Unsterblichkeit der Seele und Auferstehung der Toten,* TZ XII, 2 (März/April 1956): "Wir *warten*, und die Toten *warten*". But is waiting really the same as living?

[2] Op. cit., ad loc.

among the damned (who do not concern us here) but also among those deemed worthy of eternal life. The whole dogmatic and popular belief in the purgation and the ascent of the soul depends on a positive answer to our first question, i.e. that time exists during the life in Heaven. It is clear beyond doubt that a change in human personality, even in Heaven, can only be contemplated as long as the temporal element of life is not wholly excluded. The price exacted by simultaneity is that of immutability. Therefore, once again, the compromise solution of life before and after the final judgment—one in time, one out of time—offers an attractive though blurred answer. Christian feeling nowadays sets up its own logic and demands the possibility of progress together with the unchangeable character of the heavenly life. In the Apocalypse (ch. XX) the doctrine of the two resurrections and the Millennium seems to point the way though it is still a long way off from the notion of the progressive approximation to union with God.

THE MILLENNIUM

Unfortunately the obscurity of the Millennium is so impenetrable that no one would nowadays venture to build any doctrinal thesis on so uncertain a foundation.[1] The chiliastic speculations from of old until this day diverge, especially in their interpretation of the *place* where Christ's reign for a thousand years must flourish ere Satan is released from his chains. Those who urge that since Christ is in Heaven until the final end of the age all the departed must *ipso facto* be with him there, tend to ignore the somewhat earthly description both of the vindication of the saints and their enjoyment of bliss in Jerusalem. This celestial party of exegetes support their view against a terrestrial conception by linking Revelation chapter XX with the passage in chapter VI, 9–11, where the avenged saints are in white and among the blessed in Heaven.[2] However cogent this argument may appear it did not survive in the anti-chiliastic tradition of the Church which could not but note and oppose sectarian dangers and came

[1] Cf. b. Sanh. 99a for the Rabbis' discussion on the days of the Messiah; 40, 70, 365, 400, 7000 years are mentioned.

[2] Amongst recent, writers, e.g. J. Sickenberger, *Das tausendjährige Reich in der Apokalypse,* 1921, pp. 300 ff.

out in favour of an absolutely terrestrial and uneschatological interpretation: the triumph of the Church, to be measured from the day of the Resurrection or some other outstanding date, will last a thousand years during which the Church itself enjoys the benefits of Christ's reign.

It seems probable that the very popular notion of the Millennium is itself of secondary importance in Revelation ch. XX. The author's overriding concern is to inspire the loyalists with courage. Some have already perished, others must perish soon. Once again urgent voices question the state of the dead. It is, in fact, the Corinthians' problem all over again: how can we, the living, look forward to life after death when those who have died are evidently not alive? Does the martyrs' heroism lead to nothing better than endless waiting for the longed-for last day? Here the Apocalypse provides an answer, not wholly new, but developed in company with chiliastic expectations. The double resurrection sets the tone: it does not postulate one resurrection for all souls upon death and an eschatological one at the end, but confirms the Christian claim that the Lord's community is alive by the blood of Christ.[1] The Millennium merely stresses the paradox that the eternal community also has its existence in the passing world until the end, "as dying and behold we live" (II Cor. VI, 9; cf. IV, 11). This paradox must obviously terminate in the total triumph of Christ when he delivers the Kingdom to God.

The importance of the conception of the Millennium for the heavenly life lies in its dynamic and temporal interpretation of the reign of Christ until the end. The figure thousand is apt to mislead our attention, for what matters is that the people of Christ share his triumph for they also shall reign, and that on earth by martyrdom, and then in Heaven. They are not asleep, nor do they wait in hope or accept a passive share of enjoyment. The chiliastic hope is for them already fulfilled as "priests of God"

[1] "Die 'Welt' und die Christen haben also eschatologisch ein anderes Schicksal" summarizes H. Bietenhard, *Das tausendjährige Reich,* 1955, p. 52. Sectarian chiliasts not only abandoned this principle but even more disastrously the whole Biblical context of Christ and his kingdom. Cf. N. Cohn, *The Pursuit of the Millenium,* 1957, for the macabre currents of this extremely potent and dangerous ideology in Europe.

(Rev. xx, 6). In giving this consolation the writer dismisses ideas of progress and moral reformation after death. Since he thinks primarily in terms of martyrdom and heroism, and therefore of sacrifice, he does not even bestow a casual glance at 'average' Christians, neither hot nor cold, whose qualification for the priesthood in the Millennium must be wanting. He could hardly sympathize with their problems, which were not his and which he would have treated with scorn. His 'thousand years' are not meant to constitute a compromise, a kind of buffer between man's temporal existence and God's eternity. Only if we now determine to depart from his original intention as well as from the Church's subsequent interpretation may we cite the passage in support for the progress of souls. We may then ask, from our own, modern point of view, how the reign of the saints can mean less than the perfection of those very souls who, though aspiring to holiness, manifestly did not suffer martyrdom on earth and deemed themselves imperfect and not only capable of, but also desirous of, a growth in the stature of Christ. Thus we may attempt to replace the eschatological and the ecclesiological positions of former ages by our personal-psychological orientation, although, it must be confessed, this would make strange reading to the author of Revelation, chapter xx.

PROGRESS IN HEAVEN

The silence of the Bible does not warrant 'the ascent of the soul' as a permitted doctrine. The only Jewish authority for progress in the Heavens is late. The Rabbis are said to meet in a heavenly place (*Jeshiva*), just as they used to study the Torah in their earthly schools, and for this purpose their souls leave the cemetery from time to time.[1] But such ascents hardly support the idea of personal progress in Heaven; they merely reflect the belief that the departments of Paradise welcome, according to the Midrashim,[2] their respective occupants, who appear to retain their earthly status after death.

The evidence in the New Testament for the continuance of status and profession in Heaven is very scanty. Only the Apostles

[1] Cf. Str. B. II, p. 267; IV, p. 1035 f.

[2] Cf. Wünsche, *Lehrhallen*, III, 1, 2.

are considered to be in a somewhat different position; above all Simon Peter is given the keys of the Kingdom and his power of binding and loosing extends not only to the earth but also to Heaven. The much-discussed verse (Mt. XVI, 19) presupposes that the rank and authority, albeit of a humble, Christian office, are raised into the heavenly realm, together with the Apostle. In the Apocalypse both the damned and the saved appear before God with links strongly forged not only to their moral past but also to their rank on earth. Particularly kings, priests, and elders (ἱερεῖς, πρεσβύτεροι) build up the celestial hierarchy. Before Christ rose from the dead the priests were hindered by death from continuing (Hebr. VII, 23); death having been done away with, no such break can occur. Yet it is by no means asserted that the kings, priests, and elders are more than poetical images and that the priests of God (Rev. XX, 6) comprise only those who had attained to the priesthood on earth, except possibly in the sense that all Christians are what Israel once was, a royal priesthood (Exod. XIX, 6; I Pe. II, 5, 9). In any case progress in Heaven is never connected with notions of political or ecclesiastical advancement as on earth. The little ones and the martyrs do not have to become something else to share in the celestial life.

If, then, the crude notions of progress are not to be entertained a final glance at the evidence for progress in a spiritual sense does not reap a great reward either. The existence of the "many mansions" has already been conceded but it neither proves nor disproves their availability to striving pilgrims in Heaven. There is no celestial academy in the Talmudic sense, where souls can learn and presumably prepare for profitable examinations. On the other hand it may be argued that the brief reference to the "many things", which the disciples of Jesus could not bear until after the Spirit of truth was given (Jn. XVI, 12, 13) opens the door to the hope that the progressive ascent is one of these many things.

PURGATION

Such progress is obviously not to be thought of as occurring after the end but must belong either to the interval which occurs between the individual's death and the final judgment, or even between the final judgment and the end. In all these cases it is connected with the removal of the stain of sin through payment, punishment, or other forms of purgation. Its place in the heavenly life is warranted by the speculative tradition that Heaven provides both the time and the sphere needed for improvement. The fiery stream in Heaven is sometimes thought to assist in the purification of the departed and such a belief justifies the custom of praying and making offerings for the dead so as to help them in their progress. Above all II Maccabees XII, 43 ff., the *locus classicus*, confirms the belief and practice: Judas made a collection for the fallen to pay for a sacrifice: "in this he acted quite rightly and properly, bearing in mind the resurrection." Though penance in the beyond is denied to the wicked there is the Paradise of the Dead whose moral mediocrity warrants some measure of purgation and, therefore, progress.[1]

The New Testament contains famous passages which offer pitfalls of exegesis.[2] For example, the "loosing in Heaven" (Mt. XVI, 19; XVIII, 18) may or may not refer to the Church's power in Heaven and the progress of souls. Similarly, the themes of punishment imply in an oblique manner that the penalty may end or be mitigated (Lk. XII, 59). The sin against the Holy Ghost is here the exception rather than the rule (Mt. XII, 32) and a traffic of intercession is assumed in Lk. XVI, 9, 19 ff., just as the righteous among the dead pray for the living, according to En. XXXIX, 4 f.[3]

The two famous Petrine references to the release from death (I Pe. III, 19; IV, 6), however difficult, confirm the general impression that some Christian circles believed that the work of redemption was not confined to this earth. Those who had died before Christ were not outside his reach. Nothing, however, is said of their response and whether they escaped from their prison, which can hardly be the same as the Paradise of the dead.

[1] Cf. Str. B. IV, 1033 ff.; IV Ezra VII, 38 ff. Hillel believed in the efficacy of the intercession of the righteous; Shammai postulated twelve months of purgatorial sufferings for the 'middle classes'.

[2] Cf. H. Bietenhard, *Kennt das Neue Testament die Vorstellung vom Fegefeuer?* TZ. III, 2, pp. 101–22.

[3] For the implicit transitoriness of punishments, cf. also Const. Apost. VIII, 41; Augustine, *De Civ. Dei*, XXI, 13, 14; Serm., 172. Evidence on the Tombs of the faithful can be found in Wilpert, *Roma Sotteranea*, pp. XXI, 396 ff.

The problem comes to a head in the relevant Pauline sayings. Clearly, the Apostle is not likely to be interested in this subject *per se*, which involves no decision of any kind, but only speculation. He is quite certain that God has prepared indescribable blessings (I Cor. II, 9), the riches of his glory (Ro. IX, 23) for his elect who love him; this future glory stands in no proportion to the sufferings of the present, for it excels the expectation of appropriate vindication (Ro. VIII, 18). Nevertheless, purgatorial meanings have unjustifiably been read into Phil. II, 10, as if the subjugation of the heavenlies must also include the souls of the unworthy.[1] Safer ground is reached in I Corinthians III, 11 ff. and XV, 29 and possibly V, 5. The key themes present cumulative evidence: first, the Apostle testifies that the nucleus of true achievement shall remain permanently, when everything untrue has been burnt away. Secondly, the Corinthians' strange custom of "baptism for the dead" is by no means denounced as wrong and it must be based upon the belief that the dead can be helped in the Beyond. Lastly, a Christian fornicator, though he must be punished, probably by death, may yet be saved in the Day of the Lord. The latter instance, however, contradicts the Resurrectio Carnis altogether; it does not countenance the salvation of the whole man, Satan having destroyed his flesh; its evidential value for heavenly progress is accordingly almost non-existent. The real weakness of adducing the three themes too confidently in support of heavenly progress lies in their context. The Apostle is not directly concerned with it, but with Church unity and conduct on earth, though admittedly in the light of a future of everlasting life.

"FROM GLORY TO GLORY"

The survey of Pauline texts must reach its end with a discussion of the most difficult poetical passage of II Corinthians, III, 17, 18: the freedom of the Lord's Spirit reigns among Christians, as contrasted with Moses and the Jews and, of course, the unbelievers. Then even in revelation the veil remained (whether on Moses' face or on the scrolls of the Law): now everything is open, "our

[1] I agree with Bietenhard (op. cit.) in his argument against E. Stauffer, *Theologie des Neuen Testaments*, p. 57.

faces are unconcealed, we reflect the Lord's Glory and are being transformed into the same image". The indirect reflection in the mirror (I Cor. XIII, 12) had been frowned upon as inadequate, as belonging necessarily to this world; now the transformation is tremendous. In I Corinthians XIII, 12 we, though converted, sanctified, in Christ, were still found "looking through a mirror in a riddle" and had to look forward to the vision of the future, face to face. In II Corinthians III, 18 the vision is already within our grasp and, instead of looking through a deflecting mirror, our unveiled faces receive the light of the glory to such an extent that we reflect it *as a mirror*. Indeed, the Lord's glory is, grammatically speaking, the direct accusative object of our reflection. But St. Paul's "exalted emotion"[1] goes even further in formulating the progress towards glory, and it must be remembered that he is throughout concerned with the end of death and the dawn of life. Life is here conceived of as the reflection of God's glory, not in a general mystical manner, but in the face of Jesus Christ (IV, 6). The acquisition of life does not occur by magic or on a superficial level in an instant, ending perhaps in stagnation, but rather, going from strength to strength (Ps. LXXXIV, 7); the Christian pilgrim goes to the light of dawn which shines more and more unto the perfect day (Prov. IV, 18). The metamorphosis of the pilgrim brings an increase of light and, therefore, of reflection, from glory into glory. This progress can hardly mean "from the glory of Moses to the glory of the Spirit" (Ambrose), nor "from the glory lost and left behind in Paradise to that received in Heaven" (Ephraem), nor the gradual increase of virtuous living and piety on the part of the believer while on earth. If St. Paul was at all thinking of his own experience it is unlikely that he could have identified the first stage of glory with, say, Baptism, and the last stage with a corresponding experience, such as sacramental communion. The vision before Damascus and the trance in the third Heaven were undoubtedly glorious events, but they did not fit into a progressive line which leads to the celestial vision and reflection. He did not systematize his experiences and never claimed to be a better or more glorious Apostle as time passed.

[1] Plummer, ICC, *II Corinthians,* 1915, ad loc.—I am indebted to the whole discussion.

Such notions of progress would have been wholly alien to his conception of God and Man. Even the expression "attaining to the measure of the stature of the fullness of Christ" (if Pauline, Ephes. IV, 13) hardly warrants an evolutionary conception of growth in perfection. The work of God is dynamic; close approximations to the celestial life are not to be tolerated as steps to be taken towards an increase of reflected glory. We conclude, therefore, that the "from glory into glory" has, so to speak, two heavenly poles or terms of reference. Just as a man approaches another face for closer acquaintance and intimacy, so St. Paul thinks of the face of the Christian and the face of the Lord himself, the latter the source of God's glory, the former the recipient. But this encounter belongs already to the traffic in the heavenly realm, to the progress towards the throne in a world which is altogether glorious. St. Paul is here no longer concerned with earthly striving nor with the purgation and penances of souls, yet to be made perfect. Those who enter upon this stage of reflection of glory are contemplating God in Heaven and lead the heavenly life. Whether this still pertains to time or not, whether indeed such a contrast between time and eternity is held to exist, cannot be decided. Glory belongs to the eternal, timeless order; metamorphosis from glory to glory would indicate change and, therefore, time. The heavenly life acclaims both realms, not least because the worship of God is itself dynamic, an amalgamation of time and eternity.

Chapter Eight

HEAVEN IN CHRISTIAN WORSHIP

TRUE AND FALSE WORSHIP

ON the road from Samaria to Jerusalem, near Shechem, probably at the modern Askar (Sychar, Jn. IV, 5) Jesus is provoked into the apparently contradictory statement: "The hour is coming, and now is, when the true worshippers will worship the Father in spirit and in truth" (Jn. IV, 21). Here the alleged merits of "this mountain" (Ebal) are set against Jerusalem (IV, 20). The saying of Jesus, preserved at a time when Jerusalem was already in ruins and some Christians had 'fallen asleep', reflects the belief that neither the fall of that city nor the delay of the Parousia could hinder the coming of the true worship of God.

From the beginning Christians claimed that their worship alone was exclusively true. They did not regard the work of Jesus and their own eschatological expectation as sufficient authority to abandon the liturgical worship of God in favour of a spiritual homage, free from sacred times, places, and ceremonies. They attended the services of the Temple until its fall. Their scriptures were born into and out of the lectionaries which were taken over from the synagogue. Their rites looked back to the traditions of Israel. How, then, did the "worship of the Father in spirit and in truth" differ from everything that had been before?

The distinction between true and false worship is not a new one. Every heavenly religion must needs question both the forms and contents of its cultic tradition. It cannot regard any earthly rites as self-sufficient or even meaningful. In a world of endless variations of worship in so many pantheons the demarcation of the true from the false becomes a necessity. In his condemnation of false worship Jesus confirms the verdict of the prophets of the Old Testament that a religious cultus, practised for its own sake, is a falsehood, the epitome of a lie. God cannot tolerate the vain oblations, new moon, sabbath, assemblies and solemn meeting (Is. I, 13) because these institutions are primarily man-made and pursue earthly interests. Whenever fertility and prosperity are the end of worship the cultus is a perversion of the true end. The ambiguity of human worship is brought out well enough by the word 'cultus' itself, which denotes the tillage of the ground, the mode of living (civilization and luxury), elegance of language, splendour of clothing, and also reverence and worship. Most ambiguous of all is perhaps the expression "sacrifices of righteousness" (Ps. IV, 5; LI, 19) for these (Hebr. *zivche tsedeq*) may denote offerings appropriate in a cultic or in an ethical sense or both. Where, within such richness of possible customs and expressions, is the criterion of true worship to be found?

The attraction of Near Eastern paganism lay in its genius for combining many layers of cultic behaviour. Thus the mountain to which the Samaritan woman refers—"our fathers worshipped in this mountain"—may be taken as a symbol: here syncretism had flourished for centuries, shrines had succeeded each other in a 'high place' which must have seen more than our imagination can fathom. But one constant element was always present: the visible object, complete and final, the strength of pagan earth-bound institutions. This incontrovertible asset became in the prophetic tradition the criterion of falsehood, the negation of worship "in spirit and in truth".

Jerusalem, however, did not share these 'abominations'. Had not its cultus fought and subdued the pagan heritage of Israel? Was it not unearthly in its intention? The Jewish cultus had not only purified itself of all agricultural paganism but it had also, though but gradually and perhaps incompletely, relegated the worship of the heavenly powers and of cosmic forces to its proper place.

THE CULTUS OF THE HEAVENS

The universal worship of the sky had touched the people of Israel as it had all the peoples. The natural tendency of man to greet the Heavens with awe, trepidation, and joy had persisted throughout the centuries. The Hebrew was thus no exception in paying homage to the world above. Even after the establishment of official Monotheism in Israel there were "astrologers,[1] stargazers, and monthly prognosticators" (Is. XLVII, 13) who practised the common cultus of the sky; indeed, the "discernment of the Heavens", found as late as about A.D. 30 (Mt. XVI, 3; Lk. XII, 56) did not confine itself to a kind of weather forecast but endeavoured to read its portents.

THE MOON

It is unfortunately impossible to fix a reliable jumping-off point for the Hebrews' cultus of the Heavens. It used to be said of Abraham that he left Ur for Haran (Gen. XI, 31) because at Ur the reigning lunar deity Sin had been ousted in favour of the sun-god Shamshu. Hammurabi, so it was suggested, had caused his departure through a religious revolution, of which we still have evidence in the commemorative stele in the Louvre, where the king can be seen receiving his famous code of laws from the sun-god. But did Hammurabi or anyone else have to choose between the exclusive alternatives of sun or moon worship? There is, in point of fact, no evidence that the cultus of the moon vanished from Ur. Moreover the old equation 'age Hammurabi = age of Abraham', attractively based on Gen. XIV, 1 with its reference to one Amraphel, and a wholly wrong chronology into the bargain, has no foundation whatever in history.

The Patriarchs may be looked upon as historical figures whose traditions the Pentateuch has collected from the remote past through the tribal memories of Israel.[2] Thus Babylonian and Egyptian influences as well as Patriarchal strands of narrative and

[1] Or simply "Heaven worshippers", if *hovre shamaiim* = the rt. hbr. in Ugaritic; cf. VT, VII, 2, p. 183.

[2] Cf. M. Noth, *Geschichte Israels,* 1954, p. 188, for treating the Patriarchal narrative as part of the Aramaic migrations which are remembered in local surroundings at a much later date. Its 'Haftpunkt' is at important centres in Palestine, its origin perhaps on the desert fringes, its historicity of no value. For a criticism of Noth's 'nihilism', cf. J. Bright, *Early Israel in Recent History Writing,* 1956, esp. pp. 43 ff., for a survey of Noth's *Überlieferungsgeschichte des Pentateuchs,* 1948, pp. 58–62, 86–127. For a positive evaluation of the Patriarchal narrative on the grounds of archaeological evidence cf. H. H. Rowley, *The Servant of the Lord,* 1952, and esp. pp. 281 ff. for a rejection of Amraphel = Hammurabi; U. Simon, *Old Testament Problems: The Beginning,* CQR, 1958.

semi-nomadic customs have come down to us in a whole body of tradition which reflects the worship of the Heavens. The shepherd peoples observed a lunar calendar and celebrated the nights of the full moon and marked the phases of the moon with devotions. The Passover was before anything a moon festival after the spring equinox. The new and the full moon were greeted with enthusiasm and occasioned homage: "Blow the trumpet at the new moon, at the full moon, on our feast day. For it is a statute for Israel. . . ." (Ps. LXXXI, 3 ff.). The institution was strong and despite Isaiah's invective and Hosea's threats of gloom these high dates remained in the cultic calendar of Israel (cf. Hos. II, 11). The merchants observed them with reluctance, waiting impatiently for "the new moon to be over" (Amos VIII, 5), so as to return to normal business.

THE SUN

Lunar worship belongs to the night and is therefore only one aspect of the enticing stimulants to the worship of the Heavens. The sun, ruler of the day, was even more important. The Israelite was exhorted not to serve other gods, "the sun, moon, or any of the host of Heaven" (Dt. XVII, 2 ff.) because he was obviously inclined to do so. The royal house sinned as much as the common people. Its support of solar worship was traditional and not an innovation. In the early days of the settlement the Hebrews had had their Beth-Shemesh (Jos. XV, 10; XIX, 22; I Sam. VI, 9, 12), a house-of-the-sun or cultic place of worship. Most commentators agree that the legislation in Nrs. XIX, 1–10 for the offering of a red heifer recalls the ancient practice of a solar sacrifice. The Jebusite rock, which David captured, had also known the cultus of the sun for centuries before, and Solomon, a notorious syncretist in any case, allied to Egypt and married to an Egyptian princess, could not have embarked on the building of the temple without knowledge of cosmic worship. The eclipse of the sun in 948 B.C. may well have been a suitable moment for the dedication, granting an unforgettable impression of light and darkness. But we must not, therefore, conclude that the House was actually built for the sun, which at dawn and at sunset illumined the otherwise thick darkness of its interior, the shafts of light announcing the presence of the sun-god, with whom the king was in some measure to be identified.[1] The strange paraphernalia of the Temple, the great Sea, the pillars Jachin and Boaz, and the altar were certainly intended to be cosmic representations (I K. vii) so that Heaven was here found on earth. Yet this Temple (which was entered from the east, the *naos* being in the west) was dedicated to YHWH, for Solomon, however much open to foreign influence, intended to build a place for his own God who was also the God of the Mosaic tradition. He was wholly aware of his purpose of uniting the cosmic and the Israelite YHWH tradition when he declared: "YHWH said, he would dwell in the thick darkness" (Hebr. *lishkon ba'araphel*, I K. viii, 12). In the first Temple YHWH was to be worshipped as the God of Heaven, who by his own will consents to dwell on earth, even in "this house", though the Heaven and Heaven of Heavens cannot contain him (I K. viii, 27).

Whether Solomon's prayer renders his *ipsissima verba* or reflects the spirit of subsequent reforms is here immaterial. These reforms were frequent and short-lived and had a political background. Ahaz and Manasseh in particular provoked anti-pagan reactions (II K. chs. xviii, xxiii). In these purges the worship and service of "the host of Heaven" were outlawed and it may have been under Josiah that the school known as Deuteronomy finally promulgated its canons against the worship of the sky (Dt. xvii, 2 ff.). But legislation cannot succeed against popular feeling; Jeremiah still inveighs against the kings, princes, priests, prophets, and inhabitants of Jerusalem, whose bones they will "spread before the sun and moon and all the host of Heaven, whom they have loved, and whom they have served, and after whom they have walked, and whom they have sought, and whom they have worshipped." (viii, 1 ff.). No indictment could be more telling. Despite their nominal allegiance to YHWH in the official cultus the common worship of the heavenly powers had maintained

[1] Cf. F. J. Hollis, *The Archaeology of Herod's Temple*, 1934, pp. 132–9 for the solar thesis, and L. H. Vincent, *Jérusalem de l'Ancien Testament*, II, 1956, p. 400 for its flat denial: "Les deux montagnes mythologiques, entre lesquelles passe le soleil levant" have elicited what Vincent calls "la spcéulation particulièrement aventureuse sur un vieux culte solaire à Jérusalem qui aurait persévéré dans le Temple." For a variety of views and literature see J. A. Montgomery, H. S. Gehman, *Kings*, ICC, 1951, p. 191.

itself. According to Ezekiel VIII, 16 twenty-five men prostrated themselves in the Temple of God before the sun and renounced YHWH with a demonstration of outrageously insulting behaviour. Until the destruction of the first Temple this apostate form of worship appears to have continued.

THE QUEEN OF HEAVEN

Even the upheavals of complete defeat could not embitter the sweet taste of cosmic religion and its characteristic worship of the Queen of Heaven. Her identification has caused no little controversy.[1] Jeremiah is again our main informant in the Bible; everywhere in Judah he looks with abhorrence at the children who gather wood, and the fathers who kindle the fire, and the women who knead the dough, to make cakes to the Queen of Heaven (VII, 18). At the end the wretched survivors, who had forced Jeremiah into exile in Egypt with them, still continue the same cultus; in fact, they publicly announce their intention: they allege that there had been peace and plenty as long as the people and the nobles had burnt incense and poured out libations to the Queen of Heaven (XLIV, 15 ff.). It is not likely that this blasphemous decision was confined to them, for the last two chapters in Isaiah indicate a resurgence of paganism. The Syrian Hellenizers in the second century B.C. found many converts to paganism with its blend of the worship of the Heavens and their queen (Dan. XI, 31 ff.; I Macc. I; II Macc. chs. III–VI). The original goddess who ruled in Heaven, the Assyro-Babylonian Ishtar, never lost her central place in the common cultus of the Near East. Political powers who associated her with their conquests might fail but she did not have to abdicate in the temples. The planet Venus shone brightly as the heavenly sign of Anat of Ugarit, Isis of Egypt, and Astarte. Her secret, however, lay not only in her heavenliness but also in her guardianship of the fertility of society of which the corn and the bread were so clear a symbol.[2] The women who loved the Ashera, a tree or

[1] Cf. G. Westphal, *Jahwehs Wohnstätten*, 1908, pp. 248 ff.

[2] As Albright comments on the Ugaritic 'šrt, goddess of the sea, bride of Anu, wife of El: "The shift from sea-goddess to grove is as remarkable as any shift known in the history of religion" (*Archaeology and the Religion of Israel*, 1946, pp. 78 ff.

grove, saw and felt therein the wonder of feminine life just as they wept for Tammuz (Ezek. VIII, 14) in their devotion for the beautiful god.

THE TEMPLE

But these melancholy facts are hardly relevant to the Temple which Jesus visited nor even to the country districts of his time. Both seem singularly free from accretions of pagan belief.[1] In Jerusalem the invisible God was worshipped not as a local deity but as Lord of the universe. Jews from the whole Dispersion flocked to the centre with which all the synagogues were in constant touch. If there was opposition to the Temple—as among the Essenes and the people of Galilee—it was aroused by the ambitions of the priesthood but not by the forms of worship. The decrease of the importance of the Temple even before its fall was due to social but not to religious factors. Hence when the Temple fell the cultus of the Temple did not perish outright because the synagogues could naturally take into their systems many ancient rites and customs, but not sacrifice itself. In the reconstruction Judaism preserved its moral and ceremonial principles in the same close relationship which had characterized it before the Fall. Its innate conservatism impelled it to retain strata of the cultus which went back to the beginnings of Semitic ritual.

This genius for adaptation was already apparent before the Christian era. In many instances the old was preserved and given new meaning and thus freed from all original traces of pagan associations. Thus many heavenly types of worship and cosmic representations survived with the sanction of the priestly codes. For example the red heifer of Numbers XIX is not simply deleted nor is it what it had once been, a sacrifice to and for the sun, but it now forms part of a special lustration; the ashes yield a potent mixture against the pollution caused by dead bodies. If history had bequeathed to us an exact and well-documented

[1] When Josephus speaks of the Essenes' prayers to the sun at sunrise he does not seem to imply any criticism (War II, 119 ff.). It would be absurd to charge them with pagan practices (or, for that matter, St. Francis for his song to the sun or Christians for their orientation in worship). The East is the Eden of salvation *par excellence*. In Alexandria the Logos was contemplated under the image of the sunrise.

account of the Temple furnishings we should know how far cosmic symbolism had been admitted to its interior. As it is we have to rely mainly on Josephus, whose accuracy as a reporter may well be doubted (Ant. XIV, 72). If he may be trusted Pompey penetrated the sanctuary and saw there, apart from the two altars, the candelabrum and the lamps, the twelve loaves, vessels, shovels, etc., of which, it is pleasant to record, he did not loot anything: "Pompeius victor ex illo fano nihil attigit" (Cicero, *Pro Flacco,* 67). But nothing is said of the Ark despite its prominence in the tradition.

THE ARK

We know more about the early history of the Ark than its place in the Temple at the time of Christ (Ant. III, 134 ff.). This numinous chest had once been identified with the presence of YHWH: "When the ark set forward Moses said, Rise up, O Lord!" (Nrs. X, 35). This awareness of God's presence in the Ark probably derived from the stones within, which may have been meteors or pieces of rock laden with cosmic significance. It was no accident that the Deuteronomic version tacitly dismissed the pagan stratum and connected these stones with the Mosaic tables of stone, the Law replacing the unlawful heavenly idol (Dt. X, 2). Nevertheless, the Ark of the first Temple was the cultic representation of God par excellence. When Solomon completed his father's plan he gave pride of place to the bringing up of the Ark with sacrifice and solemn ritual (I K. VIII, 3 ff.). Its place was to be in the *Devir*, in the most holy place "under the wings of the cherubim", concealed by a veil. The resting place of YHWH and the Ark of his strength were the same, and before this cosmic shrine, at his footstool, worshippers prostrated themselves (Ps. CXXXII, 7–8). It is not surprising that Jeremiah had no respect for a fetish which in his view would become redundant: the Ark of the covenant of the Lord would be neither remembered nor missed (III, 16). Legend credits him with hiding the despised object among other things in a cave (II Macc. II, 5), but ironically the context of this passage implies that he did so in order to preserve it for the future.

After the destruction of the first Temple the Ark certainly

vanished, but whether it was revived at any time before Christ remains an unsolved problem. The Jeremiah legend, the detailed descriptions in Ex. xxv, 10–22; xxxvii, 1–9; I Chr. xxviii, 2, with references to God's footstool and the mercy-seat flanked by Cherubim (cf. also Josephus, Ant. iii, 134 ff.), the survival to this day of the scrolls of the Law in the chests of the synagogues (Meg. iv, 3 ff.) appear to make out a cogent case for the presence of the Ark in the *devir* of the Temple which Christ and the early Christians visited. Josephus, however, insists that there was "nothing whatever" (War v, 219). Could it be that he told a deliberate lie to safeguard its existence or that the priests, who were slaughtered upon Pompey's entry into Jerusalem (War i, 148 ff.) while they were officiating, had succeeded in removing the venerable structure to safety? Hardly so, if the Jewish tradition is trustworthy; the description in the Mishnah (Mid. iv) and the Talmud (b Yoma 52 b) agree that there was no Ark in the second Temple.[1]

CHRISTIANS AND THE TEMPLE

The Ark, first purified, then abolished, was typical of that assimilation of the Temple to the requirements of the prophets. Despite a record of backslidings the Temple worship must be acquitted of the charge of false worship. It fulfilled the intention of prophets and priests of providing a pure place for God's presence. Hence Jerusalem must influence the cultus of the early Church whose members in that place continued to worship in the Temple. The early chapters in Acts describe a situation which may have given rise to the hope of a compromise between the followers of Jesus and the Jewish authorities. The Christians continued steadfastly with one accord in the Temple though they broke bread in their homes (Acts ii, 46). Even "a great company of the priests were obedient to the faith" (Acts vi, 7). St. Paul, despite his break with Torah Judaism, still deliberately consented to assume the cost of sacrifices for the Nazirite vows of four Jewish Christians in the traditional manner. He did not refrain from accompanying these men into the Temple (Acts xxi, 20 ff.). To Jerusalem he would go for the feast, to worship and to make

[1] Cf. the model in JE, vol. XII, p. 95, according to the Talmud.

offerings (Acts XVIII, 21, which is not a well-attested reading; XX, 16; XXIV, 11 ff.). He thinks and argues from sacrificial presuppositions, e.g. I Cor. X, 18 ff., and describes himself as a priest (λειτουργός) of Jesus Christ to the Gentiles (Ro. XV, 16). St. Paul is certainly not the villain, nor the hero, to whom we owe the dramatic emergence of the Christian cultus out of its Jewish roots.[1] Though he often announced his intention of turning from the Jews to the Gentiles (Acts XVIII, 6), without ever exclusively doing so, he did not propose a form of Gentile worship as opposed to the Temple. If Christian worship was new it also remained in a subtle relationship of intimacy with the old. Though Judaism would not acknowledge Jesus the Messiah, and the Temple consequently did not recognize the sacrifice of Christ as worthy of recognition, thus bringing about the ultimate division of Church and Temple as well as of Church and Synagogue, the cultus of the Lamb of God not only respected but fulfilled the ancient liturgy.

HEAVEN–EARTH CORRESPONDENCE

The principle of cosmic correspondence provided the necessary bridge. Both Judaism and Christianity built their cultus around the axiom that the liturgical service of God on earth represents a divine order and that the Temple, with God present, reflected Heaven where God ever resides. Its details (loaves, candlesticks, lamps, veils, ephod, etc.) imitate and represent the cosmic whole (Josephus, Ant. III, 180 ff.). Philo says about the priests' vesture: "We have in it as a whole and in its parts a typical representation of the whole world and its particular parts (μίμημα τοῦ κόσμου), the long robe symbolizing the elements, the ephod Heaven and the heavenly bodies" (Mos. II, 117 ff.). Even the innumerable synagogues, notwithstanding the absence of sacrificial worship and of the cultic presence of God, still partook of that essential correspondence. In other words, they were not high places nor local sanctuaries, but they belonged to the people of God who

[1] It is remarkable how G. F. Moore, among others, avoids this very common and shallow assertion. Cf. GFM, II, p. 10 and the article 'Sacrifice' in EB, cols. 4227–8. What we simply do not know is whether any Christian in Jerusalem consciously broke with the worship in the Temple on what we now call 'theological grounds' as distinct from social or political pressure.

worshipped their one God.[1] Thus the Jewish service was never a mere sequence of services, held on earth, but rather a part itself of the heavenly cultus: God stands in the congregation of God, in the divine assembly (Ps. LXXXII, 1). This principle, first enunciated in Solomon's acknowledgment of the paradox that God, who is worshipped in Heaven, also chooses to dwell on earth, was eminently fitted to develop the Christian claim that God had dwelt in Jesus on earth and that the victorious Christ, now in Heaven, chose to be worshipped by his people on earth. Instead of an earthly institution, which commemorates the exploits of a departed leader, the Christian liturgy aspires to heavenliness. The Christian synagogue is visited by Christ at each meeting, for "where two or three are gathered together in my name, there I am in the midst of them" (Mt. XVIII, 20), although it is understood that Christ is in Heaven and present everywhere. Only the heavenliness of God can remain omnipresent in the universe and yet supply a localized presence in the circle of worshipping believers. The Solomonic dedication holds good of the Christian institution of worship: the Temple was thought of as an "eternal house" (*beth 'olam*), a little world (*'olam qaton*) which reflected the heavenly Jerusalem, the Temple, the altar before which Michael offered sacrifice; the Epistle to the Hebrews endorses this tradition, with the one essential difference that Jesus is mediator in Heaven. The Midrash to the Song of Songs IV, 9, which asserts that the Holiest of Holies below corresponds to that above, is written in the same spirit which made Christians consecrate altars below for mysteries which they declared to be heavenly.[2]

How far Judaism and Christianity are indebted to foreign influences in the matter of earth-Heaven correspondence it would be impossible to say.[3] One thing can be asserted, however, which

[1] This becomes very clear in the synagogues of the Christian era. Cf. the Synagogue of Beth Alpha, *c.* 5 miles west of Beisan, of the 5th century A.D., where the floor and the panels display cosmic motifs, such as the Zodiac, the scala caeli, the cloud, the rays of light, the sun and Heaven (GJS, fig. 632). Cf. also E. L. Sukenik, *Ancient Synagogues in Palestine and Greece,* 1934, p. 66.

[2] For further Rabbinic passages cf. Str. B. III, pp. 701 ff.

[3] Cf. G. B. Gray, *Sacrifice in the Old Testament,* 1925, pp. 151 ff.: "For some of the special applications as well as for the general formula [that all things on earth correspond to things in Heaven] the Jews may have been ultimately indebted to Babylon, though in the working out of the idea not a little most specifically Jewish appears."

is that Christianity did not have to go outside its Jewish roots to borrow the principle. The celestial praise, offered by, instead of to, the host of Heaven, is an ancient achievement. The Trishagion, which Isaiah had overheard (VI, 3), was a constant possession of priests and prophets alike. Ezekiel had bequeathed a similar experience (III, 12 ff.); for him, too, liturgical praise on earth echoed the celestial chorus. Thus the disgust at the idolatrous worship of the Heavens was turned to good account. The Psalms are, in that sense, celestial hymns of praise: "give unto the Lord glory and strength . . . the glory due unto his name . . .O worship the Lord in the beauty of holiness" (Ps. XCVI, 7–9) might be sung in Heaven as well as on earth. The keynote of praise on earth is the imitation of the heavenly host: "Praise him, sun and moon . . . stars of light . . . Heavens of Heavens and waters above the Heavens" (Ps. CXLVIII, 3–4), for just as the higher spheres of the universe serve and worship him so Israel must partake in the cosmic liturgy. The book of Enoch describes the heavenly cultus in these terms throughout; heavenly singers praise God without ceasing in liturgical language (XXXIX, 12 f.; LXI, 8–11; LXXI, 7 etc.). In the Midrashim the solemn seasons are celebrated by the angels in Heaven.[1] Without a break in this tradition St. Luke narrates the birth of the Saviour in Bethlehem and concludes: "suddenly there was with the angel a multitude of the heavenly host praising God and saying, Glory to God in the highest, and on earth peace among men with whom he is well pleased" (II, 13, 14). In this unique instance a part of the heavenly society has visited earth to worship on earth; after the Ascension, however, the citizens on earth visit and worship in Heaven to partake in the divine liturgy.

JESUS IN HEAVEN

The presence of the victorious Jesus in Heaven is not recognized in the cultus of the Temple but is the source of the Christian access to God in Heaven. From now on, therefore, the two religions will be divided and regard each other as false although both are dedicated to the worship of the one God. St. John writes at a time when this break is already made and considered

[1] Cf. A. Wünsche, *Aus Israels Lehrhallen,* IV, 1909, p. 73.

irrevocable; for the Evangelist Jewish worship is not heavenly, not true, not in Spirit. Only to worship through Jesus Christ is to translate the union with God, or "eternal life", into liturgical terms. Such a link is even stronger than earth–Heaven correspondence, for it is wholly personal. It is not only cosmic but also eschatological worship, proclaiming the Lord's death "till he come" (I Cor. XI, 26). In the Christian cultus the things of the new age are set forth by way of anticipation in exactly the same manner in which eternal life is begun on earth and consummated in Heaven. The things which are done and said are meaningful only because Jesus who died is alive in Heaven and at the right hand of God. Yet this worship in anticipation is not yet the final reality, the worship of Heaven itself, for the Church still looks to the same Jesus to finish his work.

ANTICIPATION AND PARTICIPATION

Since the Christian liturgy is thus at least potentially heavenly it serves the whole world. A man-made cultus only demonstrates the abyss which yawns between a sinful world and God whom it cannot worship. The Church does not propose another form of liturgy but the only available participation in the celestial worship. Christians take their share in the eternal act of veneration. Therefore "every knee should bow, in Heaven and on earth and under the earth" to the same God in the name of Jesus; for the salvation of the world is ultimately nothing else but its participation in the worship of God through the exalted Jesus in Heaven (Ro. XIV, 11; Phil. II, 9–11, adapting Is. XLV, 22–3).

THE CONGREGATION

The correspondence to, the anticipation of, and the participation with the heavenly worship can now be shown in all its aspects. The Christian cultus, in its details, compares with and yet outstrips the Jewish norms of worship. It begins, so to speak, in the synagogue and comes out of the synagogue. The early Christians are gathered out of the common assembly; hence the *ekklesia* is the equivalent of the Hebrew *Qahal*, the chosen body, made up of the appointed ranks of the people of God (the *'Edah* of the Old Testament). This Qahal or congregation of Israel is the Church, but it is not confined to the earth, a kind of religious centre for propaganda, education, and recital of prayers. It is all these things, of course, but it also partakes of that Qahal, of which it is said: "Let the Heavens praise thy wonders, O Lord, even thy faithfulness in the assembly of the holy ones" (*biqhal qedoshim*, Ps. LXXXIX, 6). The Christian gatherings are, therefore, not only co-ordinated and 'in touch' with other local congregations but they are altogether part of the heavenly Qahal and worship with "angels and archangels". Thus such possible terms as 'guild' (*chavurah*) or 'brotherhood' (as in I Pe. II, 17), which might have given an adequate description of the Church, are used as little as synagogue itself. The "Israel of God" (Gal. VI, 16) survives by election in the Body of Christ, which is both a "holy nation" and a "priesthood" (I Pe. II, 5, 9). These names emphasize that this Qahal is not tribal but cosmic, i.e. continuous with a long past and an infinite future beyond the earth. The sub-apostolic writers go very far in this direction and show how radical is the departure from the synagogue milieu; in the *Shepherd* the Church is an aged lady "because she was created first of all things, and for her sake the world was made" (Vis. II, 4). In I Clement XIV the pre-existent, spiritual Church was created before sun and moon and before she was manifested at length in the flesh. "The Catholic Church is wherever Jesus Christ is", concludes Ignatius (Smyrn. VIII). By the same reasoning the Church may be compared with the Temple, for Christians are the temple of God (I Cor. III, 16; II Cor. VI, 16).

THE CHRISTIAN TEMPLE

The Christian usage of the Temple motif, with its associations of altar, priest, and sacrifice, must recall some of the ancient features of the cultus. It is important to remember, for instance, that altars existed in Israel long before the Temple was built and that even at the time of the Temple the altar of the burnt-offerings was not enclosed by the building but stood under the sky. This altar must not be confused with the altar of incense, although it may generally be assumed that 'the altar', *tout court*, is the altar of burnt-offerings, unless the context points to the altar of incense (e.g. Is. VI). But altar and temple are never identical nor, indeed, are they inseparable. The temple which Solomon built and the pattern of the building which Ezekiel records were thought to have been constructed after a heavenly model (Ex. xxv, 9 gives the verdict of the Priestly school). But this claim of a heavenly pattern (*tavnith*) does not yet postulate the actual existence of a heavenly temple. Unambiguous references to the heavenly sanctuary are only to be found in the inter-testamental literature. The Testament of Levi (ch. III) knows of an altar in Heaven at which the archangels offer a propitiatory sweet-smelling savour to God, a reasonable and bloodless offering. According to Jubilees, chapter VI, the whole ritual of the Feast of Weeks was celebrated in Heaven from the creation to the days of Noah.

It does not follow, however, that these and later passages in the Midrashim permit us to take too materialistic a view of the heavenly cultus. It is highly improbable that people really thought that blood was shed in Heaven and that heavenly cattle had to be provided for such a purpose as on earth. If substitution played such a prominent part in sacrifice on earth it played an even greater part in Heaven: the souls of the righteous and the prayers of men were deemed to be acceptable offerings on high. The Apocalypse connects the altar of incense with the prayers of the saints (VIII, 3–5) and probably the altar of the burnt-offerings with the souls of them that had been slain (VI, 9). These two images retain the reality of genuine offerings and avoid the materialistic as well as the merely figurative use of the temple and altar motifs.

Taken as mere metaphors, 'temple' and 'shrine' tend to give the subject a vagueness which it does not deserve. The Christian claim that the old Temple was valid once but has become replaced is realistic enough. Stephen even declared the imminence of the transition and the finality of the rupture before the actual break occurred (Acts VII, 47 ff.). The building as such cannot be salvaged despite its venerable tradition and aesthetic value. The disciples' admiration, expressed to Jesus, rested upon a misconception of the real nature of worship (Mk. XIII, 1–2). Christ's denunciation here resumes the old prophetic hatred for the building and the cultus which had spread deceitful self-assurance ever since the days of its dedication. "The temple of the Lord" was not the Temple of God; it was not inviolable but worthless because of its moral failure (Jer. VII, 14 f.). It was man-made (χειροποίητος) and therefore to be replaced by "this Temple" which could not be destroyed, even Jesus Messiah himself (Mt. XII, 6; Jn. II, 19).

For the New Testament the Temple must be a problem. Significantly it dismisses the straightforward notion of a Temple and a Shrine in Heaven. Even the Epistle to the Hebrews does not refer to the existence of either ἱερον or ναὸς. There are, metaphorically speaking, temples on earth wherever Christians live together. Every member's body is such a ναὸς (I Cor. VI, 19) and every genuine and proportioned building of Christian members grows into a holy ναὸν of the Lord (Ephes. II, 21). The architectural pattern describes the mutual indwelling of Christ and the Church, the absolute dependence of each on each, and all on the Lord, who is the corner-stone, elect, precious though once rejected (I Pe. II, 4). All the Christian Churches are in their unity "a habitation of God in the Spirit" (Ephes. II, 22) because God dwells in them.

This conception of the Church renders the problem of the cultus acute. If God dwells among his people in the Spirit, what need remains for a cultic institution on earth? Wherever God dwells the true Temple, namely God himself, resides in complete holiness. But such a Temple, identified with God, is no longer a cultic institution. Possibly some Christians viewed the matter in this light (Hebr. X, 25); yet in the long run a different point of view prevailed and its success can only be accounted for by the influence of the tradition of the heavenly Temple. It was not an easy victory. The Apocalypse proves that the heavenly Temple was a difficult thing to accommodate in Christian eschatology. The seer oscillates between two opposing ideologies: on the one hand there is a Temple of God in Heaven (XIV, 17; XV, 5 ff.; XVI, 1, 17), on the other the Lord replaces the heavenly Temple in the new Jerusalem (XXI, 22). The Apocalypse thus deploys two apparently contradictory themes which lose their incompatibility against the background of the double eschatology. The first view of the Temple is in accord with Judaism: those who are judged worthy of life after death are the pillars of this Temple in Heaven (III, 12). The second view of its abolition coincides with the final act of the re-creation of the world. On the complexity of the temple motif Barth rightly says: "The reality and the relativity of this dwelling become only thoroughly visible in the New Testament".[1] It was left to the author of the Epistle to the Hebrews to use the ramifications of the whole issue and to solve the problem by taking the theme of cultic institutions furthest of all.

This writer addresses men who are partakers of a heavenly calling (Hebr. III, 1) and share by faith membership of the City which their precursors had had to be content to yearn for (XI, 16). These had served in their time what he calls "a copy and shadow of the heavenly things" (VIII, 5; IX, 23). The shadow, unlike the image, represents the celestial reality inadequately; the model can hardly be recognized by its shadow, whereas the image is in every way an attempt to guard the likeness (X, 1). The author employs here the term 'shadow' as Philo had frequently used it to bring out the contrast between degrees of reality (Som. I, 206; Plant. 27; L. A. III, 102; Post. 112). Every kind of copy is in a sense imperfect and presupposes the superiority of the genuine original. Earthly forms of worship, if they have any truth in them at all, are derived from the celestial model. Christians, having already tasted of "the heavenly gift" (VI, 4), may be expected to understand that the eternal pattern of worship existed from the beginning in Heaven; every attempt at worship in the past in Israel had been a copy of the truth, a transitory phase of the eternal verity. The earthly sacrifices before Christ had been shadows cast by the light which was yet to come. Christ had established the final type, the only true worship for the whole spiritual world. To this end Christ even cleansed the Heavens when he entered the holy place (IX, 23), removing every impurity which still adhered to them (Job XV, 15) according to the tradition of evil in Heaven.

The cosmic significance of the work of Christ has a treble effect: it assigns a reasonable place to the religious customs of the

[1] *Kirchliche Dogmatik* II/1, p. 540 (my translation). As is well-known the special difficulty in the Apocalypse concerns the ambiguity of the altar motif: (1) Does the seer speak of one or two altars? (2) Has the original been edited to such an extent that chs. XIV–XVI are inconsistent with the rest? Yet of the influence of the Apocalypse as a whole, at least in the West, there can be little doubt: it sanctioned the idea of a heavenly cultus with a heavenly altar.

past and explains their function in the preparation for the Gospel; it raises the Christian cultus on earth to a celestial level; it grants an eternal reality to worship as such. Above all, if the priesthood of Christ be taken seriously the conclusion remains incontrovertible that thus God was and is and will be worshipped in Heaven.

THE HIGH-PRIEST

The key to all cultic analogies must be found in the central concept of the High-Priesthood of Jesus. A long history lies behind the word itself.[1] The institution of a head-priest is, for instance, found at Ugarit;[2] It presupposes the existence of a college of priests who are attached to the service of a god. In Israel the title was revived to distinguish the successful leaders of the Maccabean revolt and their successors, i.e. Jonathan (I Mac. x, 20), Simon (xiii, 36), John Hyrcanus (xvi, 24). But these men hardly fulfilled the expectation placed in them, lacking in the virtue and dignity of Onias, whose repute was almost legendary (Sir. l), for their worldliness was reminiscent of the evil, unlawful high-priest Jason (II Mac. iv, 13) and led up to corruptions of which one Alcimus became typical (II Mac. xiv, 3). Hence the ideal figure of the High-Priest (*hakohen hagadol* of Lev. xxi, 10) and of the Priest-Messiah (*hakohen mamashiach* of Lev. iv, 3; ὁ ἱερεὺς ὁ χριστὸς of Lev. iv, 16; LXX) became popular and was in some circles at least as important as the Messiah of Judah. The Messiah of Levi was, like the tribe, detached from common pursuits and wholly dedicated to God, a symbol, as Philo observes, for holy service (Som. ii, 34). The Testament of Levi, which was evidently treasured among the sectarians of Qumran,[3] reviews the evils of the priesthood (ch. xvii) and predicts that the Lord will raise up a new priest to the office who will receive revelation and who will execute righteous judgment upon the earth: he shall shine forth as the sun, bring peace . . . the Heavens shall exult in his days . . . the angels of the presence of the Lord shall be glad in him: the Heavens shall be opened,

[1] Cf. E. O. James, *The Nature and Function of Priesthood*, 1955, pp. 74 ff.

[2] CML, B I VI 17–18: "Chief of the priests and chief of the shepherds."

[3] Cf. J. T. Milik, *Le Testament de Lévi en araméen, Fragment de la grotte IV de Qumran*, RB LXII, 1955, pp. 398–406.

and sanctification shall come upon him from the temple of glory (ch. XVIII).

To this expectation the author of the Epistle to the Hebrews specifically addresses himself. He does not say that Jesus is this Aaronic Messiah; nor does he oust the claims of Levi by over-emphasizing the claims of Judah. The statement "it is evident that our Lord was descended from Judah" (VII, 14) only leads up to the main point that the Levitical priesthood is altogether insufficient, having been received by physical descent and functioning according to the Mosaic legislation. These priests were mortal, sinful, priests and not high-priests. Their office was shadowy and used the blood of animals in a daily cultus upon earth. Therefore their expiations were ineffective and not acceptable to God. He who is of the order of kingly righteousness or Melchizedek (Ps. CX)[1] is appointed by God with solemn oath and does not succeed to a derived priesthood (ch. VII). He is the eternal, holy, perfect High-Priest who offers his own blood as a unique oblation in Heaven before God (IX, 11, 25). Thus he makes atonement for the human conscience (IX, 14; X, 11–14) according to the will of God (X, 5–10).

The perfection of Christ is therefore opposed to all existent priesthood (II, 10). Christ does not come to perfection by being consecrated according to the Law but by being made priest of men in his very acceptance of humanity. His espousal of human weakness and sinfulness and his passionate feeling for men on earth are grounded in his celestial origin (V, 1–9). His consecration was not a cultic event but God's unique dedication of his Son.[2] Therefore the perfector (τελειωτής, ἀπ. λ.) mediates the

[1] Philo's exposition of this perfect type of priest in L. A. III, 79–82, with its suggestive ἱερεὺς λόγος, is throughout at the back of the writer's mind.

[2] Cf. M. Dibelius, *Der himmlische Kultus nach dem Hebräerbrief,* Theologische Blätter, XXI (Jan. 1942). The verb τελειόω is applied both to Christ and the Christian. Dibelius quotes R. Wagner's motif of 'redemption of the redeemer', but admits that this is far removed from the Kerugma and approaches the Anthropos myth. But it seems that such a mythical aura is firmly rejected by our author by (a) the scriptural allegory of Melchizedek, (b) the constant allusion to the Psalms and to Isaiah. Therefore the "complete perfection" is not of an earthly dedication but part of the Incarnation, as Westcott observes under three headings: (a) the personal consummation of Christ in his humanity, (b) Christ makes his people perfect, (c) Christ's perfection through suffering the pledge of his perfect sympathy (*The Epistle to the Hebrews,* 1906, pp. 66 ff.).

faith which he has consummated in Heaven and consecrated in the eternal order (XII, 2).

THE PRIESTLY CULTUS

The priesthood of the Lord is unique. But other priestly orders and institutions are not negligible if they reflect his celestial office. The Levitical priesthood has fulfilled its functions and, as a copy, must now cease, as indeed it has ceased. The Church's priesthood is not the writer's concern, except that priesthood and cultus must reflect the true pattern. Therefore the writer even retains the imagery of Jerusalem-Zion-Temple-Sanctuary-Altar; God had dwelt and been worshipped there in the passing phase of the Mosaic dispensation. It is immaterial to the argument whether the city had fallen at the time of writing or whether the author is accurately acquainted with the architectural and technical details. Jerusalem and the cultus, as a heavenly reality, is an idea and not a topographical and ephemeral curiosity. Only the heavenly dwelling is real and replaces not only the earthly Jerusalem but also all the high places and mountains of former cults which had flourished on their tops or slopes.

Our Epistle is not alone in alluding to the prominence of 'the mountain' in religious experience. The work of Jesus is represented in the tradition as having culminated on heights: there he was tempted (Mt. IV, 8) and preached (Mt. V, 1) and prayed (Mt. XIV, 23) and healed (Mt. XV, 29); on a mountain he was transfigured (Mt. XVII, 1) and suffered (Mt. XXI, 1; XXIV, 3; XXVI, 30). From the hill, appointed for the final meeting in Galilee, he had parted (Mt. XXVIII, 16). These sacred heights were looked upon as copies of the infinite height of Heaven. Sinai had been such a mountain, now destined to pass away; Solomon's Temple had been a high house (I K. VIII, 13, *beth zevul*), built on high and evoking the height of Heaven, now replaced, for the Redeemer had come from Zion, God's mountain (Is. XLIX, 20; Ro. XI, 26). This mount Zion is now the city of the living God, the heavenly Jerusalem, the true cosmic centre of reality, where Jesus officiates on behalf of his flock (Hebr. XII, 22).

THE ETERNAL PATTERN

The earthly cultus of the Law (Exod. chs. xxv, xxvi) provides us with the parable of the heavenly (Hebr. ix, 9), for Moses had once received the pattern (Hebr. *tavnith*=τύπος, Hebr. viii, 5) of the tent and its furnishings (Exod. xxv, 9; Josh. xxii, 28). The Mosaic type could claim to be genuine as it represented the celestial antitype. Therefore its cultic ordinances (Hebr. ix, 1: δικαιώματα λατρείας) are surveyed briefly despite their imperfections and transitoriness (ix, 9–10). The earthly cultus may be compared with the celestial cultus, both as regards the places and rites of atoning worship, as long as it is remembered that the argument proceeds from the deficient to the perfect: the parabolic connexion is the "how much more" (ix, 14) of the two dispensations. The former had all the glories of worship and yet provided no access to God; the latter gives entry to the sanctuary of God by a new and living way (x, 19 f.).[1]

The cultic parable (Hebr. ix, 1–10) of eternal worship is set forth in a free manner which shows little interest in detail. With Philonic symbolism the author portrays the tent in the wilderness, itself the imaginative account of the Priestly school. The sanctuary (τὸ ἅγιον) is given the ambiguous title κοσμικόν, generally translated as 'of this world', i.e. not heavenly but physically built and visible on earth, though representative of a heavenly reality and the universe. Its tent (not two tents, despite verse 3) is again unheavenly, for it is put there by human means. Some of the furnishings are, however, symbolical of that celestial pattern whose divine order is eternal. Thus the *Menorah* or seven-branched candlestick was originally used to represent the world: this "cosmic tree" was a symbol of eternal life whose beams of light reach down to the earth. The planetary association of this Light of the world was according to Philo well known: in the *Menorah* God has given us a model of the celestial sphere and at the same time a representation of the human soul in microcosm

[1] Cf. A. Nairne, *The Epistle of Priesthood,* 1913, who calls the old relationship 'imitative', the latter 'sacramental': one is almost unreal, the other wholly real (esp. p. 354).

(Her. 216–25).[1] Similarly the strange "altar of incense" (Hebr. IX, 4: θυμιατήριον, ἁπ. λ.)[2] introduced at this point, must be meant to evoke the heavenward intentions and desires of the atoning liturgy. Indeed, the holy things behind the veil, in the Holy of Holies (Ἅγια Ἁγίων), approximate most nearly to the heavenly reality. The ark and the manna, Aaron's rod and the tables, recall with swift strokes the manifestation of the glory at Sinai; above all, the mercy-seat (*kapporeth* rendered by ἱλαστήριον), the focal point of the atoning Presence of God, had perpetuated in the ancient cultus the heavenly glory, of which the shielding Cherubim were the guardians.

The parable reaches the climax with the entry of Christ into the perfect tent. This, according to our Epistle, is the central event of salvation.[3] The anticipated pattern is fulfilled in the "greater and more perfect" tabernacle which Christ cleansed and entered, once and for all (IX, 11 ff.). This tent has sometimes been identified with Christ's body, his flesh, or human nature, or even his Mother Mary, or the Church.[4] But the writer's intention lies elsewhere and the whole context favours the identification of the perfect tent with the heavenly model, which, in that sense, is not "of this creation", but rather pre-existent, because fore-ordained by God, and eschatological, because of the new age. In this heavenly sanctuary Christ offers himself, as the perfect intercessor, not standing, but seated or enthroned in priestly royalty (XII, 2).

[1] Cf. GJS, vol. IV, ch. IV., for the Menorah which represents the Logos or Light of the world in at once a cosmic and Jewish sense; also Gunkel, *Schöpfung und Chaos,* 1895, 127 ff., for comments on Zech, IV, 1, ff. and the Menorah as a cultic symbol of cosmic reality.

[2] Rather than 'censer'; for the difficulties of the text see C. Spicq, op. cit., ad loc.

[3] "Das zentrale Heilsereignis ist nicht die Kreuzigung oder die Auferstehung, sondern die Durchdringung der Himmel und der Eingang ins himmlische Heiligtum" (M. Dibelius, op. cit.).

[4] It is difficult, for example, to follow Westcott's conclusion to his invaluable Additional Note on Hebr. VIII, 5 (op. cit., pp. 235 ff.): "The Tabernacle is indeed regarded by the writer as formed after a heavenly pattern: it has its divine correlative: it served as a figure up to the time when Christ's apostles were able to declare the fulfilment of the signs. . . . But it was not simply an epitome of that which is presented on a larger scale in the world of finite being: the archetype to which it answered belonged to another order. . . . Such an antitype we find in the humanity of Christ, realized in different modes and degrees during his life on earth, in his Body, the Church, and in the consummation in 'Heaven' (p. 242).

The author compares the self-offering of Christ with the old cultic pattern not only to dissuade his friends from bestowing their devotion on the past. His primary conviction concerns the reality of the celestial cultus itself. He does not mean to imply that the things of the earthly sanctuary are found in Heaven in a concrete, materialistic manner; indeed, it is the mark of the perishable copies that they are visible and made by hands. The true form precedes the manifestation and is perceived spiritually (XI, I ff.). The cultus of Heaven is, therefore, not liturgical in an earthly sense but in the 'ideal' manner. In Heaven the true worship replaces the symbolical which had itself given rise to earthly copies. These stemmed from the celestial original which now, made perfect, submits its forms of glory and holiness to Jesus.

How far, then, does this ideal reality of the heavenly sanctuary avail? In the metaphysical world it is an absolute reality and not a metaphor for something else or a spiritual non-entity. The author does not think in terms of incompatible alternatives, as some moderns would with regard to 'spiritual' and 'liturgical' worship. The worship of Heaven is both spiritual and liturgical. It is, therefore, impossible to agree that for our author "Jesus has gone into Heaven itself to appear before God on our behalf" while he entertained no "idea that Christ officiates before the throne of God by any sort of liturgical action".[1] On the contrary, he did entertain this idea, as his parable of the earthly institutions proves; only he entertained it by thinking of liturgical action not as a succession of 'services' but as the divine order itself.

DIVINE SERVICE ON EARTH?

Quite a different problem arises from the relationship of the Christian cultus on earth and the worship of Heaven. May the Christian sanctuary aspire to be called a holy place? Is there a

[1] Cf. R. V. G. Tasker, *The Gospel in the Epistle to the Hebrews,* 1950, p. 41, for a quotation (with approval) from W. Leonard, *Authorship of the Epistle to the Hebrews.*

For an extraordinary criticism of the Epistle cf. Phythian-Adams, *The Royal Priesthood,* CQR, 1942. Here Apollos is taken to task for his one-sided, non-homological theology which does away with atoning cult-offering (in X, 26–31) and leaves sinners without the means of reconciliation!

tent where God chooses to dwell upon earth? What is the nature of the Church's altar and how can the Christian use of it on earth improve upon the shadowy copies of the past? Naturally the voices of subsequent controversies, which would have been unintelligible to our author, must not guide our enquiry.

It has often been pointed out that this Epistle is not concerned with church services and church-going, and this is undoubtedly correct. An author who dwells upon "confidence to enter the sanctuary by the blood of Jesus" (x, 19) and who sees the Christians already surrounded by the "great cloud of witnesses", enjoying the felicities of glory (xii, 1 ff.) is not likely to break into dreary admonitions. His faith is one which looks away from immediate earthly concerns and which commends the heavenly promise. At the same time it must be remembered that the setting of the reading of the Epistle is corporate and probably liturgical. The meeting of the fellowship is not only taken for granted but even encouraged: "to meet together" (x, 25) is not a voluntary extra which may be dropped at will. Neither convenience nor duty, however, are the principles of church attendance, but the eschatological awareness of 'the Day'. All things are about to be shaken except "the Kingdom which cannot be shaken"; the Christian in worship responds to God's gift and in gratitude offers God acceptable service with reverence and awe (xii, 27–8).

This service (λατρεία) is one activity in which men join in with angels; nothing could be further from our author's mind than a sudden invention or innovation, such as cultic meetings to be multiplied on earth. The true and only possible service depends upon the pattern of Jesus' oblation in Heaven. The metaphysical basis is given in the Person of the Lord, "the same yesterday and today and for ever" (xiii, 8). The apparently impossible task of the cultus is solved by God himself, for the same Lord Jesus, who is in Heaven, is still available to men: "through him then let us continually offer up a sacrifice of praise to God" (xiii, 15). This is not a defeatist turning back to empty forms and ceremonies, to a cultus for its own sake, but the fulfilment of the anticipation and participation of the worship of Heaven. The expression 'sacrifice of praise' (*zevach todah*, Lev. vii, 12; Ps. cxvi, 17, rendered in LXX by θυσία αἰνέσεως

Ps. cxv, 8) is here taken in the sense in which Philo had interpreted it (Spec. I, 224), i.e. the ideal, heavenly offering, of which the Rabbinic tradition also says that in the days of the Messiah it alone will survive eternally. This 'sacrifice of grace' may here already be suggestive of, if not identical with, the Eucharist which becomes known as the sacrifice of praise.[1]

To share in this sacrifice involves a break with all earthly institutions: "We have an altar from which those who serve the tent have no right to eat" (XIII, 10). This verse is one of the most disputed ones in the whole Epistle. It obviously cannot mean that there is a simple choice between two earthly factions, e.g. 'their tent' (σκηνὴ) as opposed to 'our altar' (θυσιαστήριον) The tent stands for the earthly cultus, the altar for the heavenly. Some members appear to be pining for the former because they have not grasped the privileges of 'the sacrifice of praise'.

The contrast is clear: the Jewish priests and their people make or made communion through the meat offered in their ritual. The Christians cannot feast on that and at the same time on Christ. Their altar is in Heaven; it is the only altar which now exists and from which the true meat can be received. Christians cannot boast of many altars. If they have a cultus it is the common cultus of the one heavenly altar. It is not necessary to read more into this passage and to postulate the existence of a *pneumatic* group of Christians who opposed a sacramental faction.[2] It would be difficult to decide which party would in such a hypothetical case have the right to lay claim to the one altar and to the right of excommunication. The eirenic spirit of the Epistle does not envisage such hostilities. There is no hint of a Eucharistic controversy here, and the identification of the altar (θυσιαστήριον) with the eucharistic table cannot be entertained.[3] What the Christians must guard and what no one else may eat is the life of

[1] For Rabbinical passages see Str. B. I, p. 246; for early usage of the phrase, I Cl. xxxv, 12; Justin, *Dial.* cxvii. Cf. also the 'Memento, Domine' in the Roman Mass.

[2] So Schmitz, Holtzmann, Zahn, von Soden, Robinson, Moffatt, and others ad loc., no doubt due to the very common tendency among Protestant commentators to think *a priori* of the Church as non-priestly, non-sacrificial, non-cultic, as Dibelius notes in opposition to them.

[3] Cf. Spicq, ad loc.: "L'allusion à l'Eucharistie est une interprétation récente . . .".

Jesus, for he, the atoning sacrifice of the Christian, is offered outside, without the gate, in Heaven (XIII, 11–12). Thus it becomes the principle of the Christian cultus to worship in Heaven and to receive from Heaven the 'food', which the pilgrim still needs to attain to Heaven. "For the Christian there is no other cultus than the share in the heavenly mystery . . . in Heaven is the one and only cultic mystery."[1]

ATONEMENT RITES

The service of the living God (IX, 14) in Heaven can be understood only in comparison and contrast with the Day of Atonement. The *Yom Kippur* occurs annually (Lev. XVI) and its rite served to cleanse the whole people of their guilt. Then the priest was himself cleansed before he entered the Holy of Holies where he sprinkled the blood twice seven times. Both the blood and the holocaust rose up to God in Heaven to plead for remission of guilt. The immolation of the victim preceded the liberation of the life which was offered to God, as in the daily offering (X, 11).

Our author approves both purpose and ritual of earthly atonement: remision of sins is necessary and apart from shedding of blood there is no remission (IX, 22). The failure of the old way of reconciliation must be found in its lack of efficacy, the need for repetition. Both priest and victim were imperfect, the former sinful, the latter unsuitable (X, 4). The succession of earthly priests (VIII, 4) and the frequency of the offerings of the yearly round (IX, 25) prove the absurdity of the shadow-atonements and forgivenesses. But if the Priest and the Victim are united in the common purpose of achieving atonement, in the very will of dedication to God (X, 8), then the succession of blood-sacrifices is at an end. The purpose and ritual of atonement are freed from earthly limitations by such a priest and such a victim. In Heaven Christ has obtained that ministry (Hebr. '*avodah*=λειτουργία) in which he offers the gift (VIII, 3–6) of his perfect life surrendered once and for all. This gift is not the repeated immolation but the timeless and eternal presentation of himself, of which the sprinkling of blood is the genuine mark of

[1] Dibelius, op. cit. He contrasts also Hebrews—which is "neither gnostic nor catholic"—with such passages as I Cl. XLIII, XLIV.

sacrifice (XII, 24). The sacrifice of himself (IX, 26) in its completed perfection is the timeless act of the heavenly cultus to which he brings his own people by the blood of the eternal covenant (XIII, 20). From thence comes the appeal to Christians to serve the living God by worshipping in spirit and in truth. The principle of anticipation and participation now grows into that of identification with the living Christ.

BAPTISM

These three principles come to explicit fruition in the baptismal rite, but it may seem very open to doubt that Baptism belongs to heavenly worship. We can hardly conceive of the Baptism of the heavenly powers and the performance of such a rite in Heaven. The Old Testament does not foreshadow a heavenly initiation, for circumcision—whatever its origin—is not Baptism and in any case not a heavenly rite (despite Jub. XV). Such lustrations as the Law enjoins in ceremonial cleansing (e.g. Dt. XXI, 6; Exod. XXIX, 4; Lev. VIII, 6), only bear upon Christian Baptism in the accepted sense of the washing away of sin (cf. Is. I, 16; IV, 4). The Essenes made much of purification in cold water (Josephus, War, II, 129) and provided for their initiates stages of admission when the advancing member "is allowed to share purer kind of holy water" (ibid. 137 ff.). At Qumran and elsewhere it is considered important for the water itself to be clean and to cover a man (CD XI, 12–13). In the prophetic and poetic tradition this cleansing is ascribed to God; righteousness or the innocency of hands results from divine activity (Ps. XXVI, 6; LXXIII, 13), but at the same time penitence must be present: without spiritual repentance a stubborn man remains unclean despite all lustrations (IQS IV–IX); "let no one come to the water in order to attain to the purity of holy men, for men cannot purify themselves unless they turn from their evil" (IQS V, 13).

No doubt the Baptism of John and of the disciples owed much to this straightforward tradition; it can be understood as a penitential exercise and even, on some occasions, as a method of, or at least subservient to, the making of proselytes (Jn. IV, 2; Acts XIX, 4). In this the Jewish sects and the Christian Church occupied common ground. In the Gospels, however, the primary emphasis is on the eschatological character of the act. Jesus himself submits to Baptism and the time is fulfilled and the Kingdom of God at hand (Mk. I, 4–9, 15; Mt. III, 15). John's Baptism may, therefore, be regarded as "from Heaven", and not from men (Mk. XI, 29 ff.). This distinguishes Baptism from kindred Gnostic and Mandaean sectarian practices which claimed to convey men from death to life, even perhaps by means of a second Baptism before the gates of Heaven.

The Church could have developed similar features in the existing confusion, but for the emphasis on Jesus and the Kingdom of God. St. Paul discovers in Baptism a heavenly meaning, even if he himself hardly baptized at all (I Cor. I, 14). It is the supreme act of identification with Christ. The Glory of the Father which raised Christ from the dead thus imparts a new existence: "As many as . . . were baptized into Christ have put on Christ" (Gal. III, 27; Ro. VI, 1–11; Col. II, 12; Tit. III, 5). No need to outlaw the "baptism for the dead", i.e. those waiting for judgment, if they can pass from death to life in Christ by such identification (I Cor. XV, 29). Baptism, viewed as a transcending act, is something that extends beyond the earth. Isaiah had already stated the theme of a greater Exodus in the oracle of redemption: "When thou passest through the waters I will be with thee . . ." (XLIII, 2). St. Paul also linked the escape from the Egyptian bondage and the passage through the Sea with the reality of Christian Baptism: as the fathers had been liberated by passing from one side to the other, so the Christian is liberated from the nexus of sin and death. The waters of Baptism are a symbol of this new passage and a fulfilment of prophecy. Stretching typology to a fine point the Apostle exclaims: "Our fathers were all under the cloud and passed through the sea and all were baptized into Moses" (I Cor. X, 1–2); the Christian's escape follows this pattern in a time of temptation at the end of the world (X, 11–13).

Salvation is undoubtedly the main motif in Baptism. Peter's exhortation in the very early days of the Church pursues this course: "Save yourselves from this crooked generation" (Acts II, 40) and immediately about three thousand individuals plunge into the waters. How this was done and whether in view of the numbers involved the converts entered the waters themselves unaided or not is not known. The aim only admits of no doubt: by Baptism in "the name of Jesus Christ" the initiate desires to get away from the doomed earth and to Christ's Heaven. Significantly in I Peter Baptism evokes memories not so much of the Exodus but of the survival in Noah's ark (III, 21), another symbol of heavenly salvation in later Christian art. No lustrations as such—"putting away the filth of the flesh"—but the purity derived from the Resurrection of Christ, who is on the right hand of God, having gone into Heaven, brings salvation (III, 22). Baptism is accordingly practised only once among Christians, and takes its place among the transcendental unities: "One Lord, one Faith, one Baptism" (Ephes. IV, 5).

The once-ness of Baptism derives its uniqueness from the purification of the 'heavenlies', i.e. of the spheres and their members which Christ accomplished (Hebr. IX, 23). This cleansing was the beginning of his heavenly priesthood; similarly Baptism on earth is the beginning. It is not lightly regarded, but the institution is classed, together with the imposition of hands, among the first principles (VI, 1–2): "L'originalité de Hébr. est de mettre l'accent sur le progrès intellectuel comme condition du perfectionnement moral" (Spicq, ad loc.). Baptism is not one of diverse washings (IX, 10)—the plural here hardly refers to triple immersion or the number of the baptized or heretical washings but to Jewish rites—but the one effective washing with 'pure water' (X, 22). By a new and living way, the blood of Jesus, the Christian enters into the holy place (X, 19–20) or, as St. Paul puts it, into the full life of the one Body, into which all—whether Jews or Greeks, bond or free—are baptized (I Cor. XII, 13).

The principle of correspondence brings earthly baptism, within the context of the one eternal Baptism. The repeated, acts are not so many isolated phenomena, connected only with individual lives, but belong to and derive their reality from the 'heavenly enrolment'. The heavenly Church is the constant, the increase the temporal. The baptismal identification with Christ cannot be conceived of outside the "church of the first-born, which are written in Heaven" (Hebr. XII, 23). The homage which is offered by the heavenly company, which exalts God as God, is already anticipated on earth by the same confession, the beginning of credal statements. Of these the most primitive acclaimed Jesus as Lord, and Baptism was in his name (Acts II, 38). Yet already at the end of St. Matthew's Gospel this is expanded to the formula "in the name of the Father and of the Son and of the Holy Ghost". Of this Moore[1] writes, in connexion not only with Mt. XXVIII, 19 but also Didache VII, 1, that it was no trinitarian formula at that time but merely indicated acceptance of God's Fatherhood, Jesus' Messiahship, and the Spirit's inspiration. This view, widely held elsewhere, obscures the much more important fact that the origin and purpose of such and similar confessions was 'heavenly', inasmuch as the divine society confessed God's name in Heaven while the candidate to be baptized professed the same faith and thereby aspired to be enrolled together with that company. Baptism was a cultic act on earth, corresponding to, imitating, and participating in a heavenly reality, not an act in and for itself. In Hebrews Baptism is not an earthly rite—there are none; it is not an analogy—the day of copies is over; it is a symbol, a sign.[2]

THE LORD'S SUPPER

Baptism and the Lord's Supper are closely linked together, but the exact nature of that link is often disputed: if Baptism gives access to the new life this access must be whole and sufficient.[3] It is, however, also held that the life, which has been received in Baptism, is not only renewed but also developed and heightened in the Eucharistic rite. Once Baptism is given its full weight, as in the New Testament, the Lord's Supper cannot be a lesser institution, deprived of heavenly features.

EARTHLY FEATURES

The picture is, however, extremely complex. The Supper is celebrated on earth, at first in houses. It is obviously of this world, binding together certain people in a social, non-sacerdotal

[1] GFM, I, p. 188.

[2] A. Nairne, op. cit., pp. 32 ff., 53 ff., goes so far as to speak of a 'sacrament', natural and spiritual, a process of life, issuing from and leading to Heaven. The point is also made by the Anglican Prayer Book: "that . . . may enjoy the everlasting benediction of the heavenly washing".

[3] Cf. J. E. L. Oulton, *Holy Communion and Holy Spirit*, 1951, esp. ch. VIII.

manner. The New Testament does not even refer to the rite as a 'mystery'; the Gospel is indeed a secret, but the Eucharist is not comparable to the heavenly food and drink by which the initiate can be trained and sustained in his mystical progress. The pagan mysteries were more directly heavenly, charged with esoteric fancies in their pursuit of the ascent. The Christian fellowship, by way of contrast, appears to recall the perfectly normal gatherings of a friendly society. The friends of Jesus (Jn. xv, 13–15) may resemble a Jewish *Chavurah* or guild, which as a social organization was a common feature of Jewish life. Here men met together for some specific and often charitable purpose. Did, then, the society of Jesus meet to commemorate the death of Jesus which he had himself anticipated in their midst, blessing and breaking bread, pronouncing the Grace (*Qiddush*) over the Cup, as their leader had done? The rules and outlook of such a fellowship would have been altogether at variance with the emulation of a celestial pattern.

Not only Jewish but also Gentile Christians seem to have been content with an entirely uncelestial conception. The Pauline admonitions in I Corinthians evidence the same tendency, which the Apostle censures in the strictest terms. It is a falling away, a revolt, comparable to Israel after the Baptism of the Exodus (x, 1 ff.). Israel had received spiritual meat and drink, but to no purpose. The people's idolatry, as well as their privileges, had foreshadowed the trials of the Christian community, also baptized and fed supernaturally. The Christian reality is in danger of perishing in idolatrous confusion (x, 16 f.). The retrogressions at Corinth are so serious as to blot out the whole nature of the feast which has again been degraded to a level of social amusement and fellowship. The initiates come together "not for the better but for the worse" (xi, 17). Their divisions are typical of their attitude which makes it impossible to "eat the Lord's supper" (xi, 19). The behaviour of the Corinthians proves that they regard the event merely as a party of some sort, a picnic where they supply their own food and drink for themselves (xi, 21). The social love-feast, if it can still be called that, has replaced the Christian rite which the Apostle is determined to set in order when he comes (xi, 34).

The juxtaposition of the meal and the rite, which is still apparent in Corinthians XI, could not but lead to a confusion between the social, earthly assembly and the divine order. Both Jewish and Hellenistic customs of a social nature would and did interpret the key term 'fellowship' in an earthly manner. Whereas those addressed in Hebrews were altogether tired of *koinonia* (XIII, 16) and preferred to do without it, or use it at their own leisure, the Corinthian and other Churches enjoyed the cultic assembly without its heavenly, Christian implications and demands. In this sense the Eucharistic controversy may be said to have its roots in the early Church. How can the order of the Churches ensure that the true *koinonia* of the Gospel (Phil.I,5), of "the Spirit" (Phil. II, 1), and of "his sufferings" (Phil. III, 10), can be enacted by eating and drinking together?

THE HEAVENLY TRADITION

In the fluid state of those days the appeal is to the tradition, of which St. Paul says that he received and delivered it (I Cor. XI, 23). This tradition records differences, such as the order of the bread and the wine, but it is unanimous in associating the bread with the Body and the wine with the Blood of Jesus. The initiate is brought into communion with or into participation (*koinonia*) of the Body and Blood of Christ (I Cor. X, 16). This *koinonia* displaces all the cultic institutions which had been shadows of the things to come (Col. II, 17), such as the sacrificial participation with the altar of Israel after the flesh and the idolatrous mysteries of paganism (I Cor. X, 18 ff.). St. Paul does not rescind the materialism of these rites, for the true *koinonia* of the Body and Blood of Christ is not an esoteric spiritual indulgence. Bread and wine are the appropriate earthly elements for participation in Christ. Thus the cultic approach remains whilst its direction is wholly changed and therefore incompatible with the 'shadows'. It is not a service for its own sake, a competing form of *latreia*, but the divine order which exists in Heaven, where Christ is always adored by the whole assembly of worshippers. Participation in Christ cannot mean the ordering of the Lord back to earth at certain moments to be shared by his devotees but rather the anticipation, and therefore participation, of the heavenly Christ, undivided and eternally with the Father. The early liturgies (SS. James, Mark, Ambrose) make explicit this feeling of heavenly communion, inasmuch as the Church joins the spiritual powers for the common adoration of God and prays that the Spirit may descend to use the holy gifts of bread and wine and that angels may carry this pure oblation to the altar on high ("ut hanc oblationem suscipias in sublime altari per manus angelorum tuorum").[1]

But whence came this belief? How could the Jewish cultus even remotely figure as a shadow to such a development which qualified 'fellowship' as heavenly communion? It is difficult enough to reconstruct the earliest words of the institution and many doubts have been voiced about the words 'Body' and 'Blood'.[2] Whatever the original Aramaic (probably *bisra*' and *dema*') may have been, there remains the equally provocative problem how these two physical terms came to be used precisely when the communion with the living Lord was to be symbolized. How can such earthly and indeed perishable aspects of man represent the heavenly reality of a triumphant God? In this connexion the traditions of Israel, serving as copies of the heavenly altar, help to explain much, if not as much as we would.

THE PASSOVER

The closest relationship exists between Eucharist and Passover. The dating of the Last Supper appears to differ in the Synoptic Gospels on the one hand and the Fourth Gospel on the other.[3] But whether Jesus celebrated the meal or died on the first afternoon of that Feast does not alter the Paschal nature of both the Last Supper and the Passion, for undoubtedly St. Paul, perhaps citing a hymnal verse, states simply a common tradition: "our passover has been sacrified for us, even Christ" (I Cor. v, 7). It is

[1] Cf. J.A. Jungmann, *The Mass of the Roman Rite,* E.T. 1955, II, 231 f.; Const. Ap. VIII, XIII, 3 for the offering *εἰς τὸ ἐπουράνιον αὐτοῦ θυσιαστήριον.*

[2] Cf. e.g. G. Dalman, *Jesus-Jeshua,* E.T. 1929, p. 142, for *guph* as equivalent for *σῶμα*, which is opposed by J. Jeremias, *The Eucharistic Words of Jesus,* E.T. 1955, pp. 140 ff., with *bisra*'.

[3] For the former view cf. J. Jeremias, op. cit., p. 60: "Jesus used the prayers before and after the main course of the passover meal. . . ." and for the latter, G. B. Gray, op. cit., p. 389: "If the Johannine narrative is read by itself in the light of Jewish Paschal custom, all is straightforward. . . ."

more than a seasonal coincidence which links the Lord's Death with the Passover. The intimacy is complete and accounts for the ease with which in subsequent years one could replace the other. But when we investigate the infinitely complex strands, that make up the Jewish Passover, we find a perplexing blend of earthly traditions which must at first sight contradict the celestial nature of the Eucharist (Exod. XII–XIII, 9). The Passover had been a shepherds' dance, a new moon festival of the spring equinox; it had been adapted to agricultural needs and absorbed the rites of the corn; in the wake of the reform it had changed again and become half-domestic, half-public, but always and primarily a memorial of the escape from Egypt and thus an encouragement to political and social stability. Indeed the Passover belongs to the recognizable type of seasonal communion feasts which are designed to promote the good life on earth.

And yet there is, within the earthly function, a celestial layer in the Passover tradition. In the semi-nomadic days it was kept under the open sky when the full moon shone with mysterious brightness and the tradition never lost this particular solemnity. Then in the pre-exilic kingdom it became one of the feasts of the New Year in the agricultural society. The king must have occupied a high place in the ritual which may have included a dramatic representation of the creation and ended with his coronation and enthronement. Solemn and joyful were the pilgrimages to Jerusalem to be present at such a royal feast (II Chron. XXX, 1 ff; XXXV, 17 ff.). Though their fervour may have been pagan, centring on the needs of an essentially farming community, it was nevertheless the Lord's Passover which was being celebrated, and this Lord, as we have seen, was God of Heaven. The royal cultus did not detract from but rather enhanced the transcendental character of the Feast. The phenomena of nature also stressed the cosmic feeling, for light and fertility were the blessings of Heaven: the beginning of the New Year, the whole element of newness, became a guiding motif. The Priestly school credits Joshua with the keeping of the Passover when the promised land was reached (Josh. V, 10); Josiah commands the people: "Keep the Passover unto the Lord your God" in order to ratify the reform and the new beginning

(II K. XXIII, 21 ff.). On their return from Exile "the children of the captivity kept the Passover" (Ezra VI, 19). This tradition, that the Passover ushers in the New, made the rite itself symbolic for the new things of the age-to-come. In the somewhat obscure account of Ezek. XLV, 21 the Passover is surrounded by sin-offerings and whole burnt-offerings; in this context it appears that the rite is not thought of as a social communion rite at all but as a holocaust, offered solely to God for the forgiveness of old sins. That the Passover became gradually integrated in the hopes of apocalyptic Judaism is best evidenced by the expectation of Elijah, the Messiah's forerunner, to be present at the meal: "the primitive sacrificial meal thus became completely symbolical, enshrining the most precious memories and the most exalting hopes of the Jewish people in a rite not only of sacramental significance, but of singular and moving beauty".[1]

The Last Supper bears the traits of this sacramental significance. Jesus is the King now and it is the Lord's Passover which he desires to eat with his subjects. It is a meal which hails the new age, the Kingdom of God; this eschatological flavour of the new things completely departs from the notion of making a feast within the old seasonal round. All those who have a share in this Passover are no longer strangers of the divine commonwealth but are by faith in the new Jerusalem. This transition from the old to the new is rendered possible by the sacrifice itself. Jesus, who is either identified with the lamb (or more strictly, the *Pesach*, commonly but not necessarily a lamb) or perhaps even replaces it (for no mention of its being eaten occurs in the Gospel account) is the sacrifice which is offered, Godward, a whole offering accepted by God. It is this tradition which underlies the claim in Ephesians V, 2 that Christ "gave himself up for us, a fragrant offering and a sacrifice to God". This sacrifice does not lie in the past and needs no repetition, for "this he did once for all" (Hebr. VII, 27) and through his own Blood he entered into the holy place (IX, 12). Christ has fulfilled the copy of all previous burnt-offerings: "he abolishes the first in order to establish the second" (X, 9), namely his self-offering. The "offering of the body of Jesus Christ" sanctifies the believers (Hebr. X, 10), and it

[1] GFM, II, pp. 42 f.

is this participation in his Body which the Lord himself institutes at his own Passover, as Lamb of God taking away the sins of the world.

The remission of sins by this sacrifice brings to the fore another ancient strand in the Passover tradition which has nothing to do with earthly social affairs. The institution in Exodus XII itself reminds us that in this rite superhuman forces had to be placated. The little boy who asks nowadays at the meal "what is the meaning of all this?" recalls that there is a secret to be found out in the vortex of piled-up legislation. The answer speaks of Egypt and the disaster of the firstborn and the ferocity of the Lord's destruction. This kernel of the narrative originally referred to the perils of demonic powers whose night this was. They go out to slay the firstborn and only the blood of the lamb, so the tradition asserts, can save Israel by securing the door-posts. Then the enemy in the air is frustrated and cannot enter. The Christian Passover uses the shadows of this tradition to interpret the death of Christ. The only-begotten of God gives his Blood to ward off the supernatural perils, to cast out the demons, to dethrone the prince of the air, to bring to an end the rule of Satan, to cleanse the Heavens of the Enemy. "Christ our Passover" brings in the new age because by his sacrifice he has broken the power of the old. The Blood of Christ had to be shed by Christ the Priest in order to effect the complete liberation from the hostile powers above (Hebr. IX, 23). Thereafter those who share in the Blood pass securely from death to life, entering "into the holy place by the blood of Jesus" (Hebr. X, 19) who is no longer on earth but sanctifies the people by his own Blood in Heaven (Hebr. XIII, 12 ff.). The Christian resembles Moses, who "by faith kept the passover and sprinkled the blood, so that the Destroyer of the firstborn might not touch them" (XI, 28), but he partakes of the completed sacrifice. This means that the blood of Jesus is effective and available to the faithful, for remission and justification (Ro. III, 25; V, 9), because his Passover is continually offered in Heaven.[1] The earthly communion is part of the heavenly, in correspondence, anticipation, and participation.

[1] This ancient theme is still brought out in the "Libera nos, quaesumus, Domine, ab omnibus malis . . ." of the Canon of the Mass.

THE COVENANT SACRIFICE

Against this interpretation important objections can be made; the two wordings of the institution—"this is my blood of the [new] covenant, in Mark XIV, 24; "this cup is the new covenant in my blood", in I Corinthians XI, 25—though different, both prove that the primary connexion is that between the Blood and the Covenant and that the Passover background to the meal is relatively unimportant.[1] The Covenant is often likened to an earthly agreement between two contracting parties, for this impression is not unnaturally gained by looking at the *berith* concluded by God with Abraham, Jacob, and David. Although these are agreements in which God promises to act freely on behalf of his servants there remains undeniably a social and utilitarian aura attached to them and earthly rites (e.g. circumcision) and earthly well-being are their features. Only the covenant of Noah, as the representative of all flesh, has a celestial sign for its validity, the rainbow (Gen. IX, 13), and it cannot be said of this covenant that it is frequently in the minds of the writers of the New Testament (Rev. IV, 3; X, 1). Does the background of the Covenant in the Lord's Supper annul the heavenly features which the Passover has helped us to establish?

Such an exclusive approach to the covenant complex fails to take into account the sacrificial language in the Gospel narrative with its obvious reference to the making of the covenant of Sinai. Then Israel offered burnt-offerings and Moses sprinkled the altar, the book, and the people with blood and said: "Behold the blood of the covenant . . ." (Exod. XXIV, 5–8). The words of Christ's institution are deliberately couched in similar cultic terms: Blood and Covenant cannot be separated. Blood is the key term, as Hebrews, chapter IX, stresses in the summary of the Atonement. In this author's view the pattern of the whole altar worship of the old covenant must elucidate the death of Jesus, and

[1] As most radically asserted by G. B. Gray, op. cit., p. 397: "The germs of sacrificial elements must be sought elsewhere than in the Jewish Paschal sacrifice: for the Synoptic Gospels, which trace the origin of the Eucharist to a meal partaken of on Passover night, give no hint that the sacrificial element in the Jewish meal was to be perpetuated; and St. Paul and St. John, who speak of our Lord as a Paschal victim, do not bring this idea into relation with the Eucharist."

particularly the shedding of his Blood. He knows, of course, as well as anyone that Jesus was not slain on an altar but on the Cross and that his disciples are not savages who drink blood. Yet he holds fast to the old pattern to explain the new, stressing, as always, that the new outstrips the old by 'so much more' (IX, 14). He is, in fact, at one with the old prophets who did not hide their deep antagonism to burnt-offerings (X, 5 ff) and of blood in particular (X, 4). Yet the blood shed in the cultus prefigured the Blood of Jesus, the equivalent of his complete submission to God, for Jesus in the ancient Hebrew manner submitted his life to ratify the new agreement: "Lo, I am come to do thy will" (Hebr. X, 5–9, based on the LXX of Ps. XL). Jesus is the sacrifice of the better Covenant (VII, 22) for his Blood was poured out to establish that covenant relationship with God which is universal and eternal, not conditioned by outward allegiance but sustained by the living Spirit, as Jeremiah had foretold (Hebr. VIII, 6–10; Jer. XXXI, 31–3). The heavenliness of the new Covenant alone is commensurate with the sacrifice of Jesus who, himself the people's Covenant (Is. XLII, 6) "poured out his life unto death" (Is. LIII, 12).

The Blood of Jesus is, therefore, the blood of the Covenant which expiates the sins of the sinners and acquits them of their offence. But this justification "by his blood" (Ro. V, 9) applies not only on earth but also in the heavenly court, for it is in Heaven that Jesus continues to offer himself and to make intercession for the Church (Hebr. VII, 25). Justification and communion on earth in "the blood of the Covenant" are, therefore, a participation at the heavenly altar. For this astounding translation of the cultus and the worshipper to Heaven further cogent support may be found in the analogy of the Mosaic sprinkling itself. This is a fact which, though often overlooked, would seem to establish the 'heavenliness' in the original words of the institution with striking validity.

The events in Exodus, chapter XXIV, portray Moses as priestly intercessor: he alone shall come near unto the Lord. He then proceeds to build the altar under the mountain and twelve pillars according to the twelve tribes of Israel. After the sacrifice he sprinkles the blood in the ratification of the covenant, whose terms remain undisclosed until they are given for a second time (Exod. XXXIV). On the first occasion Moses climbs the mountain with the priests and elders, "and they saw the God of Israel; and there was under his feet as it were a pavement of sapphire stone, like the very Heavens for clearness" (Exod. XXIV, 10). Those present are spared and "they saw God, and ate and drank" (XXIV, 11). It is this whole picture which governs the reality of the Last Supper. At Sinai the sprinkling with blood leads up to the communion in the sight of God; in the new Israel Jesus is the Priest among the chosen congregation, he ratifies the new Covenant in his Blood. This Covenant is other-worldly, a promise to be present, not only on earth, but also in the glory above where communion is achieved. Just as the first account reaches its climax with an experience of God and Heaven so the sprinkling of the Blood of the new Covenant leads to the Banquet, so that the cultus is removed from the earth and translated to eating and drinking in Heaven.

BLOOD AND WINE

This translation from earth to Heaven underlies the liturgical language of the Church which conceives of the Blood of Christ in a new manner. The Blood of Jesus is neither the physical fluid which runs in any man's arteries and veins nor is it a mere metaphor for an ideal of sacrificial virtue. Instead the Blood of Jesus is eternal, the one spiritual reality of self-giving from which, as antitype or unchangeable pattern, all sacrifice on earth was originally derived. This life of God may now be shared, and wine is the chosen earthly substance which is appropriate in several ways. First Jesus blessed the Cup of wine at the Last Supper and identified it not only with his self-giving but also with the banquet of the new age: "I shall not drink again of the fruit of the vine, until that day when I drink it new in the kingdom of God" (Mk. XIV, 25; "with you in my Father's kingdom", Mt. XXVI, 29). He makes the wine of the Messianic age—"without money, without price" (Is. LV, 1)—the link by which he can share his sacrifice and communicate his living self which has done with earthly eating and drinking. Secondly, wine has the age-old property of acting as a symbol of blood, for this "blood of grapes" not only looks red and flows freely like blood but is actually used in sacrificial libations "at the foot of the altar, a sweet-smelling savour to the Most High" (Sir. L, 15, cf. Gen. XLIX, 11). Thirdly, Philo had already anticipated the identification of the blood and the wine to some extent when he developed the symbolic function of the wine and spoke of "the libation of the Logos himself" (Som. II, 183). Although no one would be bold enough to claim that Jesus and his followers were aware of this typically Philonic subtlety its value should not be underrated. A transcendental symbolism only could accommodate the use of earthly wine to represent the Blood in the heavenly cultus. The Eucharistic Blood, represented by the Messianic, the sacrificial, and the 'Logos' wine, may be drunk because it is not the blood of man or animal but a partaking in the Blood of Christ. Hence the Christian tradition asserts that the rational service (Ro. XII, 1: λογικὴ λατρεία) has terminated the offering of blood-sacrifices. Athenagoras specifically states that it behoves us to offer bloodless sacrifices, because God does not need blood: the noblest sacrifice is for us to know him who stretched out and vaulted the Heavens and fixed the earth (Apology XIII, dated c. 177 A.D.). Later St. Cyril's reference to the "unbloody Sacrifice" in the third letter to Nestorius, as well as expressions as "the unbloody oblation" and the "Blood of the Truth" in the Sacramentary of Sarapion, all testify to the grateful abolition of ritual slaughter in the cultus. On the other hand these pure offerings, which claim the fulfilment of Malachi I, 11, are known to be rendered possible only because "Christ came not with the water only, but with the water and the blood" (I Jn. V, 6).

BODY AND BREAD

A disquieting complication remains: how is it that the original institution and the Eucharistic rite make use of bread? The tradition asserts unanimously that Jesus "took bread and when he had given thanks, he brake it, and said, This is my body which is for you" (τὸ ὑπὲρ ὑμῶν, I Cor. XI, 24), or simply "this is my body" (Mk. XIV, 22). Bread and Body own some obvious common ground: the former may be broken literally, the latter figuratively. Nevertheless, the question remains how bread, which like wine serves as a pagan emblem of fertility and earthly concerns, fits into the pattern of the heavenly altar. The slightest acquaintance with universal mythology proves that the cult of the sheaf and the ear of corn features the pagan year. It is here of some help to cite the fact that the bread, as the shewbread of the priests or Presence (*panim*) Bread (Ex. XXV, 30), had in the Temple become part of the cultus of the Lord of Israel and that the agricultural needs of the community had naturally left indelible marks on Hebrew institutions. Though the corn harvest was celebrated in gratitude to the Lord and thus deprived of its pagan intentions it remained, however, an earthly, seasonal event.

UNLEAVENED BREAD

This monotheistic adaptation went furthest in the inclusion of the *Mazzoth*, the Feast of the Unleavened Bread, within the Passover celebration. In Exodus XII, 15 the narrative runs on as if no break had occurred, but in fact a momentous fusion has taken place: the Passover Feast and the Feast of Unleavened Bread have become united and the de-paganization is completed. Instead of stressing present fertility the blessing of the bread looks back, as did the Passover, to the liberation from Egypt, "for on this very day I brought your hosts out of the land of Egypt" (Ex. XII, 17). The old story of the sudden escape and the impossibility to leaven the dough is now woven into the arrangements of the annual memorial: leaven is not to be touched. The redemptive motif hast ousted the pagan element and prepares even for the expectation of future redemption, for God who aided his people in Egypt will do so again. Thus the bread in the Passover is charged with ideas of salvation.

In the New Testament all this is known and accepted, but the bread of the Passover plays a surprisingly small part in the tradition of the Lord's Supper. Even Melchizedek is not used explicitly as a type of a bread-offering priest in Hebrews where one might expect it. According to the Synoptic account the Lord used Mazzoth in the actual breaking of the bread and when he makes himself known after his death, again in the breaking of the bread, it is Mazzoth which he must have used (Lk. XXIV, 30). The figure of the knocking Christ who enters as a welcome guest to share a meal on earth (Rev. III, 20) also presupposes the blessing and the breaking of bread, probably Mazzoth. The Feast of the Mazzoth is either mentioned in the same breath as the Passover (Mk. XIV, 1; Lk. XXII, 1) or even stands by itself (Acts XII, 3; XX, 6; Mk. XIV, 12). It is known even among non-Jews. St. Paul, in writing to the Corinthians, brings out the traditional feeling that leaven symbolizes the evil carried over from the old year, and rounds off the Passover-Mazzoth connexion with the hymnal exhortation: "Let us therefore celebrate the festival, not with old leaven, the leaven of malice and evil, but with the unleavened bread of sincerity and truth" (I Cor. V, 8). This ethical allegory indicates the long distance which lies between the pagan origin of the corn festivities and the Christian use of unleavened bread. Indeed, the old cultic connexion has vanished; bread can be used without any scruples, independent of the liturgical calendar and considerations of harvest, for redemption having been completed by Christ the bread symbolizes the perpetual exodus from sin. The Church, freed from the old leaven, is to be the new, unleavened lump (I Cor. V, 6).[1] In order to commend Church unity St. Paul can write: "The bread (loaf) which we break, is it not a participation in the body of Christ? Because there is one loaf we who are many are one body, for we all partake of the same loaf" (I Cor. X, 16–17).

This figurative use of bread pushes the Mazzoth into the background, especially when the idea of the one loaf is pressed to symbolize Church unity. Whether it leads to earthly or to heavenly associations depends largely on the mind of the Community. Thus the enigmatic authority of the Didache does not seem to be aware even of celestial aspects of the Eucharist. There is not only no reference to any feeding on Christ, no mention of 'body', or 'flesh', or 'blood', but the symbolism of the bread is now used to portray the scattered Church and the gathering together of the particles of wheat into one loaf. The social, earthly note prevails here so completely as to give rise to the feeling that the document must be either a forgery or must stem from Jewish-Christian *Chavurah* circles or possibly does not describe the

[1] The contradiction of leaven as evil and good (cf. Mt. XIII, 33; XVI, 6) is not found in St. Paul.

Eucharist at all. On the other hand the Epistles of Ignatius use the symbolism in exactly the opposite sense; he writes: "I desire the bread of God" (Ro. VII, 3; Ephes. V, 2), which is the flesh of Jesus Christ. The Eucharist counteracts death, the broken bread being the medicine of immortality (Ephes. XX). This tradition was destined to prevail in the Catholic Church; the bread becomes the symbol of reality, heavenly and earthly, sacramental (Iren. adv. haer. IV, XVIII, 5).

MANNA

If the Passover Mazzoth of the Jewish tradition can barely sustain the weight of this development it is imperative that we look elsewhere for the conception of the heavenly bread. St. Paul in his panorama of the divine redemption in I Corinthians X passes straight on from the Baptism (to Moses) to the eating of the 'spiritual meat' (verse 3). The Eucharist is prefigured for him here not in the bread of the Passover but in the miraculous food and drink of the Exodus (ch. XVI). Similarly the central place afforded to the Feeding of the Five Thousand in all the Gospels reflects the connexion that was felt to exist between the Manna of Israel and the Bread of Christ: it is a Messianic miracle of the good Shepherd which looks back to the desert of Sinai and forward to the age of redemption. In this sign Jesus did not only feed his people out of compassion but linked the past with the future after the manner of the "golden pot holding the manna" which Jewish piety preserved in the sanctuary (Hebr. IX, 4). The Manna had long ago ceased to be thought of as a natural phenomenon—e.g. a "juice exuding heavy drops from twigs . . . sweet, sticky, honey-like"[1]—but was the mysterious "What is it?" (Exod. XVI, 15) to which Moses had replied: "It is the bread which the Lord has given you to eat." This bread was held to belong to God's gifts in the Messianic age. The Manna of the just (Ps. LXXVIII, 24) is the bread from Heaven (Ps. CV, 40); God has given his people 'angels' food' (Wisd. XVI, 20). The heavenly corn is milled in the third Heaven (b Chag. 12 b); Manna was created on the eve of the creation of the Sabbath (Aboth V, 9; Targ. Jon. Ex. XVI, 15). The Rabbinical

[1] Cf. BDB, p. 577, to justify this explanation for Exod. XVI, 31, 41.

interpretation of Exodus XVI glories in the reversal of the natural order: corn used to grow up towards Heaven, but then it descended from above. In the days of the Messiah provisions of Manna will fall again down from above (s Ap. Bar. XXIX, 8; b Yoma 75 b) and turn human hearts to Heaven (Midr. Sifr. Numb. 87–9). Philo also considers Manna to be the divine word, heavenly incorruptible food (Her. 79) which the Logos distributes (Her. 191) as wisdom for those who hunger (Fug. 137–9; L. A. III, 161–78).

The controversy in the Fourth Gospel in chapter VI affirms the rightness of this expectation; in the dialogue a comparison between the Flesh and Bread of Jesus and the Manna from Heaven ensues. The words are not merely about the Eucharist, "still less 'anti-Eucharistic' or 'anti-Sacramental' . . . The sustained and primary purpose of the Evangelist is to declare the true meaning of an episode [the Feeding] that stood importantly in the Christian tradition of the words and actions of Jesus".[1] In this setting the Rabbinic spokesmen are heard to utter the word 'Manna'; they recall the ancient sign of the bread from Heaven in order to prove that it was superior to the miracle of Jesus. Jesus accepts their challenge, but he goes beyond the simple analogy "my bread is like the Manna", or even an *a fortiori* claim, such as "my bread is even more heavenly". The attack is dramatic: "Moses did not give you the bread from Heaven" (VI, 32); it was not Moses but God who gave, and then only by way of copy of the true bread.

The tradition of the Manna must not stand in the way and obscure the revelation of Jesus, himself not the supplier of the bread but the true Bread in his Person. The criterion for the distinction between the true Bread and the copy is simple. Those who ate the Manna in the wilderness died; those who feed on the living Bread from Heaven have eternal life. The acerbity of the tone in this chapter—no doubt provoked by pressing needs at the time of writing—may account for the unique use of the analogy of the Manna, which through contrast rather than similarity brings out the dogma of the Bread from Heaven beside which none other exists.

[1] Cf. Hoskyns, *The Fourth Gospel*, 1940, vol. I, p. 323.

In the Christian cultus this doctrine of the Bread of life is empirically set forth, for it is given at the Lord's Supper to which he invites his guests: "Come, eat ye of my bread and drink of the wine I have mixed!" (Prov. IX, 5), and the Bread is his Body, himself, the Word and the Wisdom of God. Not only the martyrs who have overcome death receive the "hidden Manna" (Rev. II, 17), but even the living on earth feed on the same food. Although the gift is pronounced to be 'from Heaven', the conception of the Manna slightly changes the nature of the heavenliness of the cultus. Whereas Passover and Covenant sacrifice are really heavenly Feasts, to which the liturgy on earth corresponds by participation and anticipation, the Manna is a gift from Heaven received in the Church on earth. If, however, the abiding presence of Christ in the heavenly sanctuary be remembered, then the Manna cannot be thought of as so many pieces of heavenly food scattered down to earth in answer to prayer, but rather as crumbs from the heavenly altar which is the focus of all Christian worship. Perhaps the Johannine critique of the Manna tradition of the Rabbis should be understood as a protest against the crudity of notions of heavenly breads and an endeavour to show the unity of the Manna which is Christ.

MEMORIAL

But how does the familiar and yet so controversial phrase "Do this in my memorial" (I Cor. XI, 24–5) fit in with the celestial nature of the Christian cultus? Even if the Lukan parallel be an insertion—which is far from proved[1]—St. Paul retains evidently an important part of the tradition: the emphatic and strange εἰς τὴν ἐμὴν ἀνάμνησιν is not likely to be his own invention. But what did he understand by it? And what was the original context of the commandment? If Jesus is here overheard as striking a purely personal note—"when I am dead, remember me whenever you eat bread and drink wine"—the claims of the supernatural receive indeed a fatal blow. Such a memorial, however affectionate and deeply felt, could be little more than the commemoration of a departed friend, almost a

[1] Cf. Jeremias on Lk. XXII, 15–20, op. cit., pp. 87 ff. for a "decisive argument in favour of the longer text".

prayer for his well-being in the life to come.[1] It would lead to an extension of a funeral repast, a very earthly custom indeed. Another merely social interpretation of the words would favour the temporal realm of the survivors: Jesus, foreseeing that these followers of his will continue to meet, requests that they should not forget him in their midst, inasmuch as they had received their training and so much else from him. The words then presuppose the continuation of the practice of the Chavurah meetings and charity meals and insist that they be held not without a loyal remembrance of their source: the institution is not to change its character by the influx of new members and the oblivion of the foundation member.

Most readers and commentators, however, are too impressed not only by the historical development of the rite but also by the aura of sacrifice in the narrative to permit such a secular this-worldliness to govern the exposition. The word *anamnesis* (memorial) itself recalls the memorial-offerings (*'azkarah*, Lev. II, 2; XXIV, 7) which individuals offered through the priest to remind God of themselves, their needs in their sinful state. Part of this burnt offering was burnt and rose up to God. On the national scale, too, a memorial of sins was made on the Day of Atonement by confession over the live goat which was sent into the wilderness to perish (Lev. XVI, 21; Hebr. X, 3). The weakness, however, of linking the institution of the Last Supper with a sin-offering comes out when applied to our text. "Do this for my *'askarah*" is almost meaningless and not the same thing as "when you do this, offer me up as your special oblation". It is of course possible that the original Aramaic has been slightly distorted in the Greek and that an allusion to the atonement rite, if not an exact parallel, had been intended. In that case the interpretation given in Hebrews, chapter X, holds good: the body of Christ avails as a sin-offering in Heaven, and to make a memorial of him is in fact to unite the Eucharist to this sphere of intercessory action.

Most commentators, however, maintain that the Hebrew

[1] Cf. Jeremias, op. cit., pp. 163 ff., where he finds support in I Cor. XI, 26 and Didache X, 5 for this eschatological type of remembrance: May God remember his Messiah in that day!

equivalent here is simply *lezeker*, 'for a memorial', the memorial in view being spontaneously suggested at first by the occasion of the Passover and subsequently by Christian liturgical needs. Just as the Passover was re-enacted, year by year, to show forth the redemption from Egypt and the day is kept for a memorial (*lezikron*, Exod. XII, 14), so Jesus authorizes his disciples to keep the feast as a continual departure from sin and evil. They are to recall his work as they feast and whenever they feast in the remembrance of him they celebrate the Christian Passover. If this be the original intention of the words (Aram. *ledokran*) it must be understood to imply that the yearly rite is meant to yield to something much more frequent. Remembrance, in this or any other connexion, just cannot mean that once a year only a special effort be made; indeed, this type of memorial is excluded because it suggests forgetfulness in general and remembrance only in a cultic gathering. The whole context of the Pauline teaching opposes such notions of voluntary memorials. If the Eucharistic memorial depends in any way on the memorial of the Passover it also follows that it is freed, by these words, from a cyclic calendar even though the liturgical year itself is not abolished. The memorial is permanent because the Lord is ever-abiding; it arises from the living fellowship with him who is enthroned in Heaven.

THE HEAVENLINESS OF PRAYER

The Biblical passages, which support the participation of Christians in a heavenly worship, should not be regarded in complete isolation, for the liturgies express the same ardent desire for the worshippers to rise and ascend. Here the evocation 'Sursum Corda' (after Col. III, 1) is ancient and typical.[1] That it is not meaningless to appeal to a 'lifting up of the heart' is certainly remarkable. The dialogue presupposes Christ's Lordship in Heaven. As in ancient Israel the call to worship God meets with an immediate response in spontaneous gestures and mental attitudes which express the approach to the exalted Deity. Private prayer imitates a good deal of the Eucharistic action for it is never offered separately but always in the company of angels

[1] Cf. Hippolytus, Ap. Trad., which itself recalls earlier liturgical usage; see Jungmann, op. cit., I, pp. 28 f.; II, pp. 110 ff.

and all the host of Heaven. Therefore even the simple request, petitionary and intercessory, shares the soaring and universal quality of Christian worship. Every prayer is offered after the manner of the Lord's Prayer, addressed to God in Heaven and in conformity with the unalterable pattern; yet since it is also known and felt to be a deviation from the perfect, since it is offered with earthly limitations, it must look for consummation beyond. St. Paul therefore urges that we do not know how to pray but that God himself, through the Spirit, is praying in us, the Spirit helping our infirmity (Ro. VIII, 26). Without God himself, i.e. without the Spirit in the Church and in the individual worshipper, only a myth-ritual performance can be given and Christian prayer is impossible. The inspiration of the cultus must be taken for granted in all claims of heavenliness.

LIGHT

Of outward forms and ceremonies the most suggestive is the lighting of the sanctuary, or of the room set aside for worship (Acts XX, 8). It is perhaps the most natural expression of what the Christians felt in their worship. Candles represent everywhere the true light, and the cultus of the true God redeems the worship of the sun and all the other luminaries. In the Temple lights were lit on the great feasts,[1] for the Lord of Israel is light (Ps. XXVII, 1): "Arise, shine, for thy light is come and the glory of the Lord has risen upon thee", sang the prophet (Is. LX, 1). The universal apocalyptic hope had to be fulfilled: "Nations shall come to thy light, and kings to the brightness of thy rising" (LX, 3). To this expectation of "the Sun of righteousness with healing in his wings" (Mal. IV, 2) the ancient Christian hymn answers with the proclamation of Christ as the Light of the world: "Awake, O sleeper, and arise from the dead, and Christ shall give you light" (Ephes. V, 14). Thus the eternal principle of life is no longer worshipped in separation but in Christ himself and enters the very being of the Church.[2] The members are

[1] E.g. the great candelabra in the Court of the Women on the first night of the Feast of Tabernacles; cf. Str. B. II, pp. 806 f.

[2] Whose *Κύριε ἐλεῆσον* replaces the *Ἥλιε ἐλεῆσον ἡμᾶς*; cf. F. J. Dölger, *Sol Salutis*, 1920, p. 52.

carriers of the light and lead others in the glorification of the heavenly Father (Mt. v, 14). Christian worship, therefore, even in the dark vaults of the catacombs, radiates light towards God, towards itself, and towards the world. What is received is reflected in light, the common symbol of physical, mental, and spiritual activity and being. Only in the final unbroken Presence of God in Heaven "they need no light of lamp or sun" (Rev. XXII, 5), for in the heavenly City "the glory of God is its light, and its lamp is the Lamb. By its light shall the nations walk" (Rev. XXI, 21–3). The visible light in Christian worship indicates not only the perpetual solemnity of the rite by participating in the heavenly light but also the anticipation of the fullness of the divine glory which is yet to come.

SPIRITUALIZATION OF WORSHIP

The significance of the celestial cultus is without limit. It removes the Christian community from the immediate stress of passing turmoils and lends considerable stability to its estimate of its own existence. In the first century, moreover, it achieved an immediate social miracle. Jews and non-Jews could meet together, the educated and the ignorant could share, in the celestial reality which abolished former restrictions. It enabled Christians to believe in, and set forth liturgically, the Christ who had come and who is present and who will come, thus spanning past, present, and future. The heavenly cultus succeeded in bridging traditions almost incompatible; by sustaining the claim that "we have an altar" Christianity could supply a positive substitute for the vacuum created by the unreality of pagan sacrifices still continuing and the abolition of Jewish ritual sacrifice after A.D. 70. By removing the centre of worship from earth to Heaven Christian apologists could fight successfully on two fronts: they could attack the whole pagan milieu of crude bloody sacrifices and materialistic rites; they could defend their own worship against the extreme spiritualization of religion to which some philosophers and mystics gave the highest place although it must lead ultimately to the end of all religion. The spiritualization of the New Testament is, in fact, a fight against two equally dangerous errors, and the translation of the earthly sanctuary to God in Heaven is its most decisive weapon.[1]

The Christian spiritualization resumes all former endeavours to give meaning and ethical content to the sacrificial system. The heavenly cultus fulfils the prophetic axiom that the disposition of the offerer decides the quality of the offering. It satisfies the prophetic longing for the pure offering without rams' and goats' blood and altogether endorses the spirit of the prayer: "Let my prayer be counted as incense before thee; and the lifting up of my hands as an evening sacrifice" (Ps. CXLI, 2). Penitence and sincerity and humility are still the appropriate offerings to God (Ps. LI), gratitude prompts the right attitude: "Give to the Most High according to his gift . . . the offering of the righteous makes the altar fat . . . and is acceptable" (Sir. XXXV, 1–11). The Rabbis' emphasis on prayer and good works and brotherly charity is still comprehended in the ethos of the worshipping Christian community (Mt. V, 23–4). The devotional exercises of the sects, such as penitence and fasting, are by no means excluded from the liturgical order (Mk. II, 20; Acts XIII, 3; XXVII, 9; I Cor. VII, 5), and even the austerities of Qumran and elsewhere, which are designed to set the initiate free from the burden of the flesh, are not vetoed here (I Cor. IX, 24–7). The transmission and recitation of the sacred tradition are harnessed to the Christian mode of worship. Every type of piety can be accommodated in a cultus which is larger than each, whether it be Pharisaic in observances, or allegorical and reflective as in Philo's ideal.[2] Purity of intention and the good life are considered to be the prerequisites of worship, but they are neither enough in themselves nor indeed possible apart from the reality of the heavenly worship of the Community. This

[1] For the long and complex history of the spiritualization of the cultus, cf. H. Wenschkewitz, *Die Spiritualisierung der Kultusbegriffe*, Angelos Bd. 4, 1932. He concludes that in the Christian development cultic terms apply to processes which are no longer cultic in a ritual sense as well as to events and matters which were originally wholly uncultic (p. 228). Cf. also C .F. D. Moule, *Sanctuary and Sacrifice*, JTS, N.S. 1, 1950, pp. 29–41, for "reasonable grounds for presuming a 'sanctuary and sacrifice apologia'," (p. 40).

[2] Philo asserts that God does not rejoice in sacrifices. He regards the incense, a symbol of real piety, as better than bloody sacrifices on stone altars (Spec. I, 271 ff.) Yet Philo is believed to have offered sacrifices himself.

worshipping body of the spirit-filled Church has access to Heaven where Christ is and ministers. The Church on earth enters by the same spirit into communion with the heavenly, having "one altar, one Jesus Christ, one cup for atonement of his blood"[1] Therefore the liturgy on earth expands in the Sanctus the Qadosh of Isaiah, and adds to "the fullness of the whole earth is his glory" the very pertinent "Pleni sunt *coeli* et terra gloria tua". Heaven is not an addition for the metre's sake; rather it is the basis of true worship. The Tersanctus really breaks down the spatial parochialism of the worshippers on earth. At length neither Jerusalem, nor any other city or village, nor any angelic sphere, but the whole world together acclaims God. The solemnity of this cosmic union in worship is even more movingly brought out in the Cherubic hymn of the oriental liturgies.

The heavenliness of Christ releases all men through the Eucharistic worship from the clash of ideas and matter as well as the confines of space and time. It posits a unique religious reality whose interpretation can only be attempted in the terms of its own worship. The liturgies of the Church suffer from earthly and human insufficiencies but they accomplish the heavenly act upon earth. They voice the fundamental petition that God "may bestow upon us in Christ Jesus heavenly things in exchange for earthly" (Origen, in Luc. hom. VII). But such a petition, even in its symbolic meaning, must rest upon the ontological truth that Christ ministers in Heaven for all mankind. The liturgical action cannot go beyond the faith of the community and this faith itself must be grounded in reality.

[1] Ignatius, Magn. VII, 2; Phil. IV, 1.

Indexes

I SUBJECTS

II NAMES

III QUOTATIONS FROM THE BIBLE

A—OLD TESTAMENT

B—APOCRYPHA

C—NEW TESTAMENT

IV QUOTATIONS FROM JEWISH LITERATURE

A—PSEUDEPIGRAPHA

B—DEAD SEA SCROLLS (QUMRAN)

(References in columns and lines)

C—JOSEPHUS

D—PHILO

E—RABBINIC

V PATRISTIC REFERENCES